FROM DARK TO LIGHT

This book is in loving memory of my brother David, my mother Alice, my sister Gail, my niece Melanie, Sandra Persaud, Mary Moffat, Alfie, Snickers, Marmalade, my forever friend Kelly and Manuel De Oliveira. I will keep a candle burning in my heart till we reunite once again my loving friends and family.

A Memoir of Spiritual Awakening

Dawn M Barlow

I dedicate this book to my children Sarah and Matthew, the two pieces of my soul, who complete the puzzle within me. I love you both as much as my next breath. Thank you for being my children in this lifetime. I am very grateful for your unconditional love and support. As always promised from Grandma, better days are not just coming but they are here. We shall always rise as long as we continue to walk on a path of light.

Table of Contents

PROLOGUE

In this book, I share my personal journey, and the development of the communication with angels and others from the spiritual realm, with the hope that I can help others on their journey. The saying "What don't kill you only makes you stronger" is real. I truly believe all the pain, grief and sadness we go through, shape the people we become. It brings our souls to a new level of acceptance and empathy for others in this world, though some people don't learn from their experiences and choose to be bitter, angry or sad. We are all on this earth for different amounts of time and that time is somewhat determined by us. Some of us shorten our time on this earth by the abuse we cause to our bodies while some of us feel we are taken too soon by disease or tragedy. Either way, I believe the Lord has a plan for all of us in his divineness. Of course, I am saddened by the loss of those I love on this earth in their physical form. But I have learned that they are not dead; they are very much alive. The vessels that carried their souls upon this earth are no longer here, but their souls are right beside us each and everyday. Souls are enormous amounts of energy, light, and love. We are made from God, so in essence, we are God. I believe we choose to come to earth so that our souls may learn lessons. It's amazing for those souls to fulfill their purpose on earth in any lifetime. Because of free will, there are so many things on this earth that can distract us from our purpose. Addiction, selfishness, and greed are just a few. It is never too late though to get yourself back on track and live life the way God intended. I believe He intended us to be good to others and ourselves, then everything else will fall into place. Kindness and compassion to others is surely a life worth living and will keep you close to God. Anger or anything negative puts a separation between you and God. God forgives all and He is right there at anytime with His loving arms wide open whenever anyone is ready. I have learned this all from personal experience. I would like this book to be the kind of book you can open up anytime you are having a personal struggle, in the hopes that it will enlighten and awaken you to a better way of living and being.

Religion is for people who are afraid to go to hell.
Spirituality is for those who have already been there.   -
Vine Deloria, Sioux

ONE
Pick That Up

On a cold winter day in my hometown of Fall River, Ma the sun was shining bright through the blinds in my living room. A young woman named Heather had just entered my home for a reading in the hopes of hearing from her loved ones in spirit. As she sat on my couch I began to tell her of an elderly gentlemen who had stepped forth and said he was her grandfather. I then described to her the appearance of this gentleman. As a medium I am able to see the soul who steps forth. They sometimes make me aware of their eye color and the clothes that they are wearing. I receive messages from them through my thoughts. I also receive feelings from these souls and sometimes they can become overwhelming. As I began to give her information from her grandfather a young woman with blonde hair stepped right in and sat on my loveseat. She immediately made me feel extreme sadness. She told me that her name was Amy and she was sad because she left her daughter too early. She also told me that she passed away from a drug overdose. Heather insisted that she did not know this girl Amy. Though Heather said she did not know her Amy did not want to leave. We both felt very bad for her because of her sadness and told her it was ok to stay. A few more times during the reading Amy would say, "she knows me". Heather still insisted she did not know her. Towards the end of the reading a young man stepped forward and he showed me a motorcycle. As I was telling Heather about this young man she blurted out, "I know who Amy is". The young man that stepped forward also knew Amy in life. That is how Heather finally realized who Amy was. Heather then told me that Amy had passed away recently from a drug overdose and she left behind a young daughter. Amy then asked if Heather could please tell her family that she loves them, that she is okay and she is sorry for leaving. Heather agreed to pass this message along to her family. Suddenly a young man with piercing blues eyes who was wearing a robe stepped in near Amy. He did not speak, he just took Amy by the arm and they both left. I felt he was some sort of guardian angel. I then had a knowing that they allowed Amy to step in to ask Heather to pass her message along because of her deep sadness. Passing this message along is the start of healing for Amy. I am very grateful to bring healing to the souls who are on earth and in the world of spirit. This is a gift that I entered the world with. Unfortunately I was born into a family with an abusive alcoholic father as the rest of my family became dysfunctional along the way. My story will show you how the gift that I came to earth with was darkened and stifled by the dysfunction of my family and myself. It will also show you that regardless of where anyone stands in life there is always a way out of the dark and into the light. If I can do it, so can you.

Through the ages many of us have asked ourselves as we go through the dark times in our lives, "Is this Hell?" Darkness represents what we can't see or understand, and we question why is this happening to me? For many of us, through the sorrows of our days, wars rage within our hearts. Our weary minds wonder how, or will I even get through this darkness? As we go through these trying times it can be overwhelming and feel never ending. As children we are afraid of the dark, but I find as adults we are all too content to live our lives in the darkness. In a sadistic sort of way, darkness can be comforting, especially if that is how we are used to living. To shatter the darkness, we must surrender to the light. Anyone can climb out of the darkness even if it's just one step at a time; we all have the power within us. Often, we feel justified in our emotions because life is tough, but in reality, we are tougher.

It is so much easier to think negatively and be bitter and angry. If you want to find your way to the light, then negativity is not the answer. We can all conquer our own demons no matter what they are. Life will knock you down; just get back up and fight for your own salvation. The light within you can change the world. Another question you might ask is, how can I get through this darkness? I can only share my story with you. This is my journey, this is your journey, and we share it together. Though every word in this book is true I have changed some of the names to protect their privacy.

I was born into a very dysfunctional family of five brothers, my mother and father. Three of my brothers were older than me and two were younger. In my eyes, my mother was a saint, and my father was an abusive, alcoholic devil. I don't have many memories under the age of eight. One thing I do remember though, I was terrified of my father.

When I was age seven, and walking home from school one day, I was talking to my friends and not looking where I was walking. I turned my head and smashed it on the mailbox. Back in the 1960's small cast iron mailboxes were attached to telephone poles. I became very dizzy and almost blacked out. A huge blue egg instantly appeared on my forehead. Some woman I didn't know wanted to take me home to my parents. I immediately replied no, though I was in severe pain. I was terrified of my father because I knew his reaction would've been to tell me I was stupid, dumb, and useless. I would not have received any sympathy, and he would have caused me emotional pain on top of the physical, so I chose to suffer the pain in silence. Another memory I have is one night when I was four years old my father was drunk and threw my mother out of the house. The next morning, she was still not home. I was so scared she was never coming back. After all, my mother was my life. Some friends of my father from the bar came to our house that morning. As they stood in our doorway, and I guess because I was so scared, I told them that my father threw my mother out of the house last night. After I had said that, my father picked me up and threw me into the next room. I guess I embarrassed him, but I truly didn't understand what was going on. My mother finally did come home that day. Come to find out years later she was only downstairs at our neighbors house Mrs. Bakers the whole time.

My mother told me about an incident one day when my brother, David, was an infant. Because she didn't have a driver's license, she had to walk to the neighborhood store and leave the five of us children with my father. She wasn't gone more than 20 minutes, but when she returned; my father told her that David had fallen off the changing table. David was black and blue from head to toe so my mother took him to the hospital. When my mom returned home, my oldest brother Richard, who was age seven at the time, told my mother that the baby wouldn't stop crying so daddy threw him against the wall. The hospital never questioned my mother, and life went on as normal, like nothing ever happened. This was just another day in our lives.

Every day in school the same kids always bought cookies and milk at recess. I never did because my parents never had the money to give me for snacks. One day I don't know what came over me, but I stole some girl's milk and cookie money, put it on my chair, and sat on it. Just one time, I wanted to have cookies and milk. I was so happy thinking I was actually going to get cookies and milk that day, until the girl said her money was missing and they had everyone stand up. Of course, I got caught! I was put in a corner, and never did get cookies and milk. We were a poor family and that is life, but I didn't understand it back then. From a very young age I felt that life was not fair to me.

My brothers and I attended a Catholic school at St. Peter and Paul's in our hometown of Fall River, Massachusetts. My brother Andrew never attended Catholic school, but how tuition, books and uniforms were paid for, for five children, was beyond me. I later found out that my mother would pay whatever tuition she could, and to cover the rest of the cost, she would repair the broken statues in the church, and help out in the school any which way she could. In this Catholic school in the 1960s there was certainly plenty of abuse going around from the nuns. They would hit the kids' knuckles with a metal ruler for anything they thought was disrespectful. Through those years, my brothers had their knuckles hit numerous times. While in the second grade, though I don't remember doing anything wrong, Sister Josephine put me over her knee and spanked me. In the third grade Sister Madeline pulled me by my ear into the room because I was one minute late for class. They also put us in cloakrooms as punishment.

In the sixth grade, our male teacher, Mr. Muniz, took a day off and had his

3

girlfriend, a kindergarten teacher; take over our class for the day. She was young and pretty, and some of the boys in my class were telling her jokes. They weren't bad or dirty jokes and she laughed at them. As she walked by him, one of the boys touched her buttock. The next day Mr. Muniz came in, walked up and down the aisle, and punched every boy square in the face that had told her a joke. I remember this vividly because my brother, Philip, was one of them. He hit Philip in the head with a history book and then slammed Philip's head into the desk. Philip was in my class because he was held back a year. I felt the urge to get up and run out of that school so fast, to go home and get my mother but I didn't, because I was afraid. Nothing was ever said or done to this man because of this incident, or any other. This same man who screamed in my face at age eleven saying that I was on drugs, because I didn't realize he was speaking to me. I was a very shy, meek child, and this humiliated me and deeply affected me, especially since I was already enduring verbal abuse at home. My memories of this man are nothing but mean and cruel, and his cruelty was permitted.

One day, the principal of the school who was a nun, smacked one of my brothers across the face. He came home with a huge red mark on his cheek. My mom went to the school, smacked the principal across her face and said, 'don't ever touch my son again.' After that year we all started going to public school.

My father never held a job for any length of time and the money he did make he would use for his drinking. He would often leave us with no food, and my poor mom trying to figure out how to feed her children. Ketchup sandwiches got us through many days.

Because he never spoke of him, my mother assumed my father's father was deceased. Then one day she found out not only was he alive and well, he was also financially well off. With my mother not knowing where to turn for help, she paid her father-in-law a visit. When he answered the door she said, you don't know me but I'm Alice, your son Norman's wife. She told him that she had five small children, and no food for them, and asked if he could please help them out. He said no, and shut the door in her face. My mother said she was devastated by his lack of compassion. She also said she tried to get help from welfare but with my father living at home and working here and there, they wouldn't help. Honestly, it wasn't their problem that my father drank his pay away.

Though I don't remember, my mother told me that we were evicted many times, until we moved into a cottage on Buffinton St in 1967. Before we moved in, my aunt, uncle, and cousins were living in this house. My father and his three brothers also grew up in this same house. The house was set in the back of another cottage that were both owned by the same person. The owner and residence of the front cottage was a kind, jovial Irish woman named Sarah Partridge and her daughter, Catherine. I loved it when we moved into this house. I had my own bedroom on the second floor, and my oldest brother, Richard, had his own bedroom. The next two oldest Thomas and Philip shared a room. The two youngest, David and Andrew, shared a room. My parent's bedroom was on the first floor. We had a private yard between the houses to play in. For me, this was a dream come true. I was eight years old when we moved into this house and when I turned nine, my brother Andrew, was born. My mother was a stay-at-home mom because in that era, and with six children, she didn't have much choice.

While my mother was dating my father, she had never once seen him drunk, not even with a drink in his hand, until the night of their honeymoon when he got drunk beyond oblivion. My mother was so upset she took my brother Richard and went home to her mother. Her mother told her to go back to her husband because she made her bed, now lie in it. Back then (the early 1950's), that was the mentality. So to back track, yes my mother already had my brother Richard, but my father wasn't his biological father.

My mother was born into a poor family with an alcoholic father. She had two brothers, and a sister. My grandmother was divorced from my grandfather because of his drinking, so I guess my grandmother didn't lie in the bed she made. As a child, my mother was very thin and sickly. She told me how her mother would send her to her father's mother to eat because that was the only way she could get food. Her grandparents only spoke Portuguese and she never knew what they were saying so she said she would just sit there for a while before she left. They didn't offer her anything to eat because they probably didn't understand her real reason for the visits. When she got home her mother would ask her if she ate and she would say yes. She told me although she was hungry, and had shoes with holes in them she couldn't have been happier. She loved her childhood and her family very much.

In her early twenties my mother had a boyfriend named Russell aka Rusty. When Rusty's mom found out that my mother was pregnant she ordered Rusty to have nothing to do with my mom. Instead of Rusty sticking by my mom's side, he did what his mom wanted. Rusty's family had money, and since my mom was poor his family looked down on her. Rusty was a sailor in the service and he had gotten a few of his sailor buddies together to go see the parish priest. Together they all told the parish priest that my mother was a whore and that she had slept with all of them.

My mother was devastated that Rusty had done this to her. Of course it wasn't true that my mom slept with any of the other guys. My mom was so devastated that she tried to commit suicide, because Rusty was the love of her life, and he had betrayed her.

It wasn't long after my mother gave birth to Richard, that she met my father through a friend of hers. My father was thin, blonde hair; blue eyed and presented himself as a standup man. She wasn't in love with him but felt she needed to marry him due to her circumstances. My mother and father married in 1955, and my brother Thomas was born in 1956. Two years later Philip was born, then a year later, me. Then, two years after me, David, then finally, seven years after David, along came Andrew. In 1958 my father legally adopted Richard. By 1968 my mother had six children with a man she despised. I once asked her why she stayed and had all these children with a man she hated. She replied, "I felt I deserved it."

She never fully recovered from her true love Rusty, or what he had done to her. After Rusty was out of the service he moved to Florida and got married. He was an artist and Richard had inherited his talent. He never once attempted to see neither Richard nor my mother. Years later, Homer, a mutual friend of theirs, told my mother that he had spoken to Rusty. Rusty told Homer his wife was unable to have children. Homer said that Rusty believed God was punishing him for what he had done to my mother. I personally don't believe he was being punished but I didn't feel bad for his situation either. My belief is that karma is real, and if you don't work it out in this life, you will have to in another life. Though I don't understand why Homer said that because I later found out that Rusty had a son and a daughter. I don't know if Homer was trying to make my mother feel better by telling her Rusty couldn't have children, or if those children were adopted. I have always wanted to give this man a piece of my mind for what he did to my mother and brother, but instead, I pray for him. I have since found out that Rusty has passed away, and I now pray for his soul to rest in peace, and that my mother's soul gets the healing she deserves.

My father drank on a daily basis, and we were all very frightened of him. My mom told me I was a happy baby always smiling till the day I realized what I was living in, and then, I never smiled again. At dinnertime, my father had to be the first one to be seated and served. If he wasn't home, we didn't eat. We would hear him back his car into the driveway and we would all scramble upstairs before he got in the door. He was drunk every day and you didn't know how he was going to act that day. He was a nasty drunk, and some days he was worse than others. He would first sit at the table, and then we would be called downstairs to eat. Many times he would tell my mother that he was not eating this garbage, and demand she make him something else. Then he would proceed to tip the table over with all the food on it. He would tell us kids to go to bed and those nights we didn't eat. He spoke terribly to all of us all the time. He would constantly tell David he was stupid and a little queer, poor David was only seven years old when he started calling him this. He always told me I was ugly, stupid, and useless as tits on a bull. One day when I was eleven years old a few of my father's friends came to our house. They were standing in our doorway waiting for him and I was standing in the same room not doing a thing. My father walked into the room, and pointing to me, said to his friends, look at her, isn't she an ugly little bastard? His friends didn't respond. My father calling me ugly was just a normal part of my day. He said it so often that I truly believed him. I walked with my face down for many years so no one could see how ugly I was. He would say that my mother was a whore and I was his brother Buddy's child. The only kids he claimed as his were Philip and Andrew. As far as he was concerned, we all had different fathers.

As children my brothers and I loved spending time at my mother's sister Ernestine's house. Auntie Ernie was very kind and good to us. It was nothing like being at my house and I remember spending a lot of time there with my cousins. My grandmother lived with them also but I don't have many memories of her. I remember her voice was deep and I was kind of afraid of her. One day when I was 10 years old she practically begged me to go downtown with her on the bus. She promised she would buy me anything I wanted. I kept refusing and saying I wanted to go with my cousin Joanne to cheerleading practice, so she finally gave up asking me. I didn't know then that she was dying from cancer, and she just wanted to spend some time with me, and get me something to remember her by. Now I feel really bad, but I was just a kid then, and it still stays with me. I'll always regret that decision.

When I was around age 10, David and I were playing in the yard and I can't remember why, but he made me really mad and I started hitting him. I even broke his glasses in half. David ran up the street, I chased after him, threw a rock at him, and it hit him right on the top of his head. He had a huge lump and was crying uncontrollably. When my mother asked me if I had hurt David I denied it and I didn't get in any trouble. I don't understand why I would hurt David like that when he was my best friend. I now believe it was the environment we were living in that made us unhappy with not only ourselves, but at times with each other.

I used to always make David play a game with me in which I would close my eyes; picture a color in my head, and David would close his eyes and try to see the color that I pictured. Then we would switch it up, and David would picture the color in his head, then I would try and see the color in my head. I found this game fascinating because not once was David or I ever wrong about the color we saw. I always felt a strong connection to David, not realizing that it was a soul connection. I truly feel David is a part of my soul family, and we have lived many lives together.

My father always beat my brothers. He would punch them in the head or face. No one ever deserves to be treated that way, especially children. I was lucky in that respect because I was the only girl, so he didn't beat me. But, my mother wasn't so lucky. He would choke her and backhand her. We would get grounded for a week if we dropped our fork at dinner, or if he felt we were eating wrong, like mixing our food together. He would say that we were stupid little fucking bastards, and useless.

There were a lot of negative emotions between my brothers and myself. We were so unhappy with our lives that some of us took it out on each other. My brother Thomas had so much hate and anger towards my father that he wasn't very nice to any of us. Thomas regularly beat Philip, and said the most hateful, angriest words to the rest of us. One morning during breakfast, Thomas was causing so much chaos with his anger that I said something to him. Honestly, I might have called him a name because I was so upset with his behavior. He whipped a spoon at me and it hit me on my left shoulder so hard that the spoon bent. To this day, I don't think anyone has more contempt or hate for my father, than Thomas.

Despite everything I loved living in the house that I grew up in, though at the same time I was afraid because of the spiritual activity there. Yes, this house was definitely haunted. You could hear footsteps of spirits very loudly up-and-down the stairs, and across the floors. We would all be downstairs as we listened to the loud footsteps across the floors, and just stare at each other, frightened. These spirits wanted our attention for some reason. David and I were so afraid, before going to bed, we would put crucifixes on our necks. As I got a little older, they would call my name in a terrifying whisper. One day while lying on my bed; I suddenly started hearing whispers of, "Dawn! Dawn!" Frightened, I ran downstairs as fast as I could. That was the first time I remember ever hearing a spirit's disembodied voice.

My father loved having big parties and card games. He was quite the gambler, an incredible card player, and has never lost a card game. But what the people that played cards with him didn't realize, my father was a professional cheater. I would sit in the room while they played and watched my father's hands very closely to try to catch him cheating, but I never could. After everyone left, he would boast proudly to us how he just cheated his friends out of all their money.

As kids, many times we could not use the phone because my father was a bookie. There was no call waiting back then and people had to call in their bets. On Sundays we weren't allowed to use the phone at all. When I got my drivers license at age sixteen, he would give me huge piles of cash in envelopes and have me take it to the man who ran the gambling ring. I hated doing this, but I didn't dare say no. He was a bookie for over twenty-five years with an organization in Providence, RI.

In the early 1980's my father had foolishly spent $10,000.00 of the organization's money on drinking, drugs and women. He always had a woman on the side; I don't think my mother really cared. My father was nervous to tell them that he didn't have the money, so he came up with a lie. He told them my brother Philip stole the money. Philip was in his early twenties at the time. Two men from Providence were on their way down to break Philip's legs. My mother was very upset and told my father if you don't tell them it was you, then I will. As soon as the men entered our house my mother told them it was my father who spent the money, not her son. Surprised to hear this, they had a talk with my father and asked him why didn't he just tell them he needed the money. Of course, my father lied as to what he spent it on, but he had to pay it back and whatever other stipulations they imposed on him. I never knew what they asked of him, and I don't care to know. I do know he did some shady things for this organization, but never revealed the many things he did for them. I do remember him coming home some nights looking white as a ghost and acting like a scared little boy; whatever he saw or did wasn't good.

My father worked for a moving company in his younger days. It was owned and run by a woman named Rosemary that my father used to see socially. She came from wealth and her moving company was a family business that was left to her from her father. My father used Rosemary for her money. She always had feelings for my father, even when he was married to my mother. Unfortunately for Rosemary, she was a chronic alcoholic. She would be at my house when I was a kid and place bets with my father. She would sit there and drink until she could just barely walk.

Rosemary became a fixture in our house, and a dear family friend. David and I, and sometimes Andrew spent nights at Rosemary's house. Her house had three floors and was so huge so we would run all over the place in it; to us children, it was a playground. David and I would sit at her long dining room table and press our feet on the buzzers on the floor that used to be for calling servants. We loved doing that but it would irritate Rosemary. Every summer she would take David and me to Horseneck Beach in Westport, MA. I have wonderful memories of her taking us to an old-fashioned store on the way, and letting us each get a bag of penny candy. She drove with a six-pack of beer on the side of her, and drank as she drove us.

Although Rosemary no longer owned the moving company, she still had plenty of money. She always wore a long, tan trench coat, and always had a cigarette hanging out of her mouth, with glasses that hung on a cord around her neck. She had this certain smell to her that reminded me of bologna.

Anyone with eyes could see how she felt about my father. My mother told me that out of jealousy, Rosemary treated her bad for many years, but my mother always treated Rosemary back with kindness. Rosemary would try so hard to get my father's attention and she would hang on to every word he said. It really was very sad because most of what he said to her was mean and degrading. Sometimes she would get upset but she always came back. On one side of Rosemary's face her eye, mouth and jaw were crooked. It looked as though she had a stroke. I was always told she fell in the bathtub and that was why her face was like that. When I was older my mother told me the truth; that my father punched Rosemary square in the face, so hard that he broke her jaw, and caused nerve damage. My mother ended up becoming Rosemary's best friend. Rosemary ended up with cancer and lived in a hospice home. My mother was the only person who visited Rosemary and brought her what she needed, including comfort till the day that she passed away.

One day I was taking a nap upstairs and my father and I were the only two at home. I woke up to him calling my name. I came downstairs and he was sitting on the couch drinking a beer. There was a string on the rug in front of him. He pointed to the string and said, "Pick that up." He was always calling me to pick things up off the floor in front of him. I didn't realize the neighborhood kids knew of this till one day I was hanging out at the schoolyard with a couple of my brothers and their friends. One of them pointed to a piece of paper on the ground and said to me, "pick that up". I automatically picked it up because that was what I was use to doing. Immediately, everyone burst out laughing at me because I had picked it up. They didn't understand how cruel they were being to me.

When I turned sixteen my father would buy me little eight packs of beer. He would tell me to drink them because they were good for me. I didn't want to drink beer because it tasted nasty to me. My brother David would drink them for me so I wouldn't get yelled at. Drinking the beers was no problem for David because he started drinking alcohol at the age of twelve. Many terrible things have happened to David in his life and my father's cruelty and physical abuse was only part of it. David had Attention Deficit Hyperactivity Disorder ADHD and dyslexia. Back then this disorder wasn't understood; my father and the nuns at school called him lazy and stupid. He was far from lazy or stupid; he was brilliant, and taught himself many trades. He could do anything electrical, or fix anything that was put in front of him; the ultimate jack-of-all-trades. He had the heart of one of the sweetest souls I ever met. David and I were very close; any closer and we could have been twins. We were always together through thick and thin; I could count on him for anything. He always made me feel safe. David was very inquisitive and often wandered around our town. When he was ten years old he went down to a wooded area to walk the railroad tracks. He would actually go down there to go snake hunting. One day a man who was down at the railroad tracks raped him. The police were never called and nothing was ever done about it. It was swept under the rug like it never happened.

When I was a teenager my father would play a card game with me called knuckles. We would each draw a card from the deck and whomever had the highest card won. The loser would have to put out their hand and close their fist while the winner hit your knuckles with the deck of cards for as many times as the number on the winner's card. I never once won and my father would hit me so hard my knuckles would swell, bleed, and turn black and blue. He would laugh so hard as he hit me, you could see he truly enjoyed doing this. I don't know why I continued to play this demeaning game with him. I think it was because I wanted to show him I was strong, and could take anything he could give me. Today, as a parent I could never imagine wanting to hurt my child that way. As I write this, how could I never have realized that this professional cheater would ever lose? I always had hope I would win and have the chance to hit him back.

One day while my mother was washing dishes as I was drying them. I don't remember our conversation but we were laughing uncontrollably, which is such a wonderful memory for me. My father was lying in bed in the next room, listening to us laugh. He got up and told both of us to get out of the house and don't come back. I went to my friend Helen's house and my mother went to her sister's house. After two days he called us both to come back home. I realize now he was very jealous of the fun we were having and the closeness that we shared.

Though the words were never said to me as a child, I knew with every inch of my being that my mother loved me. She showed her love in every act of kindness she did for her children. My mother loved me unconditionally and for that I will always be grateful. My mom tried her best to stick up for us kids with my dad, but she had to pick her battles wisely.

He abused us all except for my youngest brother Andrew, who was his pride and joy. Andrew could do no wrong in my father's eyes. No matter what Andrew did to any of us, we weren't allowed to do anything back to him or we would have to deal with our father's wrath. He took Andrew everywhere he went, including the bars. He taught Andrew that if anyone touched him, or did anything to him, just let him know and he would take care of them. We all knew that my father specifically meant my brothers and I, which made us petrified of any interactions with Andrew.

One day when I was eleven years old and Andrew was two; I took him on a walk a few blocks away to the corner store. I was standing with Andrew outside of the store speaking with some of my friends. I turned around and saw Andrew standing in the middle of the road with a car headed right toward him. I quickly scooped him up from the road as the car swooshed right by. I felt the wind of it but it never once slowed down. It was like whoever was driving that car never saw him, and would have killed him at the speed they were traveling. Shaking, all I could think of is how my father would have killed me if that car hit Andrew. My main concern was not that a car would have hit Andrew but the terror I felt just thinking about my father's wrath if anything had happened to Andrew.

For Christmas we all received one gift. One particular Christmas when I was twelve years old I was ecstatic because I had received a pottery kit that I really wanted. I was sitting at the kitchen table trying to figure out how to work this Pottery kit. My mom was also sitting there conversing with our landlady Catherine. Andrew, who was three years old, saw me playing with it and wanted my pottery set. I kept telling him you are too young for this and this is mine. My father heard me saying this to Andrew so he came into the kitchen and said if Andrew couldn't have it, then neither can you. My father took it away from me and threw it in the trash. I remember the look on Catherine's face as if she agreed with my father. I was devastated and I felt so alone because no one ever stuck up for me. It was situations like this that made us kids not like Andrew. In reality it was my father's fault, not Andrew's. But as kids you don't see it that way. Andrew was given everything he wanted, and never once received a beating, or even verbal abuse. We would all say that Andrew was the "King." In the long run, Andrew paid the price for my father spoiling him and turning him into the person he became.

On Sundays in the summer months, my father would tell us that he was taking us to an amusement park called Lincoln Park. Excited, we would all pile in the car with my mother. He would tell us that we were making a fast pit stop before we went. The pit stop would always be at his hangout, Crowley's Café. He would say not to leave the car, that he wouldn't be long. Three to four hours later, he would stumble out and drive us home. I don't know why I fell for it every time. I think it is because I had so much hope that each time this would be the time we would actually go, but we never did.

When I was around eleven years old my father took me to my Uncle Buddy's house. Buddy was one of my father's brothers. We went into my Uncle's backyard where my cousins were playing in the pool. It was an above ground pool that was probably only about 3 feet tall. There was a slide to go in to the pool and all my cousins were sliding down it. My father told me to go down the slide and I told him I didn't want to. I was afraid because I have a fear of water. He kept telling me to go down the slide and when I wouldn't he called me useless, and stupid. He then told me to walk home because I was useless. I looked at my Uncle for support and he gave me a look of, "Oh Well." I walked home though I wasn't sure how to get there. It was only a half a mile away from home but at eleven years old it was scary, especially if you don't know where you are going. As a child who witnessed many forms of meanness and abuse, I never felt supported or safe by adults.

At age nine, I was a member of the National Association of Foresters. The Foresters would put on a variety show every St. Patrick's day. I looked forward to doing this show every year and really enjoyed performing. One year I made David do the show with me. He played Pinocchio, and sang Zippity Doo Dah, but he hated every second of it. That was the first and last time David was in the show. I stayed in this group till I was age fifteen because it provided an escape from all the craziness at home.

Since we attended catholic school we learned much about God, Jesus and Mary. As a child I always felt Mother Mary close to me. I can't clearly explain it but I could feel her love, and I never doubted her existence. I've always been a believer in angels and have loved them and felt them around me. In 1984 I did a novena to Mother Mary asking her for money, though as a catholic I was taught you weren't suppose to ask for money. This novena was for nine days and on the eighth day you're supposed to get what you asked for. On the eighth night I had a dream I was walking up the middle of Buffinton St., the street I grew up on. I had both my arms outstretched and in each hand was a Virgin Mary statue. On the bottom of each statue were three numbers though I no longer remember what the numbers were, but both statues had the same exact numbers. When I awoke I inherently knew I was supposed to play those numbers in the daily drawing. Since there were only three numbers and the daily drawing had four numbers I was confused as how to play them. I ended up playing them all kind of ways and won $400.00. The numbers came out that night in the exact order they were on the statue, with the missing number being a zero. I tend to overthink things, if I had kept it simple, I could have won a lot more money. I also passed these numbers on to a woman whom I knew was having money trouble. I told her about the dream and told her to play the numbers and she also won money. I was always sure of Mother Mary's existence, so this only confirmed my belief.

The novena I said to Mother Mary was: May the Blessed Virgin Mary Mother be praised, adored and glorified throughout the whole world forever and ever. Amen. You're supposed to say this prayer six times each day for nine days and no matter how difficult, your petition will be granted. However, you must promise to thank the Sacred Heart and publish your thank you, along with the prayer for others to see. In researching it so far, the author of this prayer is unknown.

Throughout my life, I've had dreams that have come true in real life. One of those dreams was that I went to work in the morning at St Anne's Hospital where I worked as a dietary aide. I walked into the nurse's station and was flipping through patient files looking for any new patients or dietary changes from the night shift. A third shift nurse walked over to me and said Yvette won't be in today, her mother died. When I awoke and went to work, my dream came true exactly as I dreamt. This really freaked me out but I never said a word to anyone about it. It was odd because I didn't know Yvette very well, so why would I dream about her and her mother? I also didn't know the third shift nurse.

Twice in my life I have had dreams of Cher. In the first dream my mother and I were in Cher's house. The three of us were sitting on a carpeted floor in her bedroom laughing and talking as if we were old friends. Cher was sitting halfway in the closet going through her shoes to give some of them to us.

In the second dream I was walking with my mother on a wooded pathway in front of stores. The era we were in was definitely in the days of the Wild West. We were both dressed in men's western cowboy clothes. I was holding a rifle as we walked and talked. We took a right turn at the end of the structure. Cher was also dressed in men's cowboy clothing and she was walking straight towards us. Though I don't remember the words spoken Cher became very upset with me for having a rifle. She turned and walked away from us. Both times that I woke up from these dreams I had felt like I actually spent the night with my mother and Cher. These dreams were so real and absolutely incredible to me. I know that I never met Cher in this lifetime but I honestly feel like my mother and I knew Cher on a soul level. I told a local medium and psychic, Tracey Lynn of these dreams and she told me that her guides said that Cher, my mother and myself have a past life connection together. Though I felt this connection very strongly it was nice to get that confirmation from Tracey Lynn.

One night when my brother David was fourteen years old, I heard him jump out of his bedroom window from the second floor. He would climb onto the porch roof and jump down. This was a usual occurrence for David so he could sneak out to drink. I was used to him doing this but for some reason that night I went into his room after he left. I found a note he had written to my mother. It said he was going to jump off the Braga Bridge and to give his belongings to his girlfriend Jean, whom he loved. My mom was at my grandfather's house taking care of him and his bed-ridden wife. This was my Father's father, the one who had shut the door in her face when she asked him for help. My mother was a selfless person with a heart of gold. I called my mom and told her of David's letter. She immediately left my grandfathers and went looking for David. She did find him and she pulled up along side of him. David was amazed that my mom was there and he climbed into her car. He said Mom, this is a miracle because I was just going to jump off the bridge and kill myself. I believe the angels guided me that night to find the note and call my mother. I also believe that the angels helped my mother find David that night to save his life. It wasn't David's time to go and for that I am very grateful. David and my mom were the only two people who ever showed me unconditional love and made me feel safe. During my entire childhood I would constantly go into my mother's room to make sure she was breathing, because I was terrified of losing her, and being stuck with my father.

Another time when I was eighteen years old and David was sixteen, he woke me up around 5am one Saturday to tell me he took my car the previous night. He then told me my car was dead on Second St., and not to tell my father. This was wrong on many fronts. He took my car without my permission, he didn't have a driver's license, and he was drunk. I was really angry with him and I told him I was going to tell my father. I never was going to tell my father what David had done. I just said that to him because I was angry. I didn't know what to do at that point so I lied in bed trying to get back to sleep. I was too upset to sleep, and I could hear David vomiting in his bedroom. I said to myself, good for you. Around 8am my mother and I was walking to St Anne's Hospital so she could get a chest x-ray. On the way there we walked right by Second St. and right in the middle of the road, double-parked, was my car with not a scratch on it. The key was still in the ignition so I turned the ignition and the car-started right up. I figured that David was so drunk he probably flooded the car with gas and didn't realize it. Relieved, off we went to the hospital.

While me and my mother were sitting in the x-ray waiting room, my father came rushing in to tell us something was wrong with David. We went home immediately and found David unconscious, vomiting blood. We called an ambulance; something my father should have done, instead of driving down to the hospital to tell us. While in the waiting room of the emergency department, my mother came out to tell me that the doctors said David wasn't going to make it. He had ingested a whole bottle of Tylenol, and his organs were shutting down. Then Dr. Harrington, my mother's physician, came out and told my mother that there was a new experimental drug that they could try if she wanted them to. At this point my mother figured what did we have to lose, so she told them to try it. David was in the intensive care unit with tubes everywhere in his body. David survived and was perfectly healthy. Till this day, I don't know the name of the drug they used, but I'm very grateful for it. David and I never spoke of the car incident, or of him trying to take his own life. Although I did feel guilt about telling him I was going to tell my father on him when I knew how much we all feared him. But I also know I am not responsible for anyone else's actions. One thing I'm certain of is that David's life being saved once again was pure Divine Intervention. His time on this earth was not done; he had not fulfilled his purpose on this earth yet. Whatever purpose that may be, only God and David's higher self knows for sure.

In my teenage years I hung out with a girl named Lisa. She was dating my brother Thomas and one day Lisa and I walked up to Maplewood Park where Thomas was hanging out with his friends. I believe I was fifteen years old at the time. We walked up to Thomas and his friends and Thomas looked at me and said, "what the fuck are you doing here, get the fuck out of here you dyke." Thomas's friends all laughed and Lisa just looked at me. I walked home alone crying while Lisa stayed behind with Thomas. I didn't know what a dyke was but I felt humiliated at the way everyone laughed at me. When I got home I told my mother what Thomas called me and she said "that bastard!" I asked her what it meant, but she didn't tell me. When I finally found out what dyke meant I knew one thing for sure, and that was that I didn't ever want to be one, because of people's reactions to it.

When I was about fifteen years old there was a knock on the door and when I answered it, two girls in there twenties were standing in the entryway. They said to me, "Is my Dad here?" and I answered, "You have the wrong house," and closed the door. They knocked again and I opened the door and, was just about to tell them that I told you that you have the wrong house, when my mother hurriedly came over and told them to come inside. This was how I found out that my father had a previous marriage, and these were his two daughters from it. I was shocked, and quite amazed at this news. My whole life I wished I had a sister, and now, here they were in front of me.

They would come over to visit my father and they never spoke to me. I would sit and watch them visit and noticed the way my father seemed happy to see them and how well he treated them. After some time went by, I started speaking to them and his oldest daughter Gail would converse with me. His younger daughter Colleen would act like I didn't exist; she never once spoke to me; she would either turn her head away, or give me a nasty look. I always tried but couldn't figure out why she didn't like me. In 1986, at age thirty-five, Colleen passed away from an aneurysm in her head, leaving behind four young children. Till the day she passed we never once spoke. After Colleen's passing Gail and I became close and will always remain that way.

When I was about nineteen years old my paternal grandfather moved in with us after his wife died. He moved into my parent's room on the first floor, and my parents moved upstairs to my brother's bedroom since my older brothers had already moved out. Sometimes during the day, while we were at work or school, my grandfather was alone. When we got home he would tell us how he could hear the spirits footsteps. He said he went to the bottom of the stairs and yelled, show yourself, you bastards. But for some reason they would walk up and down the stairs but never pass the stairs on the first floor. After my mother began sleeping upstairs, she would wake up with three bloody scratches down both her thighs.

My father had a friend named Jack and his wife Charlene. They were a very nice younger couple; nothing like his bar room friends. One night while Jack and Charlene were at my house, we all started talking about the spirits upstairs. Come to find out that Jack and Charlene were medium-psychic's. They both offered to go upstairs and speak to the spirits. They were upstairs for a short time when Charlene came back downstairs looking very pale, and as if she was going to faint. About fifteen minutes later Jack came downstairs, and they both said they would never go upstairs again.

Jack proceeded to tell us that there was a man and a woman upstairs in spirit. He said they never passed the stairs onto the first floor because the house used to be a two-family dwelling and their apartment was on the second floor. The woman was scratching my mother out of jealousy, because she didn't like her. While this woman was alive, she was very jealous of her significant other. Jack said they were a younger couple that died from a murder-suicide. My mother never slept upstairs again, and she never got scratched again. The spirits continued to make themselves known by loud footsteps and whispering my name. Somehow I knew they wouldn't hurt me but they seemed to get pleasure out of frightening me, especially the female spirit.

In my teenage years my father started taking a lot of Valium to go along with his drinking. He would drive home from the bar drunk and high everyday and not once did he ever get pulled over, or get into an accident. Even if he would have gotten pulled over, in those days he had many friends who were lawyers, Judges, even policemen. He would do favors for them and in return, they would leave him alone. Many of these men also gambled with my father. When one of my brothers got in trouble with the law they were always there to help, as the saying goes "One hand washes the other." I couldn't tell you what these favors were, but I'm grateful to have been left out of knowing the inner business dealings, I just knew it went on. Because when these men would be in our house I would watch and listen to what was said or done in front of me, though I never spoke about any of it to anyone. I knew better.

My father enlisted in the US Army at age eighteen. He and his three brothers were all in the service at the same time. They all served in World War II. Many days my father would come home so disoriented that he thought he was back in the war. He would relive it in his mind, and, as always, he thought I was a Japanese enemy. He would think my mother was a friend of his named Schumacher that he had served with in the army. I would be very frightened because he would look at me like he was going to kill me. He would often punch the walls and the stick on air fresheners thinking they were bombs. He would look at my mother and say, "Schumacher is that you?"

My father served on the front lines with Schumacher. While in a trench to protect themselves from the enemy, they could hear the enemy approaching, so close that Schumacher started freaking out and screaming. My father knocked him out to keep him quiet so the enemy couldn't hear him. It was Schumacher's turn to get ammunition but, since my father knocked him out, my father had to go himself to get the ammunition. My father returned and saw that a bayonet had slit Schumacher's throat. He ended up having a nervous breakdown from it. He felt it was his fault Schumacher was dead because he knocked him out. My father was released from the Army and came home with Post Traumatic Stress Disorder, though he was never treated for it.

My father was born in 1927. When he was four years old, his mother died from pneumonia. She was only age thirty-two, but left behind a husband, and four sons. In those days they kept "wake" for the dead in their own homes. During the wake for my grandmother they couldn't find my father. They finally found him lying in the coffin with his mother. He just thought she was sleeping and wanted to be with her.

My grandfather married another woman whom had three children of her own. He left his four sons with his mother to raise by herself, and had nothing to do with them after he married this other woman. He took on another family and abandoned his own. So, their grandmother raised my father and his three brothers. She resented having to raise her grandchildren and wasn't very nice to them. She was a screaming, raging, alcoholic. The cottage I grew up in was the same house my father and his brothers grew up in also. As I write this I'm wondering for the first time if it had any negative effect on my father raising his children in the same house he was raised in. I believe my father had Post Traumatic Stress Disorder before he even entered the army.

TWO

My Addiction

After I graduated from high school, I applied to the Drama Department at Rhode Island College. I was accepted and was beyond excited. I then applied for financial aid and was denied. My parents couldn't help me financially and I didn't realize student loans existed. So, when the semester started and I wasn't there, the school called me to find out why. Although I told them I couldn't get financial aid, no one ever informed me about student loans or any other way to get help for college. I sure wish someone would have pointed me in the right direction, or offered me some sort of assistance. Extremely disappointed, I did the only thing that I knew how to do, work, so I took a job at St. Anne's Hospital as a dietary aide.

I was working at the hospital for a year when my father told me to go down to The Corky Row Credit Union. This is a small neighborhood credit union that he did all his business with. He said the woman was expecting me and to just sign the paper. Out of fear, I did as he instructed. I didn't even question what it was for; it seemed like a simple enough requests to sign a piece of paper. I soon found out what a "simple signature" meant. I cosigned for a loan that he defaulted on, and they came after me and threatened to take me to court. I had no choice but to take out my first loan at another credit union to pay it off.

I would come home from work and many times the only person who would be home was my father. Numerous times he would be sitting at the kitchen table very drunk, playing Russian roulette. I would be absolutely terrified, not knowing what to do. He would make his way upstairs after a while and I would sit downstairs just waiting in horror for the gun to go off. One day I brought a friend home from work and my father was sitting at the kitchen table with the gun in his hand. She got so nervous she asked me if I needed help to wash the "gun" but she meant the dishes. Another time while drunk, he tried to walk down the stairs but instead fell all the way down them and hit the wall. I didn't help him; I just stared at him, and then walked away. I didn't feel bad for him; actually at that moment I didn't feel anything for him.

Growing up, there were many different parties and card games at my house. My father was the one who wanted all these social events, but my mother was the one who had to do all the work. My mother began working at a job when we all got older so the poor thing was exhausted all the time. My father would invite neighbors and friends over for these events. He was always the life of the party and he always made everyone laugh, usually at the expense of others.

When any of us children turned sixteen my father made us get jobs. My father would take our pay from us and would give us $20.00 for the week. My brothers all worked full time and I worked part time because I stayed in school. My only brother who graduated from high school except myself was Richard.

My father was very good to anyone who was outside of our immediate family, and was well liked by friends and neighbors. No one really knew how we were all living behind closed doors. Our lives looked wonderful to those on the outside. My father always got drunk at these events and then would disappear to bed. Sometimes he would stay passed out for the night, other times he would get up after everyone left and cause chaos in the house. He would throw things around, swear at us and tell us how useless we all were. He would push my mother around and call her a whore. I thought this was the way I was going to live the rest of my life. I never had a thought of getting out of there and living a different way. I used to always ask my mother, "Why was I born?" She would always tell my brothers and myself "Better days are coming." My brother David left home when he was age sixteen. My three older brothers hit the road as soon as they turned eighteen. I didn't leave at eighteen because I couldn't bear leaving my mother with my father. For some reason, I was also terrified at the thought of leaving home because that was all I knew.

When I was twenty years old I was in the bathroom ready to get into the shower when my father suddenly opened the bathroom door. I stood there naked and shocked, and tried to cover myself. My father stood there and leered at me for what seemed like forever, but was probably a minute and a half. I was embarrassed and ashamed because I knew my father shouldn't have been looking at me the way he did. Instead, he should of shut that door right away and apologized, but he just looked and never said a word. He opened that door on purpose, with the intent on seeing me naked. I don't remember if I told my mother, because I was so embarrassed.

A few weeks later I came home from work and my father was sitting at the kitchen table, drunk. He said to me, "I keep thinking about you and me sleeping together." Mortified, and scared, I couldn't respond. Instead, I went to my bedroom and locked myself in. When I told my mother what my father proposed, she said, "That Bastard." I have no idea if she ever said anything to him about it. I was hoping he was so drunk and out of his mind that he wouldn't remember what he had said to me. A few weeks later my mother was admitted to the hospital for pneumonia. At night I would close my bedroom door and lock it. Then my father said, "Do you lock your bedroom door because of what I said to you?" I shook my head no, because I was so afraid of him. Once I realized that he was aware of what he had said, I decided it was time to move out. I wasn't going to hang around to get raped from my own father. I felt bad for my mother but I had to protect myself. I stayed in that house for as long as I possibly could for my mother's sake, but it was time for me to move on.

I got an apartment with a girl named Celeste that I worked with, and a friend named Timmy. It was like a Three's Company set up. Celeste and I both worked in the Dietary Department at St. Anne's Hospital. It was perfect for me because Celeste had a car, and I didn't. She would drive us back and forth to work and anywhere else we needed to go. Everything was great; I was free, and happy. I started smoking weed, and drinking with my new roommates. We would hang out at Jake's Twin Saloon to listen to bands and drink. Timmy was a keyboard player in a local band and he knew many people in other bands. One night we were listening to a band called "Sabotage", and Donna, the lead vocalist was very good. After the band completed a set Donna came over and sat at our table.

There was a guy named Ducky at our table that I thought was very cute. I found out Ducky was Donna's boyfriend. I had a good buzz on from drinking and Donna was trying to be friendly to me but I was very cold to her. When the night at Jake's ended, a lot of people came back to our apartment to party, including Donna and Ducky. The harder I tried to ignore Donna, the harder she tried to be my friend. I was acting like a brat and I went and sat on the porch roof on the second floor. Donna followed me out there and sat with me. I can't remember what was said between us, but from that night on we were best friends.

Our apartment was a constant party house. I got drunk every single night. But I always got up and made it to work, which made me a functioning alcoholic. One night I walked out of my bedroom and there were five people in the living room snorting cocaine. I asked them what they were doing because I'd never seen cocaine before. They told me that everyone did it; that it was amazing, and then they asked me if I wanted some. Of course I said yes, and when I tried it, I immediately fell in love with it. It gave me such an uplifting feeling, and the energy it supplied me with was incredible. I continued with my drinking every night and now every chance that I got, I also did cocaine.

I left my father's house and all the abuse behind, to go into my own alcoholism and self-abusive behaviors. In the beginning it was fun drinking, and doing drugs. But after awhile it wasn't that fun anymore especially, if you can't stop.

My mother couldn't take it any longer living with my father so she took my brother Andrew and left him. She knew my father wouldn't allow it and she was afraid of what he would do to her. There happened to be an empty three-bedroom apartment where Donna lived with her mother. Donna's mother's boyfriend Armand owned the building so he let us move in. I moved out of the apartment with Celeste and Timmy, and moved in with my mother and Andrew, who was now fourteen. I had my bedroom set moved into the apartment before they even moved in. My mother planned the day of their moving in secrecy due to my father. She hired movers to come get her belongings after my father left for the bar. My grandfather was still living with my parents but she didn't tell him she was moving out until that very day. She asked him to please not say a word to my father about her moving out. As soon as my mother walked out the door for the final time my grandfather called my father at the bar and told him everything.

My father drove home from the bar as fast as he could and followed the moving trucks to our new apartment. He walked right in to the apartment and saw that my bedroom set was already there as the moving men were only moving in my mother's stuff. Right there and then he decided it was my fault that my mother had left him. He said I was the one who talked her into moving out, that I was sneaky, and planned this all behind his back.

I couldn't understand why my grandfather had told my father about my mother moving out, after everything she had done for him. Then I realized he didn't do it to hurt my mother, he was afraid of living alone with my father. My father was very mean to him, verbally abusing him just like he did to the rest of us. I also realized that my father resented his father for abandoning him and raising another family, also, that he left my father and his brothers to be raised by a raging alcoholic. My grandfather was now elderly, and not able to stick up for himself, and was afraid of being alone. Though abuse isn't justified for any reason, I believe karma is real.

My grandfather hated living there so much and was so sick of the abuse that he threw himself down the basement stairs in an attempted suicide. He was taken to the hospital and thankfully wasn't severely hurt, except for the contusions and cuts on his body. This attempt got him what he wanted which was out of my father's house. After he recovered, he was sent to a nursing home in another town. My mother would visit him at the nursing home often and he would ask for me to go visit him. I never once went to see him because I was too busy drinking and doing drugs. My grandfather passed away in 1983 and honestly I can't remember if I even went to his wake or funeral.

Two days after my mother moved out of my father's house, my father's girlfriend Mona moved in with her two daughters. I don't know how long he was seeing Mona but I knew he always cheated on my mother. I was very upset with him for this because it is one thing to hear about it but quite another to have it shoved in your face. My father and Mona were always hosting barbeques and parties; and they invited my brothers but not me. My father told Andrew to tell me to stay away from his house because he hated me for making my mother leave. Though I was happy to be free of him I was still hurt because I did nothing wrong. Even though my father abused me and put me through a lot, I still wanted his love.

Andrew was on the phone with Mona at our apartment one day while I was drunk. I started yelling what a slut she was and a "no good" whore. She said she was coming down to my apartment to beat me up. I yelled to her that I'd be waiting outside. Thankfully she never showed up because my father wouldn't let her. Mona was twenty years younger than my father. She was also the former girlfriend of someone who was in a motorcycle gang called "The Sidewinders" whom at the time had a very bad reputation. She was an alcoholic with a very tough demeanor. She would have physically messed me up, especially since I never had a fight in my life before. Then one night I was with Donna at a bar called Benjamin's, in Tiverton, Rhode Island. Of course I was drunk and Donna said to me, I think that is Mona over there. I had never laid eyes on Mona till that night. I walked over to her and said, "Are you Mona?" She said "Yes I am; are you Dawn?" I said, "Yes I am." Honestly, I can't remember a word said after that because I was so drunk. But from that night on, Mona and I became good friends, which in turn put me back in my father's life. I would occasionally go to their house and drink with them. My father and I were on a whole different level now that we were drinking buddies.

Mona and I would snort cocaine in the bathroom at my father's house because my father wouldn't allow it. I would go to the bathroom to snort a line of cocaine and leave a line for Mona. She would go to the bathroom right after me and do her line. After my father went to bed, we were free to snort the cocaine in the living room and drink all night long. There wasn't a night that I didn't drink, and it didn't matter whom I was with, as long as I was partying.

Though I had a bedroom and all my belongings at my mother's apartment, I never slept there. Part of that was because my mother didn't want any drinking at her house. On some level I resented my mother for not taking us out of all the abuse we grew up in. After I'd gotten sober, I realized she was a co-dependent with issues of her own. Her self-esteem was so low that she felt she deserved to live that life. How could she have had the courage to leave my father, take care of all those children, and live on her own when she felt useless?

Donna and her Mom lived right next door to my mother's apartment. I always slept at Donna's house and I spent all my time there. There were porches that were attached to the front of the house and I would climb over the rails to go between apartments. I only went to my mother's when I needed clothes. My mother told Donna's mother she didn't think I loved her. I didn't realize I was hurting my mother's feelings. Of course I loved my mother, but I just didn't know how to deal with life at that point. Donna and I went out drinking just about every single night. Since Donna's job was singing in a band in clubs, her place of employment was perfect for us.

My brother Philip was addicted to heroin and was living with his girlfriend who was also addicted. David was drinking and doing heroin. One day I gave my brother Andrew a gold bracelet that he absolutely loved. Andrew came to me and told me that Philip had stolen it from him. I was so angry with Philip that I confronted him, but he denied stealing it. I called him a lying, thieving drug addict. I felt so bad for Andrew that I bought him another bracelet. It wasn't long before that bracelet also disappeared. I soon found out that fifteen-year old Andrew was also addicted to heroin. Till this day Andrew and Philip both swear they didn't have anything to do with the disappearance of the bracelets and it really doesn't matter anymore.

I came out of work one day and saw that someone had taken either a bat or a pipe and smashed up my car. All the lights and windows were broken, and the car's body was dented in. I was very upset. I was just about to call the police when I realized that my mother was standing next to me. She had come to tell me that it was Andrew who had damaged my car. She said he thought I told my mother he was on drugs and this is how he retaliated. Honestly, I didn't tell my mother of Andrew's drug use, but she was not blind. I didn't call the police because my mother asked me not to. Yes, I helped her to enable Andrew, mostly out of fear of how vindictive he was, especially to me.

At the height of my addiction, I went on a three-day cocaine, alcoholic binge. During these three days I ate only one slice pizza, but drank plenty of beer. By the end of the three days I looked malnourished though I was already underweight. The amount of cocaine I had done outweighed the amount of beer I drank so I was never actually drunk. After three days of partying and no sleep I had come to the point of total exhaustion. I was at my friend's house and he suggested that I go upstairs to sleep but when I laid on the bed, I looked up and I saw a man, a woman and a little girl standing at the foot of the bed staring at me. I thought to myself, I am hallucinating. I could see them plain as day and although I thought I was hallucinating I yelled at the woman, "What are you looking at?" then I said to the little girl, "What is your name?" They continued to just stand there and stare at me. They were looking at me with a bit of shock and befuddlement on their faces as though they couldn't believe that "I" was seeing them. I finally passed out but I could never forget this incident. Due to the ingestion of alcohol, cocaine and a lack of sleep, I first considered this a hallucination. As I thought about this incident from time to time through the years, it never sat quite right with me. I intuitively knew there was something more to it than just a hallucination. I now realize that the level of consciousness that my mind was in allowed me to see the spiritual presence that was in that house. I should have had a clue because their hair and clothing were from the 1930's. Those three spirits appeared to me as outright apparitions. It was an incredible experience that was given to me so vividly and clearly till the time came in my life that I would truly understand what really happened that day. Of course I am not encouraging any three-day mind altering binges of any sort. If anything, it actually slowed the development of my gift.

My poor mother left her abusive, alcoholic husband and now had to deal with her children being alcoholics and drug addicts. My two oldest brothers, Richard and Thomas both moved to California. They were the smart ones because they separated themselves from all the negativity and addictions. I'm not saying things were perfect for them but they both made themselves a better life, and they never looked back.

When Donna and I were out at a club one night we saw one of my cousins there. I asked him if he knew where I could get some cocaine. He pointed me to a man from Nigeria named Alex. We approached him and he invited us to go back to his apartment because that was where the cocaine was. Donna and I went with him to his apartment and we snorted cocaine all night long for free. We hit the jackpot with this guy so we made this a weekly thing. Alex didn't have a piece of furniture in his apartment, but we didn't care, as long as there was cocaine. The only thing in his place was a safe loaded with money. He never once took money from us or asked us for anything in return. He would roll up $20 bills to snort the cocaine and we would stick the bills in our pockets after we used them.

One night, Donna didn't want to go to Alex's apartment to party, so I went by myself. We were doing our usual partying and after a short time I started vomiting. Then I started uncontrollably vomiting every five to ten minutes. In the early morning Alex called a taxi to take me home. The taxi driver had to keep pulling over so I could vomit. I went to my mother's apartment and I continued vomiting every ten minutes over the next 24 hours.

My mother took me to the hospital where they took blood work and gave me intravenous fluids for dehydration. The blood work revealed that I had blood poisoning. I was admitted to the hospital with intravenous antibiotics for several days. Whatever Alex cut that cocaine with gave me the blood poisoning. I don't know what his intentions were but Donna or I never bothered with him again. The day I was released from the hospital they told me to go home and rest. Instead, I went out got really drunk.

As Andrew's addiction grew, he constantly stole from my mother and me. Philip and his girlfriend didn't steal from us but would come and hang out in our apartment. They would shoot their drugs up in our bathroom then sit on our couches and nod out on heroin. David would come to our apartment very drunk, loud, and obnoxious. One day David had me lie to the police telling them he wasn't at my apartment though he was there and was really drunk. We had a back porch that was attached to the house like the front one. After I lied for David he went on to the back porch of our apartment, which was on the second floor. He started calling the police names and saying vulgar things to them. I got so angry with David that I went on to the porch and started punching him. Neighbors and police all looked on as I did this and they were all laughing. I wasn't doing this to be funny. I couldn't understand why he had me lie, and then show himself to them. I ended up letting the police in to arrest him--after all how could I now say he wasn't there. It's a good thing for my mother that I kept most of my drinking over at Donna's or at bars and clubs, because she was already dealing with my brothers and their addictions.

One night while Donna was away singing with her band at a club, I was drinking in her apartment by myself, and getting very drunk. I said to myself, "Okay Dawn, lay down and go to sleep," and I did lie down. The next thing I remember, I was sitting on my father's couch with a beer in my hand. It was about 3 am and I was just coming out of an alcoholic black out. Mona was sitting on one side of me and the television was on. As I was coming out of this black out, a commercial for a rehabilitation center for addictions was on the television. It was called Edgehill Newport and I said to Mona, "I want to go there." Mona, who was also drunk, called the place right there and then, and they said to bring me right in. Mona drove drunk to take me to this 30-day rehabilitation program.

When I woke up the next morning at Edge Hill Newport, I wanted to leave. Still drunk, I called Donna to come get me. I told her everyone there was staring at me, giving me dirty looks, and wasn't treating me well. I might have felt that way, but it wasn't true. I just wanted to get out of there. Donna's mother wouldn't let her come get me and I stayed the entire 30 days. I was happy that I stayed. I really enjoyed the program and became enlightened about alcoholism. When it was almost time for me to leave this program, I spoke to my father on the phone. He told me that he was going to pick me up and bring me a small eight pack of beer since I just learned how to drink. This revealed my father's own ignorance of alcoholism, and needless to say, I didn't have him pick me up.

Unfortunately, I didn't stay sober for very long and became a closet drinker. I thought I was hiding it from everyone, but I was only lying to myself. I couldn't drink out in the open any longer, which made it so much more difficult to drink. Truthfully, at this point it was only misery but I just couldn't find it in myself to stop. I would drink at my father's house with him and Mona because I could drink out in the open there. Sometimes I would spend days at their house getting drunk from morning till night. I would pass out on their couch and a few mornings I woke up soaked in urine. I was too drunk to wake up and go to the bathroom. They wouldn't get mad at me; they would give me fresh clothes to change into. After I changed my clothes, my father would take Mona and me to the bar where we would continue obliterating ourselves with alcohol. It was a never-ending circle that I would eventually have to stop temporarily to get myself together so I could go to work.

Mona finally left my father, and at this point her children were old enough to go out on their own. She shared an apartment with a friend of hers and I didn't see her much after this. Mona got very drunk one day, passed out on her back, and chocked on her own vomit. She lost oxygen for a while, ended up with severe brain damage, and had the mentality of an infant. I visited her a few times, but she didn't know who I was, and it was too sad for me to see her this way. She lasted two years in that hell before she passed to spirit. My father moved into a high-rise building for older people. He met his third wife there who was twenty years his junior.

The next couple of years I continued to drink and hated myself for it. I began cutting my wrists with razors because I hated myself so much that I felt I deserved it. When the blood would start to flow, I felt as though my pain was being released. I went to counseling but it didn't help. For the second time, I went to Edge Hill

Newport for another thirty days. This time I didn't enjoy the program like I did the first time I went. I met a guy in the program, and we were released on the same day. We went to a hotel, drank, and slept together. Believe it or not, I was a virgin until that day. Donna had always kept a good eye on me; she made sure nothing ever happened to me. I'll always be very grateful to her for that.

My brothers were still hanging out in my mother's apartment getting drunk and high. Andrew was still robbing us every chance he could. The landlord got so sick of it all, he evicted us. Donna's mother moved downstairs to a very small one-bedroom apartment. I moved with my mother and brother Andrew. I was still closet drinking but going to AA meetings at the same time. I found myself a wonderful sponsor in the AA program.

I just couldn't connect with anyone at these meetings. Everyone there was so much older than me. I heard of a group called NA (Narcotics Anonymous); people there were more my age, so that helped me attend these meetings. Although I tried my best, I was unable to stay fully sober. Andrew's addictions got so bad that he called a thrift store and sold them our cooking stove, refrigerator and space heater. When my mother and I returned from work, we couldn't believe that he had done this. He knew that she would not throw him out regardless of what he did, so why not continue to rob us repeatedly. My mother was a wonderful enabler, and I was no better. My mother and I called around to the thrift stores and found where our items were. We then went down to the store and bought them all back. The next week while we were at work, Andrew sold all the items once again to another thrift store. This time he also sold our grandfather clock, which actually was my grandfather's. I had a beautiful antique hope chest from my grandmother that I loved, and he sold that also. He kept selling so much of our stuff that there was no way to keep getting everything back.

I planned a trip to California to visit my brothers. I bought all new summer clothes and shoes for the trip and stored them in my bedroom closet. When I got home from work, they were all gone. Andrew had sold everything. I lost count of how many times, and how many of our television sets he's sold. One thing I absolutely loved was my jewelry. I had gold necklaces in every length with charms, and rings with diamonds, sapphires and rubies. Andrew stole every piece of jewelry I owned. I was heartbroken and to this day I could care less about jewelry; he ripped my love for it right out of me.

I was very upset with Andrew and told my mother he had to leave this house. But she said to me "Why don't you get out?" Her words devastated me. It felt like a knife through my heart, but I didn't respond to her, I just felt like crying. Instead of crying though, I went out looking for Andrew, and when I found him I demanded he give me his key to our apartment. He refused, and instead, kicked my car window in. I got out of my car and started punching him, insisting he give me the key. He was muttering under his breath that I better stop. I knew he would've hit me but at this point a crowd gathered and was watching us, so I was saved.

A few months later I pulled up in front of my house with David's four-year-old son asleep in my backseat. I saw my brother Philip running out of my yard with a coat on and the hood on his head. He was carrying something under his armpit. I noticed a woman sitting in the car in front of me. He opened this woman's car door and while getting in said to her, "Let's go." Philip is six foot three inches tall and has a very deep, distinctive voice so I had no doubt this was Philip. I said to myself, "What the heck is Philip doing?"

I carried my nephew into my apartment and saw my television set on the floor by the door, and my VCR was gone. I quickly realized Philip was in the middle of robbing me when I pulled up. I called the police and pressed charges. Philip went to prison for breaking and entering and theft. That was the first and last time Philip ever stole from me.

THREE

Divine Intervention

I finally got myself a sponsor from the NA meetings. I was drinking sporadically at this point. I did everything she told me to do but I just couldn't stay sober. Andrew robbed the girls that lived upstairs from us and in return we were evicted once again. I moved in with my sponsor and her young son. Her son and I shared a bedroom. He had bunk beds; I slept on the bottom one and he slept on the top one. I made a lot of friends in the program. Due to past connections, the friend I most relied on was Kelly. Kelly's father and my father used to share an apartment together when they were single. Kelly's brothers and my brothers hung together when they were younger so our families have a history together. I always had so much fun when I was with Kelly. I still slipped once in a while, so I still wasn't fully sober.

I would see this guy at meetings and would enjoy listening to him speak. He was funny, interesting, good looking and the only one who ever said his full name in a meeting, which always made me laugh. Come to find out he was my sponsor's brother George. George came over to visit his sister and we became very friendly. We started seeing each other romantically. I found George quite charming and easy to speak to. We really didn't have a relationship, it was more of a get together and we were both very content this way. About 10 months later I found out that I was pregnant. I never used birth control and I never had a single thought about getting pregnant.

While working one day I felt so weak and fatigued, I wondered what was wrong with me. I finally put two and two together and took a pregnancy test. About a week later I saw George at a meeting and told him I was pregnant. He became very upset with me, and told me to get an abortion. I told him I wouldn't have an abortion. George went around to the meetings and told people he didn't think it was his because I was sleeping around. This was not so. I knew positively it was

George's baby. I felt like it was Rusty with my mother all over again.

One day when I was working at the hospital, Andrew came to tell me he knew someone whom was selling a bunch of brand new maternity clothes. I was excited at the prospect of having some maternity clothes. I told Andrew that would be a wonderful financial help for me. I gave him money to go get me some clothes. But before I handed it over I looked into his eyes and said, "Andrew you are not robbing me are you?" He looked at me directly in my eyes and said, "I promise I am not robbing you." I handed him the money, but I never received any clothes. Many times I gave him the benefit of the doubt. I always believe in people and hope the best of them. I know sometimes I'm just naïve, or some people would call me plain stupid. But if you don't give people a chance, then you will never truly know if they have changed. Basically people are good, they just need someone to trust them.

I continued to live with George's sister during most of my pregnancy. I gave her money every week to live there. I let her use my credit cards and she used them all to the limit and she couldn't help me pay them back. I couldn't pay them off so I was drowning in debt. I ended up having to claim bankruptcy. At seven months pregnant I had to quit work due to severe pain from a pinched nerve in my back.

George's sister started being very cold to me and acted like she no longer wanted me there. I decided to throw her a birthday party, making it as lavish as I could. Because she was my sponsor, I truly looked up to her, blind to the fact that I was financially being used. I didn't have any more credit cards for her to use. I was feeling sad and didn't understand what was going on with her. One night, our friend Laura said I could sleep at her house because her husband was out of town. While there her husband came home so she said I couldn't stay and took me back to George's sister. When I arrived everyone was already sleeping so I just climbed into bed.

In the morning I could hear my friend Kelly and George's sister in the living room talking about me. They thought I was still at Laura's house and they were speaking negatively about the birthday party that I threw for George's sister. I heard them say that I had bad intentions when I didn't. I did not understand what they meant when all I was trying to do was be kind. I was so hurt I lied in bed crying. When they left I called up Laura and she came over and helped me move all my stuff into her house. Laura and her husband were kind enough to let me stay there until I could figure things out. Years later I asked Kelly what they meant when they were talking about me, and she said it doesn't matter.

Even at seven months pregnant I still drank some days. I felt abandoned and unloved, and I didn't care about myself or even think about the child that I was carrying. The people that I worked with at the hospital were throwing me a baby shower. Two of the girls came to pick me up at Laura's house. I remember it was a hot July day and I felt pretty cute in my cotton pink and white striped maternity outfit. I heard a car horn beep and went outside. Walking towards the car I saw my friends waving but as I waved back, my right foot stepped into a hole in the road and I fell. Instinctively, I put my hands out in front of me and protected my stomach from hitting the ground. I was in severe pain. The girls came running over to me and when they saw my ankle they called an ambulance. The EMTs put my right foot and leg in an air cast. I kept telling the EMT's that something was wrong with my left ankle also. They kept telling me that there wasn't anything wrong with it that it was just phantom pain transferred from the right ankle.

At the hospital I was taken immediately into x-ray. Shortly after my x-rays, the doctor said that my right ankle was broken in five places, and my left ankle in two places. I waited a while for an orthopedic surgeon to arrive to speak to me. The orthopedic doctor told me he didn't know if I was ever going to walk on the right leg again. He then told me I needed to have surgery on my right ankle. He wouldn't prescribe me anything for pain because I was pregnant.

My right foot was hanging, my ankle and leg was bruised up to my knee. When my mother entered the emergency room and saw my leg she immediately started to cry. Unfortunately, they were not doing my surgery till the next morning and they needed to set my foot till then. The orthopedic doctor told me to hold on to the rails of the bed because it was going to hurt. He then snapped my foot into position so it wasn't hanging, and boy did I scream. He then put a temporary brace on my leg until the surgery.

The hospital was full and they didn't have a room for me that day. They put me overnight in some sort of utility room with no windows, phone or television. I was awake all night because of the pain I was in. The next morning, I was so happy to go to surgery. They numbed me with a spinal because they said if I went to sleep then the baby would go to sleep also. As soon as they administered the spinal I couldn't breathe. I was trying to tell them I couldn't breathe but they saw it on the monitors that the baby wasn't breathing. They ran around crazily and administered some drug intravenously and I started breathing again.

After the surgery and the spinal wore off, I was in severe pain, but due to my pregnancy I wasn't allowed anything for the pain. I spent about ten days in the hospital; the first six I didn't sleep a wink, due to the pain. When I was discharged I went back to Laura's apartment till my mother got our apartment ready that she and I had found for us a few weeks previous. An ambulance brought me back to

Laura's house and every time I had an orthopedic or gynecologist's appointment, the ambulance had to transport me back and forth. Laura lived on the third floor and the ambulance workers weren't very happy about having to lift a very pregnant woman up and down three floors with two casts on her legs. It was a scary experience for us all.

I truly believe that breaking my ankles was a Divine intervention. That traumatic injury was the only thing that put a complete halt to my drinking. I'm grateful that I broke my ankles because I stayed clean and sober to raise my child. God works in mysterious ways and the pain I went through was worth getting clean for my child's sake. Finally sober, I stopped hanging out with the people I used to when I was drinking. I got a whole new set of friends and people who were in recovery. My father said because I was sober, I was no longer allowed at his house. He said that I felt I was better than him because I wasn't drinking. My brother Andrew felt the same way, but I tried to not let these hurtful things they were saying affect me. Instead of them feeling proud for me they made me feel sad. At this point, besides my mother who was right by my side to help me through everything, my son was my whole world.

When my mother finally had the apartment ready for me to live there, she arranged for an ambulance to transfer me from Laura's to the new apartment. Thankfully the new apartment was on the first floor. The ambulance workers put me in a bed that my mother had set up in the living room. She set up a television and, because it was summer, had an air conditioning unit put in the window. When I was finally able to get into a wheelchair, I was still confined to that room because the wheelchair wouldn't fit through any of the doorways.

A certified nursing assistant would come daily and give me a basin to wash up. She would then give me a bowl of cereal for breakfast and leave me a glass of lemonade and a bowl of ravioli every day for lunch. When my mother came home from work she would make me dinner. Times like these, you know who your true friends are. Donna and her sister Felicia, also a few girls that I worked with only visited me once. But Kelly visited me on a regular basis.

After my first cast was removed, I had to use a walker till my ankle got stronger. When it did get stronger I started using crutches. Kelly would come pick me up, take me to the movies and out to eat afterwards. I had the cast removed from my other ankle about two weeks before I delivered my son Matthew. I went in to labor September 19th 1989, and delivered him on September 21st. I was in hard labor for thirty-six hours. My gynecologist didn't believe in spinals for a first pregnancy so he wouldn't let me have one.

After I finally delivered him, I hemorrhaged. My poor mother walked in to the room as I was hemorrhaging, she saw the bed covered in blood and started crying. They finally got the bleeding to stop but I was left weak and exhausted. I was so happy with my healthy, beautiful baby boy. George's sister called me up right after they put me in a room after delivering the baby. Instead of congratulating me, she was kind of mean, which made me cry. I can't even remember what she said to me but I resent her for trying to take my happiness and crushing it. She later confessed that she was jealous of my relationship with my mother because she never had that with her own mother.

George came to the hospital the next day to see his son. He had been drinking and he was very angry when he found out that I named him Matthew Michael because he wanted me to name him Shawn George. I figured why should I give my baby his father's name when his father wanted nothing to do with us. George stormed out of the hospital and the next time that I saw him was at Matthew's baptism. George was on and off in Matthew's life and mine. Not only did he never once give me child support or helped in any way with Matthew, he would actually ask me to buy him things.

Me, Matthew and my mother continued to share an apartment. My mother taught me how to take care of a baby. She helped me in so many ways in raising Matthew. I would have been lost without her, and for that, I will be forever grateful. I didn't return to work at the hospital. I stayed home to care for Matthew and I enjoyed every second of it. When Matthew turned one-year-old I had a big birthday party for him. I put all his birthday money in a piggy bank in his room till I could get to the bank and open an account for him.

Andrew was now living down the street from us with his new girlfriend Gloria and her two children. She was a nice girl and I couldn't figure out why she allowed Andrew to treat her children so poorly. These children would have to do exactly as Andrew said or they would be punished and by the looks on their face you knew they feared him.

Andrew stole all of Matthew's birthday money from his piggy bank. He then stole personal checks out of my landlord's mailbox and cashed them. Thankfully my landlord didn't evict us for this. He also stole all the money my mother had. I was very angry with him and went down the street to tell him to stay away from "MY" mother. Andrew tried to kick me in the face but thankfully, Jeff, a guy we knew was there and he pulled me away in the nick of time, but not before I could feel the wind of Andrew's sneaker on my face. Andrew is six foot, one inch to my five feet, three inches. Jeff held him back as I left and went home.

Gloria started doing heroin with Andrew and it completely changed her. She wasn't taking care of her children like she used to because the drug became more important. She would leave them with their father and not go pick them up when she was supposed to, or even be available to them. Andrew went to prison for robbery and Gloria was really strung out on drugs when he was gone. She lost her apartment and her children had to go stay with their father. She ended up moving in with us.

On my mother's birthday Gloria used my mother's car to go pick up my mother's cake. She used heroin while she was gone and nodded out while she was driving. She hit a car head on, with children in the other car. Thankfully no one was seriously injured but she totaled my mother's car. She started making up stories to get money from my mother. She told my mother once that her daughter was playing and almost got decapitated by some wires. She said her daughter was in intensive care and that she needed money to help her. She had my mother in tears and my mother gave her whatever she had. Of course the whole story was a lie. Had I been around that day I would have looked into her story before my mother handed her anything. I ended up kicking Gloria out after she stole my money I had in my dresser. I had seen Gloria a few times after that but unfortunately the disease got the best of her. She passed out from drinking and drugs and choked on her vomit while lying flat on her back. She was luckier than Mona because Gloria passed away to spirit that same day.

David had moved out to California for several years and he had just returned. He moved in with my mother, Matthew and I. He came home drunk one night with some guy named Justin and told us this was his boyfriend. Though David had been married twice and had a child from each marriage we heard through the grapevine that he was gay. But he never came right out and told us till that day. I totally accepted David and his boyfriend unlike some people in my family. My father being one of them would call David a fag behind his back. My mother never once said anything derogatory against neither David nor his boyfriend. Though she would refer to lesbians as "those lezzies." She told me of her lesbian cousin Barbara who was in some sort of gang and she committed suicide. She referred to Barbara as the Queen of the Lezzies. I got a behind-the scene glimpse of how many people in my family really felt about gays. David was brave to come out.

David eventually moved out of our apartment and got his own place with Justin. They had a very tumultuous relationship of drugs, drinking and violence. But through it all you could see they clearly loved each other. I became really good friends with Justin; he was like a girlfriend to me, and David and I were as close as ever.

David and Justin lived in Portsmouth, R.I. for a while. During their unhealthy relationship, Justin would always say he wanted to kill himself. Justin kept asking David if they could kill themselves together. David got tired of Justin asking him this so one-day David said, "Sure Justin we can do this together." The plan was that they were both going to shoot up enough heroin and overdose together. They both shot up but at the last minute Justin decided he wanted to live. Justin ran outside where he collapsed from the drugs. As Justin was running outside he pushed David, who landed on the space heater. It was winter and very cold outside. Luckily a neighbor saw Justin on the ground and called an ambulance. Thankfully both their lives were saved. Because it was winter and very cold outside, David was wearing three shirts, but because his back was lying on the heater, the heater burned through his three shirts down to the bone near his scapula, and he ended up with a large, nasty scar.

A childhood friend of mine named Jean (this is the same Jean who David mentioned in his suicide note when he was younger) moved in next door to us with her children and boyfriend. She was signing up for college classes at our local community college and she was trying to talk me into signing up also. I thought about it for a couple of months and then decided to do it. I am grateful to her for that suggestion because it changed my life in a positive way.

My friend Kelly now had a son who was a year younger than Matthew. Kelly and her son lived around the corner from us. I told Kelly that I signed up for classes at the community college and she decided to sign up also. We both signed up for Liberal Arts because we weren't sure what we wanted for a major. Kelly and I took all the same classes together. We studied and did our homework together. College was so much more fun because Kelly and I were doing it side by side. During our first year in school I decided that I wanted to be a Radiologic Technologist aka an X-ray Tech. Kelly decided that she wanted to be a registered nurse. Since we were both going into the medical field, our prerequisite classes were the same. So for our second year of school we were still in the same classes together. The only difference in the second year was I had to take a semester off.

I was still seeing George every now and then. I ended up getting pregnant with my second child from George. Once again he didn't want me to have this child. He backed away from Matthew and me because I was pregnant. He told me that if I ever tried to get child support from him he would just quit his job. There really was no reason for him to say that to me because I never once asked him for money.

In January 1994 my second child was born--a daughter that I named Sarah. I was going to name her Allyson after my mother Alice. But my mother said to me if your baby is a girl could you please name her Sarah, and I agreed. Sarah slept in a basinet in my bedroom. One morning I was lying in bed and I looked over at the basinet. I had seen a bunch of white sparkly lights floating over her. I couldn't believe what I was seeing so I closed my eyes and rubbed them. When I opened my eyes again the sparkly lights were still floating over her. I got off the bed and walked over to the basinet and ran my hand through them very slowly. I couldn't feel anything but they still remained sparkling and hovering. A few minutes later they all disappeared. That was the first time I had ever seen anything like that. I told my mother about it but she didn't know what to think of it either.

While living in this apartment my mother started telling me how throughout her entire life she was able to see spirits. She could see them just as clearly as anyone could see the living. She would tell me what the spirits looked like and what they were wearing. I found this amazing and asked her why she didn't tell me about this sooner. She said she didn't like being able to see them and would ignore them as much as she could. She also said she didn't understand this ability and was afraid of it. I would always ask her if there were spirits around and she would always answer no. She later told me that she always said no because she didn't want to frighten me.

David's boyfriend Justin always wanted to have a family and children of his own. He asked me at one point if I would have a child with him. I never said yes to him but I never uttered the words no, though my brain was screaming no. I felt very bad for him and didn't want to hurt his feelings. When I got pregnant with Sarah he wanted me to tell everyone that he was the father. He figured since George wasn't hanging around, this would be his perfect opportunity to be a father. I could not tell my family or friends that lie; but he told his family and friends that Sarah was his. Sarah did not have a father on her birth certificate and I wouldn't allow Justin to go on it.

When Sarah was around five years old she started showing feelings of hate towards Justin. Justin was very controlling to Sarah. Matthew was nine years old now and he would say to Sarah, "Justin is not your father. George McGee is." I kept telling Justin to tell his family the truth because Sarah didn't want anything to do with them. For years Justin continued to tell his family and friends that Sarah was his. I did tell Justin's sister the truth when Sarah was young but she never said anything to the rest of her family. After Justin's nephew was grown up I told him the truth about Sarah. Finally, his family knew the truth and Sarah and I feel better about it. I should have had the courage to tell Justin how I felt in the beginning but

I always felt so bad for him. In my life I had to learn the difference between empathy and sympathy.

When Sarah was eight months old, I returned to Bristol Community College to finish my last semester in the liberal arts program. I then applied and was accepted to a college called Massasoit Community College in Brockton, Ma that offered a Radiology program. Kelly applied to a nursing program in Rhode Island and was accepted. We were sad to go our separate ways but we were also very happy for each other.

In September 1995 I started my Radiology Program and Kelly started her nursing program. We were both so busy with our studies and children we didn't get to see each other as often anymore. If it wasn't for my mother helping me out with my children I wouldn't have been able to go to school. Because my school was fulltime she had to quit her job to watch them.

It was a two-year very intense program of classes and clinical studies. In my class there was a guy named Paul who grew up in my neighborhood and used to hang out with my brother Andrew when they were younger. The school assigned us all to different hospitals for our clinical experience. Paul and I were both assigned to the same hospital; St. Luke's in New Bedford, Ma. Since we both lived in the same town and had the same clinical site we decided to carpool every day. It felt like I spent more time with Paul than I did with my own family.

When Sarah was one-year-old I was offered a section 8 housing certificate. Fall River housing was going to help pay my rent and I accepted the opportunity while I was in school. We moved to a new apartment in a very nice neighborhood. I went to school in the day and worked as a radiologic technologist aide at night. I was gone Monday through Friday 6 am to 8 pm. I even worked on some weekends as a tech aide in the hospital. My mother was my rock through it all. Without her I never would have been able to get a college education.

Kelly and I still hung out from time to time. When we got together it was like we were never separated. In the second year of our programs Kelly's brother overdosed and passed to spirit. I was sick over his death. When he hung out with my brothers, I had a massive crush on him. Kelly had a massive crush on my brother Richard when she was young. In my head I always called her brother my blue-eyed David Cassidy. David Cassidy played Keith Partridge on a show called The Partridge Family in the 1970's and he was the most beautiful thing I had ever seen.

I attended his wake and when I knelt and prayed at his coffin in my head I said, "Goodbye my blue-eyed David Cassidy." he never knew I called him this. When I went to sleep that night he came to my dream and it was very real. We just stared at each other and didn't say a word. It was so real that it made me afraid. The very next night he came to my dream again and this time his presence was so intense that he frightened me and I yelled, "Go Away." He did go away and he never returned. Back then I didn't understand how spirit communicates with us through dreams so it scared me. Spirit knows they can come to me because of how open I am to the spirit realm.

Kelly couldn't handle her brother's death. She ended up back on drugs and never finished nursing school. She succeeded in hiding her drug use from me for a long time. She then met this guy named Hank and they both did drugs together. Those two were not a good combination. They both came to my house one day trying to sell brand new air conditioners in boxes. I asked Hank where they got them and he said they fell off of a truck. I felt very sorry for Kelly because she looked so thin and pale. I didn't buy an air conditioner from them because I wouldn't contribute to her drug use. The healthy, happy Kelly I knew was no longer. She made me feel grateful to be clean and sober.

When Sarah was between two and five years old she would have conversations with no one standing in front of her. I would ask her who she was speaking to and she would answer, "I am talking to the angels, mommy." She would say, "Can't you see how beautiful they are mommy?" At nights I could hear her in her room talking a mile a minute and I would ask her again who she was speaking to and she would always answer, "the angels." We were at a park one day for Matthew's little league game. She was so excited as she was pointing across the street at some people's yard. She started jumping up and down saying mommy look how beautiful those angels are. I said where are they Sarah and she pointed and said, "Right there, mommy they are standing right there." I couldn't see them but I knew she truly saw them. I always believed in angels and I wished I could have seen them with her. Coincidentally the name of the street we lived on at that time was Angell St.

I graduated from the radiology program in May of 1997. St. Luke's where Paul and I did our clinical portion of the program hired both of us. We worked there for about a year when we both decided to go to night school to get certified as MRI (magnetic resonance imaging) technologist. The program was at Massasoit Community College, the same college we just graduated from. The program was two semesters and Paul and I car-pooled together once again. Though we both finished the program I decided MRI was not for me. I enjoyed running around and being in different areas of the hospital, but MRI was about sitting in the same room all day long. Paul got a job as an MRI tech through a company that had a contract with the hospital we worked in and I was happy he was in the same building so we could still see each other.

Paul ended up marrying the love of his life. They had a child together which made two children because she already had a daughter when they had met. They bought a beautiful house together and he was so happy and I was happy for him. I hadn't seen Paul in quite a while with the both of us being so busy. As I was walking down a hallway in the hospital one day I ran in to Paul. He told me how he wasn't with his wife any longer and that she was accusing him of some terrible things, like molesting her daughter. I was in complete shock to hear this and I continued to listen to him for a few more minutes but I was busy and I told him I had to get back to work. A couple of months later Paul hung himself in his garage. I'll always regret the last time I had seen him. He had just wanted my ear and I wasn't able to give it to him. I relive the heartbreak of Paul taking his life every time I remember how we went through this journey of knowledge together and the shocking end that I never saw coming. I miss my friend terribly but I know that we will meet again.

I was now making decent money as an x-ray technologist. My apartment was quite full since I had Matthew, Sarah, my mother, David and Justin all living under one roof, so I decided to get my children and myself our own apartment. My mother and David got an apartment together. Though Justin and David were still together Justin went to live elsewhere.

In my mother's new apartment, she told me of a spirit that resided there. She said that the spirit was an older woman who wore a cotton duster housecoat. While my mother was sitting on her bed reading a book she could feel this spirit very close to her back, so close to her personal space that it felt like she tried to enter her body and my mother got very frightened. She yelled at the spirit to leave her alone. Though this spirit remained in her apartment she never tried to get that close to my mother again.

My new apartment was rather roomy with a back deck attached to the kitchen, and a driveway to park in. My mother would take my children to school for me and then pick them up after school and she would stay with them at my apartment till I got home from work. My friend, Joy, the animal control officer in our city, gave us a beautiful orange tabby cat for an apartment-warming gift. He was three years old and Joy found him on the streets cut from his tail up his back. She had him stitched up, neutered, and gave him all his shots.

When we first got him he was hyperactive and would jump on my hutch in the middle of the night and knock dishes off of it but after a few weeks he finally calmed down. I let Matthew chose the cat's name and he chose Max. We all fell in love with Max and he quickly became part of our family. He was a very special cat and anyone that came into contact with him immediately loved him. I started letting him go outside because he enjoyed sitting on the grass in the sun. He would roam the neighborhood and everyone in the neighborhood knew him. While I was outside I would hear people that I never met before say "Hi Max". When Sarah was practicing for her first Communion at our church across the street, Max would sit on the side of her as the children walked in procession. When she took a step so did Max starting from the outside to the inside of the church. The day of Sarah's first communion I had to keep Max in the house so he wouldn't go inside the church.

Max would look at me with such love in his eyes. I truly felt like Max was some sort of guardian angel. I noticed one day that Max wasn't eating or drinking and he was very sluggish. I brought him to the veterinarian and the Vet said Max needed surgery for a bowel obstruction. They wanted $1500.00 before surgery but I didn't have the cash. I took Max home and the next morning he had a coating over his eyes and I knew he was dying. I couldn't bear for him to die so I brought him back to the Vet and they let me use a credit card to pay for the surgery. Max had eaten some plastic Easter hay from one of the Easter baskets and that's what obstructed his bowel.

Three days after the surgery the Vet said he still wouldn't eat or drink and they didn't know what to do for him. So I suggested I would take him home and see how he was. I took him home and the second I opened up the carrier he walked out and started eating and drinking immediately. He was just very sad and missed his family as much as we missed him. He recovered fully and was back to normal in no time.

Though the children and myself really liked the apartment we were living in there was also something scary about it. It got to the point where the kids were too scared to sleep in their own rooms at night. They slept with me just about every night. In my bedroom doorway every night stood a dark figure. I was very afraid of this presence and I could sense that it was a negative energy. I never said anything to the kids about this dark figure until they mentioned it to me. When I realized they could see it also I had no problem with letting them sleep with me. After all I was afraid, so I could only imagine their fear.

Sarah was twirling in circles in my bedroom one day and suddenly she became very frightened. She said as she was twirling around she had seen a man wearing a suit and a bow tie. She was sleeping in her own bedroom one night when she awoke to seeing someone walk by her doorway and she could hear chains clinking. At first she thought it was Matthew and then had second thoughts so she banged on my bedroom door to come in because she was terrified. I always closed my door at night because of the dark figure. When I opened my door Sarah saw Matthew sound asleep in my bed and she told me what had happened.

Matthew's friend Brian slept over one night at this apartment. Brian had seen someone who he first thought was me standing in Matthew's room in the middle of the night. When he realized it wasn't me, terrified, he woke up Matthew. Brian was so fearful he couldn't go back to sleep, and he never slept at our house again. Quite a few times I had seen a woman in spirit with a long dress (Victorian era clothing) walk into Matthew's room.

I often took Matthew and his friends to a skateboarding park in Middletown, R.I. While the boys skated, Sarah and I would shop and go out to eat. One day we went to an animal shelter and fell in love with this beautiful, graceful calico cat named Sammy. She was very timid but also very sweet. Sammy became a new addition to our family so now I had two cats and two kids.

When Matthew was twelve years old, I received a phone call from the police department saying he had been arrested. They handcuffed him and put him in a cell but once they realized he was only twelve years old, they immediately called me. Matthew and his friends were arrested for skateboarding in an abandoned mill. Other kids always skateboarded in this mill and do a lot of graffiti and damage, so any previous graffiti or damage, these kids got in trouble for it. Matthew was the youngest of all the boys involved. The boys had to go to court and they so deserved to. All of us parents had the boys write letters of apology to the owner of the mill and the boys presented these letters in court. The owner agreed to drop charges if the boys would clean up the mill every day during their school spring break. Everyone agreed and the charges were dropped. The boys reluctantly used their vacation to clean up the mill-a lesson well learned.

I received a phone call at work one day from Sarah and Matthew's aunt on their father's side. She called to let me know that George told his family that he had contracted aids and that the children and I needed to get tested for it. I went to a clinic and got the test done but my nerves were on edge till the results had come back and thankfully they were negative. The clinic also told me that since I tested negative then the children would also be negative. I found out the following year that George didn't have aids. He told his family that he had aids because he was looking for sympathy from them. He was drinking and drugging with the hope that his family would give him a place to live and help him out.

My brother Andrew also pulled the aids card on my family. He told my mother he had aids and everyone believed him except me. I told my mother Andrew is lying to you so he can manipulate you even more than he already does. It worked just the way Andrew had planned and he received sympathy, money and a place to live as he still robbed from all those who helped him. Two years went by before Andrew finally confessed he didn't have aids.

FOUR

Coming Out

Ever since I was very young I've always loved singers and celebrities. My mother said I was just like her mother in that way. David Cassidy was the first concert I ever attended. My all-time favorite band since 1978 till this day has always been the band "Heart" and I've also always loved "The Judd's". In the 1990's I was in Wynonna Judd's fan club. I traveled to many cities to see her in concert as I also did for Heart. Wynonna had the best fans and the best fan club parties. She made all the parties very personal and she was very kind to all of us. I made some really good friends in that fan club and to date, I still communicate with a couple of them on Facebook.

Through the online fan club I met this woman named Beth. We really hit it off and communicated just about every day through the computer. Through speaking to this woman and connecting to her in ways I never did with a man; I realized I had romantic feelings for her and she felt the same way. It was like a floodgate of revelations that opened up for me. I finally realized why I was never truly happy with any man I ever dated. All those years that I couldn't figure out what was wrong with me. It was such a relief to realize I could connect with another human on that level. A whole new exciting world had opened to me.

Beth and I made plans to finally meet at Fan Fair in Nashville TN. She lived in North Carolina and my plane made a stop there so she arranged to board the same plane with me to TN. We shared a hotel room and we shared our hearts. I was nervous because I had never been romantic with a woman before. We had a long distance relationship and we spoke every day and I fell hard for her. She came to visit me for a couple of weeks and I had never been this happy with anyone else before. A month and a half later we met again at another event Wynonna was performing at and I couldn't have been happier in my life. Things moved fast for us and we gave each other sapphire and diamond rings. I felt I truly loved her and she told me that she loved me. I told her I would pick up and move to North Carolina with my kids to be with her. She came to visit me again a month later. We went to meet this woman who Beth had made friends with through the fan club that also lived in Massachusetts. We met her at a mall and I couldn't believe the way Beth and this other woman were flirting with each other right in front of me.

After Beth flew back home she started acting strange. She wasn't calling me every day anymore and when we spoke I could feel the coldness in her voice. She was backing off from me and I couldn't understand why. I paid for a plane ticket for her to come and see me. She told me she was going to spend half the time visiting this other woman from the fan club. I told her I didn't think that it was right because she was "my girl" and I never get to see her. About a week before she was supposed to visit she said she wouldn't be able to make it because she couldn't get the time off from work. She kept backing away from me more and more and I was very upset about it but didn't know what to do.

I then received a letter from a woman that Beth knew from North Carolina. This woman told me Beth was duping me and this made me even more upset. I called the airline the day that Beth was supposed to fly to Boston to see me but said she couldn't due to work. I told the airlines that I was her sister and I wanted to know if her flight arrived. The woman told me that she boarded the plane and her flight arrived on time. I knew now for sure that she had lied to me because she was going to see the other woman instead of me. I immediately started shaking and crying. This was my first true broken heart and I was devastated. I called her up in anger and hurt and yelled at her and I probably didn't make any sense because I was a wreck. She told me she wanted to remain friends but I wasn't able to be "just friends" so we parted company.

It took me a good year to get over Beth. Matthew found out I was a lesbian because he had walked in on me kissing Beth. I was straightforward with Matthew and he accepted it really well. I felt my daughter was too young to tell her about myself. Though I wished I would have because children are very accepting. As of now I still haven't told my daughter but I will by the time this book publishes. I confided in a few friends who were very accepting of me.

Since Beth, I have not had a relationship with anyone. I chose to just work and raise my children instead. I didn't want my children to go through any difficult times due to my being a lesbian because people can be cruel. Through the years I have "come out" to some people that I worked with. I have never told a family member because I know how they truly feel about gay people. Many people have suspected, but I've never confirmed it for them. I can't help it but part of me feels ashamed and embarrassed that I am a lesbian. I know it's mostly because of how I was raised and had a backseat view of how others spoke of, and treated gay people. But I'm tired of hiding and being lonely. I want to live my life the way God has created me and to be free and happy. I want to find my soul mate and build a life together. It is never too late though I wish I had the courage to come out much earlier in my life like my brother David did.

In the summer of 2001 David and I drove by the house we grew up in on Buffinton St. Our landlady Catherine had passed to spirit and her family sold both the cottages. The houses were in the process of being gutted and remodeled by the new owners. Out of curiosity I pulled the car over and we walked into the yard. There wasn't anyone around so we decided to roam around the house we once lived in. Though it was being torn apart we were amazed because we could still see pieces of linoleum from when we lived there. We looked through the upstairs, the downstairs and the basement. It was actually very cathartic going through that house.

That night while I slept I had a very vivid dream. The dream was of a woman in her 30s with strawberry blonde hair who was very pale. There was also a man in his 30s with a lot of dark hair on his head and face. The man stood very solemn standing behind the woman with his head bowed. The woman was looking at me and begging me to help them. Her lips never moved but I knew what she was saying. She kept saying, "Help us." When I woke up I didn't know what to think of that dream. The very next night I had the same exact dream. But this time when I woke up I knew that these two people were the souls from the house I grew up in. I did the only thing I knew to do and called upon Archangel Michael and asked him to cross these souls over to eternal peace. I had a peaceful feeling afterward and I never dreamt of them again.

Years later I went to a medium who told me that two souls stepped forward to thank me for crossing them over. She said when I entered that house as it was being torn apart and the two souls were panicking due to all the construction. They knew my soul as a child from growing up there, so they followed me home to ask me for help.

My brother Andrew had gotten out of prison and had another girlfriend with whom he was using drugs. They had nowhere to live and wanted to live with me. I told them I didn't want them in my house. It was winter time and very cold and they slept in a car in the church parking lot across the street from me. I felt bad but I wasn't giving in for I knew it would be chaos for my kids' lives and me. They both ended up going to the hospital with pneumonia. My mother was very upset that they were sick and begged me to let him stay with me. I let them stay with me because I didn't like seeing my mother upset. I truly did not want them living with me and I didn't want any drugs around my children. But I still hadn't learned the difference between empathy and sympathy. Eventually, Andrew went back to prison for violating parole.

In December 2002 I received a phone call from my father's wife saying that he had had a stroke and was in the hospital. I drove down to the hospital to see him. When I walked into his room I saw that his eyes were wide open even though he couldn't move any part of his body. He was paralyzed from the stroke and I felt bad for him because he had such bad panic attacks and I knew the panic he must have been going through. As far as I was concerned no one deserves to suffer. I held his hand and said Dad squeeze my hand if you can hear me. He squeezed my hand, so I leaned over and said to him, "I love you, and I forgive you."

Though honestly, I didn't forgive him till many years after his death. I kissed him on his forehead and I stayed with him a short while, while he slept. In his last two years of his life my father had dealt with colon cancer twice. He had quit drinking about five years before he had this stroke. All those years the alcohol covered up the terrible panic attacks he had. I did take my children to visit him after he quit drinking. My son thought his grandfather was hilarious though unfortunately my father still sought humor at the expense of others. My father showed Matthew all kind of card tricks and Matthew thought he was so cool. He treated my children well or else I would have never taken them to visit him. I'm happy they got to meet their grandfather.

The next morning, I went to the hospital to visit my father, David and Philip was in his room speaking very loudly. I told them to quiet down because they were going to wake Dad up. Philip said, "No we are not because he is in a coma." I was taken aback by this news because no one said a word to me about it before this. I walked over to him and tried my best to wake him up. I couldn't wake him up and I felt my heart sink, but there was nothing I could do for him and I felt helpless.

After visiting my father I went to a supermarket called "The Stop and Shop" in Somerset, MA. Shopping at this location was very odd for me because I never go the next town over to food shop. I have no explanation why I went to Somerset on this day. I was walking down one of the aisles and I heard my name being called. I turned around and it was my friend Kelly and she looked healthy and happy. I was so surprised and excited to see her. Kelly had her ten-month-old daughter with her, which was another surprise for me. I had no idea Kelly had another child besides her son.

We carried on a conversation like no time had passed between us. Kelly asked me if we could go out to eat after the holidays because the last time that we did we had so much fun. I told her of course we could, and I'd be looking forward to it. Then I told her my father had a major stroke and was in the hospital and I didn't think he was going to make it. We spoke another few minutes and said goodbye to each other. As I was walking away I heard Kelly call my name. I turned around and said, "Yeah Kel", and she said "I love you" and I said, "I love you too, Kel."

Very early the next morning as I was sleeping the phone rang. I was half asleep when I answered the call. It was my sister Gail telling me that our father had passed to spirit. He went into cardiac arrest while he was in his coma. It was a blessing that he passed because he would have only suffered the consequences of his major stroke. I felt sick and upset inside but I couldn't shed a tear for my father's death. I ended up being out of work for a few weeks after my father passed because I had pneumonia.

A few weeks later I went back to work on a Saturday and cried all day at work. I couldn't control it or stop it and I knew these were the tears I was finally shedding for my father. At work on the following day I was standing in the doorway of the x-ray room in the emergency department. I looked out to the nurse's station and I saw a full on apparition of my father. He was standing in the middle of the nurse's station just staring at me. I was so shocked I bent my head down for a second to cough but when I looked back up, he was gone. I didn't tell anyone right away about this; I needed to process it first. Plus, the people I worked with already thought I was weird when I would speak of anything spiritual.

On the Friday of the following week I came home from work and my mother told me that she heard that Kelly had died. I said, "No Mom that can't be true." I called Kelly's brother Jonathan and he said, "It is too late Dawn, she is gone." Kelly passed away from taking too many Percocet's, which contained Tylenol. She took it because she was in severe pain but since she had Hepatitis C the Tylenol shut her liver down. I will be forever grateful that I saw her three weeks prior to her passing away. It is very comforting to me that we got to see each other and was given the opportunity to say that we loved each other. I know that spirit brought us together that day so we could say goodbye. It was less than three weeks between the deaths of my father and Kelly and I was much sadder at the loss of Kelly than I was of my father.

Kelly came to me in my dreams for a full week starting the day after she passed away. The first night I had seen her lying in a coffin. She got up and walked over to me, and I said, "Kel, don't you know you're dead?" She didn't say anything back to me. Then I said, "Kel, how is it to be dead?" She said to me, "At first I was mad but now it's okay." When spirit speaks to me in my dreams they never move their mouths; we communicate through our minds. Kelly continued to come to me for the next six nights and it was amazing. I would wake up and feel like we had just hung out all night. I felt so grateful and privileged to have spent this time with her on a soul-to-soul level.

Kelly came to me in my dreams a few other times throughout the years. She told me I had an incredible tunnel but it was filled with fear. I didn't understand what she meant by that then, but I now know what she meant. My tunnel is my communication to the spirit realm and I blocked it with fear. As I go through my life I am unblocking it more and more. I have had several dreams where I was flying and loved every second of it. My soul leaves my body in dreams and flies, and the feeling is beyond anything I could explain. Deceased family members have come to me in my dreams to take me to meet ancestors in the spirit realm. If I could control when my soul leaves I would go there every night. When this is happening, I am aware that I am sleeping and my soul feels so free.

The house I was living in at this point in my life had gotten sold to a man who lived next door to me. Everything changed for me after he purchased the house. He no longer allowed me to park in the driveway. He no longer let us use the deck, which was attached to my kitchen. He lived in the house next door and his children would play on my deck and look in to my windows. He said my children weren't allowed to sit on the steps of the porch. He got very angry because Max was sitting on his boat that he parked in the driveway. He then said my cats weren't allowed outside any longer. I was very unhappy living there as he watched every single move I made.

He finally told me I had to move out because he wanted my apartment for his family member. I then decided it was time to buy my own house. I didn't want any landlord telling me what I could or could not do any longer. I asked him to give me some time to find a house but he kept harassing me every week. I finally put an offer on a house I could afford. This house was a cottage situated in the middle of the block behind another house just like the cottage I grew up in. The street numbers of the house I grew up in was 209. Everywhere I went the numbers 209 came popping up and I saw this as a good sign. I felt I was being shown from the spirit realm not to worry because I was getting this house that I had put the offer on. Sarah and I went to the Shrine at St. Anne's Church to pray. This Shrine has many huge beautiful statues and we really enjoy spending time there. I was praying so hard for my offer to be accepted as I was walking towards the Virgin Mary statue. Suddenly I smelled an overwhelming scent of roses. I called Sarah over to me and asked her if she could smell the roses. She answered, "Yes I can and it is so beautiful." We were standing in an alcove where the statue was and wondered what roses were there that were giving out this overwhelming aroma. Sarah and I started to smell all the roses in the alcove. Every flower in that alcove was artificial and had no scent. I knew right then and there that the offer on the house was going to be accepted and that the house was mine. Sarah and I walked through the church a little while longer. We returned to the alcove where the Virgin Mary statue was and the smell was completely gone. A week later the house was mine.

The children and I were incredibly happy to have our own home. This house needed some work but David, Justin and a friend of theirs really helped with fixing it up. David and Justin replaced every window, along with floors and ceilings. David was working for an insulation company and he came and insulated my house. My sister and niece helped me paint. Everyone came together to help us and it was amazing. At one point I refinanced the house because it needed a new roof, garage doors, and the kitchen remodeled. It seemed like never ending work but in the end my house looked beautiful. It was a dream come true for me. I had a large porch built on the front of the house and put a three-person swing on it. Some of my favorite memories are coming home from work, and seeing my mother and brother David sitting on that swing just smiling. I was very content in my life, and loved my house, my family, my job and I now had great friends. Between my mother and David, they would take my children to school in the morning and take care of them afterwards till I returned home; everything was as perfect as it could be.

David came to my house one day with two new born kittens he had found that someone threw away near a dumpster. One was pure black and the other one was pure white. I told David I couldn't keep them, but I would find them good homes. I found a home for the black kitten and by that time I already fell in love with the white one and named him Casper. Casper had triple paws on his front and back feet. He thought he was one of my kids and he never left my side. He was like a real baby; when he was scared or wanted something from me he would say "MOM." I wish I had taken a video of him saying that but I never did.

When Matthew was in his early teens he had a lot of friends that often hung out at our house. They were all respectful to me and I liked them so I didn't mind them being there. I've always connected to younger people and children throughout my life. I made a room in the basement that Matthew and his friends could hang out in. They had a few couches, a coffee table, and a stereo system; I figured what more could teenagers want. I was in my kitchen one day and I could hear the boys in the basement. I opened the basement door and all I could smell was marijuana. I went downstairs and told everyone to leave. Matthew acted like it was no big deal; he said it was only weed. I said to him I already told you how addiction runs in this family and I asked you not to do any drinking or drugs. He convinced me it was just weed, that at least he was home, and I knew what he was doing. I honestly feel I dropped the ball on this because I should have been firmer in my stand.

When I first moved into this house Kelly came to me in a dream and showed me Matthew walking into a liquor store. When I woke up I knew she was trying to warn me that he would be partying. I didn't know what to do about it except have talks with him about addiction and warn him about consequences due to partying. It went in one ear and out the other and I kept an eye on him as best as I could.

I bought my house in 2003, and in 2004 joined the band Heart's Fan Club. Wynonna no longer had a fan club and I had been a fan of Heart's since 1978. I've attended many Heart concerts through the years. In the 1980's I wrote to them at their parent's home in Seattle. I received a letter back from their mother Lou that I still have to this day. She told me all about their fan club and thanked me for being their fan. I was excited to get a letter from their mother. While in their fan club I traveled to many states to see them perform, and have met many wonderful fans in the process. Many of us would make plans as to what concerts to attend and we would all meet there and share hotel rooms. It was a wonderful bonding experience with other Heart fans. Many of us became friendly with an employee of Heart's known as "Magic Man."

I was in California at one of Heart's concerts and I was standing at the side of the merchandise table with another fan club member. A young girl came up to me and asked me what AFW and NFW meant on the t-shirt I was wearing. I told her she was too young to know and she stepped back. A few minutes later she came back over to me and said "How young is too young?" I asked her how old she was and she replied 14. So I said okay I'll tell you, and I told her they meant Ann F-ing Wilson and Nancy F-ing Wilson. I didn't say the actual word to her. She didn't blink once and replied "Oh, okay." She then continued the conversation telling me all about herself. Like I mentioned earlier I have always connected to young people and she was a lovely young lady. Our conversation went on for about another fifteen minutes and she told me she lived in Seattle. I said to her, "Oh Wow, have you ever seen Ann Wilson around town?" She looked at me and replied, "She is my mother." I had no idea who this young girl was so I was shocked. I then said to her you must be Marie, I heard you paint rather well. She told me about an Art Gallery she was involved with in the Seattle area. I asked her if she could paint something for me and she said yes, she would.

Marie told me to contact the art gallery and she gave me a man's name to speak to. A couple of weeks later I contacted this man via email. This man would pass messages back and forth between Marie and myself. He then sent me an email that said Marie told him to give me her email so we could communicate directly. I then contacted Marie and we became very friendly. She painted one painting for me, and two paintings for Sarah. She asked her Mom how much she should charge me for the paintings. I sent her checks for each of them but not one of them was ever cashed. I got to know her pretty well and I would send her gifts that I knew she would like. This was my way of paying her back for the paintings since the checks weren't cashed.

Marie and I spoke about various things in life; this girl had quite the imagination, which made me like her even more. I found her delightful and we never spoke of her mother ever. I told Magic Man and another female employee of Heart's how Marie was painting for me; I never hid it from them. The female employee told me to beware of Marie because she wasn't quite right in her mind. Then she gestured by pointing her finger at the side of her head in circles indicating Marie was crazy. I was a little taken aback by her suggestion but I never said a word to anyone about this, except to my daughter.

Marie and I communicated for ten months. She told me she was going on tour with her mother. I was going to attend one of the concerts so I suggested to Marie that she ask her Mom if she could have lunch with me. I thought it would be fun to discuss the next painting she was doing for me in person. Ann did know we were communicating and that she was painting for me so I didn't think much of it. I didn't hear back from Marie for a few days and then I received a message that said "Beware of the Wolf." I was confused, unsure what to think of this message. I messaged Marie back and asked her if everything was okay. She told me everything was fine and that she was tired from school.

I went to their concert in Atlantic City and gave the female employee a gift to give to Marie that she was expecting. After the concert the female employee came up to me and said Ann is going to give that gift to Marie because Marie will love it. She then went on to say that Ann didn't want me to contact or message Marie in any way any longer. She then said to me it is quite odd that a grown woman has befriended a child. Then she told me not to worry because no member of the fan club would know anything about this. It never entered my mind about fan club members knowing anything because I didn't have any bad intentions. Suddenly, the drummer from Heart appeared by my side and said, "Hi, I'm Ben." I couldn't respond, my mind swirling, trying to process what just happened. Then once again he said loudly, "I'm Ben, who are you?" I said "Hello, I'm Dawn." Then Ben and the female employee started walking off together laughing. It was apparent they were laughing at me and I was very hurt by the entire situation.

In retrospect it would look suspicious that an adult would be a friend with a child, especially when her mother is famous. Ann only realized I was an adult when Marie asked Ann permission to have lunch with me, which I thought Ann knew the entire time. I only assume that Ann then went and read through the messages that Marie and I sent each other and that is when Ann wrote, "Beware of the Wolf." I realized Ann was only protecting her child like any mother would, so of course I no longer contacted Marie. I was disappointed though in not getting that last painting, or having anymore contact with Marie because I felt a connection to her.

I made plans to go to a Heart concert in Henderson, Nevada. Since Henderson is only 15 miles from Las Vegas I decided to stay on the strip. I went on their fan club message board and asked who would like to share a hotel room with me and not a single person responded back. I put the message up a few more times but still no response. I made a reservation for myself at the MGM Grand. I booked a shuttle to the concert in Henderson through a company that worked out of the basement of the Aladdin Hotel. The shuttle dropped me off at their drop off point, which was the Ritz Carlton. They told me they would pick me back up at the Ritz Carlton at 11pm. I had to take a shuttle down to the concert from the Ritz Carlton, which was on the same property. It was an outside concert in which I had front row seats and Heart was playing on a stage that floated in the water. I was so excited to be there but when I saw all the fan club members that I was friendly with they all gave me nothing but dirty looks and the cold shoulder.

We all folded up our pants and went barefoot in to the water to get right up to the stage. Some of the fan club members kept pushing me out of the way. I tried speaking to them but no one would speak back to me. When the concert was finished I asked some of the fan club members if I could get a ride back to The Ritz Carlton and one person mumbled that they were not going that way so I waited and got a shuttle by myself. When I got back to The Ritz Carlton I had an hour and a half wait till the shuttle was coming back for me. I went to the restaurant there and grabbed something to eat. Next, while waiting for the shuttle, I sat in the lobby and listened to the piano music. As I was sitting there the fan club members I asked for a ride earlier walked in to the lobby. I was as shocked to see them, as they were to see me. I said hello to them but they hurriedly passed by without a word, with looks of horror on their faces. I was so perplexed as to why I was being treated so poorly. When I returned home I messaged the female employee and told her what had happened in Henderson. She proceeded to get very nasty with me. She said I was at The Ritz Carlton stalking Heart. I told her I didn't know Heart was even staying at The Ritz Carlton. I explained to her about the shuttle from The Aladdin Hotel and she didn't believe me. She continued saying things to me like "Do you want me to tell you were Heart lives?" And, "Do you want to sleep at their house?" I then asked her if that's the reason I am being treated badly because you told them all about Marie and me? She replied, "Too Bad." This female employee blackballed me in the fan club. Till this day when I go to a Heart concert, no one speaks to me. I was very happy to have met Marie whom I feel is a special soul and I will never regret it. I honestly felt Marie could have used my help at that point in her life but I guess it wasn't meant to be. Marie was eclectic in her thinking and she fascinated me. I told Magic Man and the female employee from the very beginning that Marie was painting for me. I never hid the fact that I was an adult though I wish Ann had realized that from the beginning. I'm a very sensitive person and this all had an extremely negative effect on me. In my heart and soul, I never had a bad intention though I can see how it could be misconstrued. Although sometimes I hesitate, I'm determined to still go to Heart concerts and enjoy myself because it's all about the effing music. As I was writing this, unfortunately Heart is no longer together but they will always be my number one band and I support them separately. I have faith they will once again reunite.

As I'm releasing this book I am beyond exuberant that Heart is back together after a three-year hiatus. My daughter and I will be attending their concert In August 2019 in San Diego.

FIVE

My David

I didn't want my brother Andrew at my new house because he was still on heroin and I couldn't trust him. He would threaten my mother and say, "If you don't give me money I will go rob that bitch Dawn's house." My mother would then give him the money so he wouldn't rob my house. Once he threatened my mother for money, but she didn't have any to give him; He kicked through two doors to break into my house and rob me. He took mostly electronics, DVD's and Xboxes. Furious, I called the police and told them it was Andrew who robbed me. The police said that since no one had actually seen him break in, they couldn't arrest him. After I replaced the doors, David put huge bars of solid wood across the doors so they couldn't be kicked in again. Andrew bragged to my mother how he robbed me. I asked my mother why does Andrew hate me so much when I have never done anything wrong to him, I have only tried to help him. Her reply was that he was jealous of my life and me.

David's boyfriend Justin started going to night school to get his GED. He met a woman there that he started cheating on David with. This woman said she was pregnant with Justin's baby. Justin wanted a child so bad that he left David after being with him for 17 years. Justin married this woman who later claimed she had a miscarriage and Justin never got his child. David was beyond devastated and I didn't know how to comfort him. David moved in with my children and me. I loved having him there as he was very close to my children. He would take Matthew and his own son Kyle fishing and hunting for snakes to his favorite place in the world called Dave's Beach. He was a loving uncle, brother and father to all.

About six months after Andrew robbed me he broke into my house once again. He stole all the electronics and items I replaced from the first time that he robbed me. I called the police again but this time I found someone who he sold some of my items to. These people confirmed to the police that they bought these items from Andrew. Andrew was eventually arrested and served eighteen months in prison.

When Andrew was released from prison he called The Department of Social

Services and told them that I was a drug addict and that I allowed Matthew and his friends in my house to drink and do drugs. A Social Services investigator came to my house while I was at work. My mother and David were at my house with the kids and were very upset by these allegations that the investigator told them about. They showed him how clean my house was, that there was plenty of food in my refrigerator and that the children were well taken care of. They told him I was at work and what time I would be home, and he said he would return at that time. Earlier in the day this investigator went to Sarah's school to question her. Sarah was eleven years old and he was trying to make her say that Matthew did drugs and asked her for Matthew's friends names. Sarah said this man bullied her until she cried. He then told her don't tell your mother I spoke to you. Of course Sarah told me, and she also told me the names of Matthew's friends that she had told him about.

He came to the house to interview me. He told me that he went to Matthew's school and spoke to Matthew's friends. He then started rattling off the names of the boys that Sarah gave him. I told him that is odd because not one of these boys goes to Matthew's school. He got real angry with me when I said this. He could plainly see I wasn't a drug addict. Next he spoke to Matthew and asked Matthew if he did drugs. Matthew was never a liar and came right out and said he smoked weed. He asked both of us if Matthew was the main caregiver for Sarah and we both said absolutely not. I told him that my mother and brother watch them both before and after school. He still wrote in his paperwork that I said Matthew was the main caregiver for Sarah. He did this because there was no other way he would have a case against me. The Department of Social Services now considered me an unfit mother. This investigator straight out lied and I couldn't believe he was doing this to me.

I knew Andrew was the one who called The Department of Social Services because he bragged about it to my mother. I was trying to explain to this man how my brother was trying to get me back for sending him to prison. He couldn't care less about anything I had to say. I was assigned a caseworker that was very nice to the children and me. When she came to my house I told her the entire story. She then told me to put a complaint against this investigator because she knew that he lied about other previous cases. I received a hearing in which the investigator attended. I told the whole story in front of about six people. I received a letter stating that they denied my appeal because my main concern was that my brother did this to me out of revenge. We had an open case with The Department of Social Services for two years. Matthew had to take weekly urine tests and we had weekly visits from the social worker. I couldn't fathom the idea that I was considered an unfit mother. Knowing Andrew was very vindictive, I have feared him for years.

Matthew stopped smoking weed for those two years we were on Social Services. As soon as we were cleared off these services he resumed smoking weed. As time went on Matthew's drug use went from weed to pills and drinking. Matthew actually hid a lot of his drug use from me. I found out much later he was selling weed and hiding large amounts of it in my basement. I know that when Andrew called the Department of Social Services on me he was trying to hurt me. But in retrospect he helped us because who knows what could have happened in those two years with Matthew's drug use. I am a firm believer of everything happens for a reason.

I bought a new Toyota Camry and stored my older Toyota Camry in my garage. I opened up the garage one day and the car was gone. My mother said that while I was at work, Andrew called a junkyard and sold my car to them. He didn't need to show the junkyard a title because the car was 10 years old. I wanted to call the police but did I dare do it and reap his repercussions? The junkyard that he called to take my car was from Boston and I would have had to prove which junkyard had it. There are literally hundreds of junkyards in the Boston area. I never did anything about him taking my car. It would be impossible to list all the things Andrew has taken or done to my mother and I.

One morning I was late to work so I was speeding, driving 80 MPH on a 65 MPH highway. I was in the middle lane when a car cut me off. I tried to brake but needed to switch into another lane to avoid hitting the car in front of me. There were cars in each lane on both sides of me. The more I kept braking the more I lost control of my car and started swerving all over the highway. Suddenly my car turned right and headed straight towards the breakdown lane and the guardrail. As I saw myself going towards the guardrail, I said to myself, well, this is it! I shut my eyes because I didn't want to see myself go through the guardrail. In seconds there was complete silence so I opened my eyes. My car was at a complete stop in the breakdown lane. I was facing the wrong direction but there wasn't even a scratch on my car, me, nor anyone else. I was stunned and amazed. I have no idea how my car turned to be in the breakdown/stop lane. Now I can confidently say that it was my guardian angels that saved my life that day. It wasn't my time to leave this earth because I have so much more to do to fulfill my soul's purpose. I know I am supposed to keep telling my stories and enlightening other souls as I go through my journey.

Part of my job at the hospital was to go up to patients' rooms and take x-rays of patients who were too sick to come to our department. I often did chest x-rays on elderly people who were at the very end of their lives. Most of them were unresponsive, and on some of them I could clearly see the suffering in their faces. I would look at a patient and know it was near time for them to pass. Before I left that patient's room, I would whisper in their ear, it is okay for you to go; God and your family are waiting for you. The next day I would come into work and check on that patient and each time the patient had passed away during the night. Only once did a patient hang on a few more days. I believe she was waiting to see her entire family before she passed on, though sometimes they just needed someone to comfort them and tell them it is okay to leave. I only whispered in their ears and gave them permission if they were ready because in the end it is a soul's choice as to when to return home. I was trying to be of spiritual comfort but some coworkers looked at me as if I had placed a pillow on the patient's face.

I became friendly with two girls that I worked with. They both smoked weed but that never bothered me. One day one of them asked me to smoke weed with them while the other friend didn't think it was a good idea. I'm not really sure why but I decided to smoke weed with them that day. We had a blast laughing till we cried. From then on, every time we got together, a main portion of it was smoking weed.

I made an appointment with a man who read tarot cards. During the reading he told me he saw that someone was going to die, that he could see people coming in from out of town for the funeral. I left his house upset; all I could think of was that it was my mother who was going to die. He also told me that anytime I find coins especially dimes that they were from loved ones who passed away. That day David was sitting on my front porch, so I walked down the steps and told him everything the card reader had said to me. He gave me a slight smile and nodded his head yes, but he didn't say a word. I said to myself, he must be thinking the same thing I am, that it is our mother who is going to die.

A week after the reading David had let Andrew borrow one of his cell phones. David and Andrew were walking onto my mother's porch. Andrew, who was angry and sick from having no drugs, said that he was going to break the cell phone. David replied to Andrew, "Oh no you're not." Andrew then turned around and repeatedly punched David on his head and ear. When David got back to my house he showed me the lumps on his head and how swollen and bruised his ear was. I was so angry with Andrew for doing this to David because David was such a sweet, loving soul.

Usually when I came home from work, David would be there with my children. Suddenly he started not being there when I came home. He wouldn't come home until I was asleep, and he would still be asleep when I would leave for work. I rarely saw him anymore; it seemed like he was avoiding me. Once I did see him and he acted like he wanted to say something to me. Then he said, "Dawn." When I answered, "Yes," he paused and said, "Never mind." He then started telling me how hurt he was over losing Justin. He went over to see Justin and Justin's wife told David to never come around again. Angry with Justin, I said to David, screw them; he is an asshole.

About a week after this conversation, my two friends and I were hanging out after work at one of their apartments. I called David to let him know I would be home soon. He didn't answer his cell phone and there was a strange message that he left on his phone. I couldn't make out the beginning of the message but at the end of the message David said, "After today, no more". I called his phone back several times to try to figure out what the beginning of the message said but I couldn't understand it. I know David very well and the way he sounded when he said "After today no more," I knew something was really wrong. I called Matthew's cell phone and asked him if he had seen David and he replied no. I told Matthew about the message that I heard on David's phone. I then told him to get right home to check things out and that I would meet him there.

My two friends came with me to my house and when we arrived the house was locked up and no one was in sight. Matthew and I checked the entire house but found no one. I became nervous because I didn't know where Sarah was, and David was supposed to be watching her. I then checked the garage and the car that I let David drive was still in the garage. I started calling around to find David and Sarah. I finally received a call from Sarah telling me she was at her friend Macayla's house. David spoke to Macayla's mother and asked her if Sarah could spend the night there. I told Sarah that it was fine that she was there.

I then became very nervous that David was going to hurt himself. I called my mother and brother Philip and told them what was going on. We all kept calling David's phone and there was no answer. I left a message on the phone each time I called it. I was begging David to please come home and telling him how much I loved him. I called around at some of his friend's homes and no one had heard from him. It was getting very late so Matthew and I went to sleep. I was hoping that when I got up in the morning he would be in the living room. I had the next day off from work and I got up very early to check if David had come home but he hadn't. I started calling around to friends and family to see if anyone had heard from him yet, but no one had. I picked up Philip and my mother and we went out looking for David. Although I wasn't speaking to Justin, I went to his house to see if

David was there but he wasn't.

Philip then told me that David recently said he was going to kill himself. He said he wanted to die at his favorite place, Dave's Beach. I found out that David told quite a few family members that he was going to kill himself but no one had ever told me he had said this. David knew better than to say that to me because I would have done my best to put a stop to it.

My mother, Philip and I headed down to Dave's Beach. There are two sides to this beach so we drove to one side of it and walked all over the beach, calling his name but he didn't answer. The other side of the beach was wooded, and I had never been in there before and was afraid to enter. I went home and called the police and put a missing person's report on David. I asked the police to please check the wooded side of Dave's Beach. I couldn't just sit around so I decided to go by myself and go check out this wooded area. I walked in a little ways and I saw homeless camps set up. I became frightened so I turned around and went home.

In the early afternoon I took a ride by the wooded area once again and I saw policemen everywhere. I pulled my car to the side of the road and walked over to a policeman. I asked him if they found someone in the woods because my brother was missing and I asked the police to look in there for him. He asked me who my brother was and then he told me to wait. About ten minutes later he came back and asked me if my brother had any tattoos. I was so nervous that I couldn't remember but I told him that he had a large burn on his back. He once again told me to wait just where I was. Around fifteen minutes later in which seemed an eternity he came back and said, "Ma'am will you come with me?" I followed him around a curve and down a narrow path in to the woods. As we got deeper in the woods I could see David's lower legs and feet on the ground behind a large boulder. I stopped and said to the police officer, that is David. I knew David so well and I instantly knew that it was him. He said, "Ma'am you need to see his face to correctly identify him." He then said, "If you don't do it now you will have to go to the morgue in Boston to identify him." I didn't want to see his face but I mustered up all the courage I could find and stepped further down. There was my David with his face on the boulder; his face was white with flies and bugs all over it. It looked like he was trying to climb this enormous boulder. I just cried out, "MY DAVID". The officer then pulled me away and led me out of the woods. As I looked around there was a forensic man with a camera and several police officers and detectives around. I felt like I was in a movie with it going in slow motion.

When we reached my car the police officer asked me if I wanted him to tell my mother the news but I told him no, that I would tell my mother. I drove over to my mother's house and went inside. My mother looked so sad and exhausted. I hugged her very tight and said Mom I just identified David's body. Her body started shaking violently and then suddenly she stopped shaking. She started saying we have to get things planned and continued saying all the things that needed to get done. The way she was acting I knew she was in shock.

My brothers Richard and Thomas flew in from California. There were flowers and a funeral and everything just like the card reader had said to me. I thought of how I told David of what the card reader had said and how he smirked and nodded. When I thought it was my mother, David knew that it was himself.

Thomas was standing in one of my double parlors and the folding doors between the rooms were open. Out loud Thomas said "Damn David" and instantly the folding doors slammed shut all by themselves. I knew it was David who slammed those doors. I am heartbroken by the loss of David. I've always shared a special bond with him and I know we are soul mates. Soul mates aren't just husbands or wives; they can be a child, a sibling, or a parent etc.

During this time, everyone that I worked with was very kind to me. My supervisor Bernie and manager Elaine paid for all the food for the lunch after David's funeral. They even went to my house and set it all up while the funeral was going on. I will always be grateful for their generosity and kindness.

Before David's death I had already planned and paid to rent a vacation home in Oak Bluffs, Cape Cod. The vacation was two weeks after David's death and I was so heartsick that I didn't want to go but everyone kept saying it would do me good. So I decided it was best to take the kids away for a week since we were all having such a hard time dealing with David's death. I let the kids each take a friend with them. The house was large and very beautiful and Oak Bluffs is a quaint town but I just didn't feel like being there. I was so sick inside I didn't know what to do with myself.

The first day I was there I just stayed upstairs by myself crying. I lied down on the bed and felt someone touch my spine, their hand going up and down my back. I turned around but no one was there. I said out loud "David?" I heard nothing so I turned back around and just lied there. Suddenly my body jumped into the air from the bed as if someone had jumped onto the bed on the side of me. I knew right then that it was David. Every night that I was there, when I lied in bed he would poke my spine up and down till I fell asleep. It was comforting to know he was with me.

When vacation was over I went back to work and my life went on. But, my grief and depression grew deeper and deeper. I felt like a piece of me was gone and I couldn't get over the loss of David. I had never felt this type of loss or grief before. I thought I knew what depression was before this, but now I truly knew.

After David died my Mom was having a very hard time. Since she could see spirits she was seeing David all the time. David wouldn't leave her alone, following her everywhere she went. It was too much for her to keep seeing him. She finally told him to go away, and he did.

Not long after David's death I found out that the day he died, he visited the clinic he would go to see his counselor. I don't know what the conversation between them consisted of. What I do know is that David got very angry and screamed at the counselor that he was going to kill himself. The counselor let David walk out of there and he didn't notify the police or anyone in our family. The next day when the people at the clinic heard that David committed suicide, that counselor then called up my mother and said, "I want to make you aware that David threatened to kill himself yesterday." My mother then told the counselor that David had already killed himself. The counselor acted like he was surprised and said he was sorry. Philip attended the same clinic as David and he told us earlier how the news spread through the entire clinic of David's death so we knew the counselor had already known.

The counselor was trying to cover him and the clinic by calling my mother after they heard of David's death. Legally, when someone threatens to kill him or herself, you aren't supposed to let them leave. I hold no ill will towards the counselor or the clinic because I believe David would have killed himself eventually. We could have taken legal action against them but it wouldn't have brought David back.

A short while after David passed he came into my dream. I was sitting in a car with him and we were hugging and I told him how happy I was to see him. I looked up and saw my mother across the street. I said to David, "I have to tell Mom you are here." We stepped out of the car and when I looked across the street at my Mom she was crying. I then looked at David and screamed at him "Look What You Did to our Mother." He vanished right after I said that, and didn't return to my dreams for a while.

Around age twelve, a friend and her parents invited me to an amusement park called, Lincoln Park. My mother said I could go but I had to take David with me. I was so angry because I wanted to hang with my friend and not have to look after David. David and I went on the roller coaster and when I slammed down the bar to lock us in, I didn't realize that David's fingers were in the way and I really hurt him. I was still so angry that he accompanied me that I showed him no sympathy, and screamed at him to be quiet, not realizing just how badly he was hurt. I didn't even remember this incident until my mother told me how it affected David. While David was drinking one day he had cried and told my mother how this had emotionally hurt him. After David passed, all I could think about was this incident, and the time I beat him up breaking his glasses. Every wrong I ever did him filled me with guilt. How could I have been so mean to one of the sweetest souls I ever met? My poor David, God couldn't have given me a better brother, and I wished I had been a better sister. We were very close though, and I couldn't have loved him any more than I did. I feel like he got short changed. I hope his next life is amazing and filled with love.

It amazed me more than it did David at how connected we were to be able to do this telepathic exercise of the colors in our heads correctly each time. I never realized that it was a sign that I had some sort of spiritual gift. To me it confirmed how incredibly close I felt in my soul to David, and he to me. We only discontinued playing this game when David lost interest due to his sadness. Looking back, I now realize that through the spiritual events that constantly happened throughout my life, I was being shown my spiritual path and abilities.

SIX

Unending Loss

A co-worker recommended a psychic medium that she had had a reading with. She told me she had a group of six people at her house and this woman whom was a medium came and gave everyone there a reading. Since she spoke so highly of this medium, it really piqued my interest. She gave me the medium's phone number and when I got home that same day I called her to make an appointment. I was very excited and nervous to have this reading, hoping for some communication with David. The medium, Tracey Lynn came to my house the following week and gave me a reading. She proved to me without a doubt that I was speaking to David because of the things that she told me that only David could have known. I was absolutely amazed by her abilities and the communication that she had with the spirit realm.

Shortly after David passed, Justin told me that he was in the shower one day and felt like someone else was in there with him. He also said that he felt like someone had touched him. Tracey Lynn didn't know Justin even existed. She said to me that my brother David had a message for Justin. She also said David said to tell Justin that it was he David who was in the shower with him. I was so taken aback by this message that it gave me goose bumps. This was how she began the reading, and she didn't disappoint for the rest of the hour. Tracey Lynn is the real deal, and I have never met another medium that is as gifted as she is. Wanting to stay close to David, I made appointments with her about every six months or so. She helped me tremendously in my grieving process. Even with her help I had a terrible time getting over David's passing. David even said to Tracey Lynn that he couldn't understand why I was having such a difficult time getting over him.

About a year after David passed, I received a phone call from my mother and she said, "Dawn, do you know what I just realized?" I said "No mom what did you just realize?" and with the saddest cry I ever heard she said, "David is dead!" It took my mother over a year after being in shock to realize that her son was truly gone. I can't begin to describe to you the sadness that I felt for her.

I was hanging out with Justin quite a lot because we bonded over the loss of David. Justin felt a lot of guilt over leaving David to marry that woman. I was smoking marijuana daily, trying to numb myself, and with the grief and depression, I kept getting thinner and thinner. I wasn't large to begin with, but now I was extremely underweight. I pushed away my friends from the hospital and they never returned. I was on a steady downward decline in my life going nowhere.

Emotionally I was unable to be there for neither my mother nor my children. I felt like I could barely get through every second of every day. I would wake up and think it was all a nightmare, and that David would be sleeping downstairs. I would run downstairs to check, and of course he was never there. Matthew began using more drugs and alcohol. As far as Matthew was concerned, David was the only father figure he had known. David's passing was very hard for Matthew, also for Sarah. Matthew started using heroin and my brother Philip was the one who stuck a needle in my son's arm for the first time. Matthew's drug use just made my depression deeper.

After refinancing my house my mortgage payment was extremely high. I could have kept up with paying it if I continued working overtime but I just didn't have the strength or willpower. My house went into foreclosure and I claimed bankruptcy in 2007. At this point in my life I no longer had my David, my son was on drugs, and I lost the home that I absolutely loved. For the next two years I contemplated suicide because I couldn't endure the pain and sadness within myself anymore. I didn't tell a soul about me wanting to die because I didn't want anyone to stop me from doing it. Then one day after two years I had an epiphany, I realized I couldn't do to my Mom and children what David had done to us. I just couldn't put that pain in my children's hearts for the rest of their lives. It was like I took a small step forward and a weight lifted from my shoulders.

We moved in to an apartment building that was on the higher priced end though it was still way cheaper than my mortgage. I continued smoking weed and my depression was still in full force. Matthew's heroin addiction had progressed even further. I was so depressed that I had to take a leave of absence from work. A leave of absence meant I wouldn't receive any money for the first two weeks, then after that, I would only get sixty percent of my weekly pay. I borrowed money from my friend Amanda at work and told her I would repay her when my tax return came in. I didn't realize how little money I was going to receive from this leave of absence and I wasn't able to pay the rent. I spoke to another woman I worked with and was telling her that I had to use my tax return to pay my rent. She told Amanda I was going to use my tax return to pay my rent. Amanda was furious when she heard this because I had promised to pay her what I owed her out of this money. She left many messages on my phone threatening to beat me up if she didn't get her money. My children and I sat there and listened to her messages, which only brought me deeper in to my depression. I mustered up the courage and called her and told her I would pay her back as soon as I returned to work. It was very tense between us when I returned to work but I did repay her as quickly as I could.

Matthew was stealing whatever little money I had every chance he got. I sent him to a 30-day rehabilitation program to get off heroin. While he was gone I realized I could no longer afford to live in this apartment. Since I had signed a one-year contract and we were only six months into it, I wasn't sure what to do. I got myself together, walked into their office and told them I could no longer afford the rent; that I would be moving out as soon as possible. I found an apartment on craigslist that was affordable so I rented it. The company that owned the premises that I broke the contract with took me to court. When the Judge saw that I had already moved out and left the apartment clean and with no damage, he dismissed the case. Years later that company was still trying to come after me for the rest of the contract. After Matthew got out of the rehabilitation center he went right back on drugs.

The building that we moved into was a six-family house and the landlord seemed really nice. Every apartment in this building was empty except for a family on the first floor. The landlord gave me my choice of apartments and, because it was the cheapest to rent, I chose the third floor. Justin moved downstairs from us because his wife left him for another woman. Across the hall from Justin were two women named Nita and Emma, and their two sons. Nita was pregnant with her third child and we became very close friends. We hung together every day and smoked weed. With me in my depression and Nita being physically abused by Emma we made quite the pair. We were grateful to have each other to lean on and talk to. While we lived there, Nita and I became each other's saving grace.

Every apartment in the building filled up fast. I soon learned that the building we were living in was what I refer to as a "crack house." I never lived like that before and I never want to again. There were boys in a gang called "The Bloods" that were walking in and out of my apartment that my son was associating with. My life was out of control and I didn't know how to stop it.

Matthew's heroin addiction continued to grow. People were constantly in my apartment. Matthew and the boys he brought into my house were stealing everything they could from me. I would hide my debit card in different places. At nights when I slept I hid it under my mattress, but he would find it and take out all of my money. Every time I bought Sarah a new iPod he would steal it from her. He sold all her electric guitars and anything else that he could find.

I was downstairs at Nita's apartment one night when I saw cockroaches running everywhere. I had never seen a cockroach in my life before and I was horrified. I called up the landlord and told him about the cockroaches. It wasn't long before I started seeing them in my apartment also. It didn't take long before the house was infested with them and the landlord never did anything about them. We had to live like this till I could figure something else out. It was almost impossible to get anywhere, with Matthew constantly robbing me.

I soon found out that while I am sleeping, Matthew was taking my car and renting it out to a crack dealer. He would give her my car to use and she would give him crack in return. Some days I missed work because this woman had my car. I didn't have it in me to fight for myself or anyone else. I honestly didn't care about anything. I just felt like life was useless. My poor Sarah was caught in the midst of Matthew's drug addiction and my depression. She was depressed herself and no longer attended school. We ended up being on The Department of Social Services once again because of her lack of attendance at school. We had to go to court a few times, in which they threatened Sarah they were going to take her away from me if she didn't go back to School. Sarah didn't care at that point; the three of us were so deep in our depressions, addictions and sadness that we couldn't find a way out. Most of the time I didn't have any food in the house. Although Matthew and I hardly ate, I always made sure Sarah did. Nita always had plenty of food and would give me food to feed Sarah. Matthew and I looked like walking skeletons.

I was downstairs with Nita and Emma sitting at their kitchen table when I felt like someone was standing behind me. I turned around quick to look but no one was there. Emma looked at me and said, "Can you feel it too?" I said I definitely felt someone right behind me. Then I suddenly saw a little dark skinned girl around five years old walk into Nita's bedroom. This little girl was petite and absolutely beautiful. She was a spirit but I saw her as plain as day. When I told Nita and Emma about seeing her they got frightened and didn't want to hear it.

Emma asked me to cash a couple of checks in my bank for her that she said were given to her from people who owed her money. I cashed them for her in my bank and gave her the money. A month and a half later my bank told me that those checks were stolen. I didn't have the money in my account to cover them so since my bank was connected to my work and I had direct deposit they kept my next two weeks' paychecks to cover it. By the time this had all happened Nita and Emma had moved out. Though Nita was my friend, out of fear of Emma, she didn't dare tell me that the checks were stolen. Till this day Nita and I remain friends and she is no longer with Emma.

After Nita and Emma moved out I would go in to their empty apartment to smoke weed and be by myself. I was sitting on the floor in what used to be their living room. All of a sudden I saw the little girl again but this time she was standing there with a man who was also dark skinned. They were both dressed in gold robes and gold hats, it looked as though they were some kind of royalty. They both stared at me and without a word I knew they both wanted my help. I did the only thing I knew to do and called upon Archangel Michael to come and cross their souls over to the other side. They disappeared after a few minutes of my praying and I never saw them again.

Two detectives from the police department came knocking on my door one day. They asked for Matthew and I told them he wasn't home. I asked them what this was about and they said Matthew would know what it was about. I told them I would bring Matthew down to the police station when he arrived home. Actually Matthew was in bed sick from not having drugs. I wanted a chance to speak to Matthew before I took him to the police station.

I went in to his room and told him that the detectives were looking for him. He then told me how he received a call for a ride from his friend who lived downstairs. Matthew took my car and picked up his friend and two other boys. These three boys had robbed someone's house and they had a safe with them from the house they had just robbed. They had trouble carrying the safe so they called Matthew for a ride. Matthew allowed all the boys in my car with the safe. They took the safe to the boy's apartment that lived downstairs from us, and they somehow got it open and inside of it was $10,000.00 and some foreign currency. One of the boys pulled out a gun and held it to Matthew's head and said now get out of here, you are getting nothing because you didn't do anything. My son left and later on his friend told him if he gave him a ride to the bank to cash in some foreign currency he would get him some drugs. Matthew went into the bank with this boy to try and cash it in. The police had seen Matthew on the bank video. Because Matthew had his last name tattooed on his forearm, they knew who he was.

After Matthew told me what happened I drove him down to the police station. The detectives took him upstairs and arrested him. The three boys who did the actual robbery went to prison and have felonies. Matthew was released after he went to court and placed on probation and the four of them were supposed to pay the $10,000.00 restitution. Since the other three boys served jail time, Matthew was left with the responsibility of paying the entire $10,000. He struggled through many years and paid half of it until he was able to take out a loan and pay off the rest. He is now off probation and the case was later dropped without a finding. It was a hard, expensive lesson and fallout from his drug use.

During all of this craziness, and my depression, I wasn't the best employee I could have been. Some days I didn't go to work because the crack dealer had my car. I was showing up late for work on other days. My depression was so severe I couldn't get myself out of bed. I hardly bothered with my mother who was in her own grief over David. I felt I abandoned my mother when she needed me the most. But during this time in my life, I wasn't even able to take care of myself.

I mustered up all the strength and courage I could find in myself and sent Matthew to another drug rehabilitation program. We had only lived in this building six months when an employee from a bank came knocking on my door. He told all the tenants who lived there to no longer pay rent to our landlord. He said that the landlord no longer owned the property and that the house was in foreclosure. While Matthew was gone I found us a nice apartment in a beautiful neighborhood. Matthew was released from the program before we moved but stayed with a relative until we moved because of the drug use surrounding the apartment.

My children and I moved into the new apartment and everything seemed to be looking up. We loved the apartment and the new neighborhood. Because of the cockroach problem, I didn't take many things with me from the other apartment. Though I didn't really care because I felt free from that crack house. Life for the three of us felt so much lighter and brighter. Our new place was a two-family building and the owner's father lived on the first floor. He was a delightful English gentleman named John who took a liking to Matthew. Though we weren't very loud people John decided to move out after a short time of us being there because he wanted privacy and complete quiet in his own place.

I realized with John moving out it was a wonderful opportunity for my mother to live downstairs from me. I spoke to my mother and she agreed with me. I then spoke to the owner of the house and she also agreed. The day that we were moving my mother to her new apartment, Matthew stopped by her house very early in the morning. He was going to have breakfast with her like he used to every day. When I woke up Matthew was home and told me he went by grandma's house and she didn't answer her door. I then called her on the phone and she didn't answer her phone. I immediately got dressed and Matthew and I went over to my mother's house and rang her bell but she didn't answer. I became very nervous and told Matthew to get her window open and climb inside. After he climbed inside he opened the door and let me in and I found my mother lying in bed unresponsive. I immediately called an ambulance.

I met the ambulance at the hospital and the emergency room doctor told me
her oxygen level was 30. My mother has suffered with chronic obstructive
pulmonary disease (COPD) for many years due to smoking. He then told me that he
didn't think she was going to survive the day. I was heartsick. I called my mother's
sister, Ernestine, and told her what the doctors said. I made sure my mother was
comfortable and then I did the only thing I could think to do. I rented a U-Haul and
with Matthew and Josh's (the boy who lived next door to my mom) help, moved
my mother's furniture to her new apartment. We worked from morning till night
and the entire time all I could think about was if my mother was going to be alive
when I returned to the hospital. I'll never forget the deep heartsick I felt the whole
time I was moving her. I had no choice but to move her because she had to be out
of her apartment that day. I felt so numb I couldn't even cry. After we finally
finished moving her things, I returned to the hospital to see her. My mother was
sitting up laughing and talking with her sister. The shock on my face! My mother
said, "Why are you looking at me like that?" It was a miracle and the happiness and
relief I felt was beyond incredible. My mother had no idea how close she came to
death that day.

A few days later I picked my mother up from the hospital and brought her to her
new apartment. I loved every minute of having my mother live downstairs from
me. These apartments had only two bedrooms each so Matthew moved
downstairs with my mother while Sarah and I lived upstairs. I enjoyed things like
coming home from work and cooking dinner for the entire family.

Sarah would tell me how she could hear disembodied voices in her bedroom and
that she was terrified of them. She was the only one who heard these voices. Till
one day I was alone in the house and I went in to Sarah's bedroom and sat on her
bed. Suddenly very clearly I heard a woman's voice say, "I told her not to give her
husband the money because he would just drink it away." I said to myself, "Oh My
God, now I know what Sarah is talking about."

I had a dream not too long after moving into this apartment. In the dream I was
in a food market called the "Stop & Shop." As I looked down the aisle I could see
my Aunt Dot and my Uncle Bill that I hadn't seen in years because they had moved
to Florida. I said to a man behind the counter, look it is my Aunt and Uncle and they
look so good. I ran down the aisle to greet them but they were now in the parking
lot in a red pickup truck. As I approached the truck my Aunt was the only one in the
truck. I knew she was going somewhere, and I wanted to go with her but she told
me that I couldn't. Again I told her that I wanted to go with her and she got a little

angry and yelled, "You can't go with me." She then quickly took off, disappearing into the sky. I then looked around and it was like I was standing in ancient ruins and my brother David was there sitting on some broken steps. I looked at him and he shook his head and tapped his foot like he always did. The next thing I knew I woke up and thought wow, that was weird. The next time I went to get a reading from Tracey Lynn she said to me, your brother David is here and he wants you to tell me about the last dream you had that he was in. I told her it was very weird and she said to me your brother just said "Stop & Shop." I was blown away when she said that, then I told her the dream started in Stop & Shop. I asked her to ask David if my Uncle had passed because he was no longer in the truck when I got there. She said she could still feel my Uncle on the earth. When she asked David if my Uncle had passed all he said was, "Bye, Bye." I tried to find a way to contact their daughter, my cousin Doris, whom I hadn't seen in years because she also lived in Florida. No luck, until I ran in to another one of my cousins who gave me her number. I called Doris, told her of the dream, and she told me that her mother had passed away. I then realized that was why my Aunt said I couldn't go with her. David came to my dream to let me know she had passed away.

Because Matthew was still on probation at this point, he had to go give urine tests every week to make sure he wasn't using any drugs. He was also attending meetings at the Narcotics Anonymous program (NA). He started dating a girl he met through these meetings. I told him it was too soon for him in his recovery to get involved with anyone romantically. He ignored my advice and they both ended up getting back on heroin together. Matthew was not only taking my money now, but he started taking my mother's money also. He then had this girl move in to my mother's apartment with him. They were either constantly high or searching to get high. I hate to admit it but I was still smoking marijuana and continuously fighting to get out of this depression I was in. I was doing better than I was before, but I was by no means out of this darkness. I was still missing days at work or going in late due to my overwhelming sadness and depression. Needless to say my coworkers were not very happy with me, and I was no longer being treated nicely. It wasn't their fault; but the worse they treated me, the deeper I sank into my depression. I couldn't take a step or a breath at work without someone getting me into trouble with my boss. When we sat in our break room, no one spoke to me. I felt so alone. A few of them were not nasty to me, but the majority was overwhelmingly so. They couldn't understand what I was going through, nor the severity of my depression. I could not get over the loss of David. My grief was deep. My son was back on drugs. I felt helpless. It got to the point where many of them were trying to get me fired. Yes, I did smoke weed, but many of them needed to take a look in the mirror.

Stickers were being ripped off my locker, mean notes were being slipped into my locker, my lunch would disappear from the refrigerator, and someone stole my lab coat. I was being harassed in different ways. I told my boss about it all, yet nothing was done to stop it. The worse they would treat me, the more I didn't want to go to work. I felt like I was in a never-ending circle of misery.

I got myself together somewhat, called Matthew's probation officer and told him that Matthew was using drugs. I set it up so when they came to the house Matthew would be upstairs with me. They came in and arrested him, and I had them take his girlfriend out and told her to never come back to my house again. I went to court and had Matthew sectioned to a very tough 30-day rehabilitation program.

During his drug use Matthew was stealing my money which put me very behind on my car payments. In the middle of the night they came and repossessed my car. My mother was getting very sick and fragile at this time and was constantly on oxygen. I could see the sadness and helplessness in her face when they took my car. I started getting rides to and from work with a kind woman that I worked with. It was out of her way and I could tell that she was getting tired of doing this for me. Coworkers made no bones about telling me how I inconvenienced this woman. Quite a few days I walked the 15 miles home from work in the freezing winter. However, I will always be grateful to her for her help during that difficult time in my life.

My brother Andrew moved in downstairs with my mother while Matthew was away. I wasn't happy about this because he was still on drugs and would take any money from her that he could. She was very weak, and her health was rapidly deteriorating. Someone had to be with her at all times so in some ways it was good that Andrew was with her while I was at work.

I handled my mother's finances so I would pay all of her bills each month. I came home from work one day and she told me to give her back her bankbook and checks. She said that she was giving them to Andrew to handle her finances because I was stealing from her. I couldn't believe my mother was saying these words to me and I was beyond hurt. I was not a thief and I never stole a thing from her in my life. Andrew somehow convinced her that I was stealing from her so that he could take control of her finances. Needless to say, he never paid any of her bills, not even her rent. He gave our landlady checks that bounced. Every month when her money came in to her bank account, he would go withdraw it all and get high, and I ended up having to pay all her bills with my own money.

The end of March 2010 while at work, Andrew called saying that my mother fell and asked me what to do. I told him to call an ambulance immediately. I left work and met them at the hospital that they took my mother to. I entered the emergency room and saw that they had put a chest tube in her; she had broken some ribs and the ribs punctured her lung. An emergency room physician walked over to me and asked if I was her daughter. I barely replied yes, and she blurted out very loudly that my mother's cat scan showed her brain was full of cancer. We were only standing a few feet from my mother's bed when she gave me this horrible news. I stood there stunned as she walked away without saying another word. I walked back to my mother and acted like nothing was wrong. I didn't want her to know she had brain cancer and I wasn't sure if she heard the doctor, but she never said anything to me. I understood now why she believed Andrew when he said I was stealing from her. She wasn't in her right mind from the brain cancer.

Her doctor told me she had Glioblastoma and she had about a month to live. Next I was told that she had a tumor on the pons in her brain and the pons controls the breathing. If it weren't removed immediately, within two days she would be dead. I told my mother everything the doctors had said. I also told her she would wake up with a tube down her throat and I knew that she never wanted that tube. Much to my surprise she agreed to have the surgery. She was then transferred to another hospital for the surgery. It was my mother's 80th birthday the day that she had her surgery. Also on that day I was attending George's brother's Johnny's funeral with George and our kids. The kids and I were close to Johnny, he treated us well and always made us feel welcome. His death was quite a shock and I miss him very much. But my mother was heavy on my mind that day. My mother was never the same after the surgery. While my mother was ill, I started smoking cigarettes again, after quitting for fifteen years.

In April 2010, a few days after my mother's surgery, I needed to have surgery on my left breast. I lied in bed with her the night before my surgery and I said, "Mom I wish you could come with me tomorrow for my surgery." She replied, "I will be bright and sunny in the morning and I will go with you." She honestly thought that she would be bright and sunny and how I wished for it. The surgeon removed atypical ductal hyperplasia from my chest wall, which is pre-cancerous. It is not breast cancer but if it were not removed it would have developed into full-blown breast cancer in the future. The surgeon kept a close eye on me for a year and then released me from her care.

A week after her surgery my mother told me that she wanted to go home to die.

I arranged for her to come home on hospice. She came home April 30th 2010 on a bright, sunny, beautiful day. She was wide-awake when they brought her in to the house. She was talking, smiling and happy. I fed her scrambled eggs and pistachio pudding and she enjoyed every bite and she kept saying how delicious it was. That was the last meal she ever ate. I really enjoyed that day with her and I will never forget it. The next few days she suffered excruciating pain. Even with all the painkillers it wasn't enough to take away her pain. It was heart wrenching to watch this woman I adored and loved so much suffering so badly. Justin unselfishly helped me to take care of my mother in that time and I'll always be grateful to him for that.

May 4th 2010: I laid by my mother's side as her body was giving out. I felt someone poke my right thigh and I looked down at my leg. I could actually see the indentations of someone poking me. I knew that it was David and I said out loud, "David, I know why you are here." I was hoping that my mother's mother was with David because they were the two people she missed the most in this world. My Mom took her last breath within 15 minutes after I was poked. I knew for certain that David came to cross my mother over to the other side.

My mother lied in her bed for over three hours till the hospice nurse came and called the funeral parlor. I laid by her side during this time, talking and singing to her. Grief is so personal to each of us and it is never ending. We go through different stages of grief at different times in our lives. On any given day something that happens can bring the loss of someone right to the surface as if you just lost him or her yesterday. Everyone loses his or her parents; it is the circle of life. But I have learned that as much as I miss them, they are right by my side. A soul can never die; only the vessels that carry our souls on this earth dies. Their souls are very much alive and are watching and helping us every chance they can. Our loved ones guide us in our lives to help us fulfill our soul's purpose on this earth, until it is our turn to cross over to eternal peace, where we will all meet again.

My brothers and some of their children came in from California for the funeral. Everyone stayed downstairs at my mother's apartment. There was a lot of drinking and partying going on down there and I couldn't deal with it. I stayed upstairs in the quiet of my apartment, laid on my bed, heartsick over the loss of my mother. The day of the funeral Andrew and Thomas fought because Andrew was holding everything up, needing to get high before he went. Everyone drank a lot of alcohol after the funeral, except Sarah and I who went up to our apartment and went to sleep. The next morning when I awoke and came downstairs I saw blood on the walls. I found out that one of the young men that were drinking in my mother's apartment beat Justin to a pulp and threw him out the door in the night. This young man fell asleep and awoke to Justin putting his hands down his pants. I didn't know how to deal with this news and it just added to my sadness.

After my mother passed, I retrieved her bankbooks and checks back from Andrew. The day after the funeral I went to the bank to get the money from her last check to pay her bills and they told me that Andrew had already withdrawn everything she had. Not only did Andrew rob my mother on her deathbed; he also robbed her after she died. Employees at the bank told me to press charges against him but I knew that would only bring me retaliation that I wouldn't have been able to handle at that time in my life.

After everyone went back home, I had to clean out my mother's apartment, a very hard, emotional thing to do. Thankfully Andrew found a girlfriend a couple of towns over and moved in with her. I paid my mother's rent for the full month and in the last week the only thing left in the apartment was a couch. I would sleep on the couch because it brought me comfort to be in her apartment. Four days till the end of the month I came home from work and the landlady had someone moving in to my mother's place. I felt heartbroken because I still had a few nights left to sleep in her apartment but now I wasn't able to.

A man named Charlie and his girlfriend moved in downstairs. Charlie was a fisherman and wasn't home a lot. Unfortunately, Charlie and his girlfriend were on heroin. His girlfriend stole much of my belongings that were stored in the basement. She took items like a dresser, drapes and record albums. I was especially upset that she took my album of autographed photos of celebrities. I had been collecting them since I was a teenager and they meant a lot to me. Back in the 1970's you could write to a celebrity and ask for an autographed photo and you would receive a handwritten photo or letter. I had autographed photos from people like John Wayne, Bette Davis, Totie Fields, Jimmy Stewart, Joan Crawford, Danny Thomas, Connie Stevens, Mary Tyler Moore, and the list goes on and on.

Charlie and his girlfriend finally got evicted. When they moved out they left behind their washer and dryer. My landlady told me that due to all that they had stolen from me that I could keep their washer and dryer. I was very grateful to her for that but she changed her mind when I moved out. She charged me for the washer and dryer by taking it out of my security deposit. Actually she didn't give me any of my security deposit back, which I could have really used. The couple that moved in downstairs after Charlie had moved out wasn't much better. That man had an incredible anger problem. Someone mistakenly put our clothes in his washer instead of mine. It was an honest mistake because of the switching of washers with Charlie's washer. My old washer used to be on the side that the new people were using. When this man saw our clothes in his washer he took them and carried them upstairs to his bathroom. He put them in his bathtub and poured bleach all over them. There was no need for that because it was an honest mistake; he was just an angry, miserable soul.

Soon after my mother passed I made an appointment with Tracey Lynn to get a reading. While driving to Tracey Lynn's house I was very nervous but also very hungry. I kept thinking that I was going to stop at McDonald's and get myself a milkshake. When I pulled up at her house the first thing I thought was, oh man I forgot to get myself a milkshake. When I went inside her house and sat down, the first thing she said to me was your mother drove here with you. Next she told me that my mother said to go to McDonald's and get myself a milkshake. She also told me that my grandmother and my brother David were the ones who came and crossed her over to the spirit realm. I felt so relieved to hear that confirmation.

I had a dream shortly after my mother's death. In this dream I was standing in Kennedy Park in my town on a hill with my cousin Doris. It was as if there was a carnival or festival going on around us. I looked at Doris and she said to me, my father passed away. I contacted my cousin the next day after the dream and she told me that her father had passed away. Entering our dreams is one way the spirit realm can communicate with us and visit us.

In October 2014 I had another reading with Tracey Lynn who told me that my mother said I needed to go get a mammogram. I hadn't had one in a couple of years due to no health insurance. Since I had just acquired some health insurance, I contacted my primary care physician who scheduled a mammogram. Once again they found something in my left breast and needed to do a biopsy. They found the same thing, atypical ductal hyperplasia and surgery was scheduled. This time the surgeon considered giving me chemotherapy after surgery since this was my second time. Thankfully she decided against chemotherapy though she did keep a close eye on me for another year. In January 2016 she released me from her care once again.

In February 2015, a month after I had my second surgery, I went to pray in the chapel downstairs at St. Anne's Church. There are many beautiful life-size statues there and as I stood in front of the St. Therese statue I felt a stabbing, burning pain in my left breast that lasted for a few minutes. I could feel St. Therese's presence and I knew right there and then that a healing had been placed upon me. I called Tracey Lynn that afternoon and told her what had happened. She said that it was a healing that had been done and the spirit realm has assured her that I am done with any problems in my breast and that it will never occur again. She also told me that St. Therese is my patron Saint and she has been with me since I was a child. St. Therese also said I am to keep writing down everything I am told in my meditations and channelings. Numerous mediums and psychics have told me that I am to write several books.

At work I was doing my best each day though I was now having terrible knee pain and fatigue. I was still very much underweight and depressed. My co-workers still resented me and I was not happy working there. I was still calling in sick and showing up late sometimes. I was having a difficult time getting through each day physically, mentally, and emotionally. Matthew came home from his rehabilitation program and didn't stay off drugs. He went to see his probation officer and they asked him for a urine test in which he failed. He was arrested right on the spot. In court the Judge ordered him to a detox program and after he completed that he was to go to a halfway house for three months. With him going to a halfway house I now had some hope for my son to be free of drugs.

A month after my mother passed away, I had to put my white cat Casper to sleep. He had a tumor on his abdomen and was suffering. I was washing the dishes and crying because I was so sad, while listening to a song on a cd that had the words "Goodbye My Friend." I was playing this song for Casper. The CD player was in my bedroom so I had to keep going back and forth to keep playing the song over and over. As I was washing the dishes I realized that it was silent and the CD wasn't playing. I went back to my bedroom to see what happened because when I had walked out of my bedroom the music was playing. The CD player was open, and the CD was on my floor across the room. I was astounded at this and instinctively knew that my mother had done this. I was making myself sadder by continually listening to the song and she wanted me to stop. I did stop crying and I never listened to it again.

In November, six months after my mother had passed, I received a call at work telling me that my mother's sister, Ernestine, had passed away. I was shocked by this news because my Aunt was always so healthy. My Aunt was very good to my mother; she would always bring her food and take her to places that she needed to go. They were very close their entire lives. My cousins told me that after my mother died my Aunt never smiled or laughed anymore. They believed she died of a broken heart. Her cause of death was congestive heart failure in which I've researched on the Internet. Doctors say a broken heart can bring on congestive heart failure. I felt so guilty after she passed because my Aunt came to my mother's apartment the day after the funeral and brought me food. She stood there and looked at me so sad and lost. She said to me, "I don't know what I'm going to do without your mother." In those six months before she passed I never once went to visit her because I was in my own grief. During this time I also had to put my sweet kitty Sammy to sleep because she had rabies. Now my grief grew even deeper.

With my Aunt's passing the sadness I felt was overwhelming. It made me even sadder that my cousin's sold her house because her house represented love and stability to me. I kept driving by the house and crying and it only made me sadder. One afternoon as I was taking the corner to her street I heard my mother's voice clear as a bell say, "Don't come by here anymore." I never drove by the house again and it helped me to heal and let go of the sadness of losing that house and part of my childhood.

Exactly one week after my Aunt passed, I received the news that George, Matthew and Sarah's father, had passed away. Once I heard this news I couldn't stop crying. I felt like I didn't know how much more I could take. George was living in Key West, Florida and I hadn't seen him since his brother Johnny's funeral. Though George and I spoke on the phone every day until a couple of months before he passed, he suddenly stopped communicating with me and I didn't understand why. George had liver disease and he was on pain medication that brought his addiction to the surface and it overtook him. I now understood why he stopped communicating with me and why he passed away so quickly.

The following month after George passed, I received the news that my friend Lori passed away. She overdosed and this made me very upset. The last time I had seen Lori was at my mother's wake. I went to see her twice after my mother passed but her boyfriend wouldn't let me into the apartment to see her. The day after Lori passed, I was in my basement doing laundry. I could feel a strong spiritual presence with me. This spirit started panicking and I could actually feel this spirit climbing on my back. It was so intense that I said out loud, "Lori is that you?" I continued to speak to her and told her she needed to calm down. I said, "Yes Lori, you are dead, and you need to cross over now." I then said to her, "How long have you been waiting to see your father?" I then told her, your father is waiting to cross you over so that you may go spend eternal peace in heaven with him. Then finally I said, "Just relax, it is going to be okay my friend." I then called upon Archangel Michael to come and help her cross over to the spirit realm. I immediately felt better and the next day I felt such an incredible peace within me I knew then that Lori had crossed over and was now at peace.

Two months later I went to Tracey Lynn for a reading. She told me that there was a younger woman stepping forward and her name was Lori. She told me that

Lori had come to thank me for helping her cross over. She also told me that Lori said I was a good friend and that she loved me. She went on to tell me that Lori wanted me to know that her death wasn't accidental. She purposely overdosed because she couldn't go on living any longer. In my head I started thinking how I wished I had a picture of Lori. Tracey Lynn then said Lori wants you to go visit her sister and ask her for a picture of herself for you to have. It is amazing how spirit can hear you're your thoughts. A week later I went to visit Lori's sister and told her everything that was said in the reading. She confirmed that Lori's overdose was on purpose.

SEVEN

Awakened

When my daughter was around twelve years old, I asked my mother why she had asked me to name her Sarah. She replied that she never asked me to name her that. I was befuddled because I clearly remembered our conversation, and she did ask me to. So when I went to Tracey Lynn for one of her readings I had her ask my mother why she wanted me to name my daughter Sarah. The response she gave me was that Sarah is a namesake of someone from The Salem Witch Trials. Tracey Lynn told me that my mother lived in Salem during the trials in another lifetime. Exactly who my mother was in those days wasn't told to me. But the more I thought about this the more it made sense to me. My mother had a recurring dream her entire life. That she was running through a town, terrified, while the townspeople was chasing her to kill her.

One day when I was an adult my mother took a ride with her sister Ernestine to Danvers, MA. She told us although she had never been there before; she knew every street and everywhere to go in this town. She couldn't understand how she knew this information and it frightened her. Danvers, MA used to be called Salem Village, which is where the first handful of accusations were made for The Salem Witch Trials. There were two women named Sarah in the witch trials. Also the amazing gift my mother had of communicating with spirit all made complete sense to me. I believe in reincarnation and choosing to come back for other lifetimes.

Sarah, who was now sixteen years old, met her first serious boyfriend, Mike. Though they both went to the same high school though they did not know each other until they met at a concert that Sarah attended with her friends. When she came home after the concert she told me that some weird boy just came up to her and kissed her on the lips. She started dating that odd boy but she kept it a secret for a while because she said that she didn't want to jinx it. I finally met him after about a month. He had long hair, wore skinny jeans and was into heavy metal. He was very respectful and I thought he was adorable. Sarah and Mike were together as much as possible to the point that Mike moved in with us.

Matthew was still living in the half way house and attending NA meetings. At these meetings he met a woman in her early thirties who was living in a halfway house a few towns over from us. Against my advice, they started seeing each other. He was only twenty years old and he needed to focus on staying clean.

Matthew completed his time in the half way house. This woman started using heroin and Matthew thought he was going to be her savior. It wasn't long before they both ended up using heroin together. She was then thrown out of the half way house that she was living in. Before I could blink an eye he had this woman living in my apartment. They were the most ruthless couple I had ever met. Matthew was like I had never seen him before, threatening me and robbing me blind and I was in hell once again. Matthew overdosed many times during his drug use.

At this time, I was diagnosed with Connective Tissue Disease, which is an Auto Immune Disease. I also have lesions on my brain they first thought was Multiple Sclerosis but thankfully it wasn't. I was also having petite mal seizures. Between my depression, fatigue and this disease, it was time to quit work. I put my resignation in at the hospital on October of 2011. A huge burden lifted off my shoulders that I didn't have to fight myself any longer to go work at that hospital every day. I was relieved of many things by leaving that job. The freedom I felt was incredible and it was the best decision I ever made in my life.

I cashed in my pension to have money to live on. After taxes I received $67,000.00 from my pension. My original plan was to move to Florida and buy a house there. But while I was visiting Florida my fingers got so swollen that I couldn't bend them. Somehow the Florida weather wasn't agreeing with my autoimmune disease. It was a good thing that I didn't purchase a house there. I paid off all of my debts and I decided to move to Connecticut in July of 2012.

Matthew and his girlfriend were robbing me blind. Matthew kept threatening me with taking his life. They were relentless and he was constantly begging me for money. My brother Andrew conned me out of a lot of money. Friends were using me for money, but I was blind. By the time I left for Connecticut I was completely broke. I realized too late how I let everyone take advantage of me. I needed to find courage and strength within myself, but I had nothing left emotionally, spiritually or financially. I myself foolishly spent some of the money partying. While down in my basement smoking weed, clear as a bell I heard my mother's disembodied voice say, "Dawn, What Are You Doing?"

Matthew's girlfriend caused so much chaos and damage to our family. She was very sneakily pitting all of us against each other. The words she used and the way she spoke to Matthew was cruel and abusive. She had a daughter whom her mother and father had custody of. She became pregnant with Matthew's child and I was so afraid for this child because of the large quantities of drugs she was doing. She finally made the decision to have an abortion and I felt it was the right thing to do. I drove her and Matthew to the abortion clinic. We left her there while I took Matthew to a rehabilitation program. I didn't want her in my house any longer and I never went back to the clinic for her. She moved back to her parent's house and her father brought her to my house to pick up her belongings. I stacked all her items up in the entry, but not before I removed everything I could find that she had stolen from Sarah and myself. That was the last time I ever saw her and I'm very grateful for that. A part of me was sad over everything that went on because that was my grandchild. I kept asking myself if I did the right thing. I try not to think of her and those times because it brings me great sadness.

Matthew didn't stay in the rehabilitation program for very long. He signed himself out and continued using drugs. He and I were sitting on the couch and he was begging me to call up people to borrow money because I was broke and he was sick from not having heroin. Sarah and her boyfriend Mike walked into the apartment and heard what Matthew was saying to me. Sarah couldn't hold herself back any longer and started screaming at him. She spit in his face and in turn he threw a plastic ashtray at her. She called the police and pressed assault and battery charges on him. He took off because he was still on probation and knew he would be arrested. He never returned to this apartment again because he now had a warrant for his arrest and was afraid of going to prison. The SWAT Team came looking for him a few times at my apartment because they thought I was hiding him, but I wasn't.

Sarah's boyfriend Mike decided to join the Marines. He went to the recruiting office in our town and signed up. As he was waiting to get accepted into boot camp he would go to the recruiting office on a weekly basis and check for updates on his acceptance. It was always the same answer, nothing yet. They told him that when we moved they could transfer him to a different recruiting office in Sturbridge, MA that was near Connecticut.

A few months before we moved to Connecticut, I finally stopped smoking weed. I desperately tried to quit cigarettes but I wasn't able to at that time. I used one of the electronic cigarettes for six months but I went right back to cigarettes. In June of 2012 I rented a U-Haul truck. Sarah, Mike, my friend John and I were packing up the U-Haul when The SWAT Team arrived once again looking for Matthew. As we packed up the truck they searched for him but of course didn't find him. I wasn't sure where Matthew was at that time but I did know I didn't want him moving in with us. Though terrified that I was going to lose him, I just couldn't deal with his drug use anymore. He was underweight, malnourished; he had dark circles under his eyes and sores all over from picking himself. He was smoking crack and shooting up heroin. I had to leave him behind for all concerned. Anyone that he had to turn to for any real help was now deceased. I had to show him tough love and this was going to break him or make him.

The apartment we moved into in Connecticut was affordable, beautiful, huge, and sunny. My orange tabby Max loved it there; he just seemed so comfortable in this apartment. The town we lived in was North Grosvenor Dale; it was a very old town, country-like and quaint. It didn't have any supermarkets; department stores or much of anything else. We had to travel to the surrounding towns to buy food or anything we needed. In one way the quiet was good for us after everything we had been through. We settled in quite nicely though eventually, it proved to be too boring of a town for us. Sarah started working at TJ Maxx in Dayville, CT while her boyfriend Mike who moved with us was working at Wendy's in Putnam, CT. We found a town named Millbury, MA that had many wonderful restaurants and a movie theater. On Mike and Sarah's days off we would go to this town and treat ourselves to a movie and dinner.

We didn't have a house phone when we first moved to Connecticut. I had a cell phone but couldn't get service where we lived. To get a signal to use my cell phone, I had to walk up a hill to a park. Sarah kept asking me to call my brother Thomas to see if he could get her some concert tickets through his job. Thomas is an electrical engineer for an Entertainment Company out of Los Angeles. I promised her that I would, but I kept procrastinating. Two nights in a row I had the same exact dream. In these dreams I was hanging out with Sharon Osborne and it was like we were old friends. The dreams seemed so real that when I woke up I felt like I had just hung out with Sharon all night. A week later I called my brother Thomas about the concert tickets for Sarah. He said, "where have you been, I have been trying to get a hold of you for a few weeks?" He said he was in New Jersey working on *America's Got Talent* and that he had spoken to Sharon Osborne and she had agreed to meet me. After a couple of weeks when he couldn't get in touch with me, he told Sharon and she replied, "Oh well it's her loss. "I'll always regret that I lost a chance to meet Sharon.

I kept seeing many orbs flying around this new apartment constantly and I could feel the presence of spirit around every day. I found the orbs fascinating and took lots of pictures of them. Mike and Sarah could not see them with their naked eye like I could. One orb was huge and it stopped over a crucifix I had on my doorway.

It almost encompassed the entire crucifix but by the time I was able to take a picture of it, it moved to the right of the cross. Occasionally, we would hear a baby cry and it sounded like it was in our apartment.

After living there for a while I kept feeling sad. The sadness was turning into despair and I couldn't shake these awful feelings. I gave Tracey Lynn a call to tell her that I had moved. We barely said hello and the next thing she said to me was, where are you because there are a ton of spirits around you. She then said to me that there is a woman with blonde hair in your home and her name is Sarah. She told me this woman Sarah was distraught from losing a child when she was alive, and she carries this burden with her into the spirit realm. She also said that although the people of the town tried to help her, Sarah never got over the loss of her baby. Tracey Lynn could even see the town doctor that visited her house to help her but no one was able to. She told me to tell this spirit that she was not allowed to put her feelings of despair on me. I did as she advised and spoke to Sarah. After speaking to her I felt so much better; the sadness was lifted. Once in a while Sarah still tried to push her sadness on me but I would tell her to stop it, and she would. I spoke daily to this Sarah and tried to get her to cross over but she never would, afraid that her child wouldn't be with her if she did.

Tracey Lynn also told me that there was a portal in my apartment that all the spirits were coming through. A Native American man was there, and she said I should put something in my apartment to welcome him. I bought a dream catcher, hung it up and told him that he was welcome here. The spirits in my apartment told Tracey Lynn that they were all from a cemetery up the hill from me. I told her that I didn't know if there is a cemetery up the hill but I will check it out as soon as I could. A few days later Sarah, Mike and I went up the hill and found a very old cemetery, but we couldn't find any Sarah in it. A few days after that we saw another cemetery up the hill in back of the property we lived in. So, we went to that cemetery which was extremely old and walked through it. Amazingly, we found the gravestone of Sarah P Whittemore, born 1803 and died 1863. On one side of her gravestone was her infant son who died in 1831. On the other side of her was her husband Lyman who died two years after his son in 1833. Sarah was 28 years old when she had her son and lost him, and she lived another 32 years in that terrible despair.

Max, my orange tabby whom I love dearly, was now 18 years old. His breath was starting to smell really bad and he wasn't eating much. I made an appointment for him at the Vet, thinking he probably had some teeth that needed extracting. The night before taking Max to the Vet, we were all sleeping when at 2 AM we heard very loud drumming in our apartment that woke us all up. We got up and looked around, amazed at this drumming. It sounded like Native American drumming. This drumming went on for quite a while and then suddenly it stopped. We all went back to bed not understanding or able to explain what had just happened.

The next day Sarah went with me to take Max to the Vet. They did an examination, took blood, and told us Max was dying. He was diabetic and his organs were shutting down (why his breath smelled). Sarah and I were in shock over this news and didn't want to put him to sleep. This was a Friday and I asked the Vet if we could wait till Monday so we could spend the weekend with him. They said it was our call but Max would just suffer his death over the weekend. I told Sarah we love him so much that we can't let him suffer any further and we made the decision to put Max to sleep that day.

Max had already climbed back in to his carrier because he knew that meant he was going home. I had to fight with this gentle soul to get him back out of the carrier. Sarah and I stayed with Max while they put him to sleep. This was truly a heartbreaking day for us. We had Max since Sarah was five years old, and now Sarah and Mike was engaged to be married. We did a lot of crying that day and it was hard to get sleep that night.

During that night, at exactly 2 am once again, Native American drums started playing loudly throughout our apartment. This time there were maracas accompanying the drumming. We all got out of our beds and were astounded as we listened to the music. This time it felt very comforting and calming to us and it never happened again after that night. I spoke to Tracey Lynn a few months later and she told me that Max was a spirit animal. That Max was very special, and the Native Americans knew this and prepared for his death on that first night we heard the drumming. On the second night of the drumming they performed a ceremony to cross his soul over to the spirit realm. She also told me that since Max was my spirit animal and that God has promised that he would be returned to me in this lifetime. She said he would be another cat but just a darker color this time and I would immediately know it was him. As of now he hasn't been returned to me, but I will shout it to the world when he does.

While we were living in CT, Matthew moved to New Jersey to live with Justin and Justin's boyfriend. It wasn't good for him to be in that environment because they were not helping him in the proper way. They were freely handing him money to feed his addictions. Justin was actually getting heroin for him and Matthew. Finally Justin and his boyfriend got sick of supporting Matthew's drug addiction and decided not to give him any more money or drugs. Someone else's addiction can drag others down very quickly, especially if it takes away from your own addiction. Matthew and I spoke on the phone occasionally and he was always sick from not getting any drugs. He started drinking a lot of alcohol to try and compensate for not using drugs.

Matthew finally made the decision that he wanted to turn himself into his probation officer and get clean. I couldn't have been happier to hear this news. A friend that Matthew made while he was in New Jersey gave him the money to hire a lawyer. The lawyer that Matthew hired spoke to his probation officer before he turned himself in. Matthew was terrified of going to prison, and his probation officer had every intention of putting him there. His lawyer and probation officer spoke and came to an agreement. They agreed that when Matthew turned himself in, his probation officer would ask the Judge to send him to a rehabilitation program and then to a halfway house for three months. After the halfway house, he would then have to go live in a sober house. The judge agreed on these stipulations and I felt so much more at ease.

Matthew had done everything that was asked of him and he has done incredibly well. He went to NA meetings and he sponsored others in the meetings. He spoke at Facilities where other addicts were trying to get clean. He was very involved in the NA program and all the friends he has are from the program. Matthew got clean in November 2012. I am so very proud of my son, and the man that he is today. He stayed clean for five years but has relapsed here and there since. I am grateful to have not lost my son to this terrible disease. I will never forget this battle that was almost lost that he still continues to fight.

Sarah's boyfriend Mike was checking in on a regular basis with the marine recruiter in Sturbridge, MA. Every time he took a ride to the recruiting office the Sergeant would tell him he hadn't heard any news as yet. At this point it had been over a year and we were getting frustrated. I took a ride with Mike to the recruiter's office and his recruiter wasn't there. I spoke to another Sergeant and told him how frustrating it was that Mike has been waiting over a year to hear any news from his recruiter. The Sergeant looked very surprised and said he would look into it. Three days after we spoke to that Sergeant, Mike received a phone call saying that he was accepted into Boot Camp and that he would be leaving January 2014. Mike, Sarah, and I were so happy that he was accepted, though it was still over seven months away. Mike and Sarah could now start planning their future and they decided to get married April 11, 2014, right after Mike returned home from boot camp. Happily, and excitedly, the planning for their wedding began. While living in Connecticut, we were all emotionally, spiritually, mentally and financially healed. We spent a lot of time together just being kind to each other.

I applied for health insurance while living in Connecticut but was unable to get any that I could afford. So, after living in CT for a year, we decided to move over to the closest town in Massachusetts, which was Webster. This way I could apply for health insurance and Sarah and Mike could keep their same jobs in CT.

I rented another U-Haul and once again Sarah, Mike, my friend John and I moved us over to Webster, MA. Door to door from our old apartment to the new one was only six miles. Our new apartment on the second floor in this two-family building was like walking in to the 1970's, with shag carpeting and paneling. We didn't mind it one bit though because it was clean and quiet. The woman Lisa, who owned the house, lived downstairs from us. This was her childhood home and her father lived in my apartment before he passed. I became very friendly with Lisa and we all enjoyed living there. Spirits definitely made themselves known in this apartment. I could see orbs flying around every single day. We had both a front door and a back door to the apartment, and these heavy, solid doors with locks, would open up on their own. The bedroom that Sarah and Mike slept in used to be Lisa's father's bedroom. This bedroom had two closets; one with a regular door and the other had two sliding doors. No matter how many times we would close those closet doors, they would open back up. I constantly feel the presence of spirit in there. The feeling that this spirit gave me was that this was his house, not mine. The rocking chair in the living room would rock with no one sitting in it, which was quite freaky.

My three-year-old great niece Madyson spent a week with us. She asked me who the man was that was sitting in the rocking chair; that she was afraid of him. The next day she was sitting with me in the living room, which was outside of Sarah's bedroom. Madyson pointed in to Sarah's room and said, who is that man I don't like him. She kept repeating it because she was so afraid. I told the spirit to go away because he was scaring my niece. He did go away but only temporarily. After Sarah returned home from work, Madyson saw him again. Sarah yelled at the spirit for being a bully and scaring a child like that. When the landlady Lisa came home we told her what happened with Madyson. She showed us a picture of her father with some other family members of hers. Madyson pointed to her father in the picture and said he was the man in the house. He stayed away until Madyson went home but returned soon after. He never hurt anyone; he just made us feel very uncomfortable, and not wanted.

One day while Sarah was in her bedroom, I went outside to take the trash. When I came back in, Sarah called out to me and said, "Mom, I just saw a little girl standing in my doorway." She said she at first quickly tried to figure out if Madyson was back, or if I had brought someone else into the house. Sarah then asked the girl what her name was, but she disappeared. Sarah then realized that this little girl was a spirit. She told me that the girl was about five years old, wearing a pink skirt with a white top, and long, brown hair.

The next time Sarah and I saw Tracey Lynn we told her about this little girl Sarah had seen. Tracey Lynn said she is Sarah's daughter waiting to be born. She said that Sarah signed a contract that in this lifetime this soul would be born to her. She then said as we were speaking to her that the little girl was at Sarah's feet playing with the skulls on Sarah's shoes. Since this all happened, both Sarah and I have seen this little girl several times and Sarah has named her Allyson, after my mother Alice. Tracey Lynn said Sarah's first child would be this little girl who is waiting patiently to be born.

In January 2014, Mike left for boot camp for the Marines. While Mike was gone Sarah and I planned their wedding upon his return in April. The only way for Sarah and Mike not to be separated was for them to be married. They had already been together for four years and I could feel that they had a strong connection. I gave them my sincere blessing because I felt that they were meant to be together at this time. Although we didn't have much money, they had a wonderful wedding, thanks to Mike's grandparents who helped immensely.

They didn't have much time for a honeymoon so they spent four days in Newport, R.I. Mike had to report to base but they got lucky because Mike was assigned to do his schooling at the Naval base in Newport, R.I.; a thirty-minute drive from Fall River where both of their families lived. Mike and Sarah rented an apartment in Newport, and Mike traveled back and forth to the base.

I certainly didn't want to live in Webster all by myself, and the only people I associated with were Lisa and her friend Bill, so I moved back to my hometown in Fall River. This made me happy because I got to see my family and I still got to see Mike and Sarah. I really liked my new apartment and neighborhood. This would have been the first time in my whole life I ever lived alone, but Matthew ended up moving in with me. He had moved out of "sober living" and got an apartment with his girlfriend, but she broke his heart and he needed time to heal so he came to live with me. Matthew stayed clean during his heartbreak, which was a very difficult time for him. He did all the right things by going to meetings and talking to people. I am very proud and grateful that he got through this tough time, and didn't resort back to drug use. Matthew is an apprentice electrician, working a full time job in the day, and going to school at night to get his electrical license.

While in my new apartment I adopted two kittens from a friend who had them on a farm in Westport, MA. I got a gray male and a black and white female kitten. I named them Leo and Piper from the show *"Charmed"* because David and I really loved that show. I have many wonderful memories of David and me watching *Charmed* and it comforts me every time I see the show.

After I moved back to Fall River, I became very friendly with Tracey Lynn. She became a wonderful mentor to me, helping me on my spiritual journey. She told me that spirit kept saying for me to start a journal and write down everything that happens to me spiritually. I did start a journal and I channel messages from the angels, my guides, and other spiritual beings daily. I write down everything they tell me, even if it doesn't make any sense to me. I kept getting the nagging feeling of spirit wanting me to quit smoking cigarettes, so I finally did quit smoking and I feel so free. I then began walking each day because that was what I was being told to do by spirit. They told me they wanted my body, mind and soul cleansed. Then Tracey Lynn told me that spirit said I was to start saying the rosary to Mother Mary and I have said the rosary nearly every day since she gave me that message.

On September 13, 2014 I received messages from communicating with the other realm for the first time. I was shown a vision of me standing in front of a brick wall. Suddenly, the brick wall crumbled, and I saw many angels, with my mother standing in front of them; she herself was an angel. I then had a "knowing" that much of my negative energy and blockages come from the sadness I feel over the loss of my mother. I began to cry uncontrollably, yet this process with the communication of spirit has helped me let go of the sadness. I am now more fully open to meditation, and any kind of channeling and connecting to the spirit realm. I have received many messages in my meditation and channeling. Some of them I can share, but some messages for others are private, and I will always respect their privacy.

Since I started on a more spiritual path I have seen way more spiritual activity in this new Fall River apartment. I have seen the outline of a person in my bathroom. There was so much spiritual activity that there was a thick sort of haze in the air, with many specks of light flashing. I took pictures of them and I have one picture that has a total of nine orbs in it. It is not really good for that many spirits to be constantly hanging around because they can drain your energy. I started telling them to go away and not bother me so much and they do listen. I had to learn to put a shield of white light around me to protect myself.

Since I first moved in to this apartment I could smell cigarette smoke near my bedroom door. No one is allowed to smoke in my apartment so I knew it wasn't that. I could sense a male spiritual presence in my bedroom. He would go and hide in one of my closets. I was so afraid of this spirit I would never open that closet door. If I had to open that closet door for some reason, I would do it as quickly as I could and it was always freezing in there. I began to realize I could smell the cigarette smoke when this spirit was standing there watching me. I spoke to Tracey Lynn about this spirit and she told me that he finds it amusing how I pray and meditate. She said he stands there watching me and he laughs. I decided to try and help this spirit cross over, partly because I wanted to help him, and partly because I wanted him gone. He did not want to leave and wouldn't accept my help. After I tried to cross him over, he came in to my dream and scared me. As I was lying on my bed before falling asleep, I was being touched on my back and I was very frightened. I usually don't get afraid when a spirit touches me. I was being touched quite a bit and it felt like a bunch of bubbles but finally I fell asleep. I wrote about this dream in my Journal.

November 12th 2014: In my dream I was in a big old house with a man. I told this man I would like to see the rest of the house. I walked upstairs alone but when I entered a room the man was already inside the room. I immediately became frightened of him. I told him I had to leave and hurried downstairs but he didn't want me to leave. Suddenly, there was a distorted woman and I became frightened of her. I had a gun and shot her twice, and then I shot the man twice. Yellow fluid started leaking out of the gun holes I put in them. They were dead already so they couldn't die. The woman was wearing a white gown and floating. I went up to her, broke her forearm in half, then picked her up and folded her in half, and threw her over a rail. When I looked down at her it was my mother lying on the floor. Her eyes were closed and it looked like she was sleeping. I knew I still had to get out of that house but the man didn't want me to leave. I then woke up and lay awake in bed going through the whole dream in my head. When I got to the end of the dream it continued in my head like a movie. It was like I had no control over it. It continued with the doorbell ringing in that house and I became nervous. I told the man it was my sister at the door. When I opened the door Tracey Lynn was standing there and I was so happy and relieved to see her. She told me to step out onto the porch and when I did, she said we had to get out of there. I told her I left my keys in the house, but she said I couldn't go back inside that house. We asked the man for the keys and he said we had to come back inside to get them. Tracey Lynn then screamed at him to go get the keys and then she said, or I will call (suddenly someone said very clear and loudly in my room) "The Cops." I then opened my eyes and said out loud I need to tell Tracey Lynn about this dream. As I said this a huge orb of light sparkled directly in front of me. I knew that a spirit just confirmed that I indeed needed to tell her about this dream.

I spoke to Tracey Lynn that afternoon and told her everything that had happened. As we spoke about it the spirit realm was also speaking to her about it. She was told that this man wasn't a nice spirit and that he had murdered a woman when he was alive. The distorted woman in my dream was named Julia, the woman he murdered. The spirits said this man has no good intentions. Julia distorted herself to me so that she would scare me out of the house so he wouldn't hurt me. She then showed herself to me as my mother because she wanted me to know she was someone I could trust. Tracey Lynn came to the door because my soul called to her soul for help. Tracey Lynn and I have an incredible soul connection. The spirit world also told her that it was this man that was touching me and that's why I was afraid. She said anytime a family member touches you, you would never feel fear.

This man really frightened me in this dream and I couldn't shake the feeling. Tracey Lynn told me I am allowing all and any spirits in during my meditations and communications. I need to learn how to protect myself and only allow white light spirits in. I did exactly as she instructed; sage the apartment, told all negative energies that they were not welcome, that they must leave. I also said out loud, "I reject Satan and all his dark entities and any darkness or dark spirits." She also told me to use a night light at night and to sleep with my bedroom door open. I say a prayer before I go to sleep and surround myself in God's white light. I have not had a bad dream like that since I have done this.

That same night I had that dream Matthew (who sleeps in the next room), had nightmares of evil in the walls in his room. I must have allowed a lot of negative spiritual activity in my home, but I am learning as I go.

October 22nd 2014: I dreamt I was floating in the clouds but it was more like flying, though I was standing up straight. I was with my mother and others I didn't recognize. There was more to the dream but when I woke up that was all I could remember. I felt like I spent the night with my mother and I know that I truly did.

The next day I went to see Tracey Lynn for a reading. In the reading my mother told her that my soul astral planed out of my body in my dream. Tracey Lynn said I spent quite a while in the spirit realm and met many of my ancestors. This reading was a turning point for me in my spiritual journey. During this reading I met a spirit named Grace with whom I connected with for the first time. I could see what she looked like and that she wanted help from me. Grace was a pretty, well dressed, blonde haired woman. She told me that she wanted me to help her grandson whose life was in turmoil. That day I started a novena to Sacred Heart of Jesus and

St. Jude to help her grandson get his life back on track. I asked them to send him someone to help pull him out of this spiral he was in. Tracey Lynn told me that I am chosen by God to be a connector to the spirit realm. She was told I am to give and spread messages to people and that this is my main purpose in life. I am finally "The Dawn" God has put me on this earth to be. I accept this purpose with open arms, and I will do my best to honor God and what He has planned for me. I will fulfill my contract I have signed with God to help my brothers and sisters, and to better this planet.

November 17th 2014: The following week there was minimal spiritual activity in my home, and no sign of any negative spirit, which was wonderful. When I tried to meditate or communicate with spirit, I could not make any connections to them. I believe I have put up walls due to fear from my previous experience. I will keep working on it and try to improve on finding a happy medium within myself. So far it has been either wide open or closed shut to the spirit realm. I want to be the best spiritual connector possible by giving people messages from their loved ones. I am honored to be chosen for this journey. It took me a long, long, time to be on this path that God intended for me, but I am finally awakened.

EIGHT

Rising Out of the Ashes

As human beings we are apt to be skeptics. Amazing things happen in people's lives and we sometimes just write them off as coincidence because we don't understand. Due to fear, or lack of understanding, we are conditioned to ignore messages or feelings we receive. We avoid our fears or tune out messages that we can't define as normal. It took me a very long time to listen to my intuition and to realize that my gut feeling was always right. We should all live our lives more openly; listen to our gut instinct, and our God. God, the angels and our deceased loved ones are always giving us messages, which we should accept with faith and love. These messages are real. I truly believe and have faith in God, and the entire spirit realm, and all the messages that I receive from them. I don't really have words to fully explain how, or why these messages come to me; some of them I myself don't even understand. I receive messages from loved ones that have passed, angelic beings, Saints, and others. Some of these messages are often not perfect sentences or paragraphs. I am a communicator for the spirit realm, and it is like a stream of consciousness that I receive. They are not my thoughts, and I don't ever question any of these messages because I am devoted to God, with an open heart and mind to the universe. You may question where these messages come from, but I do not. I share them with you and others because I want to help my brothers and sisters. These messages are light, they come from light, and I share them with love. I also inherently know that I signed a contract with God before I came to earth, to better the planet, myself, and my brothers and sisters. I plan on fulfilling that contract and awaken and enlighten as many souls as possible during this lifetime, until I return home to my Father. The rest of this book will include a dated log of messages and visions I have received in my communications and connections to the other realms, and events that have occurred during these dates. As the dates go on you will notice my connection to them gets much clearer and stronger as I learn to open myself up more. When I connect to the spirit realm, I am able to see the spirit, feel their energy and emotions, and receive messages in my thoughts from them. Sometimes they communicate their name, and I see it as though it was written. Also, they show me things that are familiar to me to let me know information such as who they are. For instance, St. Jude will show me the way he looks in a statue that I've seen so I can identify him. Everyone has a main guide and other guides to help him or her at different times in their lives. During a soul's life, a new guide can step in at anytime, depending on what is needed for each soul at that time. Our guides are always there and willing to help us...all we have to do is ask them. Everyone should try to feel the energy of their guide, and get familiar with them, so that they can build a relationship with them. It is such an incredible, warm feeling.

December 3rd 2014: During today's connection I was standing in a circle with Mother Mary and another woman and we were all holding hands. We all had white light immersing from our bodies. Although they both had light immersing from their entire bodies, I had light immersing only from the front of me. The other woman kneeled, Jesus had His hand on her head, and there was a glowing green light coming from his hand. I was standing further back as an observer and then I stepped forward to see who this woman was. I was hoping it was me who was kneeling down but I was told it was St. Catherine.

December 4th 2014: In my connection to the other realm today Jesus was standing in the distance holding a stick. He kept stacking himself on top of Himself like a ladder or a rope to heaven. I kept concentrating on St. Catherine but my thoughts strayed and when my thoughts came back I was saying to myself St. Therese instead of St. Catherine. The angels said that St. Therese Lisieux aka Little Flower offers me friendship. Next, I was shown an aisle with red roses on one side. It was a wedding and I saw Matthew in a suit and Sarah was very angelic looking. I believe they have shown me my wedding in the future with St. Therese sitting on my side of the aisle for some reason.

December 5th 2014: In today's connection I was shown Jesus in a field with my mother; she was crying because there was a lamb on it's side bleeding. My brother David was standing behind my mother smiling. Suddenly, the vision changed to people from the 1920's all dressed up. A man, a woman, and a child were walking down a yard that had green hedges on both sides. As they got closer I could see that they were being filmed because I saw someone looking in front of their camera to check the lens. Then I saw a woman from the same era bent down speaking to two children. Lastly, I saw a very happy woman all dressed up, wearing a navy-blue skirt, a blue and white blouse, wearing a hat, and dancing happily. She had dark hair and wore lipstick, and her name was Bella. I spoke to Tracey Lynn of this vision and she confirmed that Bella was her grandmother, and that Bella was very happy to make my acquaintance. This was the first of many times I have connected to Bella.

December 6th 2014: Today I had a vision of St. Therese, with Tracey Lynn's head on her left shoulder. Tracey Lynn was now kneeling on the left side of Mother Mary. Blessed Mother had her hand on Tracey Lynn's head and her head was filled with sparkling lights. They were inside the clouds and Tracey Lynn was wearing white. I heard someone in spirit say that Tracey Lynn and I are to unite to carry on St. Therese's work. Next, they showed me Sarah on her first communion day standing in the front yard of The Immaculate Conception Church. I was told that the flowers that Sarah wore on her head that day honored the Lord and The Saints. This was special to me that they mentioned this because Sarah was the only girl there that day that wore flowers on her head. I remember this clearly because she was embarrassed by that fact.

December 7th 2014: In my communication to the other realm today I was shown a vision of Tracey Lynn's dining room. They showed me a young girl named Sarah with a ponytail, wearing a powder blue sweater. First she stood against the stairs in Tracey Lynn's dining room, and then they showed me her standing in front of her basement stairs. I could see Tracey Lynn standing at her kitchen sink, and her husband on the couch in the living room. Then I was shown Christmas lights on the outside of her house, and if you looked out her front door, the right side of the street was all lit up and the left side in complete darkness. Then for some reason I was shown a heart. Suddenly, a dark figure put his arm around the young girl's neck and very quickly pulled her to him and she disappeared. Then someone told me that the entity was close and to hurry up and help her. I then called up Tracey Lynn and told her everything that I had seen and heard. She told me that there has been a spirit of a young girl in that house since she moved in. She also said she could feel the darkness near her basement. I called upon Archangel Michael and asked him to please go save this young girl from this dark entity and to cross her over to eternal peace. Tracey Lynn told me that it now feels more peaceful near her basement, and that she hasn't seen the young girl since.

I had only seen my brother Andrew twice in the past two years since I had left Fall River. Andrew found out from Philip that I was back in Fall River and contacted me through him. He asked me if he could stay with me for one night but I was reluctant. He begged me and said he had nowhere to go and it was freezing outside. I eventually told him yes but that he could only stay for one night. It was a bad decision on my part, but I always feel bad for him. He was getting high in my apartment and I fought with him for two weeks to get out. A few times I thought for sure he was going to overdose as I sat on the side of him crying. I told God I can't take this any longer, I chose not to live like this, and asked God to help me. Every day for two weeks I would drop Andrew with his belongings at a place that would help him get in to a rehabilitation program; and every night he was right back at my door.

As I was sitting in the living room, I could hear my cats playing with something across the floor swatting it back and forth. I got up to look at what they were playing with; it was an uncapped syringe. I quickly picked it up and walked to my bathroom where I found the cap for the syringe, empty blue bags of heroin and a spoon. I felt so sad and helpless and I couldn't go through this any longer. Especially since Matthew was living with me and was staying clean from heroin. Andrew walked into Matthew's room and showed him a huge chunk of heroin. That is one of the meanest things you could do to an ex-heroin addict who is trying their best to stay clean. Misery loves company and this disease is cunning. I lost my composure and screamed at Andrew and finally, he understood just how serious I was. I dropped him off to get help to go into a rehabilitation program and he didn't return to my apartment again.

After Andrew was in the program for a couple of weeks, a counselor from the program called me to tell me they were going to release Andrew into my care. I told the counselor I didn't want him at my apartment and I refused any responsibility for him. They would not release him otherwise so he was very upset with me for this. I had to take care of Matthew and myself and I couldn't allow anyone on drugs into my home. I changed my phone number and went on with my life.

February 18th 2015: Today an angel who looked effervescent with a sparkling hue of pink came in while I connected to the spiritual realm and told me that I would soon be leaving this apartment. Financially, I can't see how. She also showed me a check for $20,000.00.

I dance around in my house to Stevie Nick's music. As I dance in circles I can see a group of angels laughing and dancing with me. They called Stevie a modern day muse. I find that quite amusing and I really enjoy them dancing with me.

February 21st 2015: Mother Mary appeared and said she was there for my protection of overbearing feelings that I am having. She said my overwhelming fear is due to not having my daughter close to me for much longer (Sarah and Mike are moving to California in a few days). My father then appeared and said that the connection between Sarah and myself is love; and that we are two peas in a pod. Mother Mary then handed me a rose in full bloom.

February 25th 2015: In my connection, once again a group of beautiful angels came forward; they showed me money falling all over me. They also showed me getting a new car. Again, they said I am leaving this apartment soon. Then they told me my bills will be $0, and that happiness will be bountiful for me. Lastly, they showed me a door wide open and said to step in. I feel so joyful, and the angels said that I deserve it for a job well done.

February 28th 2015: Jesus stepped forth in my connection today and said that March is bringing a new life for me. He said a new day would be dawning with daisies and daffodils. He also said I will be coming out of the dark ashes. I was told plenty more will be coming my way and to exercise my will. I was then shown a vision of St. Therese and was told to pray for healing.

March 3rd 2015: Today as I connected to spirit I was shown a vision of St. Therese and St. Anne together at St. Anne's Church shrine as they stood by the crutches of the sick. St. Anne said I was to pray for healing and that I will be guided in my healings. Next, she showed me trails of Jesus going up and down the aisles in the church carrying the cross with thorns on His head. I was then shown angels flying overhead in the church holding lights in their hands that were pointing upward. Two of the angels were boys with brown hair and wearing light blue. I then saw pink daisies in a flowerpot; was told by these angels that soil is important for it is what makes life grow. Lastly, I saw a little girl with dirty blonde hair in a green dress was running through a field with a baby lamb. I then heard someone say, "Lamb of God, take away the sins of the world."

March 4th 2015: Archangels Michael and Raphael said that a new day is dawning, and that Christ is the guide and the key to healing. They went on to say follow your heart and dreams and your soul will follow. "Be patient, and enlightenment will come to you. You are being born again with a renewed life and a positive outlook. Halleluiah, much to celebrate."

March 7th 2015: Mother Mary told me today that I am coming through a tunnel of fear with practical magical thinking. "There will be a holy turn of events and a magnificent turn around."

March 8th 2015: Three magnificent angels wearing all white that had golden sparkles of light floating around them and in them appeared as I connected today. Once again they said that my bills would be $0 and that glory days are here because a new day would be dawning.

March 9th 2015: My guide Margaret said to keep marching forward, your destiny waits. She also said numerous calls have been made on your behalf so don't quit because life lessons are hard. (Margaret reminds me of Queen Elizabeth in the way she presents herself in looks, dress and demeanor. She is definitely a no-nonsense woman).

March 21st 2015: A guiding spirit named Samantha who looks like an angel and makes me feel like she is from the angelic realm came forth in my connection today. She has blonde hair and was wearing a long pink dress. She told me to listen to Stevie Nick's music. She also said that Stevie's heart aches for love, and that Stevie is a beautiful natural soul. Samantha said a friendship will come to pass; that it was years in the making. Songs open doors to worlds in the universe and that truth prevails amongst light. April and Easter time are magnificent, and there are mounds of good to come.

March 25th 2015: As I connected to the other realm today I was shown a vision of a money tree that I knew was for me. Margaret then told me that global warming is for real.

March 28th 2015: I received this message in my connection to the other realm this morning and I wrote it down as I heard it, though it made no sense to me: I felt many beings present but I couldn't clearly tell who was speaking these words. A medium trance, a bad experience, and a transfer of souls will all occur. A human instrument of hope and transference of energy builds upon a dream. A negligent soul turned upside down. It may seem there are hopeless opportunities now but there is much more to come.

That afternoon I was just about to say my rosary when I heard someone screaming. I opened my door to the side entry and the entire entry was filled with smoke. One of the men who was living downstairs was screaming, "FIRE." I immediately closed my door and my legs started shaking. My cats started running and hiding from the excitement. I threw on a pair of jeans and sneakers with my pajama top on, and ran out the front door. As soon as I got outside, I saw the flames on the first floor and realized just how bad the fire was. My first thought was to go back in and get my cats. I turned around and started going back in when a police officer that happened to be passing by said to me," Ma'am you cannot go back inside." I told him I have to go back inside to get my cats but he said no. I moved my car out of the driveway and down the street to get it out of the way for the fireman. As I walked back to the house the fire was already in my apartment and I could see the flames coming out of my bedroom window. Sick to my stomach, I couldn't stop crying thinking that my cats were burning alive.

I called up Tracey Lynn crying uncontrollable and told her that my house was burning, and my cats were burning alive. She told me to have faith and said she had to go. After we hung up I called Sarah in San Diego and I was crying so much she at first couldn't understand what I was saying. In only a matter of minutes the fire was coming through the roof of the third floor. The entire house was now engulfed in flames. The man who lived on the third floor was on vacation. One of the men who lived on the first floor had to be pulled out of the house. He was unresponsive and his face was black like charcoal. I eventually found out that the same man who was pulled out was the one who started the fire. While wearing an oxygen mask he lit something up and it blew up the oxygen tank.

Less than an hour later, the house next door to us also caught on fire from the huge flames. Everyone living in that house had to evacuate the property immediately. There were around a hundred people outside watching these houses burn. There were many fireman, police, ambulance and Red Cross personnel there also. I called Matthew at work and told him about the fire, and he came home immediately. The firemen were having a very hard time trying to control the fire on both houses and firemen were called in from surrounding cities to help. We stood outside for five hours watching them try to get control of this fire. I was heartsick thinking of my cats, which were only ten months old.

I sat down with someone from the Red Cross who was setting up a hotel room for Matthew and me to stay at for a few days. As I was sitting there a firemen walked by me and I said, "Excuse me, but when can I go see if my cats are alive?" He told me that I would have to speak to a Chief about that and he said he would send him over to me. About ten minutes later the Chief came over and said I am sending in two guys to check on your cats but I don't want you to get your hopes up. As we continued talking I heard screaming and a bunch of excitement. I turned and looked into the crowd and saw a woman holding my gray cat Leo. I couldn't believe it and I ran over to her crying with my legs shaking. As I took Leo from her some other woman came walking over holding my black and white cat Piper. I can't begin to tell you the happiness and relief that filled me. Piper was soaking wet but Leo was dry as a bone. We wrapped them in Red Cross blankets because they were shaking. As I walked to my car to put the cats into it, someone from the local news station stopped me for an interview as I held my cat Piper.

Matthew's friend Mike, who was also his sponsor in the NA program came to the scene and gave us $1000.00 to help us get some of the things that we needed. I will always be grateful to him for his generosity. It was now dark outside and since we didn't have a thing we had to go to the store before we went to the hotel. We bought things like cat food, cat bowls, litter, and litter box. I wasn't thinking about anything else until Matthew said, 'Mom, we need to get toothbrushes and toothpaste, shampoo, underwear etc. That is when it hit me that we owned nothing, and we would have to start from scratch. At that point I was just so grateful that Matthew, the cats, and I were alive and well.

The next morning Matthew and I drove by the house to see how it looked. A lot of people were standing around outside. We got out of our car to speak to them and they told us that the people in the house next door to us lost all their animals in the fire. I was so sad for them; they lost their cats, birds and fish. It made me even more grateful that my cats survived but I also felt a little guilty that I was the only one whose animals survived. My house seemed to have much more damage than theirs so I never thought of their animals dying. Between the smoke and the fire, no one could believe or understand how my cats survived. If you could have seen this fire you would understand their bewilderment.

I called Tracey Lynn that afternoon after the fire. She told me that after we spoke she hung up immediately and went in to a very deep meditative state asking the angels to help my cats survive and to protect them from the fire. She said that she was shown angels covering my cats with their wings and helping them sleep so they wouldn't run around. I can't begin to tell you how grateful I am for this act of pure kindness and I will be forever grateful to Tracey Lynn and the angels for saving my cats.

Approximately six weeks before the fire I had switched insurance companies for my automobile. I was sitting with the new insurance agent when she asked me if I was interested in apartment insurance. I told her I wasn't. She then said that it was very cheap and that my car insurance would be cheaper if I got the apartment insurance. So I blurted out, yes, I'll take it. I was about to make my second payment on the apartment insurance when my apartment burnt. I was insured for $20,000.00. I lost everything materialistic in the fire but I'm grateful for our lives.

After the fire, I received a lot of different help from many people. After a week in the hotel Matthew moved in to his new apartment. I still had nowhere to go and Matthew's new landlord said I was not allowed to take my cats there. I stayed with my sister Gail for two nights and then I had to leave her place because of the cats. My friend Heidi and her Mom generously offered for the cats and I to stay with them until I could find a place to live. I was only at Heidi's for two weeks when I found a new apartment. I acquired the apartment through my friend Lorena-the same friend who gave me my cats from the farm. When she called her friend who she knew owned apartment buildings, he said he had only one apartment available so she picked me up and took me to look at it. I absolutely loved this apartment at first sight and told the landlord I would take it. He told me that he needed to speak to his wife first before he could give me the apartment. He called me two days later and told me the apartment was mine. They were definitely God sent, and are the most kind, generous people and landlords I have ever had. The spirit realm was truly looking out for me with these people and this apartment.

The amount of help we received from family, friends and strangers was heart-warming and overwhelming. We were given furniture, silverware, towels, clothes, kitchen items etc.; the list goes on and on. A friend of mine that I've known for 35 years named Heather reached out to me and purchased a new television for me. Heather lives in California and we haven't been in close contact for years. She purchased the television online and I picked it up at a Best Buy store near me. My daughter started a Go Fund me account for us and my friends and family were very generous. I will never forget all that was done for us.

After I received the $20,000.00 from the insurance, I paid off all of my debt and purchased items that Matthew and I needed for our new apartments. Unfortunately, the money wasn't enough, and as we purchased much needed stuff along the way, I had to max out all my credit cards once again. Starting from scratch for two people takes a lot of money and effort.

After we were all settled into our new places, I looked back on everything the spiritual realm had told me. I realized how incredibly accurate the information they gave to me was. On February 28th exactly one month before the fire, Jesus told me I would rise out of the dark ashes. I moved out of that apartment like the angel said I would. My bills did go to $0, and I did receive a check for $20,000.00 just like the angels had said. Two months after I moved in to my new place, I was in a much better position financially, and purchased a new car just like I was told.

The messages that were given to me the morning of the fire now made more sense to me. When they said "Medium Trance" I believe this was Tracey Lynn going in to her deep meditation to save my cats. The next thing they said was "Bad Experience" which I'm taking is the fire. I believe when they said "Transfer of Souls" that was from the Angels to the cats and having them rest during the fire. When they said "The Human Instrument of Hope," I believe that they were referring to me as the instrument and all the hope that I had during this entire experience. The man who lived downstairs from me that started the fire, I believe he is "The Negligent soul turned upside down" that they spoke of. Just like they said things seemed hopeless to us at first, but there were and are many more opportunities to come in the future. "The Transference of Energy that builds upon in a dream" is their way of telling me to pay attention to my dreams. Dreams are how they sometimes communicate with me and there are important messages transferred to me through energy.

Three weeks prior to the fire the spirit who occupied my apartment stepped forward to me while I was in meditation. He told me his name was Peter; he had brown hair and he was in his forties. He told me that he wanted to cross over but was afraid that God would not forgive him for his sins. I told him that God is forgiving and loving and that God will forgive him, but he must also forgive himself so that his soul can heal. I also told him not to be afraid, that when he crosses over, he would feel love, joy and peace, and that he would be reunited with his family and friends. I called upon Archangel Michael and asked him to cross this lost soul Peter over to eternal peace. And just like that Peter was gone and I felt peaceful.

Now I understand why he came to me to cross him over. Spirit has the ability to see future events and Peter knew the fire was coming. He would have been in panic and chaos not knowing where to go. I had only been living in this apartment eight months before the fire took place. I believe I was led to live in that apartment so when the time came I could cross over this lost soul. Part of my journey on this earth is helping to crossover lost souls. I accept my job as a light worker proudly and I wouldn't want it any other way. I had to experience the fire and loss, but heaven has sustained me through it all. Whether the help comes from friends, family, earth angels, or spirit, I am always right where I am supposed to be.

April 3rd 2015: Today in my communication St. Therese Lisieux told me that flowers represent the Passion of Christ and to go to mass for it lifts the negative out and I will be renewed. She also said that hope will light my path and that there is an incredible light at the end of my path.

April 14th 2015: I am now living in my new apartment. My guide Margaret told me that my landlord is God sent. She said everyone helped me upon God's request and that my life would be settled soon. Today I spoke to Tracey Lynn and she told me that St. Therese has stepped forward to tell me that she and I are the same and that she is no better than me and I am no better than her. She wanted me to know we are on the same level and that she is my friend.

April 17th 2015: My spiritual gift is getting stronger and it sometimes it drains me. Margaret told me today that I need an adjustment period.

April 18th 2015: As I was praying today a spirit came rushing into my head. I honestly can't tell you who this spirit was but what she said to me was that a woman named Maureen was hiding in fear in a closet at The Lizzie Borden house. Lizzie Borden is the woman who was accused of murdering her father and stepmother with an axe in 1892 in my hometown of Fall River, MA. Lizzie was acquitted for this crime and the Lizzie Borden house is now a Bed and Breakfast. This spirit also told me that Maureen is terrified of Mr. Borden, Lizzie's father because he is cruel. I was asked to please help Maureen. I called upon Archangel Michael to go to The Lizzie Borden house and to save Maureen from Mr. Borden, and cross her over to eternal peace. I was then shown a vision of Archangel Michael drawing his sword to Mr. Borden because he didn't want to let Maureen go. I then saw Archangel Michael lift her like a brilliant light in his free hand and cross her over. It was magnificent to see this vision and it made me feel incredible.

Since Tracey Lynn does séances at the Lizzie Borden house sometimes, I called her up and told her about what I just experienced. Even though The Lizzie Borden house is in my hometown of Fall River, MA I have never stepped a foot in that house. Tracey Lynn asked me how did I know about Maureen. I told her how a spirit came to me and she asked me to help her. She was shocked because she said there is a spirit in The Lizzie Borden house named Joseph that keeps looking for a Maureen but he can't find her. I'm guessing Mr. Borden did a good job of keeping Maureen away from Joseph. I then said to Tracey Lynn hopefully Joseph knows now that Maureen has crossed over and he can finally find her.

In the middle of April, I had seen a Facebook post from a medium named Rosie Cepero. Rosie is a very gifted medium whom had a show on TLC called "Angels Among Us". Sarah and I adored Rosie and never missed watching one of her episodes. Rosie connects to guardian angels, loved ones, and gives messages of love and comfort to many people. Every time we watched Rosie, I would tell Sarah that this woman's soul is so pure, that I absolutely love her. I felt such a strong pull to her and I kept asking my angels to somehow connect me to this woman. On Rosie's post she was offering sage that she blessed to whomever wanted to buy some from her. I messaged Rosie and told her I was interested in getting some sage from her. When you burn sage it cleanses any negative or lower energy in your home or anywhere that needs cleansing. Rosie messaged me back and asked me to send her my information and told me how to pay for the sage. A week later I realized I gave Rosie the old zip code from my other apartment so I messaged her to let her know. She didn't see my message in time and she sent it out to the old zip code. Two weeks went by and I never received the package. I messaged Rosie and asked her if it was returned to her. She apologized for not seeing the zip code correction and said she had not received the package back. Another week went by and Rosie messaged me and asked me if I had received the package yet and I replied, no I did not. She apologized and said she would send me out a new package the following week.

A week later I received a message from Rosie asking me for my phone number so she could say hello to me. I messaged her back my number and within a half an hour Rosie called me up. She told me that when she went to the post office to send out my new package they handed her the original package. Rosie had written the name of my street wrong and so it was sent back. She said the angels told her she was to call me. I then told her how I have been asking the angels to connect us. Rosie said her writing the name of the street wrong and our connecting was something that the angels set up.

Rosie then told me that the angels were telling her how I have a spiritual gift and that I am to keep telling my stories to everyone. They also told her that I am to continue writing down everything that happens to me spiritually. Rosie and I spoke for an hour, but when she forgot to tell me something, she called me back and we spoke for another half hour. Rosie appeared on an Internet show called ZENLIVE TV in which I called into and we got to speak to each other again. Once again Rosie told me I have a lot in life to do and to keep sharing my stories with everyone. I thank the angels every day for connecting me to Rosie. Though we keep in touch every now and then, we haven't yet met in person. The day that we do meet will be an incredible day for me because I feel Rosie is one of my spirit sisters, and I am grateful for the chance to connect to this incredibly pure soul.

May 4th 2015: My guide Margaret told me I have to be separated from Tracey Lynn to be able to grow and I would grow full bloom like a plant. She said it would be upsetting but necessary. She also told me that we would come together again and we would be friends for life and that it is time for me to move on and that my future is bright and sunny. Tracey Lynn can't help me, only I can help myself. She also told me to help those in need like the hungry, the poor and the sick and that the angels will be by my side and I will be guided. I was told to dig deep inside to find the love, for this is my fate.

May 26th 2015: St. Therese thanked me today for my love and admiration of her. She said I am to move forward, that there is no standing still and don't be afraid, for I am protected. She also said monetary gain is okay, but please help charities, and be kind and gentle to the dying souls.

May 27th 2015: St. Therese has been around me a lot and she said that our friendship is everlasting. She told me I have a special heart, mind, and soul. She said I was picked from the earth like a flower; like Little Rose. She also told me that we are very much alike and she will visit me again.

May 31st 2015: I was shown a vision of Rosie Cepero sitting at a round table with me to her left and Tracey Lynn to her right: "Holy, Holy, Holy" was then said out loud. I told Tracey Lynn about this vision and she believes it represents that we all travel in the same circle.

June 6th 2015: Today beautiful angels appeared and said I will be an unstoppable force and they will sing praise, "Halleluiah." They said I will be a force to be reckoned with and I will help many souls. And that love and commitment will get me through the tough times, but I will prevail, for I am an honorary member of Christ's house.

June 8th 2015: In church today as I stood in front of the St. Jude and St. Anne statues, my back was being touched and I felt as though they were doing something special to me like a healing. In my connection today St. Anne appeared and told me to behold that the Holy Spirit is alive. She said Jesus Christ our Savior had risen and He will come again. She also said these words, "He lieth in the green pastures," and "Fighteth your will and love will conquer all". There will be plentiful bounties.

June 9th 2015: A man appeared before me and I asked who he was and he told me, I am Anthony of Padua, and he said to me that "the signs you see are real. Open the door to freedom; the path is yours to take. Freedom awaits you, and the path is clear."

June 13th 2015: Margaret told me of a surprise package that would make me tearful, and today I received a necklace from Sarah made from my mother's signature which made me cry. Tracey Lynn and I no longer remain in contact with each other. I look back on messages I received from the spirit realm about us needing to go our separate ways. I will move forward in my life and do my ultimate and best good each and every day. Tracey Lynn was my first mentor and a wonderful soul. I know that one day we will be reunited, and I am forever grateful to her.

June 20th 2015: My mother appeared to me in my dream and told me that she is the wind beneath my wings. When I see a butterfly, I know my mother is around me. Today a white butterfly flew past my face and I knew that she was near. Today in my connections three illuminating angels appeared and told me that things will get better, do nothing at all, and just wait, for patience is a virtue. I'm having a hard time with hardly having any money. I was then shown a purple heart, which signifies the angels

NINE

Continued Pilgrimage

June 26th 2015: Today my guide Margaret said to me "Wings over America." She then said, "It shall be done on earth as it is in heaven. Tears of joy for the heavens are very happy with today's ruling of marriage equality passed; dreams do come true."

My friend, Amanda and I reconnected once again in June 2015. We really hadn't bothered with each other since the incident of her getting angry when I owed her money. I ran into an ex coworker who told me that Amanda's son, Eric committed suicide the previous November. I was terribly upset to hear of this news. My children and Amanda's children played together when they were young. Eric was only twenty years old when he passed to spirit. No parent should have to lose a child plus I knew firsthand what suicide could do to a family. I wanted to offer her emotional and spiritual support if she was open to it. I extended an olive branch by mailing her a card offering her my sympathy and giving her my phone number.

Amanda was happy to receive the card and to hear from me. She called me and invited me to a memorial barbeque celebration for her son in July. I attended the memorial and was happy to reconnect with Amanda. While I was at the memorial, I met a friend of Amanda's named Bob. Bob and I started discussing spirituality and I told him of events that have occurred in my life. He recommended I attend a service at the First Spiritualist Church in Onset, Ma. I told him that if Amanda would come with me then I would go and check it out. In August Amanda, my friend Heidi and I went to our first service at the Spiritualist church. We absolutely enjoyed the service and Amanda, Heidi and I started attending this service just about every Sunday. I felt like I had found my home in this church with spiritually like-minded people.

The pastor of the church is a very lovely welcoming woman named Reverend Kathleen Hoffman. The hour and a half long service consists of singing, praying and a healing portion. The church has certified healers and if you feel you need a healing you go and sit in front of one of the healers. Spiritualist healers work with the spirit, mind, body and emotions of the person wanting the healing. The type of healing you receive is not guaranteed, whether it is physical, emotional, mental or spiritual, but you will receive a healing. The healers are the vessels that are used for the unseen healing forces. It is not up to the healers as to the type of healing you will receive; it is up to the Infinite. Spiritualist healers do acknowledge the importance of the medical community. They recognize that the medical community is an important instrument of healing of the Infinite. You don't have to be present to receive a healing though the person getting the healing has to be open to it, and, accept it.

After the healing portion, a guest speaker gives an uplifting speech. The last portion of the service is when the speaker (usually a medium-psychic) will prove the continuity of life after death by bringing spirits forward for members of the congregation. It depends what spirits step forward as to who gets a reading. After the service, everyone is welcome to go downstairs to socialize and have a bite to eat.

I started attending spiritual development classes at the church on Wednesdays. I also signed up for classes on how to be a certified spiritualist healer. I was in my glory because I had no idea that churches like this even existed. Spirit works in miraculous ways to put all the right people in your life and bring you exactly where you're supposed to be at the right time.

I believe I was supposed to connect with Amanda again to help her with her difficult time of grief. Also I understand the grief process through the loss of suicide, though everyone grieves differently. I will always be there to help lift her up when she needs me. Though Amanda still goes through very hard times her spirituality has grown immensely and her inner strength is incredible. I am happy to help her anytime she needs me through those dark times the best I can.

Also during the month of June, I reconnected with a friend named Maurice that I hadn't seen in twenty-five years. I had found out that he was very ill from cancer and I went to visit him in a nursing rehabilitation home. He decided to get transferred to a friend of ours house for hospice and I would go there to visit him. I stayed with him every Tuesday night and we would watch movies and just talk. He was terrified of dying and was afraid that his parents who were in spirit wouldn't be there when he left. I had many long talks with him and I told him that his mother and father would be right by his side to cross him over. I told him how beautiful heaven was, and the incredible love and joy he would feel. I also told him how the love and joy was nothing like you ever felt on this earth. I let him know how my mother has come to me and told me how heaven surpasses everything you ever imagined. I do believe you have to see and feel what you have done to others while on earth and forgive yourself for it. I also believe that while you are in the world of spirit, you have to help those souls that you hurt on earth.

In my connection on July 26th 2015: Jesus stepped forward and told me that Maurice's soul would be delivered. I was so happy to bring him this message because he was so afraid of not going to heaven.

On September 1st 2015: As I was praying I was shown a vision of Maurice's parents standing together and holding hands. They didn't speak but I had a knowing that they would be by Maurice's side when it was time for him to cross over. I relayed this message to Maurice, and he felt very relieved. Spirits never move there lips to convey a message to me, they either put the thought in my mind or show me what they want me to know, or sometimes I can see the words that they want to say.

September 13th 2015: Maurice's parents stepped forth today and they showed me hummingbirds, which is a symbol of things good. They then thanked me for showing Maurice love, kindness and compassion.

Maurice made a decision that he would be more comfortable at a hospice hospital and so he was transferred there. As he grew weaker, I continued to visit him and give him spiritual support. Though he said I made him feel better and he believed everything that I told him, he was still very afraid of dying. His fear and the will to live took over and he suffered way longer than any soul should have to.

August 10th?? 2015: Today Archangel Gabriel came forward and showed me Maurice and the numbers 2 and 7. I immediately thought that meant that he would pass to spirit on the 27th. But as time went on I realized that the 2 and 7 that I was shown was not for the 27th. It meant in 2 months on the 7th day. Maurice passed away October 7th 2015.

Maurice's sisters took some pictures of him while he lied in the bed during the last few days before his passing. In the pictures you can clearly see him surrounded by angels and spirit. I was with Maurice for his passing. A huge smile came over his face, and then he took his last breath. I knew he had seen his mother and father at that very moment, and then he was gone. I am positive he had seen everything I had told him about. I wish I could have helped him more than I did, but I believe I did my highest and best good for him that I was able to do. Rest easy my friend.

In June of 2015 I became aware of a young girl in my hometown that was battling Ewing's Sarcoma. I kept seeing #TeamNelly come across the newsfeed on my Facebook page. I kept following her post and was amazed at the uplifting attitude of this young girl. I added her to my everyday prayers, and I kept asking for her to be healed. She became quite a celebrity in my town and elsewhere thanks to social media. I saw Nelly at a restaurant with her friends one day and I yelled to her, "Go Team Nelly," and she pumped her fist and said, "Yah." Nelly was a high school student and a cheerleader and was loved by countless people. She always had a huge smile on her face, and you could see that she loved life. At the same hospital that she received her treatment in, Nelly would visit the other sick children to cheer them up. She gave hope, inspiration and compassion to so many others in the face of her own sufferings. Just being the special soul that she was helped many people through their own struggles and grief. I was so determined in asking God for this young girl to be healed that I couldn't have prayed any harder for her.

I met this woman named Patricia Butler through the Spiritualist church in Onset, MA. Patricia is known as the "angel lady" and she does healings for people. I spoke to her about Nelly and I asked her if she could go to Nelly and do a healing on her. She told me that she would need permission from Nelly's mother since Nelly was under age. I didn't know Nelly's mother but I did know a girl named Ashley on Facebook who knew her. I messaged Ashley and asked her to call me. I then explained everything to her about how Patricia could do a healing on Nelly and I asked her to speak to Nelly's mother. I never got a response from Nelly's mother but I do understand that people everywhere offering all types of help for her daughter were bombarding her. Patricia and I prayed from afar for Nelly to be healed, and I also attended a couple of prayer groups that Nelly's mother put together.

November 15th 2015: Today my guide Margaret told me today that Nelly's illness would come to an end.

November 16th 2015: While I was praying I was shown a vision of Nelly as an angel ascending in to heaven. I had hope till the very end, but I knew now that my prayers would be answered, just not in the way I expected. Nelly's pain and suffering will end, and God will make her one hundred percent healthy and whole again, just like I have been praying for.

November 21st 2015: Nelly passed to spirit today, and it was a very sad day in my heart and in my city.

November 25th 2015: In my communication to the spiritual realm today I was shown Nelly's face with a huge smile on it. Margaret told me that Nelly was a purposeful soul and that many souls were saved because of her. She wanted me to know that Nelly had crossed over, and that she is very happy.

July 3rd 2015: Today my brother David stepped forward and said that Matthew is going to get a job offer from someone who is going to realize his potential. Two weeks later Matthew received a wonderful job, though it didn't last very long.

July 4th 2015: In my connection to spirit today one of my guides Samantha who always wears pink (so I know who she is) said that gratitude and generosity go a long way.

July 5th 2015: Mother Mary said innocence is freedom, and it would free my soul. She also wants people to realize that angels are among us and wants me to prepare to be a spiritual leader.

July 15th 2015: Today I was shown a vision of St. Therese with me as a child. Then St. Therese stepped in and told me that she has been with me since I was a little girl watching, learning and guiding me. She said hope and destiny go together and that the fellowship of souls equals united freedom of life. The sky is the limit and unity equals freedom; freedom from war, poverty and hunger. She then told me that she is united with Helene. Tracey Lynn was also told at another time that St. Therese was united with Helene. I did a little research and found out that Helene was St. Therese's sister who died when she was a child. I don't know why Helene keeps being mentioned to us. She also said divine timing is everything and the world can be unpleasant like a bridge over troubled water.

July 18th 2015: Lately I have seen a man in my city pan handling in traffic. Three different times he has come to my car to ask for money. Each time I have given him money. The third time he came to me I said to him, "This is the third time you have come to me and asked for money" and he looked at me in my eyes for a minute and then turned and walked away without saying a word. I received an uplifting feeling from this man. So I asked Margaret who this man was and she told me that the panhandler is a guiding spirit. Before she even told me who he was I had a strong intuition that he was and since that day I have never seen that man again.

July 20th 2015: Today Margaret told me that the blood moon is true, meaning adversities and failures. Knowledge is power, power means to overcome adversity. Together hope and destiny mean a lot. Terrorist troops will arrive; a window of opportunity to stop them is coming. The nation must pray to Mother Mary. Give all the goodness you can to bestow upon the world for happiness and joy precipitates human dignity.

August 26th 2015: A woman named Stephanie came to me in spirit today. She told me she was fearful of other entities around her. She asked me for help to cross her over. I called upon Archangel Michael to cross this spirit over. I saw him draw his sword to protect her while he crossed her over. Before he crossed her, she told me that she died in the water and she showed me a boat.

Though I love the Spiritual church I am only human and sometimes I doubt myself about being on the right path. I asked God if I'm doing the right thing and if I'm in the right place. On September 3rd 2015, two days after I had asked that question, I got out of bed and opened my blinds in my kitchen. Sitting in the middle of my screen was a huge grasshopper. I knew it was a sign for me to move forward in the direction I was going. Grasshoppers can only jump forward not sideways or backwards. It meant for me to take a leap of faith and I am because I know there is so much more that is planned for me. The angels, God and the entire Spirit realm answer questions by showing you signs. If you ask a question pay attention and be aware because they always answer. No one is ever alone on this earth because the spirit realm is right by our sides. You have to choose to believe.

September 13th 2015: For some reason I felt lazy today and decided not to go to church. As I sat on my couch I could hear spirit all around me. I hear a distinct frequency when spirit is around me. I really can't explain it except it is like television static but light and fluffy, if that makes any sense. The louder I hear the frequency the more they are trying to get my attention or sometimes it is just to let me know they are near me. They were getting very loud and so I said out loud to them; "What do you want? If you want me to go to church, then give me a message." Then very clear and loudly in my head I received a message that said, "message on computer desk." I went into my computer room and looked on my desk and sitting there was a newsletter from the church. I said okay Spirit, I will go to church and I left immediately for church.

At the end of the service I asked a member of the church about the healing classes I had seen in the newsletter. She said the woman running the healing classes just so happened to be there tonight and introduced me to her. That was the first time I met Patricia Butler, the "angel lady." From the moment I was introduced to her I could feel the instant connection between us.

All that night and the next day I was being shown visions of an open door with white light pouring out of it. Then I was told by angels to step into this door that has been opened for me into God's white light. They said incredible things are to come for me on this journey. I am beyond honored to be a light worker.

October 3rd 2015: Mother Mary came forward today and told me that a mentor would be coming to me soon. She told me no worries for life is good. She also said that many things are to follow because my path and I are true, kind and wonderful. I was told to allow others to help because God's work is teamwork. She also said Tracey Lynn would follow you back to Avalon, that we will be reunited one day, and our friendship will be restored. Everything will be in its place with the proper alignment of the stars. Then my mother stepped forward and said you are a daughter like no other, keep going forward. She also said she loved me, and was proud of me.

October 9th 2015: Archangel Michael appeared and told me that protection; strength and courage will follow me. He said to stay strong and be brave because courage is everlasting, and that I am a fighter and a warrior for lost souls. He also said that goodness dissipates over time, and much help is needed for the souls of the world.

October 13th 2015: Margaret told me today that a spiritual advisor is next door. She then showed me a birthday cake with pink roses on it and said Happy Birthday to Dawn. My birthday is actually October 20th.

October 15th 2015: Archangel Michael came forward today and told me that three Archangels will be helping me receive the Trinity, and these angels will be Gabriel, Raphael and Sandalphon. He also said that prejudice would bring about much pain and suffering. And colleagues would fight amongst themselves and the tragedy of human error will fall upon our backs. But mostly our descendants will pay the price. He ended by saying that families will attune to political views and there will be many rock-bashing politicians. Tonight, I kept dreaming of the number 8, which represents infinity and the universe.

October 20th 2015: Tonight was my first class at the Spiritualist Church to be a certified healer. I then attended the Spiritual Development Class upstairs which was on table tipping. Table tipping is a type of physical mediumship in which you sit around a table with a few other people and place your hands on it. The process is similar to that of an Ouija board. The intention is to communicate with Spirit by them tilting or rotating the table. You can ask the Spirit questions and ask them to thump the table once for yes, and two for no. This night was my first experience with table tipping and I enjoyed it. The table I sat at moved all over the room. Since it was my birthday, my brother, David stepped forward and gave me a piece of birthday cake and a long hug. When the table tilts directly towards you pretty much landing in your lap, which is a hug from the spirit. My mother and my friend Lori also stopped by to say hello to me in spirit, it was a very good night.

October 21st 2015: I have been asking spirit if Maurice is doing okay. My mother showed me Maurice sitting in a wheelchair and she said he is on the mend. Mother

Mary told me to keep the faith and hope that's inside of myself and miraculously things will turn around. Do not tempt fate; miracles will appear before your eyes. She then said "Hello Kitty" and that Max will be returned to me again and I would be so grateful for his return.

October 22nd 2015: My maternal grandmother stepped forward in spirit today and told me "Happy Belated Birthday," and that my sadness will go away soon. I've been sad because it is my first birthday without Sarah living here and I miss her very much, as I also miss my mother and brother on special days.

October 26th 2015: St. Therese came to me today and said she appreciates how I acknowledge her in my prayers. She also said we have a kind, true friendship and to be aware because miracles happen every day.

October 28th 2015: Today I received a reading from a medium from England named Judith Freeman. Judith told me that Spirit said that Matthew and I have saved each other's lives. I saved his life from everything I did for him during his drug addiction, and also by leaving him behind to fend for himself at the end of his addiction, forcing him to get clean. She said he saved my life because after I gave birth to him, I now had someone in my life that I loved that depended on me, so I then had a reason to stay clean.

I also attended a class Judith was teaching at the church that night. The class was called "Opening Up Your Spiritual Tool Box." As Judith opened up the class and was speaking I had a panic attack so severe I felt like I wanted to shed my body because it was being invaded. I felt sick and almost passed out. I just wanted to get up and run out of that room as fast as I could. For the first time ever I experienced a spirit that was too close in my space. I did the only thing I knew and internally called upon Archangel Michael, God, my brother David, and my mother for help, anyone that would listen. I told the spirit that they were not welcome to enter my space so closely and that they were to leave immediately. Within five minutes I felt better, and I could feel my mother by my side for the rest of the class.

We then did a meditation with Judith, and my mother was with me the entire time in the meditation. My mother handed me a box with a rock inside of it. Judith said the rock means I need to light a fire within myself. My mother also handed me a blue bag with a paper and pen inside of it; and Judith said that means I am to write more. All in all, I would say it was an eventful night.

October 30th 2015: Heidi and I were driving to the church tonight to pick up items to bring to the Elks Club in Wareham, MA for the Psychic Holistic Fair the next day. On our drive up the same spirit that was too close in my space two nights before was once again in my personal space. This time it felt worse, he seemed to get deeper into my space and he stayed there longer. Though it only lasted minutes I wanted to jump out of the moving car. It was such a bad intense feeling of being invaded, I once again called upon the Spirit realm to help me, and they did. But this time it took way longer for me to feel better.

When we arrived at the church, I told Judith what had just happened. She said I am like a beacon with light coming straight out of the top of my head. She said I'm too wide open to all the spirits and I'm like an antenna calling, "Here I am." Judith said this spirit was not a very good man in life or death, and sent him on his way. She told me I have to put a white light of protection around me each day by saying a protection prayer every morning.

October 31st 2015: My friend Amanda and I attended the Spiritualist Church's psychic fair today and there were many different psychics and mediums there. I felt drawn to one of the mediums whom was an elderly Native American man, though I didn't speak to him. After the Psychic Fair was over, Amanda and I went back to her house to have dinner and watch horror movies. I could feel her son, Eric, there, and then I caught a glimpse of him. He told me to tell his mother that he was spending Halloween with her.

November 1st 2015: Today I was in the shower listening to Stevie Nick's radio on Pandora. Just as I shut the shower off, my brother, David very clearly said to me, "This next song is for you." Out loud I said, "Okay Dave, this song is for me." I opened the shower curtain and Adele's song "Hello" started playing. I had only heard this song one time previously and didn't listen to the words. This time I listened to the words as tears streamed down my face out of sadness and joy. "Hello from the other side, I must have called a thousand times to tell you I'm sorry for everything I've done." These words were so personal to me from David because he has come through in readings with Tracey Lynn and told her he is sorry for how he has hurt me and changed me through his suicide. I cried because I missed David, but also because it was incredible to get a message in this way from Spirit. The Spirit realm never ceases to amaze me.

November 3rd 2015: St. Therese came to me today and told me that the Holy Rosary is a timeless effort and prayers must go on. She continued with her message saying "The Trinity is alive and well and that white doves are full of love. Enlightenment unfolds like a mystery, a job well done my friend. Precious life is everlasting; come unto me though many days and nights will pass until we meet my dear. Humble yourself and know that protection is all around you. Healing power is given unto you so use it well. Love and purity are everlasting. Make friends with humanity and the power ceases to overcome you. Knowledge, wisdom, power and healing will be the outcome to help you thrive in your soul."

November 4th 2015: I needed to purchase a pendulum for my class with Reverend Kathleen today. I went online and found a Holistic store in New Bedford, MA called *III Suns*. I drove to this store and as I walked in I immediately recognized the elderly Native American gentlemen. I said to him, "I know you, I saw you at the Psychic Fair." He said, "Hello I'm Ronald O'Berry." I told him my name was Dawn. We sat down and chatted for an hour and a half. The first thing that Ron said to me was there is a woman in spirit named Alice standing on the side of you. He said she wants you to know how proud she is of you and how she enjoys watching everything that you do. I then told him that Alice is my mother. I also told him how I take classes at the church with Reverend Kathleen. Ron told me that he also teaches spiritual development classes at that store. I finally realized that Ron is the mentor that those in spirit have been speaking to me about. I made a decision to quit classes at the church and take classes with Ron. I felt like I was guided to Ron, and he was the right choice for me. Also, the church has a rule that if you are in their certified healing classes then you are not allowed to take healing classes with anyone else; and I wanted to be free to take classes with whomever I wanted to. Ron teaches healing, mediumship and over all spiritual development and that was just what I wanted to learn.

November 5th 2015: Today my guide Margaret told me that the house my nephew Kyle just purchased needed a spiritual cleansing due to a spiritual swirling. When I told Kyle what my guide said to me, he then proceeded to tell me about all the spiritual activity that was taking place in his house. He could hear a child cry on the second floor of his home when his daughter was on the first floor in the next room from him. He said he felt uncomfortable in his home like he was being watched. I went to his house and while praying, burnt sage through the entire house. As I entered his basement I fell down the stairs. I was bruised and scraped but got right back up and forged on with the cleansing. I ordered all negative energies and spirits to leave immediately. I called upon the Archangels to come and help me. I honestly can't say if I was pushed down the stairs or if I just had fallen, but I wasn't taking any chances. Kyle said that his home feels much lighter and more comfortable since I cleansed it, and he has not had any signs of spiritual activity since.

November 8th 2015: I did a meditation in church tonight and a group of Native Americans appeared to me in a vision. An elderly man with long gray hair was the most prominent. He was wearing a pair of jeans, a purple button down shirt and brown cowboy boots. He wore a Bolo tie, also known as a shoe string tie, made out of a cord with metal tips and an ornamental slide. They said to me "Welcome!" I intuitively knew they were welcoming me into learning with Ron O'Berry. I felt very honored by this welcoming.

November 10th 2015: Tonight I had my first class with Ron. He taught us about doing healings on others. He also had us do readings on each other to practice mediumship. This was the first time I tried to do a reading on someone and no spirits came forth. This made me nervous about doing readings on others and I didn't have much self-confidence in myself right then. I believed that due to my self-confidence and ego, I had put up a block that did not allow me to connect to Spirit.

That night I had a dream in which my mother and I bought both of the cottages on Buffinton St where I grew up. We planned to live in one of them and rent out the other. When I woke up, I felt this dream was very significant, though I'm not sure why. I have faith that the message will eventually reveal itself.

November 11th 2015: Ron called me today to ask me what I thought of his class. He told me that his dream is to one day open up a Healing Temple. Later that day as I was praying, Spirit let me know that I would eventually be helping someone to open a healing Temple. I believe I will be provided with the finances for the Temple in the future and it will be part of my life's work. I also believe the dream I had the previous night meant that my mother is going to help me buy two properties in the future. One is a home for myself and the other is a Healing Temple. I have incredible faith and believe this will come to pass. This journey I am on is so miraculous and I am very grateful.

November 17th 2015: In my connection today Archangels Gabriel and Raphael came in and told me that between realms there is amazing relief. They also said; "They encourage opportunities to take steps and forward. As you move forward light and energy will fill you which is needed to accomplish goals and they will be right their to help anyone whom ask."

November 20th 2015: Today as I connected to the other side I was shown a vision of a Native American Chief called Eagle Hawk. He had red feathers in his headdress and he stood behind Ron on his right side. He said he protects Ron and he showed me an energy line going from him and wrapping around Ron. He said he is Ron's ancestor and he helps Ron with guidance and protection and that he is always by his side. Ron was very happy to receive this message.

November 24th 2015: In class tonight with Ron we did a past life regression. It was incredible, nothing like I had ever experienced before. I lied on the floor with a blanket and pillow. Ron slowly brought us into a meditation and a past life experience. In this past life I was in the 1700's. I was a wealthy man named Joseph W (last name possibly Wildman). I owned a bank and my brother-in-law; Daniel worked in the bank with me. Daniel was my wife's brother and we were very close, like brothers. My wife's name was Gertrude and we had three children. John was the oldest child, Mary was the middle child and Peter was the youngest. I also had a maid who was a very pleasant woman; she was short and stocky and was always smiling. I lived in a very large, beautiful Victorian house. My house was up on a hill from the town. I had dark hair and I was wearing a black suit with black dress shoes. Daniel was wearing a brown suit. I was 37 years old at this time in my life and my children were 5, 7 and 11 years old. I didn't see my wife in this regression but I knew she was upstairs in the bedroom. I knew that I loved my wife very much and that she was bed bound due to an illness.

Ron then had us fast forward five years in to the future. I could feel a deep sadness because my wife was dead. At this point in the regression I knew that Daniel was my brother David from this lifetime. I also knew that my wife was my mother from this life. I started to cry and couldn't stop because I was overwhelmed with grief and sadness. After my wife died I never remarried. I was heartbroken for the rest of my life because she was the love of my life. My children grew up and went on their own. At the age of 63 I passed away from a respiratory illness, with my children gathered around me. My wife was there in spirit to cross me over to the other side. I could still feel the sadness of losing my wife for about an hour after the regression was over. This experience enlightened me as to why in this lifetime I had a tremendous fear of my mother dying since I was a child.

November 25th 2015: My mother and David came to me today while I was in meditation and showed me Philip standing in between them in spirit. They said be prepared for when the time comes. Though I don't feel, as it is any time soon they just don't want his passing to bring me to a dark place in my life like David's passing did when it does happen.

November 28th 2015: Today my guide Margaret told me there is an angel watching over my shoulder waiting for the right time to release healing energies from heaven. She also told me that there will be a homeless man near a McDonald's near a highway and I am to give him money. She said that helping souls is helping yourself. As I type this in April of 2016 I realize about 2 weeks ago there was a homeless man near a McDonald's by a highway with a sign asking for help. Since all I had was change in my car door, I decided not to give it to him and now I regret that decision.

November 30th 2015: Today Margaret told me today that I am completely ready for devotion to Mother Mary, St. Therese and the angels. She went on to say that; "My heart is now open and filled with love and joy. She then said my next step would come to me tonight. Accept this step with open arms, heart and soul. Heaven knows no hate, only love from above so focus on the guidance of spirituality. Life may seem inappropriate at times, but changes make the difference." Mother Mary then stepped in and said to me, "Follow me and heaven is yours for all eternity and the changing of tides will bring a life like no other. The holidays are special because you share them with family. Up ahead money, love, wealth and home will be yours in abundance." She also said I passed the test with flying colors. I feel the test is my devotion to those in Spirit and on earth.

Maurice stepped forward today and said to me, "I told you I would come to visit you. He said, "My family is sad; tell them I am an Angel of Mercy and I help the souls of others. Tell them not to pity me for I am whole." He then told me thank you for befriending me and showing me the way. He said to tell his sister Robin, "don't be sad my soul sister, for we are one, and we will be united again." And finally, he told me that he loved me and to tell his family that he loves them. I told Maurice, "Thanks for coming to see me; I have been waiting to see you." He smiled and said, "It was worth the wait."

TEN

Mixed Blessings

December 1st 2015: Last night in my dream it was a beautiful day outside and I was walking on a path with trees and grass. I knew that someone was following me but I was afraid of who it was. I started running home and when I got to my house it was a large house made out of stucco with glass doors and windows everywhere. I looked into a sliding glass door and saw my father, who wasn't my father in this life, but he didn't see me. The house was surrounded by a few feet of water so I couldn't open the door. Then suddenly I was in another place that was dark. A little boy around five years old was standing in an opening in a run-down house and then he fell into the opening. I was so terrified and then a man ran in the house and caught the little boy as he was coming down a chute in the basement. As this man handed the little boy to me through the opening there was also a woman in the basement that was touching the boy's leg. I was very frightened of this woman and her face was green. But she looked directly at me and said, "Thank you" with so much appreciation. As soon as the boy was handed to me he was now a newborn. The man told me that because the woman touched him he would always stay a newborn and never get older. I have a knowing that this woman was Sarah P Whittemore and she was thanking me for crossing her son's soul over to eternal peace. I believe that crossing souls over who need my help is the step that Margaret told me about a few days ago to accept with open arms, heart and soul. I do fully accept helping the souls who need me.

Sarah P Whittemore had appeared to me while I was in mediation one day. She had blonde hair and wore a white dress with a white bonnet on her head. She thanked me for my friendship. Till today I still drive up to Connecticut and go to the cemetery to visit her, her son and husband and I leave flowers on their graves. I don't want Sarah to ever think that she and her family are forgotten.

December 5th 2015: In my connection to the other realm today I was shown a vision of men sitting on benches in a park wearing white robes. There were trees, grass, and a path around them. Mother Mary told me that they are men of God. They all had long hair and reminded me of Jesus. Tracey Lynn then appeared with them wearing a white robe with a ring of white flowers on her head. There was a little arched wooden bridge over a body of water. I was standing on the bridge wearing a white robe and flowers on my head, except my robe was sleeveless. I had a rainbow over me and there was a beam of light coming out of my heart. I was smiling and very happy and waving to everyone like they were my fans. Next, a beautiful angel with blonde hair was hovering over me covering me with sparkling light, and telling me that I am ready to be a healer. Archangel Raphael was also there and he told me that I have an innocent pure love in me and he said he is helping me get ready to be a healer.

December 14th 2015: Archangel Gabriel came to me today and told me to trust in and follow God. He then said my brother Philip's soul would shine in happiness with the reunion of David and your mother when it is his time. He went on to say that life will beat you down, but the love of God will pull you back up. Faith, hope, trust and love are the combination that will get you through. Lastly, he said that Philip's penance is being paid here on earth before his return home and the timing will be as it should be.

My mother then came to me and gave me a message for Matthew. She said, "Grandma has your hand, and Uncle David has your back." She continued with telling him to get under the umbrella in the rain and that bright sunny days are coming. My mother also said, "I will hold you through this my boy. Keep going forward one step at a time. Life isn't perfect but life is good. Clouds of doom are over your head Matthew, so wash them away with positive thoughts and smiles. Roses can prick you but when they bloom, they can be beautiful. Everything happens for a reason Matthew--have faith and trust."

I thought my mother was telling Matthew these messages because he cut his hand pretty bad at work and needed stitches, and was out of work for a few weeks. A few weeks later he lost his job and was sinking into depression. He almost lost his apartment and I had to remind him of what grandma had said. He forged forward and got a new job and a boss that he loves just in the nick of time. Spirit can truly get us through the tough times if we listen to their messages and allow them to help. Always pay attention to your intuition because spirit whispers in your ear.

Bella, Tracey Lynn's grandmother, visited me today and said the price is too high to be paid for friendship right now. She said time will heal and the flow of energy will come back to you.

December 15th 2015: In class tonight, Ron did a meditation where we went to a crystal-healing palace. In the meditation the entire palace was made of crystal, even the stairs. The palace had beautiful colors beaming from it. I climbed the stairs and went onto the porch where people were gathered. My mother was on the porch and I told her that I wanted to see the healing of children. My mother and I then stepped inside to a large foyer-like room. There were many children all dressed in white playing in this room. The room was bright with lots of light. I got a feeling that this was some sort of waiting room. There were angels wearing white walking and floating around. When an angel passed by a child, white light from their wings would fall onto the child. All the children were playing and seemed very content. I saw one child holding a lollipop made out of pure white light. I walked down a hallway by myself that was off of that room. Down this hallway there were rooms on the left and the right. The rooms to the left were filled with white light and children that were laying in beds with cherub angels flying around the children and tending to them. The rooms on the right were dark and I knew those were the rooms of the children who weren't going to survive. I didn't enter the rooms on the right; I just knew I was supposed to look in there but not enter. I looked down the hallway and at the end of it stood Mother Mary and she motioned for me to go to her. When I got to Mother Mary she opened up a larger wooden door. Sitting behind a large wooden desk in that room was Jesus. Mother Mary then said to me, this is my son, Jesus. Jesus stood up and said to me, "Thank you for your prayers and your service but there is much more to be done." I never spoke a word during this meeting. I then turned around and St. Therese was standing there and without saying a word she walked me back to the room I first entered. The children in that room were all still playing. My mother was bent down playing with and speaking to one of the children. My mother turned around, saw me and stood up. We both exited the Crystal Healing Palace on to the porch; I walked back down the stairs by myself and left.

January 5th 2016: While I was praying today I asked for a healing on my friend's son who has a tumor on his pituitary gland. I also asked for a healing on his mother, Heather, to have a better quality of life because she is disabled. I was shown a vision of white light beaming on the top and back of her son's head. I was also shown white light being poured on to Heather and it was filling her entire body. I knew then that they were both receiving some sort of healing. Heaven is so amazing to me and all you have to do is ask for their help and it shall be done.

In class tonight with Ron we did healings on each other. While I was doing a healing on a woman in my class, I felt someone touching my back. I asked who was touching me and Archangel Raphael showed himself to me. When it was my turn to get a healing, I did what is called an absent healing and I sent my healing out to Heather's son for his tumor and all the headaches he was getting.

January 6th 2016: Today I woke up with a severe headache, especially in the back of my head. I kept waking up all night in pain. The pain was so severe that it made me nauseous. I never get headaches like this so I believe it was related to the healing I did on Heather's son the previous night.

January 7th 2016: I woke up this morning with my head still in pain. Though I felt better than yesterday, I still kept waking up all night in pain. I called Ron to ask him about the healing I sent out and the headache I now had. Ron said I absorbed his pain and sickness inwardly and that I need to take his pain and illness and send it out to the Universe. I called up Heather to ask her how her son was and she told me that his headaches had disappeared. I was very happy to hear that his headaches were gone. I continually learn as I go, and Ron and any other mentors that I encounter will continue to teach me to heal others for I believe this is another part of my journey.

Today I keep getting signs from the spirit realm. I can feel them strongly around me though I'm not sure what they want. I found a dime in my luggage as I was unpacking. I know positively that it wasn't in there when I packed. I also found a penny on the ground. My mother and brother always give me coins to let me know they are around especially if I am having a hard time in life. Also, I keep seeing 444 everywhere I look. The more 4's that you see the stronger the message is that the angels are helping you. Seeing 4's is a very positive sign and it is the angel's way of letting you know that you are being helped, protected, and watched over.

Matthew and I went on vacation to the West Coast. While there, Matthew posted our location on social media. He then received a message from my brother Andrew saying that he was living in the city we were visiting. Honestly, I didn't even believe he was in the same state, much less the same city. After all it was 3000 miles away from home-the last place I had seen him. We made plans to meet up with him though we didn't expect him to show up. Andrew wasn't the most honest person and was always telling us stories. But lo and behold, we couldn't believe our eyes; there he was walking down the street towards us. We were astonished that Andrew was in the same exact small town in this entire country that Matthew and I were visiting. We were both happy to see Andrew because we really didn't know if we would ever see him again, besides, I did feel guilty stopping communication with him. I feel like Spirit had a hand in this meeting, and more than likely it was my mother who arranged it.

Andrew was homeless, and had lost a lot of weight since I'd last seen him. He was carrying a little adorable Chihuahua dog with him that was only about five pounds. We took Andrew out to get something to eat. Matthew and Andrew were in the front seat and I was in the back seat of the car. While we were in the car eating, the dog urinated on Andrew's lap and he became furious. Andrew got out of the car and whipped the dog on the cement. The dog was yelping and crying and he picked the dog up again and whipped him into the car door. I was screaming at Andrew to stop. I took the dog from him and hugged and held that dog till he stopped shaking. I couldn't stop crying and shaking and I felt physically ill. I didn't want to give Andrew back the dog but I had no choice. The good thing is the dog wasn't Andrew's. It was his friend's dog that Andrew was on his way back to give him. I know for a fact that Andrew has nothing to do with the dog any longer. I couldn't stop or change what happened to the dog that day but if Andrew was the owner, I would have made sure the dog was out of his care. I assure everyone that the dog is now in good hands.

I felt so sick that I had to get away from Andrew because he just showed me he hadn't changed at all. As Matthew and I pulled away, Andrew and I were both crying. We do love each other but I just can't handle his anger and addictions.

Andrew repeatedly apologized to me by text for what he has done to the dog. Though I was happy he had remorse it didn't make what he did any better or change anything. Before Matthew and I returned home, we visited Andrew one more time. We took him out to eat and went shopping with him to buy him new clothes. This time he didn't have the dog, which made me happy. Though this time he was high on drugs and that alone stressed me out. I left feeling so sad for him and the life he lives. He has done so many terrible things that no one in the family will have anything to do with him. I love him but though his suffering and sadness tears me apart, I can't have him close in my life. I no longer felt the guilt over stopping communication with him, and I was happy for this "coincidence" that brought the three of us together. Andrew was down and out and clearly needed to be pulled into my life. Though it was only temporary it was long enough to let him know that Matthew and I cared about him and love him. Andrew and I are on different paths but the Lord brought us together out of nowhere in the most unlikely place. Andrew is still on his travels; I wish him the best and I hope I get to see him again.

January 16th 2016: Last night while lying in bed I heard a bell ring in my apartment. It was 3:44 am. When I connected to the other realm, I asked what the ringing of the bell meant. Margaret my guide told me that it was a message from God delivered and that I would know in the future. I also asked her that in my dreams the last two nights, what did the bears and cats mean? She said that they are vibrations and frequencies to bring me out of the dark. Mother Mary then stepped in and said amazing, incredible times are to come, peace be with you.

January 18th 2016: In my communication today an angel told me that they deliver divine guidance. This beautiful angel also told me that a job related opportunity for Matthew is coming. Then I was shown a vision of angels, my mother and my brother David lifting Matthew up and pulling him out of the darkness and that he would have another job soon. Then I heard; be grateful for better days are coming.

January 26th 2016: St. Jude stepped forward today and said that a blessing is coming to me very soon. "Love, hope and honesty are instilled within your heart. Life as you imagine will be beautiful beyond your dreams. Help those who help others. The mastermind of peace and healing is within you. You will do much for the souls of others. Make people smile, lend them a hand, and divinity will be yours. This land is to be worshipped and fed upon, not to destroy or kill the forest. Animals have rights and they belong to the earth. Don't linger a single second--do all that you can do, your job is plentiful and wide open. Go forward and do God's work for you are one with God. Be a friend to all, others will follow, and your life's accomplishments will be many. Your soul's purpose will be met. Eternal life is yours my child. You are not alone for we are with you. Peace on earth and good will towards men, and love and blessings to you."

January 28th 2016: Mother Mary stepped forward today and said that; "Fantasy could be reality for the angels work together to make things happen. Anything is possible and disappointment is a part of life. A magical mentor will enter your life. There is much to be done for the souls of the world. A lifetime of memories will fade and never again to love within the same realm. Hope and conflict will be tremendous in the world. Life can be turmoil and filled with prejudice. Many backward leaps of faith will turn against each other. Nobody knows the outcome within the divine eternity that is in all of us. Protection from the enemy is going to be love, peace, and happiness, and most people will value this. Property, real estate, and forest, will come to a halt. Carry on in the name of God the Father in each one's own Divine guidance. All will see."

January 30th 2016: Mother Teresa stepped forward today and told me that plentiful bounties are ahead. She went on to say that; "Many obstacles have been overcome and life's path is open, keep trucking forward. Hope comes in many assorted colors and pure magic, joy, hope, and happiness is all yours. With big money come big opportunities and responsibilities. You will receive money in the future but you will be overcome by the greediness of others. Help those in need; feed the hungry and clothe the poor. Help the shelters financially. Take your time; there is no rush to spend money. Quietly do your business and don't involve others. The truth shall set you free; just do your highest and best good. Be wise in your decisions and make wise choices. Smell the roses for Mother Mary is with you. Be loyal to your friends, life is good, and life is amazing. Be proud, and stand strong, we in the Spirit realm are behind you.

As I was praying in front of the Mother Mary statue today at St. Anne's shrine, I looked at the statue and the blue curtain behind seemed to become one with her. All I could see was Mother Mary's face and it seemed to me that her head nodded up and down as if to say, "Yes" to me.

January 31st 2016: I received a phone call today from Matthew telling me that the police pulled him over and towed his car. They also took his plates because his registration was inactive. His registration renewal was never mailed to his new address and he didn't realize it was inactive. This entire situation upset me because Matthew and I are both struggling financially. We are just like everyone else on earth and sometimes we feel like we can't catch a break.

I received a reading from a medium from Scotland that came to the church in Onset in August 2015. He told me that in five months' time I would know of a financial abundance that is coming to me. He said I wouldn't have it in five months, but I would know of it. I have been anxiously waiting for word of this "abundance" through the mail or a phone call. So far I haven't received a call or anything in the mail telling me of money I would be receiving. The last day of the five months was yesterday and I feel disheartened and let down. I cried and felt an overwhelming sadness and despair today. By nighttime I was angry and I yelled at God and the angels. But while I was yelling at them, I kept saying I was sorry. Though I was so angry I still felt like goodness is coming my way. I also prayed to God, Mother Mary and the angels to take away anything that hinders my soul from fulfilling my soul's purpose, whether it is fear, anger or doubt.

I went to St. Anne's church to pray in the shrine again. As I was kneeling in front of the Mother Mary statue once again the blue curtain was one with her. For a split second I was shown a baby that was sitting on top of her head in place of the crown that's there.

When I connected today, the angels told me not to worry about a thing for they are here to help. "There is nothing too strong to bring you down. Heaven is at your door and goodness waits. You will behold a magnificent present. All too soon you will feel the joy and the light of the Lord. Many kindred spirits are at your side to behold the newborn King. Your life is meaningful, and light will be shed upon it."

When I was told behold the newborn King, I truly felt that was baby Jesus shown to me on Mother Mary's head this morning.

February 1st 2016: As I was praying this morning I became totally enlightened which was a wonderful, freeing feeling. Ron O'Berry had been telling me the whole month of January how abundance is coming my way. The Spirit realm keeps showing Ron how they are stacking up on the abundance and they are going to open the gates when the time is right. All this time I was waiting for a letter or a call when the answer was straight from the Spirit realm through Ron. When the car situation happened with Matthew, I felt overwhelmed. It released any doubt, fear or anger I had within me and brought it to the surface. It was festering so slowly that I didn't even realize it was there. Today I feel free of any doubt, fear, or anger. I know wonderful things are coming my way and that everything will be okay. I can truly step forward towards my life purpose, which is to help other souls in any way they are put in front of me--whether it is to enlighten them, feed them, or just give someone a hug. It is now time to go forward with writing the book to show other souls the path. I have faith that God and the heavens will put the right people in my life to help me do this. I'm constantly connected to the Spirit realm and I'm always protected. I am truly grateful for everything in my life.

Today as I was praying in front of the St. Therese statue, a purple glow of her outline appeared to the right of the statue. This outline only appeared for about a minute. I instantly felt St. Therese's presence at that very moment. Purple is the color for those who seek spiritual development.

February 2nd 2016: When I woke up today I walked in to my dining room and opened the blinds. When I turned around, I noticed that my Mother Mary statue that had been completely facing forward was now completely facing sideways. Mary was now facing my Jesus statue. No one except myself had been in my house. I was very happy to receive this sign because in church yesterday, although I got a sign from St. Therese, for two days now I have been expecting one from Mother Mary. Though I'm not clear as to what it means, I know this is a sign from her.

February 3rd 2016: In my connection today I was shown a vision of Jesus turning the Mother Mary statue. Jesus told me I am in her and through her; this is the word of the Lord. Jesus was revealing to me that though I pray the rosary every day to Mother Mary, it is actually Jesus who helps through her.

February 4th 2016: In my communication today, a beautiful angel appeared and said help is on the way, hold steadfast, it will be here all at once. Move quickly and gently, for we the angels will be at your side. This is the year of incredible feats. Don't overindulge in food and sweets because healthy living is a plus. Longevity is what you need for your soul's purpose. Many children have sorrows; you must lift their hearts, souls, and spirits to all eternity. Muslim people cry unfair but in reality hope is all we need. Don't exert your heart in state affairs. Love is on your side, and you are equal to all.

February 5th 2016: St. Therese came forward today and told me that I would connect to other mediums through her. "Believe it and it will happen, I will guide you my child. Take my hands and trust me. A magical mentor is almost here. Better days are coming so don't slip into negativity. Stay strong and have courage, all good things come with time. Spread your wings, it is time to fly. You will meet many in your field. Success is yours; welcome to the club my friend."

February 6th 2016: In my connection today I was told from my guide Margaret that today's faith goes a long way tomorrow. Such is the deed of others as life's circle continues. Miraculous events unfold throughout all creation, but people have blinders on so they don't see. The illusions before us are real. A friendship will occur, and its love is everlasting. The presence of others will lift you high. Don't doubt or be fearful, go forward. Your next step is huge, we will accompany you; the grace of God is with you. Do all you were sent here to do, and the end result will be magnificent. We will be proud beyond compare.

February 7th 2016: Mother Mary came forward today and told me that heavenly messages come in threes. Look for the taped box; inside will be overwhelming love from us in heaven. Most people create fantasy within the realm of life. Loops of magical wire command your attention. Pay attention to the markings on the calendar. Most days are vivid in color while some are black and white. Homeless shelters need assistance.

February 8th 2016: I woke up this morning and was all knowing what to include in my book and how to start it. In today's mail I received a check for $150 in a taped package. Heaven always has my back. I also looked at the markings on the calendar today like Mother Mary said to, and it is a new moon. In my connection today my guide Margaret said that the Merciful Almighty God the Father looks down upon us with kindness and flawless imperfections. A hundred deeds done in acts of kindness are worth so much in heaven. Tulips will bloom, roses will bloom, and heaven is awaiting the circle of life.

February 9th 2016: In class tonight Ron gave us all a reading from the spirit realm and my message was that I am taking a trip down South. We also did two meditations in class tonight. In the first meditation I flew with grandmother Eagle. I went five years in to the future and it took me outside of the First Spiritualist church of Onset, MA. I was wearing a blue robe and Reverend Kathleen was wearing a black robe. We were standing near the steps of the church, with a lot of people around us. I don't know why but I didn't want to be there. So instead I went into the present and I was standing in front of the house where I now live. There was a U-Haul moving van in front of my house filled with my possessions. Heidi was standing there with me saying goodbye to me and I knew I was moving across the country.

In the second meditation I did, I met the gatekeeper to my soul. He was a dark haired male named Christopher, though I never saw his face clearly. He said that wonderful things are coming for me.

February 10th 2016: As I was sitting on my couch today watching television, I heard someone say that magnificent news is on the way. In my communication today I asked my gatekeeper Christopher to step forward. I asked him what is stopping me from being a medium as good as Rosie Cepero, Theresa Caputo or Kim Russo. He said that fear stops me, and I must meditate every day. He also said I must practice mediumship every day.

A woman named Olga, who used to live in the house I now live in and is now in the spirit realm, visits me often. Olga was a very frightened timid spirit until I welcomed her and told her that I am her friend. I tell Olga not to be afraid and she can hang with me anytime she wants to. Today Olga kissed me on my cheek and we now have a mutual friendship with peace and kindness for each other. She is going to sit on the couch and watch television with me today.

In my connection tonight, Archangel Haniel stepped forward and told me that my development will be abundant and fast. She said that others would see my gifts as an abundance of favors. "To thine own self be true, do your highest and best good. The light will shine through the window of your soul. The darkness will fade away and nothing will stop you. A train of thoughts will go on and on and your book will be filled with chock full of energy and love. Keep going forward, love and kindness is yours. You're about to experience so much gratitude and love; it's like a never-ending story. Hope comes to the hopeless through you and your book. Greatness waits and finances will be plentiful. Your book will be true words of wisdom throughout all eternity."

February 11th 2016: In my connection today Archangel Haniel said, "The blessed are amongst us. There is much to learn in life so go forward and seek the truth within you. Help yourself by helping others. Be wise, kind, and caring, and it will come back ten-fold. Your spiritual development is extravagant beyond measure. Nobody knows or understands the level to which you will rise. Your soul will suffer great defeats, but your purpose will be served. An honorary King (I was then shown my orange tabby cat Max who is in spirit) will come to your aid once again."

Today I noticed that the Mother Mary statue has moved even closer to the Jesus statue. It is so close there is only a sliver between them. I have not touched these statues since Mary turned sideways. I'm hoping that the deeper meaning of her moving forward will eventually be shown to me, I have great faith that it will.

I can feel Archangel Haniel with me today and I believe she is helping me develop my spiritual gifts. I can also feel the heavens around me, and I also feel surrounded by white light and love.

February 12th 2016: The Mother Mary statue has moved forward again, and it is now touching the Jesus statue.

In my communication today I was shown a vision of Jesus moving the statue forward. Jesus then appeared before me and said, "Two hearts that beat as one, I am Divine Light that shines upon the Universe. Freedom from pain comes easily to those who have faith. Don't ever forget your worth. A stone's throw is where I am. Do unto others as they do to you." I believe today's message is the deeper meaning of the statues moving together.

February 16th 2016: In my connection today, St. Therese stepped forward and told me that she is there for me for guidance, support, disappointments and troubles. "A windy road is ahead, do your highest and best good and you will be rewarded with great blessings and healings. Daisies and tulips are a passion from Christ. Don't agonize over the fury of the beast for it will reveal itself. Be proud of yourself because your mother is."

February 17th 2016: Today an angel appeared to me and said that Theresa Caputo would light up my life, bright like a shining star. Amanda and I are going to see Theresa do an event on February 28th so hopefully Amanda will get a message from her son Eric. I have recently asked the angels if they could please make sure she does get to connect to her son that night. The angel went on to say that, "Judgment would award me a new life. Personal traits overcome a miracle of faith, live and let die. Mother Earth needs our help; the forest and trees must be saved. Pollution is ruining life as we know it, it will be too late in this stage to recognize it. A beautiful magical turn of events is yet to come."

February 20th 2016: Today in my communication to the other realm I was shown my father and the many things he had done wrong to my mother and me. My guide Margaret said I was shown this so I may heal and move forward. My father then told me that he is sorry, and he asks for my forgiveness (I do forgive my father). I then saw my father in a white robe, and he says he is forgiven. I believe by me forgiving him I have helped him to move forward some. They showed me my mother, brother and father standing together. Margaret said the trios of them all help me. I asked my mother if she has forgiven my father and her response was, "He is my friend." My mother said that happier times are ahead for me. Opportunity is almost here and for me to reach for the stars. She said it would be emotional at the event with Theresa Caputo and that they love me; trust me and have faith in me. She went on to say that Sarah is an emotional roller coaster and her gifts overwhelm her though she needs to know how to use them, for fear is her enemy. She finds comfort in everyday life and the normalcy of life with no surprises. Great awareness of the world is within her. She will be a spiritual leader one day." My guiding spirits, which include my family, are always supporting me, and will help me get the work done that is needed on my journey.

Jesus stepped forward and said, "Rewards in heaven are abundant for you my child. The purpose of your life is yet to unfold. There is plentiful abundance to all who seek faith. A child of God is pure white light. There are unicorns in a magical universe, which exist in time and space. The end of your career will be in the change called death. Until then, you will change many lives and help many souls. Miracles and divine interventions will come through your vessel. The world will grow in faith and confidence in God the father because of your work. Love, hope, and divine light will exist in the hearts and souls of the faithful. Recognize the awareness of one another for in the green pastures of the land; the sheep and lambs will be slaughtered for a divine purpose. Their blood will serve as medicine for those who believe in God the Father. Believe child, and it will be."

February 21st 2016: Today I called in again to ZENLIVE TV to speak to Rosie Cepero. I kept calling but I couldn't get through. I asked my guides and the angels to help me get through and they did. On the show they wanted to hear of miracles that had happened in people's lives. I told them the story of the time that I drove on the highway and lost control of my car and someone from spirit saved my life. Rosie said it was my guardian angels that saved me because I have much more to do in life and advised me to keep telling people my stories.

February 25th 2016: In today's communication, Margaret said that my friendship with the angels is magical. The angels enjoy me, and I enjoy them. She said there are many U Turns in my life to come. Finances will be raised up tremendously and that financial freedom is almost here. There is much work to be done and those in the angelic realm will help. Keep going forward for life is precious.

February 27th 2016: In my connection to the other realm, today Mother Mary stepped in and said to me, "A magical mentor is on your path. Keep walking towards your path and you will find your mentor."

February 28th 2016: Margaret told me that today is a day of awakening for me and that my hopes and dreams are filled in advance. She also said that my spiritual awakening is marvelous and mind blowing, and that this is what I have been waiting for. Last night Amanda and I went to see Theresa Caputo at The Providence Performing Arts Center in Rhode Island. This 3000-seat theater was completely sold out. As Theresa stepped down from the stage the first thing that she said was; I am looking for the mother of the young boy who killed himself. I said to Amanda, that is you and out of fear and anxiety she didn't raise her hand, it was like she was frozen. For a minute I kept thinking I should raise my hand for her, but I didn't. When no one claimed that reading Theresa quickly moved on and Amanda lost her one chance at a reading with Theresa that night. Amanda kept hoping during the rest of the show to get another chance but she never did. When the show ended and Theresa left the stage, Amanda cried uncontrollably, so upset with her self for not claiming that reading, she felt as though she had denied her son.

We met a woman there that was going backstage to have a meet and greet with Theresa. Because Amanda was so upset this woman offered to give Theresa a message from her. Amanda wrote her message to Theresa on a piece of paper and later the woman texted her to let her know that Theresa had received the message. Amanda never did hear from Theresa. I didn't expect Theresa to understand the message or what had really happened that night. I am the one who invited Amanda to see Theresa in the hope that she would get a message from her son. I'm the one who asked the angels to make sure she got connected to her son. I should have stepped forward for her when she wasn't able to. Amanda was devastated by the events of this night. I feel responsible for it and the angels told me how Theresa was going to light up my life. It was meant for Amanda to speak to Theresa but I dropped the ball that night and I'll always regret it. She was afraid to speak up, and I was afraid to speak on her behalf. This was a clear example of how fear can change an outcome.

February 29th 2016: Jesus came forward today and told me that He Himself is the grace of God. The kinship of others will shine brightly upon the spiritual realm. Stay close to Me my child; the rewards are limitless." Also, a guiding spirit named Earl who helps me with finances said that financial stewardship is available within hours.

March 1st 2016: Today my guide Earl who helps me with finances said that hardship comes with rewards. "Plentiful abundance is coming your way, but boundaries and limits will be set. Divine light will shine brightly upon your heart to guide you through." I've only recently become aware of another guide of mine named Agnes, who will help me to get my book started, she told me "Start writing your book my dear, and your heart will follow."

March 2nd 2016: Today I started writing my book. In todays communication my new guide Agnes stepped forward (she is a gentle, and sweet, elderly nun. The habit on her head is very old fashioned; the sides of it stand at a 90-degree angle, straight upward). She said I was to lead by example and work hard, that others would follow. "Follow us through the window of your heart. The essence of God is a true believer within itself and there are many true believers in God, family, and relationship to self. Ron is a wondrous healer from ancient times, but things go askew in this lifetime of healing. He is not always on the mark or keeping his eye on the prize. Many distractions in life had led him astray. His heart is golden at this point in his life, which is why he is now the mastermind of healing. Ron will uplift your life in many ways, so stick to him for now so he can show you the way. Communication is the key and many spiritual gifts will unfold for you. Ron is pretty impressive for a boy from a small town and is a powerful mentor of sorts."

March 3rd 2016: My mother, father and brother David visited me today and told me that they are always with me. They said I have to keep going forward, have patience and live in the moment, that I need to learn to separate my ego from my higher self, and determine which is which.

ELEVEN

Helene

March 8th 2016: While I was in Ron's class tonight as he was speaking a spirit entered my personal space. The feeling was way worse than a panic attack and I wanted to jump out of my body. I internally called upon Archangel Michael, Raphael, my mother, my brother or anyone who could help. The feeling was so bad that I needed all the help I could get. I asked them to take this imposing spirit away from me. I told the spirit that he was not welcome and I demanded that he leave. Within 10 minutes I started feeling better. I believe this spirit has been attached to me for a couple of weeks. I have been incredibly angry for two weeks and I couldn't figure out why. Since the spirit left, I feel back to my normal self. I'm so grateful that all that anger I was feeling is gone because I couldn't take much more of it. I really need to protect myself better spiritually.

March 9th 2016: A guiding spirit named Rose told me today, "You are blessed my dear, an opportunity is coming your way. She also told me that I would be traveling."

 March 11th 2016: Today I was shown a vision of my soul mate and myself walking together and hugging. I was told a publisher will somehow come through her and it will be financially rewarding. St. Therese stepped forward and said that Divine guidance and protection are mine and to just ask for it. She also said that we are soul sisters, and together, we can make miracles everlasting.

March 15th 2016: As I connected to the other realm today my guide Agnes told me of a woman named Patricia who is a wandering soul who needs help on her journey. While in Ron's class tonight, I realized Patricia is the woman in my class who needs the help. While we were practicing mediumship tonight, I connected to a family member in spirit for every person I read. I hope that I helped Patricia in someway with the message that I gave to her. I'm really opening up and developing spiritually.

March 19th 2016: As I started my communication to the other realm today I saw a circle of angels surrounding me as though they were guarding me. Christopher, my gatekeeper, came forth and said to me, "I am allowing someone to step forth." The gatekeeper is the one who decides who is able to step forth in your space. A woman then came forth and I wasn't sure whom she was, though she reminded me of the Blessed Mother because of her clothing, but I knew it wasn't her. She then told me, "I am Mary Magdalene. Nothing is a coincidence. You have recently read something about me and that was done in preparation for my stepping forth. The people of the world have not respected our Heavenly Father. The belief and devotion I have felt upon earth is a feeling that should be spread worldwide. There is disappointment in the hearts of many in my realm and sphere, which are connected. I am pleading with the souls of the world to open up and to have faith and trust in the Creator's plan. Love, devotion, and faith, are of great importance to the signing of the cross, and to the prayers that are received by our Father. I was once a black sheep but now I am considered a sacred lamb. Anyone, at any point in his or her journey, is able to change for the better. We are both proof of that, my dear. Go forth and spread the good word of the Lord by working closely with the angels and those of us whom sit in His glory. You have been chosen for your faith and devotion, and it is an honor to have you within the fold."

March 21st 2016: In today's connection to the other realm, my guide Margaret told me to harvest my energy to shine on and enlighten people. She said I was to spread the word of God and the afterlife. She went on to say, keep telling your stories and others will follow; you are a storyteller for God. More communication to the spirit realm will open soon enough.

March 22nd 2016: I am so excited in the development of my mediumship. In class tonight I connected to Ron's father, and Patricia's grandmother, and I gave them each a message.

March 24th 2016: A beautiful angel with long brown wavy hair wearing a blue dress appeared to me today. She said her name was Sarah and she told me that help is on the way. She said eventually others will stop in their tracks at the sight of you, and I will be looked upon as an earth angel. She continued with telling me to go forward and help as many souls as I can with faith, hope, love and trust in God the Father. Miraculous events will unfold; go with the flow of the Universe.

March 25th 2016: I dreamt last night of a small rhinoceros charging after me in a house. There were a lot of people in this house, and each time I entered this particular room, it kept charging me and I was filled with fear. Yet, I wanted to go back in that room because the people that I wanted to be with were in that room.

In my communication today I asked the angels about my dream. They told me not to charge through my book and to take my time because it is not a contest. They said to think about what I want to write, and, the fear that I have is of failure.

March 28th 2016: Today is the one-year anniversary of our apartment fire. Matthew won $1,000.00 on a scratch ticket today. I keep seeing the numbers 222, which mean to keep the faith. My seeds are planted, and though I am not able to see it, I have faith that everything good will be coming to me.

When I connected today an angel of abundance stepped forward and thanked me for my love and faith, and to keep going forward on my path. He said my endeavors will be fulfilled and I will be filled with light.

March 31st 2016: Archangel Gabriel came forward in today's connection and said that my book would start a revolution of spiritual beings and connections to people. He said modesty would take place in my hometown. Go forth in faith and the struggle will be real but worth it. Jesus then showed Himself to me as the Sacred Heart. Sacred Heart means the apostleship of prayer and I felt that He was showing me this due to my daily devotion to prayer.

April 1st 2016: Today I was shown a vision of Jesus as a shepherd in a field with many followers. He said, "Follow Me and lie down in the green pastures," then I was shown a black sheep. Then I heard someone say, "Hooray for Hollywood and that I was going to California soon," but I could not see who it was.

April 2nd 2016: Mother Mary came to me today and all she said to me was to light a candle and make a wish. So I did, and I wished to visit my daughter in California.

April 5th 2016: In class tonight my communication with spirit has really opened up. I connected to someone's loved one in spirit for everyone that I read. Ron gave me a reading tonight and he told me that a spirit named Walter said that the book of my life is closed, but the door is wide open. He also told me that I'm going on a trip, and that this trip will lead to other trips. He then said that an opportunity would be presented to me and that a guide named Grace said that I am to consider this offer very carefully. Ron then told me that he feels someone might try to take advantage of me and that Grace doesn't want me to take this opportunity (I did receive an opportunity of someone wanting to look at my book to help me get it published. I passed on the opportunity because I felt negativity around the offer).

April 6th 2016: In my connection to the other realm, Mother Mary appeared and told me that she loves me, and to go forward on my path and soar like an eagle. She said they would all help me with any difficulties on my path for there is much to be done and opportunities are limitless. "There are pennies from heaven all around, catch them. The time is here and now, don't be afraid to take life by the horns. Projects will arise from the darkness and light will shine upon them. Go forth in trust and faith with our blessings."

April 7th 2016: In today's connection to the other realm my mother stepped forward and told me that when Philip comes home that she, David, and my grandmother will greet him. My father told me that he would then repair his relationship with Philip, that it is time to take responsibilities for his own actions. My mother then said that though finances overwhelm me, my gratitude is amazing. She also said powerful enemies would seek revenge against my brother Andrew. It will be like hide and seek in the future and his life will be in danger.

April 9th 2016: My grandmother came to me today to tell me she is proud of me, and that she loves me, while my Aunt Ernestine was standing on the side of her. Then my mother appeared with them as she waved to me. It gives me such comfort knowing they are all together.

I went to the Spiritualist's Church Psychic Fair again today and I received a reading from Alan Acton, a medium from England. They have a Fair every six months to raise money for the church. Alan told me that I would be writing a total of four books and they will all sell. He said that my mother was there, and she said to tell me that she was sorry for something that she had said to me in life. She wanted me to know that she only said what she said because she was stressed. I believe my mother was apologizing because she had seen something I was writing about in my book; about when she told me to move out of her house because I wanted Andrew to leave due to his drug use. Souls in the spirit realm realize how their actions and words have hurt someone when they go through their "life review."

April 11th 2016: Sophie, another one of my guardian angels, stepped forward today. Sophie has blue eyes and brown hair that she wears up. She always plays a musical instrument. She told me that my path is a long winding road, and to go forward on this spiral path for my dreams will come true. She went on to say that when Family members leave for the spirit realm, don't get depressed, just keep going forward on my path. There will be many changes in the years to come. People will follow you; just show them your soul, goodness, kindness, and inner peace. In the future a lake near a summer home will be peaceful for writing.

April 12th 2016: My mother came to me today in my meditation because I have been asking the spirit realm why I haven't seen or felt my brother David around. My mother told me that David is busy working on his higher self. I was also told that my guides would visit me soon to enlighten me on my path.

In class tonight we did a meditation climbing inside a healing crystal. Once I was inside the crystal, I slid down a slide made out of crystal. When I reached the bottom I was in a park with grass, picnic benches, and a beautiful tree. Many people were standing around in the park, my mother was also there, and we casually went on a walk. On our walk I had seen a beautiful male angel with blonde hair that was petting an orange cat. In the distance I could see a temple, and said to my mother that I wanted to go to the temple. She stayed behind while Archangel Gabriel took me to the temple. Inside of this temple there was a large room with a sunken fire pit in the floor, and basins of water throughout the room. Everything was made of marble, and I just inherently knew that everything in this room was holy. I entered another room where many children were sitting on the floor with their legs folded underneath them. The children all wore white, and were looking up as if someone was speaking to them, though I never saw whom they were looking up at. My brother David was one of the children; he was about six years old. David stood up, walked over to me, and then he hugged me. I could feel how much his heart loved me, though he never spoke a word. I said to him, you do your higher learning David, and I will fulfill my soul's purpose on the earth. I told him that when it is time we would be together again. I then left the temple and went back to the park. In the park I saw the beautiful tree again and realized that it was a money tree. Someone then handed me a canvas bag and I opened the bag under the tree while someone shook it. When the bag was full, I closed the top of the bag and it was then time for me to leave. I turned around and looked one more time at this magical place that I didn't want to leave but knew I had to, and then swiftly left.

April 18th 2016: A magnificent angel wearing white and illuminating golden specks of light appeared to me in my connection today and told me that an orange and black Monarch butterfly is a sign of the coming of the Lord deep in your soul, with the power to help others. Reach beyond the stars and open your heart and soul to those in need. He then said that I am making a life of leisure and joy for myself. I then saw Jesus step forward and he said, "Don't be afraid to be judged by others for I am the only one who can Judge you. Beyond the borders of the realm there are important details to convey. Magnificent and majestic waters will fill the holy land and the world will be as one. Listen as I speak the truth and don't harbor your neighbor. The lay of the land will rise up to meet the sun and all will be well.

This is the word of the Lord."

April 19th 2016: We did a meditation in Ron's class tonight where we flew with grandmother eagle. After we flew, we landed on the grass, and there was a special tree there that was mine. This tree had pink flowers and gold leaves. The tree then turned into my gatekeeper Christopher. Standing in front of Christopher was a little girl in a pink dress. She was eating a candy apple and she was very playful. As I walked away to leave, I turned around quickly and she stuck her hand out and waved goodbye to me. After the meditation was over, I asked Ron who he thought the little girl was? He said to me don't you know, that little girl was you. After he said that to me it all made so much sense. It is the playful child inside of me that wants to come out because this child has been hiding ever since the day my brother David passed away.

Ron gave me a reading tonight and he said that St. Therese was with me and she said to tell me: two times six. Ron said he doesn't know what she meant and neither do I, but I'm sure I will eventually find out.

April 21st 2016: A woman appeared in my connection today and said her name is Catherine of Augustine. She told me that beyond the light let us journey towards our soul's purpose. "I have chosen you to be the light to show others the path of love and recognition of their inner selves to battle the addictions within them. Your true self will shine brightly for all to see. Go forward with courage and strength; your faith will be rewarded. There is much to see and much to do for there is a lot of work ahead. I trust in you my child for you have the Christ spirit within you."

April 23rd 2016: I did a meditation today from the Internet with Emily Stroia medium/psychic/intuitive. During this meditation I went up an elevator to the 44th floor. I entered a room, sat down and my mother sat across from me. Mother Mary stood directly behind me and St. Therese stood behind me to my right. There were also other's in the room that I didn't recognize but I knew they were my family. My brother David was sitting on a couch smiling at me and my father was sitting beside David. Archangel Gabriel was also present.

Again I saw this beautiful young blonde angel boy. I was told that this boy is Christopher Michael. He is Matthew's son who had been returned to heaven and is waiting to be born. I also saw Sarah's daughter, Allyson, who is also waiting to be born. Allyson had a huge smile on her face. She was about six years old, with long brown hair, and wore a white dress with pink flowers on it. I am beyond grateful for the chance to see my future grandchildren and I was given the information of who the blonde angel boy is. The ability to receive all this is a gift from heaven that can be matched to no other.

April 25th 2016: St. Therese stepped forward today in my connection. I asked her about my financial abundance that I'm supposed to receive. She said trust, have faith, and follow your heart. "Magical moments will happen in the right time. Live your dreams, write your book, and you will keep going higher, for our faith and trust in you is divine. Everything is coming up roses, just do your best and belief in yourself. Love yourself, and the world is your oyster." (I am only human and sometimes I have no patience in waiting for what they promise me).

April 27th 2016: In my meditation I was shown white angel wings with the numbers 777, which in angel numbers mean you are on the right path.

April 29th 2016: I was in the shrine at St. Anne's church today when a slender young man around 25 years old came up to me. He had dark hair and some facial hair. He asked me if I worked at the church and where could he leave an item he had found? I told him that I did not work there and then I directed him to the church rectory so they could help him.

A week and a half later at the shrine, I again saw this young man. He walked up to me and once again asked me if I worked there, and again I told him that I did not. He had a very humble, mellow energy coming from him. I thought to myself that he looked like John the Apostle.

Two weeks after that, I saw this young man once again in the shrine; this was now the third time I had seen him there. He walked up to me and asked me if I knew where the groundskeeper was? I told him once again how to get to the rectory. He looked at me in my eyes, extended his hand and said hello my name is John. As soon as he looked me in the eye and introduced himself, I knew he was sent from heaven. The feeling I received was comforting, and familiar somehow. He thanked me, then walked away, and I have never seen this young man again. I truly believe there are times that those from heaven do walk upon earth.

Since then, whenever I go to the shrine and see that it needs sweeping or cleaning up, I do it. It also makes me feel useful to do this because I so enjoy the shrine. If there were something more I need to do there, heaven would surely let me know.

May 2nd 2016: I saw a beautiful angel wearing a blue dress who told me her name was Clara. She said that an angelic mentor would arrive and that my devotion will be rewarded. "Good things come in two's like twins. Harvest the faith and surround yourself in beauty and nature. Admiration of the cross is the path to all you that seek. Don't let others' journey throw you off of your path. Your family watches you and admires your loyalty to God and to us angels."

May 5th 2016: Archangel Gabriel came to me today and gave me this message.

He said the plight of the world rests upon the shoulders of the incarnate. "The eyes of the world will see it as the leaders throw their holiness to the wind. Many people will come forward to reconcile. Hope and trust will never be able to be forged upon humanity by those who distrust themselves. The weak will never go forth and the strong will become stronger, strong of mind, body and soul, this is the word of the Lord."

May 17th 2016: During class tonight, a woman in my class named Sandy gave me a reading. She said that she sees me going to San Diego to visit my daughter, that my path is clear, and she sees no obstacles. Ron also gave me a reading and told me that my sister Colleen was there, and that Colleen said for me to grab my hat and coat and get ready to go, because I'm going on a trip.

While in the shower today, quite a few orbs were floating around me and I could feel that my mother was one of them. Though I'm happy to have them around I sometimes have to ask the spirits if I could have some privacy.

May 20th 2016: Mother Mary stepped forth in today's connection and she told me that life ahead is a clear path with nothing but bright light. She went on to say to make myself known to the world and step forward with social media. "The time has come and there are big changes around the corner. Many artistic people will grow in your presence. Be humble and have patience, for your life is amazing. We recognize your soul from a million light years away. The harvests of fruits fall upon the hearts of many. Beyond your dreams the manifestation of magic appears. Behold Jesus the Savior and the Son of God our Father. Mountains can be moved, and life can be miraculous and belief is all that I ask of you so come forth my child and fulfill your soul's purpose. Together we will accomplish all that is good; I am proud and have faith in you. Believe in yourself and there is nothing we can't do."

May 21st 2016: As I connected today two male angels who looked like twins appeared and said that they are by my side and that my destiny has arrived. They went on to say that many Archangels will help you succeed along the path of your journey. "Your soul will blossom like an onion, peel the layers and release the tears of happiness, joy and love. Many awkward moments will arise, but always be your true self. You are a conduit for the Most Holy, be proud to serve the Lord with utmost dignity. Tame the beast that comes forth in the form of fury; help souls who cry in pain." I was then shown souls in emotional and spiritual pain.

May 24th 2016: In class tonight Sandy from my class told me that her guide says I am not to worry about where anything in my life is going to come from. He also told her that I am to just keep writing my book and keep going forward. He also showed Sandy a pigeon and a dove to let me know that they are my spirit animals.

The dove and pigeon are interchangeable for they are one and the same.

Today Matthew asked me if I would take the girl who he is seeing to a clinic to get an abortion. Though it is upsetting to me I will take her because it is not my body or my choice. Now I understand why I have seen Matthew's son in two of my previous meditations, which makes this even sadder for me.

Sarah called me today and told me of a dream that she had last night. Her dream was about Matthew's previous girlfriend that he was on drugs with whom I took for an abortion. She dreamt that the girl was pregnant once again with Matthew's baby and she was going to have another abortion. In the dream Sarah was crying saying why are you killing Matthew's baby again. Sarah has never met Matthew's current girlfriend and didn't know that this girl was pregnant with Matthew's child. Sarah has always received information through her dreams from those in spirit.

May 29th 2016: In the Spiritualist church tonight I received a reading from a medium who told me that my Aunt Ernestine stepped forward and said that I have a heart like hers in helping people. She also likes watching me write my book. He also told me that my aunt said the first part of my book is personal, but the second half of my book will attract many people. Although I'm a medium, I still appreciate confirmation of information given in messages from other mediums.

May 30th 2016: My guide Margaret told me today to turn the page for prophets are in the highest regard. "Magical moments will arise before your eyes so bathe in the words of wisdom, and you too shall rise in the highest mountain. Many people hope for the best in the world but only few will actually take action. Take care of the suffering souls beneath the surface of the spirit realm. Help them to go forth in their journey and to measure the dignity of those who fail. There are forthcoming rights towards the sea of all nations. Hope and dignity are measured beyond emotion. Don't let those souls who control the lives of many control you, and have no fear for their destiny will be cruel. Your life will be plentiful."

May 31st 2016: Today as I went outside for my daily walk there was a dead pigeon on the lawn. He was face down, with his wings spread wide. I had a strong feeling that this was a message for me, especially since Sandy told me 2 weeks previous how spirit showed her a dove and pigeon for me.

I asked my guide Margaret about the dead pigeon and if there was a reason for it and she said that there is a fight or flight protocol for monetary gain. "Your soul flies free without a shadow of a doubt. Friends will appear by your side in your path as a light worker which is open, and the tunnel is filled with light."

In my class tonight Sandy told me that when a spirit animal dies like the pigeon they are giving their power up to you. Also in class, I connected very clearly to Sandy's boyfriend who is in spirit. He wouldn't leave me alone; he gave me anxiety and kept making me feel agitated. I told him to back up from me and I called upon Archangel Michael to back this spirit away from my space. He was making me feel physically ill. When it was time to give readings, I told him he could step forth. I gave Sandy a lot of information from him in this reading. He committed suicide, which is the reason I was feeling agitated and ill. As a medium I can see spirit and feel their emotions. My connection to the spirit realm is really opening up, and I am very pleased.

June 1st 2016: Archangel Gabriel came forward in todays connection and said most of what I do will first be taken with a grain of salt but move forward because that grain will grow with the help of the angels. He also said bottoms up and to celebrate with joy and music. Also in the future, a proprietor will ask me to move for family, but there will be many options to me at that time.

June 2nd 2016: Today I took Matthew's girlfriend to the clinic for her abortion. On the ride there I told her of Sarah's dream and of how Matthew's son has appeared to me. I didn't tell her this information to guilt her. I thought it was fair to share this with her especially since she has the same spiritual beliefs as me. She did go forth with the procedure, which is her right.

June 5th 2016: In today's connection I was shown a vision of a Jesus statue that I have on a long table in my dining room. On the side of the statue I have the receipts for Matthew's probation. I pray daily for heaven to help him get it paid off so he can be free of it. They showed me someone who bent down and touched the statue and said "all taken care of." I got the feeling that this person that was bent down was Jesus, but I never saw who it was. I was also shown a vision of the Mother Mary statue that I pray to in St. Anne's shrine. Then Mother Mary appeared to me and said, "I heard your prayers dear, now go forward in love and grace."

June 6th 2016: In today's communication John the Baptist stepped forward and told me to pack my bags for the trip is on, surprise. You will eventually drink from the Holy Grail in the presence of the Pope. He then showed me on my knees in front of the Pope drinking from a chalice. He then said welcome to the holy world of all that is good. "A humble beginning has brought you to the future and into the light and beyond. Many people will thrive upon the existence of the darkness and fall in to the outer limits where there is no tomorrow. Please help heal those who ask for help, and those who offer themselves for service to the Lord. Be kind, honest and generous with the abundance that will be bestowed upon you. Your life matters to complete the silence of the lambs. Many moons will be thrust forward before your mission is complete." I was then shown a vision of my mother and brother David standing with pride at all that I have accomplished, and all I will accomplish. Then I was shown my friend Heather, and I was told to pick my friends wisely.

My friend Heather called tonight and told me that she is paying for my trip to San Diego in July. Spirit truly amazed me with the message I received today and the phone call I later received from Heather. This is incredible confirmation for me that the spirit realm always has my back regardless of how they send help to me. I'm so grateful to Heather for being so incredibly generous to me. I do choose my friends wisely for not only is she generous, she is a pure soul.

June 8th 2016: Today, 3 glorious angels with white light beaming from them appeared before me. They were in a circle holding hands and they told me that the triple 3's mean, the Father, the Son and the Holy Spirit, and that there is a never-ending supply of energy and love. They also said Heather's daily life will get tougher each year till she succumbs to her disease. Heather is disabled from juvenile rheumatoid arthritis since she was a child. They also said to let the sunshine in and that squirrels are over taking her yard and then they showed me a vision of Heather standing on her porch watching the squirrels. And she will 'hob knob' with celebrities one more time. They also showed her in a maroon dress standing on her porch and said that by the time she passes, she would be happy with the way life has gone and how her life is currently. They went on to say that we are lucky to know and have each other. Heather's road had been windy and rocky but her exit will be marvelous and that Heather and myself need to be grateful, for each day is precious.

Heather called today and I told her the message I received from the angels. She was flabbergasted because she said a few hours before we spoke, she asked the angels what does the triple 3's represent. She said she was standing on her porch earlier watching the squirrels and looking at the ramp on her porch that was just painted maroon. Heather and I have some sort of special spiritual connection to each other and the angels always confirm these connections through the messages I receive.

June 10th 2016: My guide Agnes told me that the medal I have of St. Therese is appreciated. She said I would be sitting with Tracey Lynn again and that harmony; peace and friendship will all come together in the future. She also said that I will have a dream of the other side and while I dream, the other realm is coming to whisk me away to teach me as my body rests.

June 12th 2016: In my connection today, Mary Magdalene stepped forward and said that the plight of the world is upon the shoulders of man. They must step forth in faith and for the protection of other souls. The most common mistake is that we don't value our freedom more. "Behold amongst you is the Lord." Be cautious in all you do because he may be standing at your side. There will be tests of strength, courage, and hope within the realms of your decisions. In your work you will help bring peace to a whole new light to envision the world that was meant to be.

June 14th 2016: While I was in the shrine today in St. Anne's church, I could hear the spirit realm around me. As I paid closer attention, I could see angels flying overhead in the church. They told me that happiness and joy are here for me. They also said that everything is working out. As I stood in front of the Archangel Gabriel statue, I was told "surprise!" I'm not sure what that means, but I'm sure I will find out eventually. As I stood in front of the St. Joseph statue, a spirit of an older gentlemen named Richard asked me for help to cross him over. I called upon Archangel Michael to come and cross him over. I saw Michael scoop Richard in to a ball of light and put him in some sort of a jar and then they were both gone. That was the first time I had ever seen Archangel Michael scoop someone into a ball of light like that.

In today's connection Catherine of Augustine came forward and said that my soul is connected in ways that I will understand later in my life, and that my connection is deep and powerful by my choice. She also said that I am a light worker by choice and the contract that I signed with God will never be null and void. My life's purpose is closer than I think. Then she said that my mother is at my side helping me through the difficulties of my journey. She went on to say that most men will accompany their fears into the dark forest but only some will come out in light on the other side. "You my dear have forsaken all your fears and darkness and your light shines brightly. The full moon will be upon all those that stand heavy in their soul. Be glad for your life on earth for you are among your brothers and sisters who will conquer freedom for the souls of the future."

June 16th 2016: My guide Agnes told me today that faith, courage, and strength, would be mine for the asking. She then said she is behind me and in front of me, and I will be protected as she stands by my side. Protection comes from the love that dwells inside our hearts. She also said don't be afraid to show my true colors to the world: beauty and the beast.

June 17th 2016: St. Therese stepped forward today and said that fantastic dreams come true like wishes from the spirit realm. Many shards of glass are invisible on a shattered soul and the soul is ultimately unbreakable. Wisdom can come through many obstacles of fear. Walk the path that is destined for you, don't worry about your brothers' and sisters' paths. Most likely your survival depends upon your inner peace, but procrastination of your inner soul will lead to self-destruction. I was then shown a vision of a white dove for inner peace. She then told me to do my highest and best good in each situation. She also said some will try and tear you down but I will build you back up, my sister. There will be moments of disappointments and tears but don't fear for I am at your side and together we will conquer.

June 19th 2016: My guide Agnes stepped forward today and told me that they eagerly await the choices and decisions that are made out of love between what is deep inside the treacherous and the illumination of a soul. Treachery can be avoided if you take a minute to cleanse the aura. There will be many possibilities of freedom to break through the walls of a boxed heart. She also said that Queen Elizabeth has made us proud for her years of service to the people of England. "She has lived a legacy like no other. Though there are too many people waiting to put their hands in the pot." I was then shown a vision of Queen Elizabeth as a young woman transitioning to an older woman.

June 20th 2016: When I connected today Archangel Michael stepped forward and he told me that trustworthy people would enter my life. He said don't be afraid to step forward, courage and strength are instilled within you. "Your fears will disappear.

Awkward moments will bring you clarity of an on-going situation that interrupts the summer solstice. Angelic beings surround you for your protection from harm of those in the darkness. I was then shown two rows of angelic beings, with me in the middle of them all. He said we stand like soldiers at your side. Heavenly forces will guide you through any storm and magnetic strips of light will appear before your eyes."

June 21st 2016: As I connected today my guide Margaret came forth and told me that moments of tragic revelations come between space and time. "However, love and unity can ignite the fire deep in our souls. Help those who seek heaven on earth. Magical moments appear each day if you look with your mind, body and soul. Helter Skelter: Charles Manson is a soul of the darkness that cannot recover, it is his choice, his path, and there is no light."

St. Therese stepped forward to tell me that happy days are here my friend. Pleasurable memories have yet to unfold in this journey on the earth. Be confident in the knowledge that is instilled within you and that I have taught you. On many levels your soul is exquisite beyond others. Your hard work and dedication is a tribute to your honor. Very clearly I heard St. Therese say to me, "We will be united again one day Helene." I sat there for a few minutes to realize that she had just called me Helene. I then asked her if she called me Helene as in her sister while she was on earth and she answered, "Yes." Which means I am St. Therese's sister from her last life on this earth. I was filled with deep emotion over this revelation. Now I understand why she has always been with me to help me through my life. And I now understand why she only spoke of Helene to me and not of her other three siblings who passed away. Helene passed away three years prior to St. Therese being born so they never met on the earth plane. Everything is revealed in divine timing, and I believe it was time for this information to be revealed to me.

June 22nd 2016: While I was in the shrine today at St. Anne's church St. Francis of Assisi came forward and told me that prejudice is in the hearts of those who have darkness and that illumination is the key. "Distinctive demonstrations among fellow protestors are considered acts of violence in the spirit realm. Protestors of peace bring harmony. The Yulin dog festival is an abomination. Animals big and small are God's creatures and earth is their home. If the roles were reversed, would animals then be considered savages? Peace on earth toward all men and creatures worldwide."

June 23rd 2016: St. Therese came forward in today's connection and told me that the flight of the lonely would immerse in the darkness of eternal damnation. "Bring forth and immerse yourself in the light of all creation, the light that burns in the Christ spirit within you. Many years in the making are the outcome of the population of the people that will outweigh the mere existence of the kingdom to come. You will need strength and courage for the good fight, the fight to battle other people's demons. Look within and pull out your deepest darkest secrets to build upon a new you. Procrastination is a trait not worthy of most circumstances due to cowardice. Step forth and be ferocious in a loving, kind way. Most will be proud and honored to serve by your side. The knowledge and wisdom beneath the surface will rise on the request of God. Till then my friend be wise in your choices for ultimately the price paid will be too high. Don't risk all that we worked for, for the solidarity of one soul." My mother then stepped forward and told me I am her treasure and a precious soul. She told me to listen to the birds for they are singing me a song. I didn't realize it till she said this but the birds were chirping right outside my window.

June 24th 2016: Archangel Michael stepped forward today in my connection and he said that the angels are helping me behind the scenes. A higher energy of the evolution of mankind is similar to world dominance. Predominance, whether it is good or evil, will shine a path to The Holy Land. And it is nothing compared to the relevance of the Lord as the Master of the Universe. It was a cruel feat; the twin towers, but the angels and myself has carried them all home due to your help and others who work in the light. I was then shown a vision of angels flying around the towers carrying souls. I am very happy to get this information because a few years ago when Tracey Lynn went to the site of 911, she could see and feel the lost souls that were stuck there. The souls were following Tracey Lynn around the site asking her for help. One of the souls attached themselves to Tracey Lynn and went home with her and made her physically ill for two weeks. She called me and asked me for help to cross over this soul, and other souls from the 911 sites. I went in to a deep meditation and prayer, calling upon Archangel Michael and all from heaven who could help to cross these souls over. I did the praying and meditation while Tracey Lynn and I were on the phone together. Tracey Lynn could see and feel not only the soul that was attached to her, but also many other souls from the tragedy, as they were being released and crossed over to heaven. I could see all the angels flying around collecting the souls and helping them to cross over. I felt good about crossing these souls over but part of me was afraid that what if some souls were left behind. The information given to me today confirmed that all the souls have been carried home. I truly love working hand in hand with heaven; there is no better feeling of accomplishment for me to know that I am fulfilling my soul's purpose while I am on this earth.

Michael went on to say to develop the courage that's within the human spirit to fill the soul within. "Mystical magical people will step into your path soon. They will be Spiritual beings that hold secrets to the other realm and an unfolding of greatness will occur. A pleasant surprise is coming your way through others. Accept it with open arms as a gift from God. You have pledged your allegiance to Almighty God and as requested Grace is your favor. Your bond with St. Therese is like no other, sisters in heart and sisters in soul. Most likely your grace will lead you to a path beyond illusion. The price is too high to be paid for those who walked a downward path. You must try to lift them to new heights with your books, healings, and mediumship. Your words can ease the pain felt by those who suffer needlessly. Do your highest good and the rewards are limitless."

June 25th 2016: In my connection today my guide Margaret said that tragedies would befall London in the perils and hopes of a brighter future. An explosion was shown to me in a building that had a huge clock, which could be the clock they call "Big Ben." She also said the enemy would tear down hope and the future. "Money will play a big role in all that is to come. There will be chaos throughout the streets and the police will lose control. Things will get worse before they get better." I don't know when this will happen for heaven's time and our time are very different, which is called divine timing. Divine timing can sometimes be frustrating when they promise something that will better your life.

June 26th 2016: St. Therese stepped forward and said though we never shared hearts on earth, we share our souls that are beyond great wisdom.

June 27th 2016: In church last night I received a message from a medium named Karen Daley who is from the Quincy, MA Spiritualist Church. She told me that my mother was apologizing to me for not always knowing what was the best thing to do for me while she was on earth. She also said that my mother wants me to get my book finished so other people can see how amazing I am, just like she can see it. My mother also said I will be writing another book right after this one. My mother loves being around me all the time and watching what I do, though she feels that when I channel her, my energy gets nervous, which blocks me from getting all the messages I'm supposed to receive. She said she would back off from me when I communicate with others.

Today in my connection an angel came forward radiating a beautiful golden light. He had locks of blonde hair and beautiful blue eyes. I felt such intense peace from him. He told me to be grateful for memories of family unit and that there is strength in numbers. Beyond the universe there are waterfalls of love; everything is made of love; everything you touch is love and the moon doesn't set because the sun always shines. Then I heard someone say there is a peculiar voice that comes over the intercom, peculiar but soothing. I was shown a vision of a beautiful waterfall with flowers and trees everywhere. People were standing under the waterfall wearing some sort of canvas robes just past their knees. Everyone there was happy and enjoying themselves.

June 28th 2016: Mary Magdalene came forth in today's communication and said that with hope and dignity, trustworthy souls would enter my life. "Enlightenment and white light is the meaning of true love in its purest form. Harsh words behind your back won't hurt you, so rise above with love and light to be your true self. Due to irresponsible people who are careless about human life, there will be many outrageous outcomes. Don't let those who quickly intrude upon your steps in life become the friendships that you seek. Be optimistic about the joy that can come from the existence of others. Hopefully, the distraction of the irregularity of personal deception will put a stop to the taming of the beast and his protégé who no longer serves the Lord. Beware, for their sting and bite are deadly, and only trust those in God's white light."

TWELVE

Whaley House

June 29th 2016: Jesus stepped forward in my connection today and said that some days are better than others, like today is. "The shift of the cosmos in the universe is a well-kept secret, most likely to develop when Uranus meets Mars. The prejudices amongst men are equal to terrorists. Attacks of terrorists will be never ending; it is part of the world structure that brings us downward. Destiny and hope are huge pieces of the anatomy of the world. People fight the Savior against the turmoil of their own souls and the jurisdiction of the people whose lives will be saved and go on a quest and a journey to fulfill the prophecy of all souls united. Many will fail and those who thrive will be leaders for the new Kingdom. The new world will be bountiful in peace, love, and harmony. Justification for the outcome is a desirable one. Peace on earth and good will towards ALL men. No need for worries, the future is bright. Trust me my children, for a new day is dawning but hundreds of moons will pass till the outcome. Till then, suffering souls are to be prayed for. United we stand, divided YOU fall."

I took a walk tonight down to The Battleship Cove in my town. I was feeling very warm so I decided to take a break and sit in the shade under a tree. As I was sitting there looking out into the Cove at The USS Battleship Massachusetts, also known as "The Big Mamie," I recalled an event from my life. As a child I would hear the adults speak about "The Big Mamie." Though I didn't know what "The Big Mamie" was, they spoke about it as if it was special. One day when I was 10 years old I was riding in the car with my mother and father. My father asked me if I wanted to see "The Big Mamie." I was very excited and of course I answered yes. My father slowed down the car and pointed out the passenger side window. I said where is it and my father said it is right there. I didn't know what I was looking for because I had never seen a "Big Mamie" before. I said to my father that I couldn't see it and he became very angry with me. He screamed, "it is right there," and I became so frightened I said, "Yes, I can see it." He said, "No you can't, you fucking stupid bastard," and drove away. It was years before I learned what "The Big Mamie" actually was.

At first I wasn't sure what relevance this story would have to my book. I was a confused little girl harshly scolded by her father for not seeing the obvious. I was so excited to see this "Big Mamie." It was as big as can be but I didn't know what I was looking at, or looking for. The lesson here can be as obvious as that giant ship that was in front of me. Sometimes when we are searching and looking for something, we miss what is right in front of us. But what's more important is if we can't see it, it would be very lovely for kind words of guidance. My father could have said look at the giant ship, or he could have told me the history of the ship. Instead he took the harsh and easy way out, and just humiliated me. He called me names for not seeing what he could see. Kind guidance and shared love is how I want to express myself. It's how I want us to experience this journey; to share with all of you what I can see and what we can all see together. I promise anyone that if you have a hard time seeing something that is obvious to me, I would treat you with love, kindness and respect. We are all children of God for we are all equal.

June 30th 2016: While I was in the Shrine today at St. Anne's church I knelt before the St. Jude statue. As I knelt there, I saw a pamphlet, picked it up, and saw that it was a pamphlet of novenas to St. Jude. The front of the pamphlet said, "This Man Can Make Miracles Happen." Since there was only one pamphlet, I decided to put it back in case someone else really needed it. As I looked up to the statue a very bright yellow, white orb of light appeared and it traveled over the pamphlet. I knew instantly that the pamphlet was meant for me to take. As soon as I picked up the pamphlet the orb of light disappeared. I didn't understand why I needed this pamphlet of St. Jude, but as I write this it became clear to me that it is for a young man who is having a hard time in his life. He is conflicted within himself and Agnes told me that in order for him to find a resolution, he must surrender. St. Jude can help him surrender if he allows it. Agnes also told me that there needs to be spiritual preparedness for the souls of turmoil. "Help those who seek God's white light and turn their faces against the darkness. We need preparedness for the future, watch for the signs of the Most Holy. Bring forth the levity of all those souls in the future. There are many possibilities of turmoil in the souls of those who seek God's guidance. Serve the Lord upon request of your own volition, and do unto others as they do to you." She then said I was to share these messages for the world to see.

July 1st 2016: My guide Agnes told me today that thoughts are processes erased over time in the mind. Happy thoughts are created through the expression of your inner love. An expression of gratitude can be wholeheartedly felt in your gut and children feel the difference in the levels of love from others.

July 2nd 2016: In today's communication Mother Theresa came forward and she told me that the most prominent young people in the United States have a shield of energy that protects them from the harshness of the world. She said the angels help protect them with shields from Christ the Lord. "Their job is to unite for a more powerful future that will better this planet. Halleluiah, the mold has been broken. Protection is the key to unlock the Universe and all its forces from the damnation of those who are in power and are evil. Step forward with courage, strength and determination to seek the ones who need elimination from their position in power. Do all that you need to do to bring down the dark forces that reside in the souls of many. We are all equal; it is our choices that make us differ from one another. Your road is your own, and you can see the forest from the trees. Be proud of yourself, for we are. The turmoil within yourself has settled nicely and the levels to which you will rise will be miraculous."

When I awoke this morning, I lied in bed and got onto my phone. I went on Facebook and the first thing I had seen was a post about signs from the angels. One of the signs that I read about is how angels can come to you in your dreams to give you a message that they want you to know. The more clearly you remember the dream, the stronger the message. The dream I had just awoken from included several people that I worked with at the hospital. I was shown one person in particular and that was my boss Elaine. I knocked on her door and when she opened it, she was standing there with a huge welcoming smile on her face. She was wearing the most beautiful vivid purple outfit I had ever seen. The color purple is closely associated with spirituality, healing and humanitarians who like to do good for others. I inherently knew that Elaine was being shown to me because she had been an earth angel to me during all the difficulties that I went through in my life while I worked at that hospital. Elaine was the one person who was consistently kind, considerate and treated me fairly and humanely. I will always be grateful to Elaine for her kindness and her pure soul. She is the main reason I made it through those difficult times and kept my job. Heaven puts the right people in our lives to help us through our tough times, and make our lives a little easier to get us to where we need to be.

Another sign I read about was when you see little flashes of light that is mostly in your peripheral vision; it could be visits from the angels and the spirit realm. This brought up a memory for me of when I was working at the hospital. I kept seeing an incredible amount of little flashes of light in my peripheral vision but when I turned to look at them, they disappeared. It was an ongoing thing and I thought something was wrong with my vision. I made an appointment with an eye doctor and he performed a thorough examination on my eyes including dilating them, and then told me nothing was wrong with my eyes. I told him that I was definitely seeing little sparkles of light that hovered. He got irritated with me, and treated me like I was crazy and making up a story. I now know that as I went through my life the angels and spirit realm were trying to reach out to me in many different ways.

The third sign that I read about was butterflies, and how they can just flutter by, or even spend long periods of time with us. Butterflies symbolize amazing changes and transformations coming forth in your life. You can actually feel the message that they bring. Today as I went on my walk, I saw a white butterfly as I came to a street crossing. I stopped at the curb and a driver signaled for me to cross the street. As I crossed the street, I could see the shadow of the butterfly on the ground following me over my head. When I reached the sidewalk I looked up to see the butterfly and he flew into the hedges. I received an incredible feeling and I knew that the spirit realm was letting me know that they will be with me every step of the way on my journey.

Angels, guides and loved ones in spirit leave us signs to either just let us know they are around us, or to comfort or guide us. If you ask them for assistance or guidance through some difficulty, then pay close attention to the signs you will receive. They will always answer us in one way or another. If a sign is meant for you then it will draw your attention and you will feel it in your heart. Have faith and trust in yourself and those in heaven. Other signs that I have actually seen are coins from loved ones. I have had coins show up in the most bizarre places. I was feeling very sad over the loss of my brother David one day. I went to the supermarket to get my mother some lunchmeat. In my head I thought to myself, I'll get her some rolls for the lunchmeat. I picked up a package of rolls and sitting on the package that I picked up was a dime. I knew immediately that it was from David and I instantly felt him around me and at that moment it brought me some comfort. Another time I was cleaning out the freezer section in my refrigerator before I sold it when I was losing my house. When I reached up to clean the top shelf on the freezer door, I found two dimes. I knew that they were from David, and he was close by. Till this day I find coins, as it is a way of spirit letting me know they are with me. Angels and guides also give us signs to let us know that they are helping us spiritually, physically, emotionally and financially. We just have to pay attention.

Numbers are a big way the spirit realm communicates with us. Seeing the same numbers and patterns are wonderful signs. You can see the numbers on clocks, televisions, license plates etc. The number 1111 is a sign of spiritual awakening. It is letting you know to keep your thoughts positive because what you are thinking about is being manifested. While 444 means your angels are sending you blessings and are helping you behind the scenes. The more sequence of numbers you see the stronger the message is. Those in spirit always communicate with me through numbers.

Other ways the angels can communicate with you are through feathers. Feathers are referred to as the calling card of the angels. My angels for some reason don't communicate with me through feathers. I never find feathers anywhere as of yet. They can communicate with messages through clouds to show you their presence. If you're loved one in spirit is around, you may feel goose bumps, a temperature change, or hear a song on the radio. There are so many different ways the angels and our loved ones can communicate with us. Some of our loved ones in spirit are definitely our guardian angels and are always by our side.

July 3rd 2016: St. Therese stepped forward today as I connected to the other realm. She told me that the babies are waiting to be born, Allyson, and Christopher Michael. She said they must be wanted in order to fulfill their souls' purpose upon the earth. Matthew and Sarah's wills are purposeful and that part of Matthew and Sarah's purpose is to bring these children into the world. Contracts were signed but free will is their choice. Most of heaven's travelers are neglectful in their contracts. You will fulfill your life's purpose and much more. Give thanks to the many who have come before you to clear the path of adversity. Some will envy you while others admire you. Step back and look at the picture as a whole before you take steps forward. You make us all happy and proud. I was then shown a vision of me as Helene about 2 years old sitting on my mother's lap while she was sitting in a wooden chair. There was a lit candlestick in an old-fashioned candleholder nearby. St. Therese said I was healthy then and that she was showing me a loving moment with my mother.

St. Therese also told me that our mother and father have been honored by the world. Since she told me this, I have done some research to learn these amazing facts about Louis Martin and Marie-Azelie Guerin Martin who are St. Therese's parents. They married in 1858 and had nine children, three died in infancy, and one at the age of five. The five remaining children entered into religious life. Louis and

Zelie, as she was called, would attend mass daily, pray and fast, visit the elderly and sick and welcome the poor into their home. They both served God with their lives and led their children down the same path. On March 26th 1994 Pope John Paul II declared the couple venerable, which means heroic in virtue.

The couple was beatified, which means Cardinal Jose Saraiva Martins declared them blessed on October 19th 2008 in Lisieux, France It is a declaration that the deceased is in a state of bliss and is a step toward canonization. Though they are the second couple ever to be beatified, they are the first parents of a Saint to be beatified, highlighting the important role parents' play in their children's spiritual upbringing. Before beatification a miracle has to be recognized after prayers for the couple's intercession before God. The Catholic Church had recognized the 2002 miracle of Pietro Schiliro, an Italian child cured of lung trouble at the intercession of Louis and Zelie. The doctors and family anticipated this child's death because the child was in such crises of respiratory failure. The child's parents started a novena to Louis and Zelie and asked friends and family to join in. During the time of this novena, the child's improvement came abruptly and he was taken off artificial respiration. Pietro has survived and he is healthy.

Before they could be canonized a second miracle had to be recognized that occurred after prayers for the couple's intercession before God. In 2008, a little girl named Carmen in the diocese of Valencia; Spain was born prematurely with multiple life threatening complications. Carmen suffered a major brain hemorrhage, which could have caused irreversible damage. The little girl was very sick and wasn't expected to live. Carmen's parents, their loved ones and many Carmelite sisters prayed for the intercession of Louis and Zelie. Carmen survived and is very healthy today, thanks to the intercession of Louis and Zelie Martin. Pope Francis canonized the couple on October 18th 2015.

July 5th 2016: Today when I went outside today, once again there was a dead bird lying in front of my window. In my communication with spirit I asked if the bird had anything to do with me. Mother Mary stepped forward and said that the strength of God's love was carried upon the wings of the little bird for you. "It was carried to your heart and soul for the challenges of the souls of turmoil that you will meet. You are a child of God who walks in divine light and will show others the path. The Monarch builds walls of self-esteem for a brighter future. If you are shown a Blue Jay, then an enemy is approaching. There will be battles to fight in the hearts of those with a strong will. Keep concentrating on God's love and power within each other. A telltale sign of an accumulation of souls divided will be particular moments of silence but hope will lead you back to the promise land."

July 6th 2016: John the Baptist stepped forward in today's communication and told me that happiness is an abundance of love, peace and harmony. "Beyond the majestic mountains you will seek a mentor who is like no other and he is considered royalty in the spirit realm. He said I will see a robe, a crown, and a scepter and I will immediately know it is him. It is destiny that the two of us meet. It is a connection for a brighter future for the world. There will be a roadblock of thugs but they will not be as tough as they look. Advance on your journey as Jesus did through the desert."

July 7th 2016: Today I can't quiet my mind to hear the other realm. St. Therese showed me white roses falling in my mind to try and help me quiet my mind. I was then told to be humble and pray to St. Louis and Zelie Martin for the sick children.

July 8th 2016: In my connection today Agnes said that those you seek shall speak the truth of God our Father with confidence. The darkness runs through our lives like streaks of lightning: some catch them while others don't. Feel free to widen the gap between our world and yours. Show others the eternal light within all of us that is forever. Broaden the spectrum and scope of your mind to open a dialogue with others. Connect to your mother and father and ask them for help (I was then shown Louis and Zelie Martin).

July 9th 2016: In today's communication I asked for Louis and Zelie Martin to step forward and connect to me. Zelie said we are here my child. She told me love is the key to all communication and don't hesitate to bring peace to the world. "Go forth in your unrequited journey for this is the life you were born to live. We are proud of your courage and strength in this world and this life. You will make progress rather quickly as we stand behind you. Your sister is of great service to you. Our little flower watches over you with honor and love. Your soul connection is greatly bonded throughout all eternity. Pray to us and we will intercede for you to bring hope to the weary souls."

July 11th 2016: I arrived in San Diego, California yesterday. I will be here for a month keeping my daughter company while her husband is gone for training in the Marine Corps. Sarah was at work while I was cleaning her house and listening to music. I could feel my mother's presence and she whispered to me that the song playing was for me from her. The song was "You Are the Wind Beneath My Wings." As I listened to the song, I cried with sadness because I miss my mother but I also cried with joy because I was grateful to get the chance to connect to her and receive a message. I am so very blessed to have this gift and I thank the Lord every day.

Archangel Gabriel came forward today in my connection and said that the majestic mountains that they have been speaking of are here in California. He said my guardian angels and the spirit realm are celebrating with joy for a new chapter in my life. He also said hold your head high and spread your wings for the world to see. "Opportunities are coming your way and the progress through your lifetime is amazing. Souls will step forward to trace the steps of your journey so that the path may be embodied for all eternity. Others will learn through your mistakes and your willingness to sacrifice yourself for your children. Your generosity for your children comes from your heart with the purest of love. Your children are pieces of your soul and your existence for now and forever."

July 16th 2016: Jesus stepped forth in today's communication and said that in truth, memories go unnoticed in the spirit realm. He said hopefully communication with the spirit realm would lead to bigger and better things for the world. "Our hope is to take you higher and higher so you may be a leader and have followers to brighten the future of those who have sorrow and grief deep inside their souls. Many angelic beings surround you to lift you as one of us."

July 17th 2016: Today I went to a party for my friend Heather's son's 30th birthday in El Segundo, California. While I was at this party, I practiced my mediumship and gave readings to five people. I did well on all of the readings except for one of them. I was upset that I couldn't connect and get enough information to give a better message to a man named Tim. Tim is Heather's friend and he has been a writer for television shows for the last thirty years. Tim wrote for the show Dexter, and that is how Heather met him because her son, Brando, acted on Dexter for a couple of seasons. After I finished all the readings, Sarah and I sat down with Tim and had a great conversation with him. We explained to him about many of the spiritual things that have happened in our lives through the years. My daughter Sarah also has spiritual gifts but she chooses not to use them. Tim had many questions for us and I believe we all left feeling better about Tim's reading. As I laid in bed that night I asked the spirit realm to reveal to me why Tim's reading went the way it did.

July 18th 2016: Last night in my dream, someone from the spirit realm told me there will be a block, that was all that was said to me. After I woke up and was going through my day Agnes came to me and said that it wasn't a block with Tim or myself. She said the spirit realm put the block on us for communication. She said the block was put there; otherwise Tim, Sarah and I wouldn't have had the conversation that we had. She then said the conversation had to take place and that more would be revealed in the future.

She went on to say that the connection between Tim and I was orchestrated by those in her world. That Tim and I will collaborate together and it will be the biggest success of his career. She also said the benefits Tim and I will reap would be incredible. Creativity and ideas will fill Tim's head and his work will be amazing. The right time will be revealed to the both of us. She then told me to keep an open line of communication with Tim and build a friendship, and that bond will help ensure our success. There will be a jealousy over our friendship but the bigger picture is to reveal much light to the world where there is darkness. The soldiers are lined up and will fall into place one by one, so go forward one step at a time.

July 19th 2016: St. Therese stepped forward in today's communication and said that my communication and delivery of messages has vastly improved. "It is time for others from our world to step in and introduce themselves to you. You bring comfort to the broken hearted and give strength to the weak souls. The freedom that ignites children's laughter will open the hearts of many souls who roam this earth. Don't worry, you will be seen and revered in great light. Your family is by your side, and they sustain you for you are loved and protected, so don't be afraid of what others think. Unity among the spiritual community is important. Your hopes and fears will be conquered and the world is your oyster. Magical moments will appear out of nowhere to show you gratitude. I am by your side and will uplift you and support you. You can lean on me for strength and courage and I will assist you. The way you feel today is only temporary and you will be bright and sunny in the morning." (I was feeling rather down today).

July 20th 2016: Archangel Michael came forward today and said that there is much to be done for there is a heavy dark curtain that drapes over the world. "Fill their hearts with light and love and never stop trying; for you will be rejected by some but welcomed by others. Happiness and joy can thin out the darkness between worlds, and love is the key to all questions answered. Dark memories provoke hatred among men, they must let go and let God's will be done. Hope and love will retrieve a person's anguished heart from the dark side. Listen to your guides and angels, they protect you, guide you, and lift you up when you have fallen from Grace."

July 21st 2016: St. Therese told me today to pray for the weak of mind and soul; the souls of turmoil.

St. Louis and Zelie Martin then stepped forward and said that they watch over me as they guide me and protect me. They then told me to transfer my thoughts and energy into the world and I will heal and improve others and myself. Surrender your will to the Almighty and heaven restores balance within your soul.

July 23rd 2016: St. Therese stepped forward today and told me that determination is the key to a successful outcome, beginning with the slightest act of kindness. "Know the power that you hold within yourself and that an act of kindness equals an act of God. The knowledge and power of belonging to a spiritual group will rise beyond expectations. In the future you no longer serve the Lord alone; a partner will be at your side. Take the hand that will guide you to the next step forever into the land of the Holy here on earth. Congratulations, you have softened the hearts of some souls who were hardened. The imagination of others will produce great results. The harmonic rhythm and flow of music produces serenity and peace for our earthly bodies.

July 24th 2016: A man stepped forward in today's connection and I was not sure who he was. He had about shoulder length brown hair. He was wearing a brown robe-like garment. I asked him who he was and he replied, "I am John, an apostle of the Lord." He began by telling me that I have seen a sign of the Holy Spirit that embodied the water in Galilee (though I don't know now what he is speaking of, I hope to be enlightened on this in the future). He then said a most Holy Tribune would come forth to show the world His earthly powers. "Disappointment comes to those who seek evil and revenge opposed to those who seek truth and justice with love in their hearts. Many followers of our Lord Jesus shine brightly in heaven's sky while others are dampened by the darkness that surrounds the entire force field of our souls. Heavenly creatures will surround those who are light bearers and bring truth to the goodness of mankind. It is important to stay focused, with a clear mind, body, and soul, so that your path is free of hatred and prejudice. Bring light to the unfortunate souls who cannot find their way alone. The rewards in heaven are limitless just like the love of our Lord and all the angelic beings. Keep going forth my child your devotion is amazing. You will find what you seek and much more, and the world will eventually adore you."

July 25th 2016: Archangel Gabriel came forward today and he said that love bridges the gap between two worlds. I was then shown a beautiful vision of an arched bridge with white light sparkling all around. There were beautiful flowers, grass, blue skies, and Jesus, in a white robe standing on the bridge. He was extending his hand to someone to help him or her over, though I was not shown whom it was that he was helping over. He then told me that the angels surround me with love and devotion towards my life's purpose. He went on to say that heavenly assistance is at my side and they want me to feel and understand their loving support. "Greatness awaits you; don't neglect what is right in front of you. Seek the truth and you shall find the answer to calm the storm that rises beneath the evolution of the earth. Earthly angels have arrived to assist you in your quest of greatness, so pay attention to the signals and signs that are laid out for you. Momentary lapses of judgment can prove to be fatal in the eye of the beholder and we are at your side to always lift you up. Part of your journey has been negative to teach you to enjoy the positive side of what is to come. A brilliant white light will appear in the form of an angel. Be wise in your decisions as you step forward on this spiritual journey."

July 27th 2016: My guide Margaret stepped forward to tell me that hope and destiny are two things that eradicate all else that matter. "Hope and destiny are so powerful that it makes fear drop off the side of the earth. Generous amounts of love are given to the weary of heart and soul. An expedition beyond our realm is like going through the twilight zone. It is a zone of freedom, freedom from hatred, prejudice, violence, and anger. Step in to your journey and release all your inhibitions for that is the first step to freedom within the confines of your own soul."

July 28th 2016: Yesterday Sarah and I had a tough day together. I am still in California with her and sometimes I don't know how to handle her anxiety and panic attacks so I ended up yelling at her. She is having a hard time with her husband being away on training. Matthew is also having a bit of a hard time right now, financially, and otherwise, which is also stressing me out. Matthew has been sharing my car with me for the past six months and I am finding it to be difficult, but I will do whatever I can for my children.

Today my mother stepped forward to tell me that I am an amazing person. She asked me to have patience with my daughter for she is in need of emotional support. She also told me that Matthew is going forward on the fast track to a better life.

My brother David then stepped in and he said that he wants me to tell my children that he supports them with a bounty of love. David showed me him sitting on Sarah's couch with her as he wipes her tears. He said, "tell Sarah she is never truly alone for Uncle David and Grandma are always with her." He said to tell Sarah to speak to them and then look for the answers. David said as she walks alone in the desert, it is then that they carry her like Jesus did. David also told me that he would be sitting shotgun with Matthew as Matthew drives his new car in the future.

As I remained in meditation connecting to spirit, I was shown a vision. In this vision I was a small, blonde hair child named Grace. I was sitting in a sort of wooden wagon that was being pulled by an animal. Something was physically wrong with me, like polio. I was in front of a convent with a short pudgy nun who was looking at me like she was angry that I was there. Then another nun came walking over to pick me up. She was the Reverend Mother, she was filled with light and I felt her love for me. I lived at the convent till age 5 when I passed to spirit. This vision amazed me because a few years ago Tracey Lynn told me of a past life that I had in which I was a little girl named Grace.

Then my guide Agnes stepped in and said that angels guide me through the spirit realm as I sleep. "You walk through paths of love filled corridors enhanced with the beauty of your ancestors. Your struggles in this life were above and beyond what was planned for you. There will be smooth sailing for the rest of your earthly days. Don't worry about anything; just-go forward as we guide you towards brilliant devotion to God and all your brothers and sisters. You will make a big difference in all that you have done, and will. A magical mentor is on its way; he is closer than meets the eye. A wonderful surprise is about to erupt from the heavens very soon. You will be very excited about your life to come. It is goodness wrapped in a ball of light, like an orb that travels with energy."

July 29th 2016: Jesus came forward in my communication today and told me that there is a dwelling place in the house of the Lord that connects us all to our own egos, soul mates and families. "We convene there for the purpose of planning and connecting us in many ways to the entire Universe. We have all visited there five times each per year, to reconnect and check in with our families and the progression of our souls. The level of our souls determines the amount of sacrifices we must make in order to be whole. The destiny of our whereabouts upon the earth are called placement therapy as to where you will be placed according to your mission and your soul's purpose. Each being will be filled with love and joy upon their entrance. It will drop off at different rates based upon the experiences you go through. The more difficult life you lead is determined by the amount of pain you project into the world. As you change your life, you change your destiny and you will have accomplished your soul's growth. Do unto others, as you would have them do unto you."

July 30th 2016: Yesterday I went to Los Angeles to do readings for six people. I felt I did well with my communication and messages, and that I am improving. Today, I also met someone who offered to help me with my book. I am very hesitant of this person and I believe this is the one who Grace was speaking of in a message given to me on April 5th 2016. Grace said don't take the opportunity, and consider it carefully because someone is trying to take advantage of me.

My guide Margaret told me today that the seeds have been planted and to make the best of my friendships because they will carry me far on the path that I seek.

She also said I am going to get help with my book, but beware of contracts to be signed.

August 1st 2016: In today's connection a gorgeous angel appeared in all white. She had curly; honey colored shoulder length hair and huge green eyes. I asked her name and she told me to call her Lily. She then told me to notice the blue skies, the green grass and the majestic mountains because they help to fill and heal our souls with the power from the earth. She went on to say that Mother Nature is far more important than meets the eye. "The connection between the earth and us is formidably higher in life than so-called death. Daisies bring power to those who are more than the average soul and also to those who leap in bounds as to their souls' purpose to help weight-bearing souls. Weight-bearing souls are souls that dip into the darkness and drag themselves in the dirt."

August 2nd 2016: Today I went to The Whaley House in Old Town San Diego, California. Thomas Whaley had this house built in 1857 for himself and his family. The building was known as the finest brick building in San Diego costing $10,000.00. Before Thomas owned this land there was gallows where the house now stands. The final hanging on that land was of a man who was convicted of attempted larceny in 1852. His name was James Robinson aka Yankee Jim. Jim was a very tall man and when they hung him, his feet dangled on the ground due to his height. He swung back and forth for over half an hour as he slowly strangled to death as the entire town watched. Thomas Whaley was one of the spectators at the hanging. Even with its history, Thomas Whaley still brought the property to build a home for him and his family a few years later. After living in the house with his family they would hear unexplained heavy footsteps moving around the house. Mr. Whaley and his family believed those were the footsteps of Yankee Jim Robinson.

Thomas and his wife Anna had six children, Francis, Thomas Jr. who died at 18 months, Anna Amelia, George, Violet and Corinne Lillian. Violet took her own life due to depression from a failed marriage. She shot herself in the chest right outside on her father's property, where her father found her still alive, carried her into the house, and laid her down in his study where she died.

Many visitors to The Whaley house over the years have encountered ghostly experiences. People have seen apparitions of Thomas and his wife, Anna. Psychics and mediums have entered The Whaley House through the years and have come across spirits of young girls, even animals.

When my daughter, Sarah and I first entered the house, we went into the first room on the left (originally built as a granary but had multiple uses through the years-was last used as a courtroom). I immediately felt spirit there very strongly. The spirit was so strong and so close to me that they were in my personal space, and I felt panicky. Once again, I forgot to surround myself in white light for protection before I entered the house. I asked spirit to please take a step back from me but they would not back up so I called upon Archangel Michael, the angels, my mother, and my brother to please get this spirit away from me. The feeling was so terrible and strong that I wanted to run out of that house as fast as I could. After a very long five minutes I finally felt better. I felt fine as we walked through the rest of the house. As we approached Thomas's study on the first floor, I could sense a female presence there. I then saw a younger woman in spirit with light brown hair wearing a very long cream-colored dress, with some dusty rose color in it. I could feel that she was Violet Whaley.

Sarah and I left the house and went out to eat. After we got back to Sarah's house I wasn't feeling too well. I was feeling weak, just not right, and needed to lie down. I was lying on the couch and could feel a spirit with me. This spirit was trying to attach to me as he was definitely in my personal space. He then caused me to have what felt like a very bad anxiety, and panic attack. Though this doesn't happen to me often, I usually don't tell anyone about them till they are over, but this one was so bad, and made me so frightened that I had to tell Sarah. I called upon the spirit realm for help and they came in so quickly, within minutes I felt better. I then asked for a shield of light to protect me and I also asked Archangel Michael to please escort this spirit out of my daughter's house and away from me and so he did. I also burnt sage in her house that day just to cleanse out the energy. My big mistake was not putting a shield of light protecting me before I entered that house. I don't know whom that spirit was I only sensed he was male and that he was a negative energy. I leave myself open too much to the spirit realm, but I'm still learning and I never want to stop.

August 3rd 2016: In my connection today Archangel Michael came in and said that a spiritual divide exists in The Whaley House. He said it is a battle of negative and positive energy that resides there. Violet Whaley is sad and regressed while Thomas Whaley is going about his business organizing all that goes on there. He then showed me a vision of Mrs. Whaley sitting in her bedroom in a rocking chair with a young child on her lap. He went on to say that there is an Indian Chief on the premises who oversees things for his ancestors. "The heart of the house has a connection to the spirit realm, and all who enter walk through its path. Violet cries for the loss of her dignity. The Whaley family wants to heal and be reunited as they once were in life. Positive energy can uplift the spiritual activity within those walls and help is needed for their souls' progression." He then had shown me many positive uplifting people in The Whaley House, all holding candles praying for the souls in the house so that they may all move on and progress in spirit. I myself will pray for those souls and I asked Archangel Michael to please cross over the confused, lost souls that reside there.

August 5th 2016: St. Therese stepped forward in today's connection and told me that angels and angelic beings raise me up when the dark times surround me. "Be strong, confident, wise and healthy in all you do. The decisions you make are important to your well-being. Your brother Philip will be freed from the pain of his human body when the time is right. His soul will heal and he will be reunited with his family when the time is right, for his life cycle must fully complete first, it is in his contract. His suffering has not been for no reason. His karmic balance must come to full fruition. Everyone's life cycle is different; everyone has his or her own path, some succeed, while others fall flat. We are responsible for our own pre-destiny ritual. Everyone starts with a blank slate and a neutral beginning. As life piles on, so does the incredible energy that makes this world swirl. Everything, and everyone are connected, and are of equal importance to God and the heavenly divine mission. If you could remember your mission on a soul level, then peace on earth would be a reality."

August 7th 2016: Today, after four weeks of visiting my daughter, I left San Diego and headed home to Massachusetts. Since I woke up this morning, everywhere I look, I keep seeing the numbers 44 or 444. This is a good sign because it means my angels are with me and I can feel them very strongly today. While on the plane on my connecting flight to Philadelphia, I was reading Kim Russo's book, "The Happy Medium." While reading about clairaudience (being able to clearly hear when spirit speaks to you), I was on page 188 titled, "Hears To You." As I flipped to page 190, I suddenly heard a group of female voices chanting. They were soft, friendly voices, and I could feel they were heavenly but I couldn't make out what was being said. I looked around at the other people on the plane and clearly, I was the only one hearing them. This lasted for about three minutes, then it just stopped. I wished I could have understood what was being said.

August 8th 2016: As I connected today an angel with an incredible presence came forward. She was wearing a green robe and her wings were magnificent silver. I could tell by her presence and energy that she was special. I asked her what her name was and she told me that she was Archangel Haniel. She then said to me that a financial advisor would be coming through the book. She then said an angelic prayer was being sent through the air yesterday and that the prayer was for peace on earth for mankind. (Now I understand what the chanting was that I heard on the plane). She went on to say that the angels surround me with white light to be free of harm, lighten my load, and to give me enlightenment. "The angels are also connecting you to others, remember the soldiers are lining up and falling into place one by one. You are all part of our angel team, the ones who will rule the universe with your staffs of white light. The empowerment of white lighters has yet to come to fruition. Many disabled bodies will rise in their spiritual selves to find the truth and become one. Hope will venture far and wide as will the epitome of the oxymoron and for those who are truth seekers."

THIRTEEN

Spiritual communications

August 9th 2016: In my connection today, my guide Agnes told me that the higher soul within myself needs nourishment. She went on to say that you need a group of like-minded people to fill that space that is connected to the spirit realm. "You will meet a person who is an unlikely candidate for spirituality but you must console and help her to bring forth her inner peace, courage and strength to endure the trials and tribulations on her journey. All we ask is that you do your highest and best good, and you will be rewarded. Let the games begin, go forth at a fast pace, and make decisions quickly. Help her to get settled in her soul; we love you." The following week I connected to an old friend I hadn't seen in years. To put it nicely, she was a "hot mess." I instantly knew this was the person Agnes spoke of that I was to help. I listened to her, I consoled her, and I spoke to her about changing her life for a more spiritual path. I do believe I have helped her in some way. We can show others the path of light, but it is up to them to walk it.

August 11th 2016: Mother Mary stepped forward in todays connection and told me to help the people of Santo Domingo and the Dominican Republic by praying for a better life for them. She said for me to go forth in my daily prayers. She then told me that the souls of The Whaley House have been delivered and it is now pure and cleansed of negativity. Thank you for your work, job well done. Violet Whaley then stepped forward to thank me for my help; she told me that I am blessed to do this work. Jim Robinson also came in and stood on my left side but was apprehensive about leaving. I told him that God would absolve him of his sins but he must first forgive himself. I also told him to go feel the joy and love on the other side because he deserves it. He then turned around and was gone, and I have never seen them since.

Then St. Therese stepped forward and we greeted each other. She said, "Hello Helene" and I said, "Hello Therese." She then brought forth Louis and Zelie Martin.

I told Therese that I don't feel a strong connection to them and I asked her if she could help me feel closer to them. For the next few minutes all I could see in my head was the color purple. Then Therese said the connection is there and the bond can never be broken.

I was then shown a vision of school children from a long time ago watching what looked like a guillotine swinging back and forth. I couldn't control my head also from turning back and forth and watching it swing. Then as my head turned to the right it stopped, and all I could see was red. This sort of thing has never happened to me before where I felt I couldn't control what I was doing. I felt as though I was really there watching whatever this event was, with no idea why I was shown it.

August 12th 2016: Archangel Gabriel came forward today and told me that the messages I receive are transference of energy through the space-time continuum. They move so quickly that there is no detection of the energy flow. Most people won't realize the interference of a message during their lifetime. We send many messages but only a small amount is received. It's like riding a bicycle; you will never forget how to receive these messages. Pope John Paul failed to receive our messages while Pope Francis is more attuned.

August 13th 2016: In my connection today my mother, father, brother, aunt, my mother's cousin and many more people that I didn't recognize stepped forward. There were several souls just standing there looking at me. I then heard someone say that my ancestors have stepped forward to let me know that they guided me through the toughest times of my life. They said to me, "We helped you through the rough patches." Then they all stepped back and I was about to say, "Where are you all going?" when suddenly Mother Mary appeared. She told me, "Your devotion my child is unbelievable. Follow your path and your soul will open like a light filled room on a bright sunny day. There will be so much light; it will overpower the darkness that tries to behold you. Find courage and strength in our love for you. Don't let those who want to drag you down, win. You are our savior for the frightened weak souls that need you. Don't go astray my child, for drugs will call your name once again but cast them aside and go forward on your journey. Most people won't see through the darkness of our times. Your ancestors are here to guide you. Pay attention to the signs as they appear in front of you." (As I was reading this message back to myself, several orbs appeared and floated over the page).

August 15th 2016: Today in my connection three angels all wearing blue appeared to me and they said that doves will lead me to a new understanding of being a light bearer. Follow them through the veils of the walls to reach your eternal destiny. Us angels will guide you on both sides so you make it safely to and from. This is part of your journey my dear, and each step is a step closer. The path is clearly marked for your entrance and exit. (Then I could hear the song "Just Like the White Winged Dove" by Stevie Nicks in my head). They then said the clearer the path, the brighter the future. (Then I could hear a song from Annie that said; Clear away the cobwebs and the sorrow till there's none). Then they said we love to use metaphors and songs, for that is how you better understand us. We are playful, joyful; we love to laugh and are filled with love. There is no greater joy than to help others and we wish for peace for all.

August 16th 2016: John the Baptist stepped forward today in my connection and said to me that falling through the cracks of eternity is something that will never happen to most of us. "Our obligation to the universe is of freewill, mind, body, and soul. The mastermind behind the veil of light or dark can be uncovered by just looking under the veil. Don't be scared to step forth and do what's right for the universe, for we are all connected throughout the entire universe and beyond. A small particle of the earth settles largely upon the cosmic wave. Other life does exist (he then showed me fairies and aliens) though not the way it is seen in the human mind. The human race is far behind in technology as the rest of the universe. Humans are closed-minded and cannot see what others can, and are light years behind. Cancer can be cured and the cure is right in front of you. Relax; take a moment to think of the simplicity of it all. Money hungry souls live in turmoil and darkness, and they cover those who have light with blankets of darkness. Those who stand strong must fight for the weak. Those who are in the darkness will suffer in their karmic balance. To all those in need of light and love, it is offered by God for the asking. You do not have to beg, just ask and it will be done. Have faith and believe in all that heaven offers."

August 17th 2016: Since I returned home from California, Tuesday I went to my first spiritual development class with Ron. It didn't feel right to me, like I didn't belong there anymore. Though I have respect and love for Ron O'Berry and the people in my class, I don't feel they are my spiritual tribe. I have been asking my angels and guiding spirits to please help me find my way and my tribe. I will try to continue to go to classes with Ron until I find my tribe and community because my soul aches for spirituality and the development of it.

Mother Mary stepped forward today and she told me that a new day is dawning. "The mentor you seek is abroad and there is a lot of shuffling around for the both of you to meet. You will go on a magical journey for your soul's progression. You have earned this journey of enlightenment and you will be filled with happiness from head to toe. Many white lighters will rush to your side to accompany you on this journey. You will bring great hope to the sick, the tired, and those souls who feel empty. Bigger and better things are coming down the road for you. Obstacles will be knocked down, doors will be kicked open, and hope will lead many to a new destiny. The world will feel new to those who open their hearts to God the Father. Light a candle and light the way for your predecessors and for those who are blind to the ways of the Lord."

August 18th 2016: I asked my guides Agnes and Margaret this morning to help me decide if I should continue classes with Ron. I then asked them to help me progress my gifts, spirituality, and my soul's progression. They said the highest level of the soul can be accomplished with great devotion and Mother Theresa accomplished this. Don't act like a weed in a garden of roses waiting to be pulled. Your courage and strength have gotten you to this point and you must forge forward. The divine essence of Jesus is in all of us. Don't allow negativity to drag you down. You asked for an answer my child and this is what we are offering. Keep doing your highest and best good and when the time is right, we will show you the path. They then said that sea salt is a healing property for many diseases. A token between worlds is as simple as saying, "I love you," and that every spiritual awakening is more important than the next one.

August 20th 2016: Today, an angel in white came forward in my communication. I asked him his name and he seemed hesitant to give me a name though he eventually did; he said call him Angelo. Angelo told me that spirituality is a form of God's being. "It is all that holds us together; it is like the glue of our being. Many tyrants have been set free from the will of their own being to bring about their own power. The willingness and powers combined are great assets. The conjunction of the willingness of those who walk through the door instead of those who keep walking into walls is admirable compared to the tunnel of enlightenment that you must pass through to be a whole being. The angels can guide you through the tunnels; all you have to do is ask. We help all those who are willing to do their highest and best good in all they do. For those who are ready for the tunnel of enlightenment we are waiting for you to break the seal and show us your true self."

August 20th 2016: In today's connection, Archangel Gabriel stepped forward to tell me that he has a message for me from God. Next, I heard someone say, "Your duties upon this earth are trivial compared to those in heaven." Next what I heard being said was, "You are an impersonator as a white lighter." I got very upset and couldn't understand why this was being said to me, so I then said, "No, you are the impersonator. Now get out of here and leave me alone for you are not in God's white light." I then heard, "Congratulations, job well done. Follow only those in God's white light. Your next steps require you to recognize the light in others for the ambiance of the night will bring forth many unknown entities. Protect yourself well, and do all you can to surround yourself in light. Dark souls will appear when the curtain is lifted. Remove yourself from the environment upon their entrance."

Gabriel then told me to say this prayer: "Holy Father, I, your beloved child, ask for forgiveness, absolution and enlightenment for the dark souls. May they be one with God and find their brothers and sisters."

He then said, "You must help all souls, good or bad, to become enlightened. Your prayers are a direct stream to God's consciousness. The light that burns within you is more powerful than the energy of the moonbeam. Truths will be revealed through the eyes of the beholder who roams this earth. Go forward in peace my child and do what is asked of you."

I had seen today that Radleigh Valentine, a spiritual intuitive who connects to the angels, was doing a Facebook live reading. You may also know Radleigh by the tarot cards he creates with Doreen Virtue. I hardly ever go on the live chats but today I was told by spirit to go on and check it out. Radleigh was answering questions that people posted by pulling tarot cards and connecting to guiding angels. I put up a question a couple of times asking if I should be doing more spiritually. Everyone's questions quickly went by, but he either never saw my question, or he just didn't choose it. I then intuitively changed my question to: am I going to find my beloved? I didn't hit the send button till the angels told me to. As soon as I hit the send button, I heard Radleigh say "Dawn, you want to know if you are going to find your beloved." I adore him so I was very excited to get a message from him. He pulled three cards for me and told me that I am definitely going to find my beloved. He told me if I am invited somewhere and I feel like I should go, then I am to go, because I can't find my beloved sitting home. He also said that the angels said that I have healed all my past relationships and it is time for me to have a love. This reading lifted me up even though earth time and heaven time are quite different. Working with the spiritual realm, I have learned to have patience.

August 22nd 2016: Archangel Haniel stepped forward in my communication today and told me the commitment of one's soul is devotion like no other. "Transcendent light will beam from the moon to give you power. Go under the full moon and ask the universe to instill the power within you to help you accomplish great feats. For the safety of the angelic realm upon earth, they are helping those who abide by the laws of the universe.

Animals are our protectors; our guides, and we must treat them with great respect and honor. Those who abuse animals are likely to fail themselves in their soul's purpose, and their karma goes unbalanced. Tears of joy are in the eyes of God when his children show love in any form."

August 23rd 2016: Today, I kept feeling someone touching me between my shoulder blades. I didn't mention this earlier in my loggings but someone has been touching me for a very long time between my shoulder blades and some days more than others. Actually, as I write this, I am being touched right now. I am bringing this up now because in class with Ron tonight, I received a reading from Sandy who is in my class. She said that the spirit who is always touching me between my shoulder blades was a twin of mine from another lifetime. Though she didn't come with me into this life she is always close to me. She said she believed her name is Athena or something similar to it and she is very shy and embarrassed that she didn't follow me in to this lifetime. Sandy also said that she saw a vision of us as little girls with dark hair being hugged by our mother while we were giggling. She believed we lived in Switzerland due to our clothing, and the mountains behind us. (I have learned that you never know what is going to come up in a reading).

August 24th 2016: Agnes told me today that the light of the divine is the mere essence of love. She went on to say that souls, who have created their own interpretation of God's will, are the souls that cannot see what is before them. The branches on the tree extend from family to family and are everlasting. The possibilities that are in the minds of some scientists are so overwhelming that they burn out before their purpose is accomplished. In your world Harry Potter is a fantasy but in our world is a reality. The human mind has trouble ingesting things on a spiritual level if they aren't able to communicate with the spirit realm."

August 25th 2016: John the Apostle came forward today and said to me that the Divine Protector would seek a mentor for my work, for you have asked and it shall be answered. "The coming of a Sabbath in the future will bring joyous news to your family. The energy ball of light will be passed from one generation to the next. A child will be born with magical gifts like no other. The world will be amazed at the depth and creativity of this child's gifts. Ocean water will prove to bring healing powers to the world.

The Knights of the Round Table are real and will rise again. Make the most out of this life because it determines your eternal fate and your soul's growth. Fill your soul with white light so you may light the way for others to see. The souls are dim of those who walk on a dark path. Be a leader, shine bright, and show the way for your brothers and sisters. Heavy hearts fill this earth with too much space. We will help you find a way to clear out the negative energy that pulls them down."

August 26th 2016: My guide Margaret stepped forth and told me that the bright light that shines upon the face of those who seek God will bask in the glow of eternal peace. "Brilliant minds have been torn from the earth due to unexpected tragedies at the hands of mankind. Our brothers and sisters who came before us walk upon the holy land. Joyous events are coming through Rosie Cepero. The moment between worlds when you and Rosie meet, there will appear an army of angels, and an unbreakable bond between your souls."

Today I finally started my social media Facebook page, Twitter and Instagram to get a following like the spirit realm has been telling me to do. I put a message from spirit each day on social media. I also choose tarot cards with the guidance of the angels and put them up on social media. I tell the people to choose a card for some daily guidance and then I post the meanings of those cards later in the day. I hope by doing these things I am helping people with this guidance. I am trying to move forward and do my highest and best each day. I also am getting some requests for readings though I am still learning but I do the best I can for each reading. I am learning, as I am also helping others by giving them messages from their loved one.

August 27th 2016: Mother Mary came forward in today's communication and told me that I shine brightly like a star in the dark sky. "You have opened up a new world in which you will reap fantastic results. Others will follow, so have patience my dear. You will see what will become of your life and the doors that have been opened for you. Kim Russo will notice you in the future. Your mentor abroad is waiting upon arrival of your heightened gifts. Work each day to help those around you and you will be rewarded with incredible love. The world needs and seeks white lighters like you to help protect the internal flame within all of us. Don't let those who hate disturb your path. Walk with your head high and show your faith to all that you meet. Your light is burning so brightly and we are very proud of all that you have accomplished. There is much more to come and you will be pleasantly surprised. Show the world the greatness that is in you, and that can be in all of them. Bless you my child."

August 28th 2016: Jesus came forward in today's communication; he said that a telltale sign of a broken soul is someone who has deviated off his or her path. "They must align their chakras to match their environment so that they can open up to those around them. The difference between souls upon their arrival on this earth depends upon their awakening, and midnight is a variable in this. The stars are aligned when the souls who are awakened have crossed paths. Most people will never recognize the truth about their destiny or the destiny of others. The reality of most awakenings depends on the actual soul. Each soul has control over all that is to be, but most souls will release their power to the universe.

"Troublemakers who reside on this earth doom themselves in all that they encounter. The ability to reset your soul is available upon request. The broken, chopped minds of addiction are working out a karmic balance. Some win, some lose, but all will be redeemed. Our paths get boggled with things of destruction. Strength, courage, hope and faith are all needed to clear that path. Many winding roads have led us all down the path of destruction. To turn around on this winding road has been all up to us. As long as you have hope and faith, you will prevail. Go forth my followers and I will meet you in the Land of the Holy."

August 29th 2016: Today my daughter called me and told me that one of her friends was sarcastically asking her. "Since when has your mother been a medium?" It upsets me that people are so closed mind and negative in this world. I know I will encounter much of this in my path and I will rise above it all because I have faith and I believe in every single thing I do. I asked the angels and my guides to help me ignore those who are doubters and haters. In my connection today I received this message from St. Therese. "Troublemakers will always be a way of the world. Take flight and be free, don't let those who underestimate you drag you down. Be solemn in your demure and don't let them ruffle your feathers. You bring light to dark corners, so much that even the blind can see: the blind of the heart and soul.

Many quests will be asked of you. Be open to them all and your life will follow the path that was meant for your soul's progression. You are on a higher learning journey upon this earth. The next step in your life is to listen and avoid the negativity. Be in your own zone so others don't affect your energy. The book of your life will be hailed as wondrous. We guide you, protect you, and love you every step of the way. Stay close to friends and family, but above all be happy. We only want the best for you dear."

August 30th 2016: Mother Theresa came forth today and told me that the light at the end of the tunnel could illuminate even the darkest of souls. "Education is vital to the world to save the environment. Like a train on the tracks we must go full force to end world hunger. The desperation in those who are suffering is beyond anything a human should feel. Love conquers all and should be included in every action that is set forth by mankind. We all hear the prayers of the devoted souls who weep for many reasons. We uplift all those souls but freewill puts a halt to their awakening and enlightenment. Please my brothers and sisters, go forth in faith, belief, and devotion without question so that you may be free of all that keeps you down."

August 31st 2016: Mary Magdalene stepped forward in my connection today and said that humanity is a word that kind souls use more often than others. "Steps must be taken to move forward so the next generation will accomplish more than they could ever realize. These children need support and love to go forth in leaps and bounds and do the work that measures the love of all humanity. Problems will arise in the future for these children so we must bond together to help them succeed. It will be a long haul but worth the sweat and tears. Angels will rejoice, a celebration will begin and the heavens will ring in happiness as the world is filled with peace. The spirit realm will dance and the Sacred Heart of Jesus will bleed no more. There will be more to accomplish but the base work will be laid. Halleluiah, Glory to God in the highest."

September 1st 2016: John the Baptist came forward in my communication today and said the way of the world can be obnoxious beyond repair. "But as long as there are souls who cooperate with the universal laws then hope will always win. Determination is the key to success in many endeavors. Go forth with pride and inspiration and you can do the heavens no wrong. The moment you awaken souls will be an interchangeable event between worlds.

Every country in this world has to abide by the laws of God to exist in peace. Together we can conquer world destruction and stamp out what no longer serves us. Every person has their faults; no one is perfect in their actions but together we can overcome the imperfections within us. Teamwork is God's work. The land of the living and the land of the Holy will unite to make one kingdom where everyone shall be set free." (Then he recited these words) "Thy kingdom come thy will be done on earth as it is in heaven."

September 2nd 2016: My guide Agnes stepped forth today and said; "Keep going forth on your path, we will lead the way. You are ready for the next step; so step back and behold the beauty of all that is to come your way. Some people may underestimate your abilities but you will shine upon request. Your life should be maintained throughout your entire journey. Many people risk their lives without ever knowing their purpose, or the contract that they signed upon their entrance in to this world. You are lucky if you have awakened before your time is up. Do your part and all that we ask of you to better the planet. Life on this planet is worth living if you follow the guidelines of your soul."

September 3rd 2016: St. Jude stepped forward today and he told me that the necessity of trials and tribulations in life are important to reach the destination of our souls' purpose. "Each person must come through the other side of all that is handed to them. The life expectancy of those suffering can be a lot longer than expected due to circumstances beyond our control, which is free will. Absolutely no one can cross the realm without permission from his or her guides. It doesn't mean to stop trying because determination makes all things possible. The best solution to world events is to stay neutral. Don't let politics bring you down for it isn't the end of the world. The best possible solution to end world hunger is to free your souls and remember there is one nation under God."

September 4th 2016: I have been doubting myself lately. I wish I had a mentor that I could turn to when these negative feelings and this thought processes happens. I can't help but wonder if I'm truly on the right path of my journey. I have been feeling very alone and stressed out about finances and my future. I speak to the angels, my loved ones on the other side and God and tell them exactly how I feel, and I know they are listening. Sometimes that is not enough, as opposed to having a person standing right in front of you that loves you and supports you. I am human and, like everyone else, I have my off days. Most people in my life can't identify with the fact that I communicate with the other side. When I start to talk about something that I feel was spiritually spectacular that happened that day, I get a lack of interest from people. I keep a lot to myself and this is part of the loneliness that I feel. I hope I find my spiritual family, mentor, and my beloved soon. I know that patience is a virtue and I will continue to go forth each day and do my highest and best good for myself and my brothers and sisters.

Mother Mary came forward in today's connection and said that financial support is a means to an end. "Don't stress, for your life has just begun a whole new journey. You, my dear, will find your niche. The way of the world revolves around your thought process so don't think negative, think positive. We are lifting you up my child. The cries of the crows' voices could be obsolete just like the cries of a human. Pondering your thoughts in the spirit realm is much like lighting a candle and making a wish. The objectivity of faith is built upon ideas like a staircase to heaven. The thoughts of the human mind cannot comprehend what is right in front of them. Reach out and touch the veil between worlds and feel the presence of those who found their way home. Many of our brothers and sisters stand right before you. Though you don't see them with the human eye, you can feel them with your heavenly soul. Take a step forth and try to find the meaning to their worldly presence. Whether you realize it or not, the veil between the two worlds can be torn upon request. Beware, for not all on the other side have been awakened and enlightened. Manifesting powers are here, so think power, think big, and think money and success." (I feel that Mother Mary gave me all this information because the manifesting full moon is very powerful right now. Believe in the power of the moon for it can really help you go forth in your life and empower you.)

September 5th 2016: Jesus stepped forth in today's connection and said that the hope and dignity of the world relies upon the courageous souls who choose to step forth in the name of God the Father. "The righteous souls can be freed from the bowels of the earth upon request from your brothers and sisters who are light workers. Help the needy; donate to those less fortunate to redeem your souls from being trapped in a world of neglect. The mighty sword may be sharper than the pen, but the outcome can be gruesome beyond our control. The Almighty God the Father is pleased with the recognizing of souls of the light workers. The light workers honor God by all that they do. Between the chaos from the lost souls, and the purity of light workers, it helps to even out the tragedies of the world. Your heart beats to a different drum so that those who follow you will see the light to become awakened. Don't fret my child; your purpose will be seen throughout the world. You are a saint in our book and don't let negative souls turn your face the other way. The light of the world burns upon your shoulders." (Suddenly I received this message from someone I could not see but only hear who I believe is God the Father). "Come to see me in faith through the eyes of Jesus Christ. You shall not want any more for I am your Father, all forgiving and full of love. My daughter Mary sacrificed her life to raise My Only Son upon faith and belief in me. The rewards in heaven will be great my child. You have earned my trust and confidence in all that you do. Keep going forth, for the path that you have created is magnificent. I am a proud Father who is joyous for the success of his daughter. Believe and trust in yourself and in the words I speak." I then said, "Bless me Father," then I heard, "You are blessed my child."

September 6th 2016: Archangel Gabriel came forward in my connection today and said that spiritual growth is required for the health of your soul. "Anyone that is at a standstill will suffer within himself or herself. They won't appreciate all the beauty and magnificence that the world has to offer. Frightened souls are like children who have never learned to live properly. The outcome of these souls is going to prove to be devastating to their entire being. Whatever lingers in the air will not dissipate but will be soaked in from the lonely souls who feel despair. Most ladies and gentlemen have arrived for the show too late to watch the King get crowned. The crown of thorns placed upon Jesus's head was a sign of human pain inflicted upon the holy by the souls who were blinded by their own fear and despair, and no one can truly understand God's sorrow. Every piece of information that we give you is to be put in the book, as there is a reason for it."

September 7th 2016: Catherine of Augustine came forward today and she said to me that the fortitude in the people upon earth makes for a more gracious flow of energy throughout the universe so that others can live in harmony. Miraculous, marvelous events will unfold at the altar of Jesus Christ our Savior. The Promised Land is beyond your wildest dreams. Beggars will come forth to beg for forgiveness for the wrong that they have done. They will be forgiven for all of God's children are worth saving. A predictable theme upon the earth would be a tragedy. Most tragedies could be prevented and are the fault of mankind. We must align our souls with the high frequency energy of the Universe so we can travel at the same wavelength that was meant for humans to be at their highest and best good. The future holds much more unfortunate tragedies for those in a low frequency level. We must lift up our brothers and sisters to go forth in a world of confusion and pain. Most days we can see how obsolete love is and it separates us from God and His word. We can come together and lift this burden from our shoulders and the shoulders of each other."

September 8th 2016: A beautiful angel came forth today shrouded in a pink light. I felt an immense love from this angel but I wasn't able to differentiate between male and female. I asked this angel his or her name and I was told I am the archangel called Chamuel. This is the message I received: the distance between two hearts knows no sorrow in the spirit realms. "The magic between souls is amazing beyond anything you could compare to on the earth plane. Jealousy and other negative emotions are not known in these realms; only joy and love and they bring exceeding happiness. The choices made at the time of our birth makes us surrender our will to the evolution of mankind. Most day's souls are open to suggestions brought forth on the wings of angels while other days they are closed to all that is sent forth from the other realms. Live each day gallantly like the next one and you will see and feel the rewards of positive living. We ourselves are our own worst enemy for the damage to our souls. You can all make a big difference in the lives of those you encounter on this planet if you open your hearts and have mercy on the souls of those who are less fortunate in many different ways. Bring forth the weak in mind, body and soul so that we can repair them and they may stand strong right before your very eyes."

September 9th 2016: Archangel Gabriel came forth in my connection today and he said that direct sun light upon your soul will lift you on the wings of angels to heaven. "Pour out your negative emotions so your soul may fill with light. The angelic realm welcomes those who choose to enter from the opposite direction.

Your soul will be cleansed upon entrance. Your willingness to separate from the dark is enough to make you pure. Don't hold onto any negative emotions for they will cause you distress and keep you off the track of your life's purpose. The Monarch butterfly will roam the earth, free to help stamp out disease within the follicles of auras."

September 10th 2016: I have been feeling lonely and sorry for myself today. Sometimes I feel I don't get enough respect or time back from the people close in my life that I give it to. In my communication today I was having a hard time connecting because of the way I was feeling. I did finally connect to my guide Agnes and she told me to facilitate the needs of those around you. "Your job is to bring happiness and peace to those who need it. Your friends will be grateful for the gifts that you share. Resolve the loneliness and anger within yourself to move ahead."

September 11th 2016: Archangel Michael came forward in my communication today and he told me not to shy away from conflict because it will make me stronger in the end. Then he went on to say that the brilliant light that shines upon the darkness as a whole would ultimately win the fight of light and dark. "Many people will assume the worst as they look back at the history of the world but they can't defend the moral compass by which it was run. Derogatory remarks will be made about Kings and Queens though they must run their course in history. The most obnoxious person alive will lead this battle. Ropes will be strung along the mainland to keep out the so-called enemy. The pope will get involved and try to break the pressure between the two opposing forces. It will lead us to a newfound land of never-ending tragedies. The weak get weaker and the strong get stronger and it will be like Armageddon."

September 12th 2016: Mother Theresa stepped forth in today's communication and told me to take the high road when it comes to all that concerns mankind. "The heavenly powers that connect the world to the Universe are beyond anything you could possibly imagine. It is all so simple as is the connection from soul to soul. There is no breakage in the connections, just bumps upon rocky roads. The connections are unbreakable and the forces within them are of pure love and light. Dreams that seem impossible are only impossible due to fear, and we can accomplish anything that can be imagined. Most budding stars shine so brightly in the sky as a way to be found. They shine so brightly to show their brothers and sisters that they have been awakened and enlightened. The trust worthiest person you can find is the one who twinkles at the mere essence of God. Trust yourself to go forth and be the soul who you and God have agreed upon. Miracles will happen to those who stand strong in their faith. This life happens to be an educational experience that can only bring us higher in our learning before we return home."

September 13th 2016: St. Jude stepped forth today and said the light of the world relies upon much more than meets the eye. "Hopefully souls will be awakened before the end of this era so they can become God's followers and future light workers. The magic of light that projects through the core of the tunnel is more powerful than a nuclear bomb. There is no surprise as to the number of souls who have passed due to circumstances of their own doing. The epidemic of drug use in your world has saddened everyone in the cosmos. Brilliant marketing research can obliterate the drug use. Drug companies are offended by the words of others but the blame is to be put on all of mankind. As a whole group you must stick together and save the next generation from this impending epidemic. Souls are leaving before their time and it is upsetting the karmic balance. You must fight from deep within your souls to win this battle. The battle of addiction is tough but your true selves are tougher. You all need to band together to lift this blanket of darkness from the world." (Then I suddenly heard the song, "Come Together" by The Beatles playing in my head. I love when the spirit world communicates a message through music).

September 14th 2016: In today's connection I saw what looked like an army of angels. I felt they were all banding together as one to bring me today's message and it was said with assertiveness, yet lovingly. They told me that boundaries must be set for your happiness and to go forth. "Protect yourself from the bad energy in the flow of the Universe. Take the time to assess the most important journeys in your life. We will help you to divulge the truth about your existence on this planet. The most effective way to reach others is through your heart and soul. Be protective of your family upon this journey. You will make the best decisions of your life soon. You will be filled with light, honor, and respect. Take pride in the work you do. The Mother Mary cards were a good choice and that is what is needed right now. (They are referring to the daily tarot card readings I do online in which I have chosen to use Mary Queen of Angel cards by Doreen Virtue this week) Stay strong in faith, have courage and hope for this too shall pass. Take the high road and don't let anyone bring you down. We need you in our army of soldiers to stand strong against the darkness. Our motto is to hear no evil, see no evil, and speak no evil. Stay pure and stand in the light so others may follow your way. Do your highest and best good and we will continue to lift you up, wipe your tears and give you love You are never alone and don't be afraid to ask for help. We will rush to your side to be of assistance."

September 15th 2016: Mother Mary came forth in my connection today. She told me to say this affirmation: "Cleanse my soul to fill this body with light and love." She said that if you say this on a daily basis, any soul would be cleansed and filled with light and love. "It is never too late for the sick suffering souls to be whole again. On your behalf let the heavens and spirit realm impede upon your soul for forgiveness and resolution. Trust and give of yourself to God the Father for He is our only Savior and there will be no other. The Divinity wrapped into one is all that is needed. There is slow progress for the souls who are not willing to fight for their own salvation. The path you seek will be revealed upon your entrance on this earth, though during your journey, small bits and pieces will be revealed along the way. Some souls will ignore the truth that is right in front of them, while others ravish just a thought of white light. Each person has their own free will, which determines their soul's growth and their journey upon this earth. Words of wisdom upon your journey are to open your heart and soul to all that is good. Turn your back against anyone or anything negative that tries to get in your way." (Then I heard the song playing in my head "Carry on my wayward son, there'll be peace when you are done").

September 16th 2016: Archangel Haniel came forth today and told me that the angel messages that I put out on social media today were wonderful. She said that I light the fire in the hearts of those who were burning dimly. "Many rewards are ahead for you, my friend. Don't let people needlessly take advantage of you. Help people who you can offer words of encouragement and hope to. Your path is lit with love and kindness, which will bring you to a higher soul level my dear. Cherish your children for they stand by your side with great enlightenment and words of wisdom. Your track record shows us the empathy you have placed upon the hearts of others. Your love for mankind goes exceedingly beyond the outer limits of your soul's purpose. We are proud to call you an angel guider in the spirit realm. You guide souls to the angels so that we may lift them up. The future ahead holds much love and joy, coupled with strenuous spiritual work. Take things as they come and don't overwhelm yourself. Go forth in love and light my child for we are at your side."

September 17th 2016: St. Francis of Assisi stepped forth today and said that those in his world can offer help and hope to those in need through the universal portal. "It shines brightly from the hearts and souls of those who have faith in God the Father. Be diligent in your offerings of hope to those who need it. The beauty and magnificence of the mountaintop of Mt. Everest holds many secrets to everlasting life upon this planet. Those who seek its beauty and magnificence shall take on a whole new meaning of life. The souls that have conquered Mt. Everest and all that it offers will be freed from the pain, turmoil and suffering of there own inner demons. If we acknowledge the imperfections within us, then we can move on towards absolution, resolution and forgiveness. Take the hand of the Almighty as He leads you down the path of eternal peace. Make the most out of this lifetime and treat your brothers and sisters with dignity and respect."

September 18th 2016: My guide Margaret stepped forward today and told me that the heavens are open to all who step forth towards the light. "A miracle of sorts is about to unfold for you. Don't hold on to the negative people as we lift you higher. You must go forth-full force in order to achieve your soul's purpose." Then she said, "We asked you if you were ready and you answered yes. Keep doing what you're doing for people, and in the end, they will see what we see."

"World events will be recognized as a sign of the times changing for the better. Politics will play a huge role in the changing of the times. There will be obedient followers who will obey their every move. The most gentile people will become vicious in this circle due to circumstances out of their control.

There will be a wasteland of medical supply that will affect the air quality in a certain area causing illness and ultimately disaster to many. The government will hide facts and details about the on goings of this disaster in order to control the rest of the population. There will be rebels who go against the government and spark a revolution. The entirety of this will be due to the carelessness of mankind. Peace on earth and goodwill towards all men." (It wasn't made clear to me what country or government this would be).

September 19th 2016: John the Baptist stepped forward today and told me that the most progressive souls in the world are the souls that show their empathy to others during their trial, tribulations and tragedies. "The weak of mind, body and soul will not progress to the light until their debtors and they are forgiven. They told me to help raise the frequency and vibration so others may hear, feel and see the angels who are closely connected to them. An arbitrary sign of the times means nothing as compared to the signs from heaven. Follow those who have light in their hearts and you will see the truth unfold before you. The parliament has the power to veto what is known as judgment day in the spirit realm. Judgment can only exist in the minds of those who are trapped in a swirling vortex of negativity. When the crows caw, those in darkness listen for it is their call to power. We must align ourselves with the universal laws so we may bring justice to the deserving souls who walk a thin line. The most prominent of people can go haywire when the power of the moon is at its strongest. The most recent events in the news of terrorism have been brought upon us like a plague throughout the Muslim people.

It has spread like wild fire amongst them for the destruction of America. There are many white souls in the darkness of their hatred for mankind. We are making a plea for everyone to pray and stop the hatred to save the innocent souls." (I intuitively know that they are speaking of the explosions on September 17th in New Jersey and New York). The future relies upon how everyone can come together. (In my head they started playing the Beatles song "Come Together").

FOURTEEN

Heavenly and Earthly Mentors

September 20th 2016: Jesus stepped forth today and told me that at one time all of creation was divided amongst the pure souls until light turned to dark, then the power had to be switched. "The evolution of these souls was more than likely due to karmic balances. The hope and dignity of these souls hung in the balance. The propaganda of their lives became anew when it was officially time for judgment. People ran amuck in this new world, which led to destruction. Hope and dignity was the official motto of their true selves. The light at the end of the tunnel is deep and wide to absorb every ounce of cellular activity within souls. It is meant to cleanse and purify before entering the first level of our dimension."

Tonight, I attended a class at The First Spiritualist Church of Onset with renowned international medium Gail Moffat from the UK. This class was supposed to be on Deep meditation. I was the only person who showed up for this class. My friend Heidi was supposed to attend with me but ended up having emergency gall bladder surgery. Gail said that the spirit realm was telling her that they had set it up for me to be the only one who attended. She said the spirit realm also told her to give me a private class on mediumship. I gladly accepted this class because I kept asking the spirit realm to please help me be a better medium. Sometimes in my mediumship I would have spirit step forward but I wasn't always able to get the message they were trying to tell me. Gail told me it was because I was a dipper that I didn't know how to hold my energy up and it would just dip. She taught me how to sit in the power and hold my energy up. I truly believe this was the miraculous event that Margaret was speaking of that was about to unfold. It might have been a small miracle but it was a miracle nonetheless. Heidi jokingly said you mean they made me have my gall bladder out so you could have a private class. Really, it wasn't that they made Heidi have her gall bladder out, but they knew she was going to have it out and set up the timing of it all perfectly. I don't know why others did not show up that night for the class but I'm assuming that their gallbladders are all intact. I do know that I am truly grateful that the spirit realm has my back, and that they are always helping me take a step forth on my path every day.

Gail is the mentor abroad that the angels told me about in the message I received from August 17th 2016, and in this message, they said there would be a lot of shuffling around for us to meet. As these messages and experiences go on you will see how Gail does become my friend and mentor.

September 21st 2016: Today I gave two separate readings over the phone that was long distance. These were the best readings I have ever given to anyone. The details that came through from the spirit realm were incredible. The comfort and help that I gave these ladies made me see just how important my work is.

In my connection tonight a guide of mine stepped forward. I asked him his name and he said it was Joseph. I told him he looked like a King because he was wearing a long king-like robe, a crown, and he was holding a scepter. He said to me, "I am King of the angels." He wanted to show himself to me and let me know he was there. I then realized this was the mentor that John the Baptist spoke of in my communication to spirit on July 6th 2016. He said the mentor is considered royalty in the world of spirit.

Joseph then told me that no one particular soul can come forth to claim the throne for it is for all of God's children. He said they sit like children at the feet of their heavenly father. He went on to say that the love that we feel for each other on earth is similar to the love our God feels for us though his love is an unbreakable bond that goes on for eternity. "We must follow through the doorway to reach the steps to heaven. Every step you climb is a step closer to eternal bliss and reformation. The Holy Land will reunite you with your ultimate hopes, dreams and ambitions. There is no room for negativity in the spirit realm. Most days seem inappropriate to those who cannot conquer the quest they have been given. It is like a jungle fever that runs rampant through hearts and souls with the most inadvertent outcomes."

September 22nd 2016: Today I received a one-hour private reading from two internationally known mediums from the UK, Alan Acton and Gail Moffat. I learned a lot in this reading and so I will share some of it with you. It also confirmed some things those in the spirit realm had told me previously.

My maternal grandmother was the first one to step forward. The first thing she said was she didn't like my father or the life my mother had lived with him. She wanted to explain to me that she didn't like my mother having a child out of wedlock and that there was a sense of respectability back in the day. She said it just wasn't how we did things back then. Then she said she regret the day she ever wanted my mother to marry my father. She said he caused my mother a lot of pain and grief to the point where her life was unbearable and she felt she couldn't go on any longer. My grandmother is furious that my mother had to live that sort of life. I believe my grandmother stepped forward to tell me this because of what I had written in this book about her telling my mother you made your bed, now lie in it. She wanted to explain the reasoning to me and since she has, I have now let go of any resentment I had towards her with this situation. I now understand the situation more clearly and realize she really didn't want this life for my mother, and it was considered a huge embarrassment that came with those times. My grandmother also told me that I was very good at turning my life around when the situation arose in my life with drinking and drugging, and how I walked away and that she is very proud of me.

My brother David stepped forward next and told Gail that he has been on a higher learning journey. Which confirms the vision I was shown and everything that I was told about David on his higher learning journey from the angelic realm. Gail said David now helps those who come over to the spirit realm that have passed from suicide and he now works with the angelic realm. He has had a lot of learning to do and he had to understand the healing in the angelic realm in order to do the job properly. She said the earth plane wasn't the right place for David and he could never achieve happiness here and that my father had destroyed him. My mother and all my family in the spirit realm said they are very proud of David and all he has accomplished, and he has done exceptionally well since he has been in the spirit realm. Gail said she believes there are two forms of suicide; one that is meant to be and the other one is opting out. David's was meant to be; it had been decided that David was going to do this kind of work before he came to the earth realm. He needed to live this type of life before he could understand it, so he had to walk in those shoes in order to help others. He had to come to the earth plane and endure the suffering to reduce him to suicide in order to do the work and help suicide victims who cross and give them that healing. She said he was given one of the most difficult challenging lives that you could possibly have because even as an adult he had enormous challenges. Even when my father passed to the spirit realm, David's challenges didn't stop and they also didn't stop when he left home, it just continued on for him. It was one challenge after another for David. David was also apologizing to me for causing me pain over his death. He felt guilty because of the trauma that we suffered as children and he didn't want to give me any more traumas so he was sorry for that. Alan then told me that David asked me to listen to the song, "What Becomes of the Broken Hearted." David said this song has a lot of meaning in it and it would help me understand how he felt upon this earth and it would help me to move on.

The angelic realm told Gail that they have given me insights into their world on a deeper level and I've been able to put these insights into print. They said this is very important because they want to get these words out there to the world. They also said in the process of my book that it has been important for me to meet Gail. They said further down the line Gail and I will be more involved with our work and we will work together on some level. They kept repeating how important it was for Gail and I to meet. They also said Gail and I will be very instrumental in advising the world that there is a better way to think and a better way to be in our world. They said I will be doing humanitarian work and they called me an Ambassador of the carry on with the work of Mother Theresa.

Next Gail said she sees me spending 75% of my time in California and that it will be good for me. She said I have a healing energy around me from the angels and I will be very healing for my daughter who needs it. She also said I will meet people in California who will be instrumental in taking me to the next level. The spirit realm said Sarah needs healing and I am to ask the angelic realm to heal her. They said I would come in contact with some hands-on healers in California. They also said the West Coast is going to be important, and I would be spending increasingly more time there. The more I meet new people it will excite me to move there and it is quite important for me to be able to freely move around the world.

My father then stepped forward and kept asking for my forgiveness. He said, "I am sorry for what I did to you and your brothers and sisters." I told him I do forgive him but they said he is in a space where he is torturing himself for the pain he has caused so many people. He is in a space of contemplation about his life. My father's mother then stepped forward to tell me that my father had a very problematic upbringing where he was beaten quite regularly. She then said that our family has reconciled a lot of differences among them, and that our family is on a different basis now. Gail said my father is struggling to forgive his mother for dying when he was four years old. He told his mother if you hadn't have died then I wouldn't have had to go through all that I did. Gail said my father is a selfish brat that is blaming his mother for his troubled life. Gail also said my father will come through a lot of his misdemeanors in the spirit realm. That by the time I pass into the spirit realm, there will be a great reconciliation, and he will be able to prove to me he is the father he should have been. There is much important work being done with my father right now so he will be ready when loved ones come over. They also said that David has had a meeting and a conversation with my father though they are living separate lives.

Gail then told me that one of my guides Joseph has a very important role to play in my life with his work. Joseph is with me to connect me to the angels, but on a more angelic realm. Joseph is also to bring me to a more humanitarian way of thinking. Gail said they told her that over the next four to five years, I will be looking at more charitable adventures and thinking of others. They said a lot of work needs to be done in our world and it is an important journey I am embarking upon. They also said they have chosen me because everything about me is just perfect for the job. They went on to say that I have had so much thrown at me in life and I have so much experience in life that I will be able to empathize and understand every single person out there.

Gail said my family was standing there waving and saying how much they loved me. My father said he promises by the time I go over to the spirit realm he will be the reformed character that I need. Gail said my father is a wounded man as a result of his upbringing. The alcohol was a sickness that he needed as a crutch in order to cover up his enormous pain. My father said if he could do it all over again, he would be the same because that was the person he was then.

I am not sharing this information with everyone for entertainment purposes. I am purging my soul to tell you of my experiences. Thanks to my gift I have the added communication and help from the other realms. The other realms and I come together to show you it matters how we treat people, it matters how we talk to others whether cruel or kind. Karma is 100% real, you do not leave it behind; it follows you into the next realm. All of your deeds, all of your kindness, all of your actions of the people you have loved or hurt…it matters. Our bodies may die, but our souls go on for all of eternity. There is no way out of any negative actions you have done in your life on earth. The kindnesses you have shown to others will also follow you into the next realm. We can either get stuck in the darkness or open ourselves up to all that is around us. None of us are alone; the Lord, the angels, our guides, and loved one on the other side are always with us. They sit patiently by waiting for a chance to help us; all we have to do is ask. No one has to go through this life alone. One of the biggest responsibilities I feel in writing this book is to let everyone know we all have a responsibility to ourselves and each other to put positive energy, love, joy, and kindness out to the world. I realize we can't always stay at a high loving perfect energy because that can be exhausting. Sometimes what is around us is heartbreaking and at times can be soul crushing. We can try our best and start by being kind and loving to ourselves and to those around us. Remember, we are never alone; they are always with us; all we have to do is open our hearts. Not only do we fight on the outside, many souls also fight on the inside; we can win the fight. Have faith; believe in yourselves and God the Father, and the beautiful angels around us. I have learned from my connections to spirit just how loving and caring the other realms are, and how they all want to help us but we must ask for it, and be willing to help ourselves.

Mother Mary came forward in my communication today and said to me: you have a clearer channel now, my dear. "Priorities in this world are thrown to the side like trash in a barrel. The most important things to the people of this world should be each other. Instead of helping each other you all try to climb over each other like they are hills, but instead they are bridges that bring our souls together. Joy and peace should be found within our inner selves. The hierarchies of people in your world come through channels of disillusionment. Your chosen leaders that are in place in this hierarchy will not serve a quality purpose to this world. You should all take a moral high ground to take care of your brothers and sisters to show God your love and appreciation of each other. Though it will never be too late, you will not have reached your soul's growth or your soul's purpose. Then there will be a need to rewind your life as you go in circles. This Pope is kind, gentle and loving. Follow him on your journey and you won't go wrong. The abstract feelings of tomorrow will bring a renewed purpose to your life for all of eternity. We send you love and light our brothers and sisters. Go forth in your day and bring happiness to another's heart by just a smile."

September 23rd 2016: Last night my brother David came to me in my dream. I was incredibly happy to see him and I was hugging him as tight as I could. He said to me, "I have to go now; they are calling me." I said, "David, please don't leave me." He said, "it is okay, we will be together again when you go through the vortex." I can't tell you the happiness and peace of mind it brought me for David to visit me.

In my communication today 3 beautiful angels appeared to me. They were wearing white but there was a haze of pink around them. The first thing they said was the most appropriate moments come when the timing between two worlds is open upon request by the Almighty. (I feel they told me this because David was allowed to come visit me from the angelic realm last night.) Next, they said the joy experienced in a newfound land would bring hope to the hearts and minds of all who enter this three-dimensional world. "The monastery relies on lost hope and faith to keep people on their knees. I was then told to tell the world how incredible each and every soul is, and their purpose on this earth is worthwhile. Every soul, every cell is intertwined in a unique way. The bigger picture of everyone's life will be revealed to each individual as is deemed necessary whether it be upon this earth or in another realm. Each moment of each day causes a ripple effect throughout the Universe. Don't take your lives for granted for it causes harm to the greater good."

Also, today I listened to the song that David had told the medium Alan Acton to have me listen to, "What Becomes of the Brokenhearted." As I listened to the song, I felt David beside me. I also felt the incredible sadness, hopelessness, and distraught feeling that David felt while he was on earth. David came to me during the song and had me feel what he felt every single day of his life on this earth. I cried uncontrollably for what I was feeling, and I cried knowing that David had to live this life with this feeling of complete and utter despair. I now truly understand why he had to leave, and now I don't blame him at all. I can't begin to make you understand the horrific feelings that he felt on a daily basis. I will never forget what I felt as I listened to that song. I'm so happy my brother is home where he should be and doing wonderful work in the angelic realm. My heart and soul are at peace for him. My heart breaks for those in this world who experience utter despair and hopelessness. We must all band together to help those who suffer instead of shoving them aside like they don't matter. For every soul does matters. The hatred, prejudice and not understanding what others are going through must end. We must be kind and loving to each other regardless of race, skin color or beliefs. We all have the same color soul and it is full of God's white light; if we would just trust and open up our hearts to all, then peace on earth would be very attainable.

September 24th 2016: Today I attended a class up in Onset, MA at The First Spiritualist Church. This was a six-hour class taught by Gail Moffat on developing mediumship. The first part of the class we had to give each other a reading. Me, and another member of the church named Beverly were to give each other readings. When Beverly gave me a reading, she said my paternal grandfather had stepped forward. He came to apologize to me for not being in my life or being there for me at all. This was the first time in any reading I ever had that he came forward to apologize to me. Once again this proves to me how my family is stepping forward to apologize and set things straight with me since I have been writing about them and their wrong doings in my book. They all see what I am writing, and after I write it, they step forward to either apologize or explain to me the situation or circumstances that led to their actions. I feel this was part of my grandfather's cleansing as well. Do you all see how much our families are still part of our lives after they cross to the spirit realm? They never leave, they will always be a part of us no matter what. They don't miss us because they can visit us at any time, but we miss them because we are no longer able to interact with their physical bodies. If you just sit quietly in your mind, try to feel them and speak to them in your thoughts, and trust me, eventually you will feel them or even hear them. When you feel someone touch your cheek or your head, or whisper in your ear, that is your loved one. Have faith, trust, and believe, because one day it will be you in the spirit realm trying to let your loved ones notice that you are right beside them.

Mary Magdalene came forth in today's communication and said that the magnificence of this world is the common denominator between realms. "Both worlds are magnificent in their own rights. The choices we make in our lives makes the difference whether you see beauty or feel pain. The opportunities that are presented before us are of vital importance to the overall health of our souls. The best way to enlighten others is to show them their purpose on this earth so that they can flourish. The objectivity that our angels and guides help us to stumble upon is so we may see our paths clearly. It is important that we don't look through rose-colored glasses at each other or ourselves. We must see our true selves in order to go forward with every minute task. Be true to yourselves and don't let those in power change your thoughts or ideas and stand on a high moral ground.

September 25th 2016: My guide Agnes came forth today and said that the most affluent people in this world should lead by example. If their example is not of sound character and mind, then the process of the flow of the Universe is harmed. She said everything I know about the spirit realm is because I am of sound character. "We trust in the ones who are chosen to spread the word of God and to enlighten and awaken as many souls as possible upon this earth. Every soul that is awakened and enlightened will go forth with peace in their souls to spread it to their brothers and sisters."

September 26th 2016: My guide Joseph came forth today and he said that the swirling vortex of light that connects the two worlds is a simple construct of light and energy particles. "When you pass through this vortex you will become whole again at a rapid speed of light. Time does heal all wounds, and in the end, it heals all of time. All of creation can be linked to incarnations. If you would be willing to sacrifice yourself for your brothers and sisters, then the lesson has been taught and your life would be worth living."

September 27th 2016: A man came forth today that I had never seen before. He had light brown shoulder length hair and I could tell from his clothing he was from the biblical days. I asked him who he was and he answered, I am Matthew, apostle of the Lord. He began by telling me there is a constant coordination of the earth realm, particularly on comprehending all that is done to keep this world going forward instead of backwards. "The increase or decrease in economic rate depends upon the soul's commitment to the upcoming of the world's main purpose, which are goodness, kindness and love for all of mankind. Many souls have lost their way upon the journey of economic growth, and this shall be of great importance to find your soul's purpose in this world. March on like soldiers of God the Father, and go forth in your lives. Each day, try to seek your purpose, and uncover the hidden truths that lie before you. The spiritual realm is always at your beck and call; all you have to do is ask. We also are the children of God, and are here to help our brothers and sisters. Try to look within yourself, and don't get stuck in the atrocities of your world. If you step outside yourself and take a look around, you will see all that needs to be seen, and feel the essence of all that is good."

September 28th 2016: In today's connection my guide Agnes told me that this message was for Gail Moffat and me. The first thing she said was that transportation and communication between worlds is as easy as blinking your eyes. "The traveling of souls from one dimension to the next can be taught from experienced white lighters who have had glimpses into other worlds. Don't be afraid to take the first step into another world to experience nonjudgmental beings that are filled with pure light and love. You will be shown a time to step forth upon this journey and you must enter with an open heart, mind and soul. Be aware of the setbacks that could arise on this journey due to broken souls. Go forth with your utmost highest character with pride and honor to enlighten your brothers and sisters. This message is for a future endeavor that you will both embark upon. You are blessed my children and protected from the energy of the angels."

September 29th 2016: Archangel Chamuel came forth in today's connection and said that the conjoining of two souls and hearts feels to them like the sunshine that makes sunflowers grow tall and strong. "The beating of these two hearts contain white light and energy to fill the voids in the Universe. The King and Queen of Egypt were two souls that ignited a fire and shone a ray of light upon their people and out into the solar system. Never underestimate the strength of pure true love. Love can rule the world and bring peace throughout all the lands. As a lamb is a symbol of purity and love, so are good intentions thrown out to the world. Every ounce of integrity within our souls can bring forth the ultimate warrior of God the Father, for peace on earth for all men. The next full moon will bring great rewards to those who believe. Stay close to the Archangels for their protection is everlasting."

September 30th 2016: St. Jude came forth in today's communication and said the inevitable darkness that surrounds those who stray from the path can hinder the souls of those they come in contact with. "The prohibition brought about much pain and suffering that was needless and unwarranted. People reacted without thinking about the future consequences. These consequences have trickled into today's world. It was the start of the war against drugs or chemicals ingested without proper use. The guilt lies on everyone's shoulders in all of history and all the way down until today. We must be united in a stance against anything that alters our mental status. We must cleanse our hearts, minds and souls to walk forth on the path of God the Father. Free will is something that will hold mankind back for all eternity. The right choices aren't always the easiest ones though our struggles will make us stronger. When you come across a dark soul, don't judge them, just love them from afar, and the peace that will reside in you will bring you comfort in your time of sorrow. Do unto others, as you would have them do unto you."

October 1st 2016: Because Gail Moffat was still in the US, and doing another six-hour mediumship class in my town I decided to attend it. My friend, Heidi attended with me and we met a few other women who also attended. Heidi and I connected with these women, Tiffany and Robin, who lived in our area. Robin told me about a Spiritualist Church in East Providence, R.I., and about a medium named Gladys Ellen who connects to the angels like I do. This has really excited me because it is hard to find anyone who lives nearby that connects to the angels. Robin and I will be attending the service in East Providence on November 20th and then attending Gladys's workshop with the angels right after. I will let you all know how that goes. Those in the other realm are amazing because they are always putting wonderful people in my path to help me along this journey. It was all meant to be to meet Gail and go to her classes and meet other like-minded souls. It all lines up and the other realms surely know what they are doing. I didn't do any connecting today because I was exhausted after class, after using a lot of my energy.

October 2nd 2016: I have been feeling down for the past week and not having any confidence in myself. Then last night a few spiritual people who I looked up to snubbed me and it really hurt my feelings. Today my guide Agnes told me that the tigress could no longer rule without the strength, courage and support of her cub. Mother Mary is the tigress and you are her cub. "The strength and courage you seek is dwelling within yourself. Don't let other's actions bring you down. You have the power within yourself to lift your spirit to the highest mountain. We may bring forth those to you who will help you on your journey, and sometimes they are just meant to pass through your life at that time. Others' actions do not define the quality of your soul; it defines the quality of their soul. Go forth with our blessing, you are not alone for we are here at your side. The amazement of this world and all that you do in it will set you free."

October 3rd 2016: My guide Joseph stepped forth and he told me that the compromising in this world to accommodate selfish souls is abominable. "The needless, careless treatment of lost souls is cruel, and there will be a high price paid during the recycling of the karmic balance. We must all band together to comfort and love the suffering souls. Our free will is abused on the earth realm and not looked upon lightly by the other realms. Trust in yourself and the God deep within you to make the right decisions upon this earth to help the spiritual balance go forward. Seek the truth within yourselves to place yourself on the path of mercy and love for your brothers and sisters. Make the most important decisions in this life with love in your heart and we won't steer you wrong. We will guide those who have the best of intentions and we will help you succeed at every God-filled thought or action. It's as simple as just ask and you shall receive. We must all better this planet for the future of mankind and we start by bettering ourselves. The highest moral value you can learn is when you are called upon, step forth with courage and strength. Be good to others and freely share what is needed to those around you."

October 4th 2016: My guide Agnes came forth today and said that the confusion in this world is due to preposterous amounts of negative energy; its main purpose is to turn those from light into dark. The energy that seeps within our souls determines the outcome of our future lives. Many unpleasant people will pass through the tunnel of light upon their return into a world of havoc. You must follow God and all that He represents in order to create a sacred space within your soul. This space will keep you safe from others actions so you may turn inward to protect yourself. The highest mountain in the Universe is the mountain that you can stand upon and be free to love, honor and respect yourself and those around you. Show your true self to others and you will find that acceptance was always there.

October 5th 2016: Mother Mary stepped forth and told me that the compromising of souls on this earth is a disgrace to the spirit realm. "Those who wonder if they shall be forgiven shall not pass through the open doors of light until they have forgiven themselves. Each and every one of you is responsible for your own purpose and morals while you are on this earth. We accommodate the souls that suffer needlessly at the hands of others. Forgiveness is the key to eternal bliss. You all ask, "Why must we suffer tragedies?" and the answer is simple. Every ounce of tragedy comes from each other and yourselves. We do not bring tragedy to the world; it is encompassed in your lives by everyone's actions. Do not blame the Lord for tragedies that were brought upon you all by yourselves. Free will trickles down and affects everyone. Even the tragedies that are caused by Mother Nature for all of the negativity that fills the earth. Peace on earth for all of mankind is the only way to reverse the effects of all that is wrong and to save each other and yourselves."

October 6th 2016: Archangel Raphael came forth in today's communication and said not to be afraid to step forth on your journey when the road is rocky; for the path might not always be clear, but the intentions are. "Wise decisions are based upon the purity of your soul. Good intentions are first and foremost the ultimate weapon in the war of darkness with the help of the angels. All you have to do is ask and you will receive our help. We will help guide you to the tunnel of light so you may join your brothers and sisters in everlasting peace. Your journey upon this earth is none too great that you're not able to stop and lend a helping hand to those in need. Empathy is part of the fabric of your soul when you enter this earth, but when it drops off, for some, that is where the connection to God is broken. All can be healed and repaired with willingness, desire and good intentions."

October 7th 2016: An angel in all white came forth in my connection today. He or she would not give me a name for this angel said my name does not matter. I got a very neutral feeling from this angelic being and this was the message I received: the light from the candle that lights the world comes from within each of us. "We show each other a way to a better life and to be better souls. We are each other's salvation upon earth. We must rely upon the goodness of our brothers and sisters in this world. False hope is something that we give to each other. Our inner strength and the beauty within will lead us to a new world. This world will ignite the flame of love and bring peace to the entire nation. This is not just a wish but also a dream come true if we all band together as was meant to be. The separation of colors and races go far beyond the truths that are hidden deep within our souls. Release the beasts to free yourselves from incarnation."(I was then shown a vision of balls of pure white light floating and I instantly knew these were souls that were free. The feeling I received with this vision was sheer bliss, with great peace and love).

October 9th 2016: Mother Mary came forth today and told me that the plight of human kind is more of a burden to those who stand strong in their convictions against the souls that encompass the darkness. "White doves fly freely to bring peace to the hearts of those who need it. We have sent out many signs and symbols for the world to embrace, but those who truly need it mostly ignore them.

Those who fight the darkness within them torture themselves and this is not needed. If those people would truly open their souls and hearts to God and our realm, then we could purify their souls so they may feel peace. You have to fully trust, let go, and let God. The unwanted and needless suffering that goes on upon earth is far beyond anything that God wants for his children or any part of this Universe. Just taking care of yourselves and not throwing rocks at your brothers and sisters would turn your world forth for the better."

October 10th 2016: John the Baptist came forward in today's communication and said that the projection of love and light that comes through the Universe is more powerful than the atomic bomb. "Love and light always win over anything negative. The best possible outcome in this world for all involved is a hands-on approach from every soul willing to commit to our Heavenly Father. The more spiritual muscle that is put into the world will create peace and love like you have never known upon this earth. We must band together like soldiers of God to fight for a new world. Everyone's hopes and desires should not include selfishness but the desire to help others so we may all succeed upon this journey that is called life on earth. Before each of us left the spirit realm for the earth realm we were all taught what our journey entailed and the lessons we were to learn. But the longer our bodies inhabit the earth our free will takes over and we no longer follow our soul's purpose and we become lost on our journey. Some souls find their way back and some souls don't. Those who don't find their way back will have to repeat these lessons again until they can find the strength within them and overcome anything that is self-serving. These messages that we give you are meant to help you all go forth and find your way. Also, this is to let you know that we are right here to help you; all you have to do is ask."

October 11th 2016: My guide Agnes told me today to follow your heart's desire to the path of happiness. "Make the most out of each day, each moment and each action, for the world is your oyster. We do not judge you upon your false hopes and dreams, but upon the way you live your life on a daily basis, and the kindness you show others. Though this in itself is self-judgment, for you are free to choose your own path. We might stir you on your path when you have disregarded or blatantly stepped off, but it is ultimately up to you. You hold the reigns to your final destination."

October 12th 2016: Mother Theresa stepped forth in my connection today and told me to focus on the energy of a spiritual awakening and that to find a soul's purpose is amazingly beautiful. "There is no problem that can't be solved when your heart is open to accept all that is good. The majority of souls will lean towards the negativity of a situation instead of trusting themselves for a positive outcome. We must look beyond what holds us back in this world to rise to a new level of acceptance, love, joy and a whole new way of thinking. You must all believe in yourselves and forgive yourselves for any misfortunes that have arisen in this life. Don't look back; look forward to a new way of life, a new way of thinking and being. Be the souls you were meant to be for it would mean peace on earth for all of your brothers and sisters for all of eternity. Follow those who we send you and you will be set free."

October 13th 2016: St. Therese came forth in today's communication and said that the energetic forces that lie beneath the soil of the earth constitute the true energy flow of the Universe. "The magnetic pull of this planet is much stronger than the atomic waves of energy that are flowing throughout the solar system. Dandelions have magical qualities that are prevalent on the earth. It is pure and simple when compared to others in the solar system. Use this knowledge wisely and help save this planet. The more mechanical things we throw at you will only cause confusion. Don't stray away from the type of lineage that connects you to each other. We must band together in order to bring peace throughout the nation. My fellow brothers and sisters take this world by the reigns and take control of all that passes in front of you. Some days will be better than others, but it is today that counts. The most human experience you can feel are the good deeds you will incur on your paths"

October 14th 2016: Matthew came home today with a bag of medical marijuana, given to him by a customer who he did some electrical work for. He didn't know what to do with it but we both agreed how absolutely wonderful it smelled. I kept going back to smell it because the smell was so enticing. I asked Matthew if he could give me some of it for my brother, Philip who smokes it because it helps him with pain. Matthew agreed to give me some for Philip and he gave the rest away to a friend of his. I had to double bag it and store it in a Tupperware container because the odor was so strong that the smell still filled my apartment. I kept it in my apartment two weeks before I gave it to Philip. During these two weeks I played around with the idea of taking a couple of hits of it. I told myself after all it is supposed to be good for you. I was literally torturing myself with it in my house and I was also having dreams of smoking it. But in all reality, I knew with my addictive personality that it was not a good idea. After two weeks of torturing myself I finally took it to Philip. Though during those two weeks I had in the back of my mind a message I was given that had something to do with drugs. I finally looked back on the message, and it was from August 13, two months prior to this event. The message was from Mother Mary and she told me: "Drugs will call your name, cast them aside and go forward on your journey." There is always a reason for the messages that I receive and the heavens will always continue to amaze me.

My guide Joseph told me today that the magnificence and beauty of this earth plus the freedom that is given to every soul should be enough for true happiness. "Depending upon how we use our free will it can either destroy us on our path or raise us up to a new level. The choice is yours and we will not interfere with it unless you ask. The soul relationship is simple compared to the human mind. The mistakes that humans make are due to not being able to let go of earthly connections, unimportant things or possessions. The most common mistake made is when you tear yourselves away from the most important things, which are love, kindness, forgiveness and joy. Our hope for the future of the world is that people will see how important it is how you care for your brothers and sisters. The foundation of the entire earth consists of being good to each other; it is the one lesson that evolves around everything."

October 15th 2016: As I was waking up this morning, and still half asleep, coming out of a dream in which there was a brown wooden door with the numbers 444 on it. I stood in front of this door and knew I was supposed to enter but woke up before I could. I instantly knew that this dream meant something wonderful was behind that door for me and it is coming soon. I was filled with feelings of great faith and hope for what is yet to come. Also, while doing laundry today, I found a dime in the washing machine, although there were no pants in the clothes I was washing. I knew that this dime was from spirit, whether it was my mother or brother. Finding this dime verified for me that what I'm feeling today is right on track and I'm very excited.

Archangel Gabriel stepped forward today and told me that to bring me to a new destination they are watching over all that happens in the world. In life you have prevailed amongst many tragedies and it is time to be rewarded. He went on to say that the messages I deliver to the people are very Important for the well being of those on the earth plane. Your job is crucial to our plan. You are much more blessed than many others so step forth in your path without trepidation and do what we ask of you. Your career path will switch as we guide you to a new level of learning. Take the hand of those who offer it for they will guide you to a brighter life. The Archangels surround you and are here to help."

October 16th 2016: Matthew the Apostle stepped forward today and said to me that the best things in life are free. "Materialistic people cause setbacks on their paths and journeys to being better souls. The cause of all that is good or bad comes from within our connection to material things. When we let go of earthly possessions, then our souls will truly feel the freedom that was meant for us. Every instrument of hope that lies within the human mind makes a connection to the spiritual plane and all its earthly possessions. A cord of light similar to an umbilical cord keeps us connected to the spirit realm from the earth plane. It is as simple as cutting that cord to free us from these possessions and for us to realize just how unimportant they are. Those who are blessed with great finances and help others are revered in heaven. Our journeys are to help each other and ourselves with kindness, empathy, love and understanding. It's not about the collection of material items. We want each of you to live well but you must also help your brothers and sisters."

October 17th 2016: I went to the shrine at St. Anne's church today and as I was kneeling in front of the Virgin Mary statue and looking up at it, I was asking Mother Mary to please help me in my journey upon this earth to do my highest and best good. As I moved my head to look down, I saw Mary's praying hands open up. I couldn't believe what I had seen; I immediately looked back up, and they were closed again. In my head I asked if I had really seen Mary's hands open and I heard," Trust yourself." I truly believe that Mary opened her hands to me as if to give me blessings and to show me she is helping me.

An angel came forth today in my communication. She was wearing a pink robe and was quite exquisite in her beauty of long brown hair and gleaming green eyes. I asked her what her name was and she told me to call her Samantha. She said that the law of the angels constitutes true religion. I was then shown a vision of a beautiful baby girl about three months old and sitting on her mother's lap. I wasn't given a clear vision of the mother's face but I knew she was young and beautiful. The mother and child were of African-American descent. I was then told this little girl is an angel on earth. I believe she was shown to me because I will somehow connect to this child on my path, and I must tell the world about her.

She continued with the message in telling me to never mind those who stand in the background and throw insults for they are of weak mind and body. "Pay attention to the strong that are by your side for they will be the ones who take you to the next level. Justice will be served to those who prey on the weaker souls of the world, the souls who aren't able to take care of themselves. Sexual predators are deemed monsters upon the earth and shall not return to the earth realm until their souls have been purified and they have redeemed themselves."

"The Muslim people honor God with such greatness. But those of their people who stand in the darkness do not outweigh those who stand in the light. Though

God is one, He is many to all people. The light of the world falls on the shoulders of each and every single person upon this earth. Stand together; stand strong, become one and that would be the equivalent of peace on earth."

October 18th 2016: Today, after I asked the angels to help me choose the cards for my daily angel readings (I was using the Guardian Angel tarot cards from Doreen Virtue and Radleigh Valentine), as I was putting the cards back in their box, a single card fell out on the table. I then clearly heard someone say this card is for you. I excitedly looked at this card to see what message I was getting from the angels. The card was the Seven of Abundance that said, "Have patience. A time of harvest is coming, but it will take some time for the plants that you have put down to bear fruit. Sometimes dreams grow slowly. It may seem to you as if little is happening, but beneath the surface, great roots are reaching out and expanding. There will be rewards for your hard work. In the meantime, take a moment to review your progress and decide what your next steps will be. When your time of prosperity arrives, you'll need to be ready to move forward." This card made so much sense to me because many times I don't have patience and I wonder if I should keep going forward on this path. This message from the angels gives me renewed faith and hope and I'm truly looking forward for the harvest that's coming in so many ways in my life. Also, today, as I was walking home from visiting the shrine at St. Anne's church a white butterfly flew right in front of me. A butterfly represents spiritual rebirth, transformation, and a whole new life.

My guide Agnes told me today that the signs are all around you my dear. "Magical moments are happening everywhere. March on like a soldier of God for freedom of the souls. The aging process won't slow you down; it will only lift your soul higher to the next level of learning. There is so much for you to accomplish but remember patience is a virtue. The angels are of assistance to you at any time. Your life long plan has been established and is already set in motion. Perseverance is a key factor of the longevity of your time on this earth."

October 19th 2016: Archangel Haniel came forth today and said that the law of attraction is similar to the law of abundance. "The most direct way to connect to the energies of these laws is to open your heart and soul to the Universe. You must completely turn around your way of thinking and throw out positive energy on a daily basis. All your lives can be full of abundance in so many ways if you practice this way of being each day. Don't let the negative energy slip back into your lives. Your strength, courage, and determination can raise you up to the incredible joy and happiness that God the Father has gifted you with. Take advantage of all the good in the Universe and all it has to offer, instead of being comfortable with the negative. Negativity has become a common way of people's lives but the time has come to be aware, stand up, and change it for the better. The angels are always here to assist those who ask."

October 20th 2016: A man came forward today that I have not previously seen in my communications. I immediately knew he was from the biblical days. He had brown hair but was bald on the top of his head. When I asked him who he was he said I am Thomas servant of the Lord. I then asked are you the one they call Thomas the apostle and he nodded yes. He began by saying that the plight of the world lies on the shoulders of those who are no longer self-serving. "Each and every person in this world chooses his or her own convictions. These choices are what led them down the road to either their success or destruction. A simple turn of events in this world will either make you or break you. The most arrogant human beings are the ones who take no responsibility for their lives or actions. The miracles you all seek upon this earth are inside of you and can be pulled out with trust, faith and belief. Free yourselves of self-hatred and self-prejudice and accept yourselves in your human body for your soul is what defines you. Stop being hard on yourselves and let your inhibitions free to conquer the world. Set good examples for your fellow brothers and sisters and lead them down the path of righteousness."

October 21st 2016: My guide Joseph stepped forth and told me that the names and origins of the people on this planet have no impact on anything, for we are all one together. "Your forefathers have all paved the way so your lives would be easier. You must always keep the next generation in mind for the entirety of it comes back full circle. The thoughtfulness, kindness and ingenuity of others are what keep this world going on a daily basis. Your love for each other is what fuels the energetic flow throughout the world and when hatred rises, the flow of the universe feels the effects. The most humane thing that can be done for each other is to consider others' needs above your own. Let peace reign throughout your hearts and souls so white light can fill the world and then there will truly be peace on earth. The most prevalent thing that we ask of you my brothers and sisters is to be good to each other. If you truly understood the impact it would have upon the world, then there would be no second thought in your mind."

FIFTEEN

Michael Jackson

October 23rd 2016: Archangel Gabriel came forth in my communication and said like the flowers that blossom in the spring, so will the hearts of many who step forward to do God's work. "The rewards are limitless if you can only open your hearts and souls. Open your hearts so we may pour in the light that will runneth over your cup and open you up to a new way of living and being. Take one step at a time to better yourselves, which in turn will better the planet. Break the molds so that your children and grandchildren don't know the pain of suffering and the tragedies brought on by humankind. Make it better for the future but not just for the next generation but also for the return of others in future lifetimes. Set the precedent to a gold standard so everyone can reap the benefits for many lives to come. There is hope for the future and it begins with each one of you. Take the hand of your brother or sister and show them the way as we the angels guide you to a better world." The entire time I was receiving this message I kept hearing Michael Jackson's song "Heal The World"). The spirit world has been around me today more than usual; they are making me feel like something good is going to happen.

Every communication and message that I receive from the spiritual world is quite amazing to me. So, I will preface this next communication with the intent that I make no judgments on the messages that are given to me via channeling. You are welcome to judge, if you like. I mean in reality we are all welcome to do so. I can only tell you if I stand back and observe what has been communicated to me through my communications, sometimes it gives me pause. Occasionally I say wait a minute, should I write this? Sometimes as human beings it's hard not to second-guess. And the answer is, of course, I write it because these are the messages that I proudly receive from the spiritual world and I write them down not just for me but also for each of us.

Gabriel continued on with his words saying that Michael Jackson was sent from the angelic realm to this earth. His job was to bring awareness to people and to enlighten and awaken souls through his music. He was given an incredible talent in order to do his job. He said Michael was a pure soul that was childlike because he was an angel on earth. "Michael did the best he could upon this earth but the way that mankind treated him, broke his soul. All Michael wanted was to do good for everyone but in the end his experiences caused him great sadness. As an angel who had been put on earth Michael wasn't used to all this negativity, hurt and pain. His suffering had gotten too much for him to bear so he was called home to recover and become whole again. The actions of people upon earth have brought sadness to the angelic realm. The judgments that people put upon each other are very wrong. Everyone must be good to each other on earth because you never know who is standing by your side. It could be someone from the world of the angels who has been damaged by those in your world." Once again it had been stressed that kindness, acceptance and love is the key to peace on earth.

In January of 2019 Jesus came forth to me and asked me the pray for the children of the light who have been damaged. I have dutifully been praying and sending love and light to them when I say my daily rosary. Since the release of the HBO documentary, I have been seeing snippets of it. I have seen the hurt and pain from Wade Robson and James Safechuck that seemed so genuine. I immediately received a sick feeling in the pit of my stomach. At this point I hadn't seen the documentary but I was listening to others who had and were big supporters of Michael's innocence but were now changing their minds. I have always been a huge supporter of Michael, and thought that he was being taken advantage of due to his fame and fortune. I felt so confused by the message that I received from Gabriel about Michael. I asked the spirit world, "How could Michael come from the world of the angels and have committed such abuse, especially to children?" Archangel Gabriel came forth and said, "The message that you received of him coming from our realm is true." I was still very confused with it all. On March 2nd 2019 while I was saying my rosary I forgot to send healing to the children of the light who have been damaged. I heard a voice say, "Don't forget the children of the light who have been damaged and I was then shown Michael Jackson. I then had an immediate all knowing that Michael was one of these children.

I also now realize that it doesn't matter what world you come from for not one soul is perfect, especially if they have been damaged in some way. I in no way condone anyone's bad behavior or acts. I am only happy to be able to understand the mystery of it all. I not only pray for those children of the light but I also pray for the souls they themselves have damaged. I am amazed at the foresight that spirit has into our world by telling me months previous to the release of the documentary to pray for the children of the light who have been damaged. The day after I was shown Michael as a damaged child of the light, I started receiving these following messages from Michael himself.

March 3rd 2019: In today's communication from the world of spirit Michael Jackson has come forth in the first of several messages I have received from him. He said; I am truly sorry for my actions upon earth. My heart was pure but my soul was damaged. I could not overcome the demon within me. I knew what I did was wrong, that is why I kept myself mentally and emotionally in a state of childlike existence. If I convinced myself I was a mere child than my actions were justified for I myself was one of them. I was drawn to children my whole life for their purity and innocence. Children are similar to the world of the angels were I came from. In my life as a child I myself was molested from a man in the music industry. (He then showed me a recording studio). As I grew I no longer trusted adults. Deep within my psyche I remained a child for I did not want to grow into one of them. Unfortunately, I never realized what I actually grew in to. I convinced myself that everything I did was with the purest of love and best intentions. In my eyes I did nothing wrong. I now understand the error of my actions. Part of my redemption is that I helped this documentary come to light. These boys need the world to see the truth so that they may be able to heal. I accept all responsibility of my behavior. I am healing and allowing my true self to be seen so that I may evolve into a state of purity once again. My only solace is that my friends and family find the peace within themselves in the knowledge that even though I was a great entertainer, my soul was flawed. Now I am shedding what damaged me as I go on to find the peace within myself. No apology can fix what harm I have caused to these boys. As I stand in the world of the angels I offer them my unconditional assistance for all eternity.

March 4th 2019: Today Blessed Catherine of Augustine, Elizabeth who is the cousin of Mother Mary and a guide named Osteria said that they all stepped forth as part of Mother Mary's soul family. Catherine did the speaking and she said: "We come forth together in support of the damaged children of the light. In your world there is much commotion over the allegations of these two men. The harm that has been caused to them is irreversible in your world. Upon there return home the healing of these souls will be of the utmost importance to us. As they stand on earth it was our world that worked with Michael on shedding the light upon the truth of it all. If the truth was not brought to light than there was no chance of healing for either Michael or the souls who have been affected by his actions. Because Michael is a child of the light we work closely with him in repairing not only his soul, but also the souls that he caused damage to. His actions have not gone unpunished in our world. His penance to atone for his sins will be in helping the souls he has hurt as they live their lives on earth. We have not swept aside any of his wrong doings just because he is a child of the light. On the contrary he is looked at more closely than others in all that he has done. We also do not forget the good he has done for the many in his time on earth. But that does not in any way negate the bad. We have banded together today with the blessings of Mother Mary in showing the souls of earth that no matter who the soul is we don't allow sins to be hidden. The truth is what allows souls to be at peace and grow. May the truth of your sins set you free.

March 5th 2019: Michael Jackson came forth again today and here are his words; the convictions of my soul were innocent. The love in my heart was pure but the knowledge in my mind was jumbled. I was a trustworthy servant of God who had fallen on his trust. The struggles of mankind are real and are hard for any soul who goes to earth, regardless of how much love and light they are filled with. I went to earth with the best of intentions but as my soul became damaged, so did my thinking. I was overwhelmed by the need for childlike innocence around me and I sought it in all areas of my life. I am not asking for forgiveness from your world. I am only stating information so some may have an understanding of my immoral actions. It has brought a better understanding to those of us in our world at how easily a soul of light can go dark. On one hand I did the work of God that I was sent there for as I felt my commitment to him. On the other hand, I hid my darkness and the pain and hurt that caused damage to my soul. I come forth to you Dawn, as I see that you stand in both worlds at the same time. I also see no judgment from you in one-way or the other. You once believed my innocence but you now gracefully accept the truth. Thank you for allowing me to express my words.

Michael then presented me a gift of protection. A figure in a black hooded cloak came forth and as he took off his hood he looked like a sort of gargoyle. Michael said as a soul of the light you need all the protection you can get in a world saturated in darkness.

March 6th 2019: Michael Jackson came forth again today and I asked him to further explain this gargoyle to me. He said that his name is Zorin and he is from the light and love of God. His soul is attached to the world of light. He will attach this light to you so that you are protected at all times, especially if you're in the public eye. His protection stems from the core of heaven and it is spiritual and physical. He will guide you through the darkest of storms as you open yourself to the world.

There will be much backlash in all you say about me, regardless of which side you stand on. I guarantee that you will sit in the chair that I considered my throne. Go forth with your heart and soul open as I help with your future.

Mother Mary also came forth today and spoke these words: the time has come to move forward in your life. Your soul has reached it's potential in this home. Your life will explode with excitement in the upcoming future. You will support the claims of these men in the truth they speak, as you will also honor them as the hurt little boys they are within. Their true healing will begin the day they walk through the doors of this childhood pain in releasing all the darkness into my arms. Our world does not hide from mistakes; it fixes them. It won't be long till all is as it should be.

March 7th 2019: In today's communication Zorin has stepped forth looking like Hagrid from Harry Potter. He told me that he could show himself in any form he chooses. He chose to show me himself as Hagrid because he wanted me to know how he lived in his world as an outsider. He also said that he was put aside a lot because of his true appearance. He went on to say that Jesus feels we needed to get acquainted since he will work closely with protecting and guiding me for the remainder of my time on earth. My true appearance can be disturbing, almost frightening to some, which is why I hide under the cloak. But my soul is as pure as they come. I am honored to work with you and your acceptance of me. I am the one who worked closely with Michael in his time on earth. Keeping him safe from himself was the hardest job of all. This is a huge sacrifice for Michael to allow you the gift of myself. I am his "security blanket" no matter which world he stands in. Please allow me to wrap you in the comfort of my safety. You have always stood in the shadows without anyone seeing or realizing the light and purity that is in your soul. It will soon be time to shine your light into the world. I promise I will always protect you in all ways until your last breath upon earth.

March 8th 2019: Today Michael Jackson stepped forward and showed himself to me at around the age of nine. He told me this is when the sexual abuse started happening to him. He then said these words: I am not condoning my actions. I am watching the anguish that my family is going through. Some family members protect me so gallantly as I can see the doubt starting to seep into some of them. My family should not have to pay for my sins. I am angry at myself for my mother is suffering due to my actions. Her life is unpleasant right to the very end. Upon her arrival home I will bear my soul to her and work on healing the pain I have caused her in my life and death. I am disgraced on earth and looked at as a monster. In reality I went to earth to do good with the best of intentions but I failed. In doing so, any good that I did will be forgotten by mankind. My actions have ruined not only my legacy but also the lives of those I've harmed in different ways. My heart bleeds for those that I harmed.

March 9th 2019: Zorin came forth today as a man in his hooded black cloak. When he took the cloak off he looked like Sean Connery. I was surprised at his appearance and he said, "I told you I can look anyway that I choose to." He went on to give me this message. I will not only protect your soul but I will protect your physical being from the cruelty of the world. This chapter of your life might seem quite mundane right now. As time goes on you will look back and realize how peaceful you were. In the upcoming months, relax and enjoy each day. You have a life of leisure and peace, which is just a dream for many souls who trudge through life on earth. You have a battle of wits that has not yet been explored but will become useful in the future. Do not take others negative words and actions against you too seriously. Always focus on the purpose that took you to earth. Remember, you are royalty in the eyes of many in the world of spirit. I don't mean as a king or queen but as a pure soul of light. Keep your head high and never forget were you came from.

Michael Jackson then stepped forth and said to me: "you must watch the documentary." He then told me that he was with me while I was watching the thriller video the previous night. He went on to say; I see all, which is how I know that you have never spoken against me. I applaud your willingness to open yourself up to my wounds by allowing me a platform in your book. Many will speak against you. This is why it is important for you to have Zorin by your side. He is a great deflector of negativity, both spiritual and physical. Zorin was my muse in much of my music. He will serve as a wonderful inspiration to you in many ways. I stand by your side as you embark on this journey. To be upon earth as you stand in the light is like throwing yourself to the wolves. Some might consider myself a wolf but I will continue to rectify my wrongs. I am happy to be home as I heal myself, and those that I damaged.

Tonight, I watched the entire documentary of Leaving Neverland, since Michael seemed insistent for me to watch it. As I was watching part one, I was amazed when I heard Wade Robson's mother mention how she was sitting on a bus next to Sean Connery. It is no coincidence why Zorin came forth today and showed himself as Sean Connery. That is why I felt the insistence from Michael to watch the documentary today. This is spirits way of giving me confirmation of all the messages that I am receiving. They wanted me to watch it on the same day that Zorin stepped forth as Sean Connery. Spirit always finds a way to continue to amaze me.

March 10th 2019: I closed my eyes to connect to spirit today and when I opened them, Michael Jackson's face was right in front of mine and he said "HI!" He then gave me these words. Now your eyes are wide open to all that I've done. I can see and feel the essence of your soul. I can feel the empathy that you have for those on both sides of the fence. This is why you were chosen to express my words to the world. Others have damaged your soul, though not in the same way as mine. You are still filled with the understanding of a damaged soul. Your empathy and kindness for others is pure and deep. It can sometimes be overwhelming troubling to your spirit. This empathy is especially deep for souls who are pure and innocent like children and animals. Others might say "why you?" Well, all this is why you. It is human nature to question others and their motives. This is something that you will do in the future as your wealth rises, and your fame explodes, as your presence on earth is known.

March 11th 2019: Michael Jackson came forth today and showed himself as the monster in the video Thriller. He said; I see that some are questioning if I actually made Thriller from the monster within myself. There is a little bit of darkness in all souls. The question is whether or not you want to bring that darkness to the surface. In my case the darkness grew within me from the emotional harm caused to me from my father, plus the sexual abuse from another. I chose to hide that darkness from all and it manifested in ways that hurt children. I did not have the courage to get the proper help that I needed. Instead, I allowed it to manifest within me and darken the light in my soul. Helping the children of earth is the main reason that I went there. I started out helping them but ended up hurting them as I allowed this sickness to overtake me. I shall never return to earth again. I will spend eternity helping those that I harmed and others that have been hurt like them. In answering the question of Thriller; subconsciously I was trying to show the world the monster hidden within me. I could not function properly in life because of what I became. I disliked myself, and the world that I lived in.

March 12th 2019: Michael Jackson stepped forth today but he did not speak. Instead he brought forth his father Joe Jackson who wanted to speak. These are the words he gave to me; I have done many wrongs in my life. I may have been too tough on my family but no one can say that I didn't love them. Michael and I are working out our differences. My biggest regret is how I disrespected my wife

Katherine by stepping out on her. She is a woman of God and I didn't deserve her and she certainly didn't deserve my actions and me. I stand by the side of my son Michael as I take responsibility for his damaged soul. I was neither kind nor gentle to him in his childhood. I pushed my children into the spotlight as a way to gain wealth. All that happened to Michael in his life as a result of his fame lies on my shoulders. In one sense I am proud but in another I am saddened by how I pushed all my children to their limits and beyond. I did not realize the extent of what my actions had upon their lives. The man that touched Michael inappropriately as a child will have to not only answer to Michael but to me when he returns home. I might regret my actions to my family but I will never regret having that family. Please tell the little girl that I'm ok and that I love her. Then he showed me a butterfly and a humming bird for her. He then tipped his soft hat to me and left.

March 13th 2019: In todays communication Katherine Helmond came forth and she gave me these words. "I'm speaking for the community of souls who lived their life in the spotlight. Life in the public eye can make good people do bad things. I have witnessed the fall of many young stars. Evil lurks in the darkest corners of Hollywood. I myself was tempted briefly by this corruption that runs deep. Though I handled myself in such a manner that would not be me in such a position. My only offense is that I seen it going on around me and kept silent. It is not only sex and drugs; it is more like a secret society. If you are not part of this society, you will be thrown to the wolves. I loved acting and I loved most of my life but Hollywood is not glamorous. It is more like who can beat out who. The saying "Dog eat dog," is the most appropriate saying relating to Hollywood. I spoke soft and I kept to myself and this is how I survived that lifestyle. If you are in, then you are in. But if you are out, then forget about your dreams in Hollywood. Now I am out, but if I had to do it all again, I say, Maybe."

Mother Mary and Jesus came forth today also though they didn't speak. Zorin then came in and showed himself to me as half horse and half man. He said he shows himself this way to me because it is fun for him. Zorin then gave me this message; "I am a muse and a mythical legend in the minds of some. I was created by God and have always existed in the world of spirit. I have been the muse for not only Michael Jackson but for many brilliant minds. Mother Mary and Jesus accompany me today as we say congratulations. You have weathered many storms, as you will now step in to the light of a new day. It is during this new day that I will work with you more closely. As you step in to the future your soul will become more enlightened to your purpose. It would have been overwhelming if all were to be revealed at once. This is why everything in life plays out slowly over time as it is meant to be. In the future take your time with your newfound finances, as I will show you the best way to use them. Stay grounded in your heart, mind and soul and you will do well."

March 14th 2019: Michael Jackson came forth again today and gave me this message. "I am ashamed of how I manipulated others as I rose higher in my fame. My self-preservation was about hiding myself deep within the innocence of children. I felt safe and understood by them in a way that I could not connect to adults. The essence of their purity is what drew me to them. In my mind the damage of my own soul allowed me to damage the souls of these children. I no longer stand in the darkness and I no longer hide under a sheet of lies. My heart breaks for all those that I left behind who are affected by my actions, including my family. I'm hoping to alleviate some of the pain and guilt of these boys by speaking the truth. Even though I am not on earth it is not any easier to speak the truth. I am stripped of my human body; my soul exposed for all to see, as I stand before God and all who are in the world of spirit including my father Joseph as I confess my sins. There is nowhere to hide and nowhere to go. There is only the truth and I. Those on earth can judge me and say the words they feel about me but no one will judge me as harshly as I have judged myself. My road to redemption is long but as long as I stay on it all the good that I've done will have some meaning to me. I come forth to not repeat myself but to explain a little more each time."

March 15th 2019: Michael Jackson has come forth again today and gave me these words. "The cornerstone of my legacy is built on my music. For that I will always be proud. Regardless of what they think of me, those in your world can never take that away from me. Souls on earth have a habit of punishing others by trying to strip them of their humanity. Every soul has human basic rights regardless of what crimes they have committed. Judgment flies around earth as freely as love should. Those who judge the harshest are not the ones who walk on a path of light. When a soul is looked at as evil, it is hard for them to redeem themselves. Many have closed minds as they look upon another with tunnel vision. There are few on earth who truly understands the meaning of forgiveness. To have this forgiveness you must willingly walk on a path of light as you unselfishly release another from the shackles of the pain that they caused you. By releasing what binds your soul to anger, hurt or resentment will help with any future afflictions that are brought on by others. I never felt at home on earth.

March 18th 2019: As I connected to spirit today, I saw an ox that stood up on his back feet. I wasn't quite sure who or what this was and so I said, "If you are not from God's white light then I don't want you here." He immediately changed into the gargoyle sort of looking creature and I felt innocence from him as I realized it was Zorin. Jesus then stepped forth to let me know it was safe. Michael Jackson then came in and said; "This is how people on earth are viewing me, as a beast. Tell my family that I cannot control the thoughts and actions of others. I can only speak the truth and tell you all how sorry I am for the hurt and pain that I caused. I slowly drifted apart from some family members in my life. I was not able to deal with the family relationship and the dynamics of were I stood in the family. Tell Janet it is okay to let the truth be told for the sins of my soul must come to light in order for me to heal. The healing of my soul is more important so I can go forth and help others who suffer. My penance will be repaid time and time again, as I will help others for eternity. The life and times of my work will never be forgotten. As time goes forward my music will be passed from generation to generation and this in no way degrades the lives of those that I've hurt. Those who have hurt me will have to answer to their sins for no soul is free of the damage they have caused to another. My soul is set free as I speak the words of truth. The cries of a child are a far greater sin on ones soul than I even imagined. I send peace and light daily to those I have hurt upon earth.

March 19th 2019: Jesus stepped forth and Zorin came in behind him standing as a man in his black hooded cloak. But Zorin was wearing a mask that had a long bird like beak. Michael Jackson then came in and gave me this message. There is hope in the light of each new day. The monstrous image that some people have of me is no greater than the image I had of myself before I passed to the world of spirit. After I myself had children it is then that I realized the extent of my actions. I had a hard time facing each morning after I realized what I had done to innocent children. The guilt overwhelmed me, as I could no longer sleep even with the help of alcohol and drugs. I was having a nervous breakdown towards the end of my life and paranoia was setting in. I felt like a broken bird that fell from its nest and I could no longer be fixed. There is hope for a new day for those that I've left behind, my children, my family, and my victims, for my sins are not there sins. My hope is that they all have a new day that begins with forgiveness and ends with peace in their hearts. I blatantly lied of my innocence out of fear and what I now understand as shame. I do not want my children or family to wallow in self pity. I want them to hold their heads high and go forward as they all remember the man I was to them. As long as they hold me close to their hearts the memories will last their lifetime. I am never far from my family; all they have to do is think of me and I'll be there.

March 20th 2019: Michael Jackson came forth again today and gave me these words; the explanation of the actions in my life may not be suitable for all on earth.

Speaking the words of truth has cleansed my soul so I may heal. I have settled some scores with my father Joseph. I am preparing myself to face the one who sexually abused me, upon his arrival into our world. It is then that I will start to prepare myself to face those that I've hurt upon their arrival home. Till that time I will continue to help them in their lives on earth. This includes all members of their family that I have hurt in some way. I no longer profess my innocence in either world. I am hoping this helps to release my victims from the scrutiny of others. I want all to know that Oprah is a true friend in my eyes and in the eyes of God. She goes forth with courage and strength to help victims of abuse be heard. She is not afraid to speak the truth, as she has always been a faithful servant of our father. I applaud Oprah for her part in helping the world to see what I've hidden for so long. She is guided daily by the Lord as he bestows his Grace upon her. I ask anyone who has questions of my actions to turn to God for the answers. I do understand that I have let down many people and have left them heartbroken. Never put anyone so high on a pedestal that you view him or her as a God, because not one soul is perfect.

March 21st 2019: Michael Jackson came forth and told me he had a personal message for me. I would like to share this message with everyone. Your courage and strength will be challenged as you speak the words of truth. Whether they are my words or the words from any of us in the world of spirit. Your acceptance of us is a friendship that will last an eternity. It is a privilege to come forth and speak our words to you. I must bid you farewell as I have important work to do. I will never be far away if you need me you may call upon me. I leave you with Zorin as your protector. I love you Dawn.

St. Therese then came forth and gave me this message; when someone is considered a legend and their faults or sins are put before them, they are destroyed by the impact of their downfall. It is not right to put souls on pedestals and then kick the pedestal out before there very feet as the earth crumbles below them. The undertaking of raising one so high up is the fault of all. When this soul is to be found less than perfect then this soul is treated poorly and disregarded as worthy. There are many on earth that should look at their own reflection before casting others aside for their actions. There are many souls on earth who commit sins and hurt others. It is those who are put on pedestals that pay the biggest price by the ones who put them on this pedestal to begin with. The problems of earth are wider and deeper than you all realize and all souls need to take responsibility, for no soul is without sin.

April 1st 2019: Michael came forth today and gave me this message. "The allegations in the documentary and the publishing of your book were brought together by Divine timing. The release of your book could not be until the world had seen the truth in the film. Those of us in my world, work through those in your world. We do so with the best possible intentions in order to help all the souls involved. My hour of darkness has been brought to light and in this light may no shadows be cast upon the innocent. I take full responsibility for my actions and they are my actions alone. They should not be attached to my family or those who were around me. I understand this is the end of an era for my loyal fans. I sincerely apologize to anyone that I hurt from the fallout of my actions. I've always tried to come from a place of love because I really do love you all. Thank you all for your devotion but never be blinded to what you cannot see.

SIXTEEN

Words Of Wisdom

October 24th 2016: This morning I was asked by a woman from England named Michelle Darbyshire if I could please help out with a group she helps run called Heavenly Angels. I told her I would post my daily messages from the angels and my daily tarot card readings on her site. I also told her I would offer two free readings a week to her members. Michelle seemed happy with that offer and she made me an administrator for the site. This group has over 700 members and is a wonderful opportunity for me to help grieving souls and to possibly get more followers for my book. I now know why the angels were around me so much yesterday. I know beyond a shadow of a doubt that those in spirit set this entire thing up because helping others is helping yourself. Though my time with this group didn't last long it was a helpful learning experience and I'll be forever grateful to Michelle for it.

Mother Mary stepped forward today in my communication and said you have your wings dear, now fly free like you were meant to do. I was then shown a vision of a white dove. She then said that a door has now opened so step into it with great self-confidence. "You have asked for help to be on a more charitable and humanitarian level and we have listened. Like we always say, ask, and you shall receive. The work of the Lord is in your capable hands. You are blessed with an abundance of trust from those of us in the spiritual world. We won't abandon you and we will follow you closely on your path as you awaken and enlighten souls to a brand new way of living and being. Halt any friendship with those who spread hate amongst others. We want you to have tunnel vision and only see the light when it comes to haters. Desperation is a key factor in the way some people behave. Remember, the best things in life are free, and your service is included in that category. The most memorable times of your life will be through helping others. Watch for an ambush of people on the earth plane telling you to charge for your services in the early stages but stand strong for your rewards will be from within. It is not about money, it is about helping others. This is one step toward being a humanitarian. In the future you will receive monetary gain for your services."

October 25th 2016: John the Baptist stepped forth in today's communication and said that the highest wave of energy that can befall any one person is the energy of love. "It can encompass your whole being and fill your soul with so much joy and happiness that it automatically brings you to the next level of truth on your journey. Love is way more powerful than hate or any other emotion that is within any of us. It is also the fundamental key of our true essence that will unlock every door you try to enter. Every moment in this life is fueled by an emotion or an action. If the fuel were a constant flow of love, then anything negative would cease to exist. The most reverent days ahead will require hope and faith in God the Father if all of mankind is to survive the impending wars. Make the most out of your lives and dare to be someone who makes a difference in this world."

October 26th 2016: Mary Magdalene stepped forth in my communication and said that the afterlife is more rewarding than life on earth. "The human experience is a learning tool to evolve your souls on higher learning levels, to bring you to a new understanding, and to widen your perception of the Universe. The human experience is a very important part of the process of eliminating negativity from your soul. The freedom that freewill allows us all can hold back your development in your soul's growth. Even in the spiritual realm you must choose to forgive yourself and to forgive others for the wrongs committed. Your choices can either bring you higher or make you stagnant. Your desires can lead you on different paths than what was planned for you. In the grand scheme of things, you all have a hand in your final destination. Always choose good over bad because in the end it will be you who reap the benefits."

October 27th 2016: Catherine of Augustine stepped forth in today's communication and she began by saying that the comfort zone in many people's lives relies on the back fall of tragedies. "We must all begin to think of a new way of living and being. There are many vast destinies in this world and each one is important to keep the Universal laws aligned, and these laws aren't as complex as people imagine. The flow of the Universe is of utmost importance to keep the moral standards of mankind as high as possible. If you choose to look the other way while help is needed, then your moral compass is off kilter, and this action affects every aspect of the Universe. The most appropriate time for you all to come together would not be just for world tragedies but on a daily basis. These are steps for peace on earth. Our wish for you is that you all aspire to the same common goal of creating our worlds in such a similarity that it is heaven on earth. Anything is possible in this Universe by setting the best of intentions on a daily basis with an open heart and soul."

October 28th 2016: In my connection today, I was immediately shown a white dove flying with his wings spread wide open. My guide Agnes then came forth and said to let go of fear, self-doubt, and to trust yourself, for you have the power to climb the highest mountain. "Each step you take is one step closer to being one with the universe. Every day you linger based on fear, is a day wasted of opportunities to further yourself upon your journey. Be kind and gentle to each other because life can be rough enough without the negativity of others. Don't pull at others' heartstrings unless you are willing to comfort them when needed. There will be a consequence for every action taken upon this earth, whether positive or negative. Some of the most obscure thoughts that people have are whether they will be punished for their actions in the spirit realm. The answer is no, though self-punishment and self-forgiveness is something there is no escaping from. The work is hard, true, and pure, that has to be done on yourself to become a better soul and to raise you to a higher level in many ways."

I found out today that I would be leaving next June to stay with my daughter in San Diego for 10 months while her husband is on deployment. It is scary being away from home for that long but I believe everything happens for a reason and I feel many positive things will come from this trip. Gail Moffat had previously told me that I would be spending a lot of time in California with my daughter.

October 29th 2016: I keep getting a strong feeling there is something more to Joseph than just my guide. I know that he first presented himself as a king and said he was King of the angels. Today I asked him if there was more to him than meets the eye. He then told me, I am husband of Mary. He then said remember there is always a reason for all that happens.

October 30th 2016: My guide Earl stepped forth today and said that one positive aspect is that the economic growth in the United States will rise to a higher rate over the next four years. Unfortunately, every action that is taken by the government will increase the odds of financial success for those who are already high in finances. Eventually there will be a shift of energy in the White House with the help from other realms and this shift will enlighten many members of congress to be more open to the needs of the American people. The negative energy will be forced out and the positive energy will remain. There will be everlasting years of wonderful exciting things in, and for America. There will be groups that will ambush trying to bring down and destroy the happiness, but they won't prevail. This will help Americans come together more as a close unit and not be pitted against each other. Have faith in yourselves and other realms because together we can conquer anything.

October 31st 2016: As I connected today, I saw two incredible angels who had specks of sparkling white light surrounding them and falling off of them everywhere they moved. I felt such peace and tranquility from these angels. I asked for their names and they said all that you need to know is that we are angels of God. These are the words that they spoke: that the altering of two worlds when the veil is lifted depends upon the magic that is felt in each soul. "Though it is a time of great communication, it is also a time when negative energies take the opportunity to slip in to your world amidst the entrance of other souls. Beware of whom you let in for they can cause great havoc and chaos in your lives. The angelic realm is proud of the angels on earth and the assistance and guidance of the souls that are helped to bring great joy to our realm. We watch with great anticipation for the future of your world. We sit on the side of those who feel hopeless and want to give up as we wait for the right words to come out of their mouths for help. In most cases we cannot intervene unless we are asked. Patience is a huge virtue for those who do ask and want the help instantaneously. We help in the ways that are best for each of you though it might not be the help that you had in mind. We ask for your faith, belief, and the patience from within yourself. We the angels truly are here for each of you. We don't doubt you and we ask that you please don't doubt us."

November 1st 2016: St. Therese stepped forward in today's communication and she said to let the light of the world shine upon the darkened corners of our souls to awaken and enlighten the way life is supposed to be. "You must all learn a new way to be and live so that peace on earth is possible. Take the outstretched hand of those who offer a better way of life. Don't be afraid of change or of switching paths at any point in your lives so that you may walk more freely through this kingdom God has created. If your soul's purpose is to switch paths and you have done so, then you have done your part in this world towards a better way to live. Many angels walk upon the earth while others only visit on a daily basis. We are all interwoven through your lives to guide you. Though our guidance isn't always accepted, we accept you all with non-judgment and love. Know that we stand by your sides as we did your ancestors, also with the hope of a brighter future for all. Trust in us and we will lead you down roads you never knew were possible."

November 2nd 2016: Mother Theresa came forth today and said a true testament to our Lord would be that kindness is shown to everyone you meet along your path. "The most reverent of all kindnesses is a smile. A smile, along with a hug or a handshake upon greeting your brother or sister, sends the energy of love to the other worlds. The importance of every action you take upon this planet seeps the energy into the universe whether it be a positive or a negative flow. Mankind does not realize the impact this earth has upon the cosmos and the effect that trickles in to other worlds. It isn't just about mankind and the earth; it is about the entire universe and the effects that are felt throughout, whether positive or negative. Take care of this planet because there is nowhere to escape the after effects. The inhumane slaughtering of animals deeply saddens all the realms. If each soul could be a little kinder each day, the positive impact it would have upon earth would be astronomical."

November 3rd 2016: My guide Agnes told me today that the highest and best good you can do for anyone is to show them love and kindness. "There will be an explosion of anger and hatred over the results of the presidential election. The country has been divided and the lack of solidarity is ruining what makes this country great. You must all rise as one to overcome the falling of your country. Opinions can differ but not to the extent that we have witnessed. Not only have you given up on each other, but also you have given up on yourselves and the good within each of you. If this Presidential election is a testament to how the anger is being spewed so freely then we are afraid of when all will be called upon to stand together for the uprising of the world. Politics has always been considered dirty and underhanded but the deceit has trickled out into the everyday lives of your loved ones, including your children. We cannot let politics separate us from the core of our beings or the goodness of our souls. Everyone must open their eyes and their hearts regardless of others' beliefs. Be good to each other for you're all that you have through out all eternity."

November 4th 2016: An angel came forth today and I knew by his energy that he must be an archangel. I asked him his name and he said I am Azrael and I have come to speak words of truth. He then told me that the souls upon this planet weep for their loved ones who have departed. "What they don't understand is that their loved ones are standing right beside them. Your loved ones can act as guardian angels that give you guidance and support through your journey. They do their jobs without a physical body, which allows them to do more than any human body could ever endure. Your departed loved ones do not feel saddened that they have left the earth realm, for they have gone to their true home. They have the ability to see each of you, and spend time with you while they wait for you to come home."

"Once a soul crosses over, many things are revealed. Everything will become clear to you and you will wonder why did I ever worry so much about money or anything materialistic that has no meaning to our soul's purpose upon this earth. Food, water and shelter are the basics of what we need to survive as human beings, but love and kindness are what feed our souls to thrive and grow. It is true that many soul lessons come from suffering and pain, but they must be learned in order to keep the karmic balance flowing smoothly. Some of the soul's lessons we learn are agreed to before your entrance on this earth, and these lessons are important for your soul's growth. Once you have gone through them and learned them, then it is not necessary to repeat these lessons. Everyone's free will plays a large part in the lessons chosen though karmic balance also plays a part in the final decision. There is nothing more important on this earth than each other, and that is what is at the basis of each lesson learned."

November 5th 2016: Today I attended the psychic holistic fair that my church runs every six months at the Elks Lodge in Wareham, MA. I received a reading from a Psychic Medium named Tom Foley. I had never met Tom before and I felt drawn to him spiritually due to his hippie soul. In my reading Tom said to me, this is something odd because Jim Morrison is here. I then told Tom that in my prayers I pray for Jim Morrison's soul everyday. Though I was never a huge Jim Morrison fan, he just happens to be one of the celebrities that I pray for. Tom said Jim came forward to thank me for praying for him and he really appreciated it. I found this to be amazing and it made me feel good to know that my prayers are appreciated.

My guide Agnes told me today that the force of the universe is so strong that it counteracts the negativity within each soul in any realm. "When the sky is filled with sunlight, it's when the universe is most vulnerable to negative emotions or reactions from the world. The souls that deviate from their paths on earth are overwhelming. We cannot force any soul to stay on their path; we can only offer assistance and guidance toward a better way. A better way to live is to follow your heart because each soul knows the truth on some level. The most common desire of human beings is to do what makes you happy in the moment, with no regard for the future. You must all learn to look at all aspects of situations from a past, present, and future perspective, in order to have a strong foundation that will keep

218

you more on an even keel in the many dimensions of your life."

November 6th 2016: I have many magnets on my refrigerator door that I have collected over the years. I was lucky enough to be able to get them from the refrigerator in my last apartment after the fire. I opened up the door to my refrigerator like I do countless times in a day, but today I heard something drop on the floor as I opened it up. I bent down to pick up what had dropped and it was a magnet from the band "The Doors." As I looked at this psychedelic magnet that I chose to purchase years ago due to the colors of it, I could feel the spirit of Jim Morrison with me. It was a feeling of intense appreciation for being remembered. I will never forget this experience because the spirit realm never ceases to amaze me.

John The Apostle came forth today and said that a spiritual uplifting is needed in this world. "When you turn your backs on the homeless or a so-called beggar, you never really know who you are turning your backs on. Remember that the angels and messengers of God walk upon the earth for many different reasons. When you find it hard to be kind to someone due to his or her actions, distance yourself and do not partake in their negativity. One small act of kindness can have a domino effect and make a positive difference in many lives. Every soul upon this earth was created from the loving father and therefore, every soul has God within them. Your thoughts and intentions are more powerful than any of you realize. Trust yourselves and go deep within to pull this power out to better this world for all of mankind. All you have to do is ask to be shown and we will guide you every step of the way. Remember patience is a virtue and faith is above all. We will keep you safe in these spiritual travels, just open your hearts and souls to us and we will show you the way."

November 7th 2016: Archangel Michael came forth in today's communication and said that the light of the world falls upon the shoulders of the many who step forth to help conquer the plight of those who suffer. "The angelic realm opens their doors to allow love, peace and joy to flow freely into the world. The poetic justice for some souls was derived from following the anti-Christ in another lifetime. We must help each other to stand strong against any negative influences in all aspects of our lives. Do not be fooled by those who make false promises of miracles, for you know in your heart and soul the right choices to make. The truth will always be revealed so that the light may shine through. Be forceful in your convictions and don't let others tear you down."

November 8th 2016: Joseph came forth today and said that the disillusionment of many souls upon this earth that think they have a greater purpose than God is humiliating to our Savior's being and existence. "May the light workers go forth and pull these souls out of the darkness with devotion and love for your fellow brothers and sisters. An opportunity had risen for a brighter day and you have seized it. You will be amazed at the profitable gains that will now enter your life. Let go of emotional financial negativity so you may move forth in many endeavors that are planned for you. Trust us, my child, and you will be shown miracles. The trust in God, yourselves and each other will be obsolete if souls aren't opening themselves up to the faith within them. Purgatory is real, it is where the souls go to congregate and ponder upon a higher journey and the next step in their soul's growth. A higher-level journey is prepared for you upon your entrance into the spirit realm. It is your decision based on your free will whether you accept this journey or not. There are many ways and many journeys for your soul to grow, but that growth is completely up to each soul. Your journey depends upon the lesson that each soul chooses to learn."

November 9th 2016: Yesterday was the Presidential election in The United States and today many people woke up to find that the candidate they voted for was not elected to office. Many people are reacting with fear and anger at the outcome.

Jesus came forth in today's connection and said don't despair for the doors to the kingdom are open and we are pouring white light upon the world. "Against all odds a miracle has prevailed and there is a reason for it. The world will not end because this man is the chosen leader. You all have to open your hearts and souls and welcome him as the leader of your country. It won't all be a bed of roses and there will be thorns along the way. Every human makes mistakes, and his will be scrutinized. The electoral vote was rigged and there will be light shown upon that in the future. Make the most out of the next four years for it is a time to build yourselves up to a new level of economic growth. The more sustainable you are, the further you will get ahead in your lives. Preach only things of a positive nature, which will spread love and kindness toward each other. In reality the flaw of any president is that their promises are inconceivable in their presidential term. We ask courage and strength of you all and to stand together and unite, as we from the heavens will guide you every step of the way."

On a personal note, and with a clear head, the observations of my communications show me that turmoil doesn't affect just us but the other worlds as well. Jesus, the angels, and other beings sense everything that we go through. When it is a global or national event, they are right beside us feeling the heaviness of it all. It is very important for my readers to understand that I connect to the other world and write down whatever comes to me. Afterwards I may wonder or think my own thoughts or questions. My understanding with those in the spiritual world is that what I receive, I write. There is no judgment or questions asked even if there is initial confusion. During the Presidential election of 2016, I spoke to a couple of my psychic friends and they both have opposite reflections and forecasts of how this presidential administration will affect our country and our world. I wanted to make it perfectly clear that my communications are not my feelings or thoughts but they are what I convey from the other world.

November 10th 2016: Catherine of Augustine has come forth in today's communication and said that a transcript of a book of the world would read as revelations in warning others of mistakes made upon your paths. Though your journeys may seem zigzagged at times, you are always on the path of Creations. We pick up those who have fallen from their paths further than they should be. The final destination for everyone is to fully love yourselves and each other and then you will truly have learned your lesson upon this earth. Do not judge others for things unseen, or project negativity due to your expectations of someone. When you are filled with fear, it is the greatest time that you must have faith within yourself and that of your brothers and sisters. We are watching above at how hate is spewed unnecessarily on both sides." (The angels are speaking of the Republican and the Democratic Party due to the outcome of the presidential election). "We cannot stress enough how unification will raise this world up to a better way of living. Though it might not be what you had in mind, have faith, for better days are ahead. Pick yourselves up and go forth; this too shall pass."

November 11th 2016: Today I visited the shrine at St. Anne's church. After I was done in the shrine and was walking across the church parking lot, I was walking in between two parked cars and as I looked down, I saw a dime and a penny, which I thought, was amazing because today's date was 11-11, which are very powerful numbers. What I have learned about angel numbers is that 1111 means to keep your thoughts positive because your thoughts instantly manifest. The more ones you see, the more powerful the message. As I bent down to pick up the eleven cents, I realized there were more coins on the ground. I picked up all the coins (3 dimes, 5 pennies and 2 nickels). I then searched the ground very closely several times to see if there were any more coins but there were none. I then turned around to walk away and low and behold there was a dime and a penny right in front of me where I had just previously looked, and there wasn't a soul around. I started out by finding eleven cents, and I ended by finding eleven cents. The angels and the universe were speaking loud and clear to me and I paid attention. I kept my thoughts uplifting and happy and I could feel the positive energy around me.

November 12th 2016: Today while he was at work my son Matthew sent me a picture via text of 11 cents lying on the floor that he had found. The spirit realm is also telling Matthew to keep his thoughts positive. I also have a strong intuition that the universe is trying to let me know that Matthew is going to be somehow connected to me on my spiritual journey and I can't wait to figure it out. I feel Matthew and I are connected more than either of us realize.

Jesus came forth in today's communication and he said to follow the light, for it will shed truth upon the purpose of the leaders of your country. "The work that has to be done for the United States of America has to be done by someone who is willing to fight and go up against those who say no. You must all understand that unity is the fundamental key to a better America. Dividing yourselves will only harm the outcome of Trump's success in building up America for the better. Stop the violence and accept each other's opinions to go forth, for a new day is dawning. I do not want these words to fall on deaf ears. Many have prayed for a solution to rise up your country, and now it has been handed to you. Help doesn't always come in the form you would like, but nonetheless it is here, so please accept it with open hearts and arms. If you fight against the help we give you, then it will make it more difficult for the outcome to be a success. Time really does heal all wounds."

November 14th 2016: Today Matthew sent me another picture at another job he was at because he found another 11 cents. To me, it reiterated the heavens and universe saying to us, he is connected to you. Matthew and I usually only find dimes or pennies but never a dime with a penny. Being that it is the 11th month, it is the universe's way of communicating, whether it is our loved ones in spirit, angels, or our guides.

Mother Theresa came forth today and said the price paid for Princess Diana was her life and that is one example of the media frenzy and the harm it causes for the safety of everyone. (She is saying this due to the media frenzy and all the chaos surrounding the outcome of the Presidential election). She went on to say the horse drawn carriage has arrived, and you must accept the passenger. "Put aside the hatred and the prejudice and become united for the good of the nation and the success of America. Each drop of negativity in the air causes great harm to the universal flow and balance. Outrageous comments are being said from the mouths of those who are ignorant to the final outcome of Trump for president. Please come together as one so we may help America stand strong instead of falling to shambles. Open your eyes wide and look around and see the hatred that is being spewed like they are everyday words in conversations. Follow the paths of those who have opened their minds, hearts and souls to unite and support the man before you. We are asking you all to give your brother a chance. Eventually the light will be shown upon the truth and everything will fall in to place. For now, accept and believe that heaven has a plan and it is the best for all of God's children."

November 15th 2016: Archangel Michael came forth today and said that an ultimate warrior of the Lord is someone who protects his name and honor with love and kindness for all of mankind. "Those souls that are non-judgmental are the souls that are way beyond their years of learning and developing their souls to higher levels. It is those without prejudice that have walked in the presence of the Lord. Hope will help you to rise with dignity to feel the essence of your true being. Every soul upon the earth has encountered rocky paths but it is how you handle it that is of importance. When midnight falls, we sprinkle grace upon the earth so every soul has a chance to start anew. The magnificence of this world starts with each of you, and we have faith and trust that love and kindness will prevail and the future of this world will be brighter than imagined."

November 16th 2016: St. Therese came forth in today's communication and said that the challenges you face as a nation are restricted due to the leadership of your country. "Each and every decision should be based upon how underdeveloped countries can benefit from these decisions. You should help other countries rise up without neglect to your own, then you the people can rise as a nation. Everyone will profit from the benefits that these actions offer. Coming together as communities based upon love for each other is the start of a new world, and a better way of living. Each soul that takes a step forward to a better way of living will be a better soul for it, and the rewards you reap will be endless, whether upon this earth or in heaven. Do not despair for the world's eyes are wide open. A heavy hitter for his administration will eventually rise to the occasion to set things right. The flow of tears from heaven depends on the flow of negativity and violence upon the earth. Do your part and send out love to the universe on a daily basis to help you strive for peace on earth."

November 17th 2016: Mother Mary has come forth today and she said we see people throwing judgments at each other with hatred and no recourse for their actions. "Once that negativity is thrown out it bounces around the universe out of control. The only way to curtail this negativity and hatred is with love and kindness. Once it is in the universe it spirals out of control and can cause great harm to the universal flow of balance and energy. If we overpower the negativity with love, it will snuff it out like a smoldering fire. To make an immense impact for a new beginning of peace on earth would include a small leap of faith forward for each soul towards kindness and love without judgment for your brothers and sisters. Peace on earth is such a reality and is right in front of every single soul. It is the choice of mankind to not live side by side and accept each other for the souls that they are themselves. You must all start anew and keep your minds, hearts and eyes wide open in order to go forth toward a better way of living."

November 18th 2016: Three beautiful angels radiating love and a brilliant white light came swirling around me today. They told me that "The Angelic Channeler" is a name suitable for my soul's purpose. They went on to say that enlightening souls upon this earth is of great importance to the angelic realm. "Every action or word an angel/angelic being speaks is pure love that radiates from our heavenly Father. The assistance that the Angels receive from the light workers are of the utmost importance in keeping both worlds connected. Those chosen to walk on light filled paths have an incredible responsibility to every being that has existed. Light workers are filled with the burden of helping souls who are stuck in darkness. The uplifting of every soul possible, takes us closer to the ultimate goal, the promise of a better way of living, which is peace on earth for all."

November 19th 2016: Archangel Gabriel came forth today and said the grace that is bestowed upon the world many times is given in vain due to the fact that many people ignore what is right in front of them. "The angels spread a sheet of light on the earth's ground to help guide the lost souls who can't seem to find their way. Every soul has the courage and strength within them to pull themselves out of any situation or desperation of emotions. Sometimes you must dig deep inside to find it but that is part of your soul's growth. Take a step forward, my dear, you are ready for a new part of your journey. We walk beside you and guide you with light, love and grace. You must be open and willing to accept the plight of the world as you move forward. Don't worry about the minute details of earthly responsibilities, for the time has come for you to rise up and be the light worker you were sent to earth to be. Your outlook on life will be different than the rest. The heavens are fully open to you my child, and we are at your service; all you have to do is ask and you will see miracles from heaven."

November 20th 2016: Today I attended a service at The First Spiritualist Church of Rhode Island for the first time. After the service I attended a class on past life regression with a spirit medium and angel intuitive named Gladys Ellen. During a guided meditation with Gladys, the first thing she told us was to go back to a recent meal that we enjoyed. I went back to a simple meal of burgers and fries with my son Matthew at Sonic. She then said to look with whom you are eating. I looked to my right to see Matthew, but it was my brother David sitting there instead of Matthew. I immediately felt like crying, overcome with sadness, joy, and confusion though I held back my tears. Every time I have a dream of Matthew, I am shown that Matthew and David are the one and the same. I believe I understand why I am being shown the oneness of the two. When I pray and speak to David, I always thank him for making me feel safe when he was here. David's death was such a loss for me and I also feel that I lost that feeling of ever feeling safe again. I am being shown that I have Matthew to keep me safe, and to help me feel safe. The angels always have a way of keeping Matthew close to me. I also have this strong intuition that there is an even deeper meaning in showing me the two in one. I'm sure somewhere along my journey it will be shown to me more clearly. Like I stated earlier, I do believe Matthew has some connection to my spiritual journey, and he has his own spiritual gift but fear has held him back. I have faith that eventually all will be revealed.

Gladys next had us go back to either a wonderful childhood memory or in utero. I could not find a wonderful childhood memory so I tried to go back in utero. I could instantly feel my mother's pain, sadness and loneliness and immediately backed away from it. As this past life regression went on, I walked down some stairs and saw a beautiful door. I opened the door and Jesus was standing there; He took my hand and He started walking with me. I could see the both of us from behind as we walked and I was a ten-year-old girl with brown hair in braids, wearing a red and white dress. Suddenly Jesus was gone and I was standing in a village. I looked around the village and saw men, women, and children busily doing daily chores and duties. I then looked down at my feet and I had the feet of a man; I was standing on dirt with no shoes on. I looked down at my clothing and I was wearing a sort of tunic or robe, the kind that was worn in biblical days. I desperately tried to find a mirror to look at myself and I found something like a mirror to see my refection in. I was a rather handsome young man with brown shoulder length hair. I also had some sort of material on my head that I was wearing like a hood. I became aware of something extremely heavy that I was carrying on my right shoulder. It felt like I was carrying the cross that Jesus carried but I knew it wasn't that cross. I kept trying to see what it was that I was carrying but I never did see it. I then tried to see what my name was and I heard someone say, "Robbed Peter to pay Paul."

Next Gladys told us to look around where we were and look in to the eyes of someone next to you. I looked in the eyes of a young woman and suddenly it was a deer's eyes I was looking into. Now I was in the woods with a group of men and I believe we were there to hunt for food. The weather was colder because we all had on heavier clothing, like some sort of a long fur over my robe.

Lastly Gladys told us to go back to the last day of that lifetime. When I went back to the last day I was kneeling on a dirt ground while a group of men were throwing large stones at me for my beliefs and I knew that I died that day.

Today my guide Agnes said do not waiver in your faith as you step forward, you will meet your kindred soul. "A mystical land in the heavens where souls grow like trees that are planted firmly and have great strength are in existence due to reincarnated kindred souls. Souls go there to learn and grow while they wait for their other half. Some soul's main purpose is to be a kindred spirit. While these kindred souls are apart from each other on the earth plane, they feel lost and lonely. If these souls don't stay on the right path on earth, then they go through their entire lives searching for their other halves to no avail. Their mission and journey is to seek and become one. Every soul has a different mission and journey but in the end, love is the fundamental key to any door."

November 21st 2016: In my prayers today I asked my angels to please give me a sign as to where my journey is headed because I am feeling lost and stuck. I also said to them I know that patience is a virtue and I have to just keep my faith and keep going forward each day. Immediately after I finished all my prayers I turned on Pandora to listen to music and I chose the shuffle category, which is a variety of artist. The first song that played was "Lady" by Stevie Nicks. Very loud and clear the angels gave me the message to my prayers through her song. In the lyrics she says, "And the time keeps going on by and I wonder what is to become of me, and I'm unsure I can't see my way, and he says, Lady you don't have to see." The message was well received from my angels. I am not to worry about what is ahead, and I am not to see it, or even know it. I am to keep going forth and keep doing what I'm doing for I'm where I need to be right now. The angels love music and their favorite way of communicating and giving messages is through music. This is the second time they gave me this message from the song "Lady." I am human and I have days where I have self-doubts, so I ask for guidance and help from my angels who are always there for me.

Jesus stepped forth in my connection today and he said that precious memories are gifts that help you get through difficult times in your life. "Instead of using these precious memories to feel sad about the changes in life or the loss of a loved one, use them as a more positive way of thinking. They help you get through difficult times, and appreciate people and the way things were at a certain time of your life. People use these memories to wallow in self-pity and sadness instead of using this gift to remember and feel the love, appreciate, and accept the life that you now have. Life is about constant change, and it is all part of the human experience. Accept each change and transition with open arms and celebrate the lives of those who are no longer with you on the earth plane. Be grateful that you have these memories. Use the gift of memories to rise yourself up, and not bring yourself down, for that is one of the purposes of this God given gift. As long as you have shared time and space with another soul, then there is no separation. It is only your emotional heaviness that will cause you to have a false feeling of separation. Celebrate, love, live, laugh and feel the joy that was meant for all of mankind. We all rejoice in the heavens when we see joy upon the earth plane."

November 22nd 2016: In my connection today, I saw a brilliant yellow light and in this light appeared a stunning angel who seemed very tall. I felt peace and love in her presence. I asked her name and she replied Jophiel whom I recognized as an archangel. She said to me, seek the truth and you shall find it. "Open your heart to love and you will feel love. Be kind to others and kindness will envelop you for what you give to others and the universe is what will bounce back at you. You reap what you sow is the truest of statements. As the world spins on its axis and our lives upon this earth go on, we must open ourselves to change and accept each other for the souls that we are. The magnificence of our true beings is something that a human mind cannot comprehend. It is so simple, subtle, and pure, yet so brilliant from the essence of our Heavenly Father, the Creator of all that is good. In the light of our souls, there is no cellular molecule that is the same. Each and every one is different and that makes us who we are. The structure of the molecules within our souls is limitless through God. Everything God does in the entire universe is never-ending. He could create for eternity and there would be no end to the beauty or the love he possesses in every cell of his being. Jesus taught us to have faith in God the Father; and when that faith wavers, so does our love for each other, our Creator, and ourselves. Be humble and kind, and an abundance of rewards will open up to you."

November 23rd 2016: My guide Joseph came forth today and said that one certainty is that our souls and the love of our heavenly father are never-ending. We leave the home of our Heavenly Father to come to earth for a human experience. We come to learn and grow as we do, until we return home once again. Love, kindness and empathy are the key factors to what is important on earth. But not much more than that is important for the soul and its growth. Each step you take is a step closer to the succession of your journey and the reason you decided to come to earth. When someone says, "I didn't ask to be born," is an untrue statement, for every soul has agreed upon his or her entrance into the world. Human emotions are lessons to some and can be big obstacles to others. They can be joyful or burdensome but either way, they must be dealt with in order to fulfill one's purpose upon the earth plane. Every soul is connected and united and while we are in heaven, we automatically know this. But while we are on the earth plane, souls forget and feel disconnected, and are not able to deal with being a human. The unity is forgotten which makes life on earth much harder. Some souls never feel comfortable, or never blend in on earth, and that makes their journeys and purpose much more difficult. Others return home earlier than planned because of this. That is one reason light workers exist on earth (to remind the souls where they come from and that no one is ever alone). Everyone's guides and angels are always at their sides helping, nudging, and guiding you all to find your way. May every soul feel the love we have for each of you."

November 25th 2016: John the Apostle came forth in today's connection. He told me that I seek the truth in others, although the truth is actually in myself. "You are the one that will light the way for others as a spiritual mentor. Take the path that you feel in your heart, and the growth that you experience will be amazing. Each newcomer will light your flame a little more. Teach what you were taught, and live what you have learned. Each moment in time will prevail over the next. The everlasting gift of love is the one connection that binds us in the unity of togetherness."

He went on to say that the extremists of the world will believe they have conquered all that is good when in actuality, each member of society are the conquerors, whether good or bad. "No soul stands alone, but those who feel they stand-alone are the ones who make their journey more of a struggle than needs to be. If you were openly accepting to all, then every aspect of your lives would be so much easier. The saying, "The apple doesn't fall far from the tree" is true in the fact that you are all of God's children, and are made from pure love and divinity. You carry God within you at all times, though it is up to you to bring this pureness to the surface. There is no break in the bond between God and his children. The break is only in the minds of those who are not willing to accept all that is good."

SEVENTEEN

Heavenly Visits

November 26th 2016: Mother Mary stepped forth in my connection today and she told me that earth angels will be coming my way for assistance in my life. She said that the poor will need assistance and those who sinned will need help with self-forgiveness. She also said that I would be a mentor, in many ways a trailblazer of sorts. "Share your plate of food with the hungry and help to stamp out hunger in your lifetime. Give a dollar to someone in need even when it is your last. Bring comfort and joy to those who seek it. We, my dear, will put you on a pedestal as a shining light of hope for the world to see. Trust in our guidance and have faith in yourself. Be the soul you came to earth to be and unite with those in the spiritual community. Your work will be revered in heaven, with a huge celebration the day you return home. Go forth my child with the Grace of God, you are loved, and we thank you."

Today I had a class in my apartment that was given by Gail Moffat from the UK. The only other person that attended this class was Robin, who I met at Gail's last class. We had a "marvelous" time, as I learned new aspects of mediumship. Today I learned that when someone I am giving a reading to ask me questions to prove it is the person they are speaking to, it then puts my mind in panic and throws me out of the connection with spirit. As I get to be a better communicator with loved ones, everything will become easier. During the class Gail asked me who the picture of the woman was on my wall. I told her that it was my mother. Gail said I thought it was your mother because she is here and she keeps telling me to look at her picture. I replied that I know my Mom is here because I have felt her close to me all day. Robin then gave me a message from my mother. She said my mother wanted to shake me because I have no faith in myself, and I don't trust in myself enough. My mother wishes I had half the trust in myself that she does. My mother hung around for the rest of the day and I could feel her loving energy.

After the class the three of us started conversing. I began telling them that from where I lived, the famous Lizzie Borden home is three corners down from me. Gail asked us what were our thoughts on the Lizzie Borden case. We both said we felt that Lizzie was innocent and Gail agreed. Gail then proceeded to tell us that Lizzie Borden had stepped forward and was in my house. Gail said she had stepped forth to thank us for our belief in her innocence. Lizzie went on to say that we couldn't understand the life she has lived after the murders, and the persecution she felt from the entire city. She said she was depressed and lived in seclusion due to it. She also said that her sister lived with her for a while but due to Lizzie's depression and stigma attached to her for the murders, her sister moved out. (At this point Gail, Robin and I were all receiving information from Lizzie). She then spoke of her father, who she said was a cruel, mean man and he never treated her well. She said her father was very demanding and cheap and that he made them live like paupers when they were very wealthy. Lizzie said her father physically hit her and sexually abused her. Mr. Borden was mean and cruel with his words to everyone he encountered, but Lizzie was like a prisoner of it. She then spoke of an Uncle who always thought of himself as Lizzie's guardian after her mother passed away. He was terribly upset all those years at the way Lizzie was being treated. When he found out about the sexual abuse it was the straw that broke the camel's back. Without actually throwing her Uncle under the bus, she let us know that it was her Uncle who had committed the murders. Without hearing the actual words from Lizzie, it is a knowing that you receive from spirit. After we received all this information from Lizzie, she then asked for our help. She asked the three of us if we could please clear her name. We all agreed to help Lizzie and she said that she was very grateful to us and she then thanked us. I will do whatever I can to help Lizzie clear her name. I feel putting my communications and conversations with her in this book are a good start.

Robin had to leave so Gail and I started to chat about my work with the angels. Gail asked me if I could tell the difference of when it's an angel, or a guide that is giving me messages during my connections. I explained that they almost always identify who they are, and when it is someone else like Mother Mary, a Saint or an Archangel, the feeling is quite different; they give me feelings of complete peace and love. Gail then asked if I knew the work of each Archangel and I told her that I knew the work of the ones that I have worked with. For example, Archangel Michael is a protector, and Gabriel is the messenger. She then asked if I knew what Archangel Uriel's job was because she kept hearing the name Uriel. I didn't know Uriel's job so I looked it up and she is the angel of salvation. Gail then said

Archangel Uriel was with us. Suddenly a wave of complete love wrapped around me and the room was filled with such a feeling of love and warmth that I started to cry from the overwhelming feeling of it. I could tell by the look on Gail's face that she felt the same way I did. Gail then told me that Uriel has come forward because the angelic realm has been waiting for this day to happen. Uriel said since the first time that I had met Gail the angelic realm had been waiting for us to reconnect. Uriel said this was the first day of our journey together. She also said that Gail and I would be doing humanitarian work on a world level. Uriel said the angelic realm had tied knots together that day to bind Gail and I to each other. She also said we would be intertwined as we come together to work, and then separate throughout the years. Lastly, Uriel said that I would learn a lot from Gail and that Gail would learn a lot from me, and that we would be the best of friends. It is days like today that makes me feel ever so grateful to be one of God's light workers. There is no other way I'd like to spend the rest of my life.

November 27th 2016: Archangel Uriel stepped forward again today and said that part of Gail's and my journey will include helping Uriel with the salvation of the souls of the world. She went on to say that there is no end to the depth of the love from the angels. What I felt yesterday was a small sample of their love for each soul in the universe. "Go forth and know that we stand beside you with all the love and guidance you would ever need. Each soul is programmed to be open to the love of all the realms. But as lives go on upon the earth realm, souls close off to that love, which in turn causes turmoil in their lives in many ways. When a soul becomes awakened and finds enlightenment, there is much joy felt in the angelic, and all the other realms. It is a time worthy of celebration. Moving a mustard seed is just as hard as moving a mountain, if your heart and soul is not open. The benefits you would reap by being open are immeasurable to anything else. If your heart and soul are not open there is no chance of enlightenment. Be willing to at least look at a new way of being and your chances at a better life are much greater."

November 28th 2016: Archangel Sandalphon stepped forth today while Archangel Uriel stood in the background. Sandalphon told me this message is from the world of the Archangels: "Each soul is filled with pure love and as the soul evolves, the purity of this love slowly drops off. As time goes on, hatred and anger replace the purity and love that was once there. Souls can be born into bad situations, but it is how you come through the other side of it that matters. Those who live in the dark have chosen the dark; those who live in the light have chosen the light. You, my dear, are a prime example of the negativity and wrong doings that have come your way and you have, by far, chosen the light. The awakening and enlightenment of souls upon the earth is a huge undertaking. We have great faith in you, my child. On completion of your succession on earth, you will be greatly rewarded. Go forth on your path and you can feel within you the right steps to take each day. We love you, support you, and guide you."

It has been said that Sandalphon was once a mortal man known as the prophet Elijah. He is an angelic ambassador of prayers, music, earth and personal ascension. Sandalphon has a twin brother known as Archangel Metatron. They are known as the only two Archangels who were once mortal men. The two brothers are the only Archangels with names ending in "on" instead of "el" like the rest of the Archangels. I then asked Sandalphon if he and his brother were once mortal men, and if they were twins. Sandalphon told me he has been on the earth as pieces of the earth but not in human form. He then told me that he and Metatron are twin flame souls and not twins as we think of on earth.

November 29th 2016: Today as I started my connection a man stepped forth. He had a hood over his head with his head facing down. When he first looked up I thought, "could this be Jesus?" I then asked him "who are you?" He replied, "I am Moses." He then told me that the people of this planet are eager to destroy the place they call home. He went on to say that each individual is responsible for his or her part in keeping this earth clean and saving this planet. "The nocturnal resistance on earth is what brings us to the level of destruction that will be witnessed if people are unwilling to do their part. The hope that we have for mankind is the willingness to open ourselves to a new way of living and being. Our wish is for peace on earth for all of mankind."

November 30th 2016: Archangel Michael stepped forth today and told me that the hours in a day aren't enough to hold all the magic, love and blessings he possesses. He went on to say that freedom from our will gives us much authority in the land called heaven. "Congratulations on your success of connecting to our realm. You will watch many events unfold for the rest of your days on earth. You are now an official communicator for the Archangels and all the realms. There will be many different souls who will step forth like Moses has done. Your job is to spread our word to the souls on earth. We have great trust and faith in you, my child. Our door has been opened to you, and you are welcome in at any time. You have earned the title, "Angelic Channeler," throughout all eternity. Your soul is soaked with the light of the angels and your path is clear and bright. Go forth to show the world new hope and new beginnings for everyone. You must all come together to shine your lights upon a new world."

December 1st 2016: Today Archangel Uriel stepped forth. I was then shown a vision of me as a child sitting on the ground-playing jacks with all the Archangels standing around me in a circle. Suddenly I was an adult standing in the circle of Archangels. I was shown this vision so I would understand that they have always been with me. They were waiting for me to be awakened and enlightened fully, to do the work that I have come to earth to do. Then each Archangel came forth to tell me what they have given me. Michael said he has given me courage and strength. Uriel said she has given me peace and love. Sandalphon has given me the uprising of myself. Gabriel said he has given me the gift of messages. Haniel has given me the gift of true enlightenment. Raphael said he has given me the ability to heal other souls. Raziel said he has given me laughter and joy. Raguel has given me health and blessings. Azrael had given me a boost of self-confidence and self esteem. Metatron has given me the ability to carry on. Haniel has helped to awaken and enlighten me. I was told the ability to see clearly has come from all of them. Then Mother Mary stepped forth and said she has given me the Grace of God. She then said that the turmoil that is in the hearts of many is caused by a twist of their faith. "As a leader of the light, you must show the way to restore faith in the hearts of the lost souls. Each individual creature represents certain significance to the world as seen by the eyes of the creator."

December 2nd 2016: In today's connection, I saw a vision of a man wearing a long king-like robe. I couldn't clearly see this man's face. Then he quickly started changing in to the many ways we portray God upon earth. I then asked this man, "What are you the King of?" The reply was, "Heaven" and then I heard, "I am in all things, I am in the pen that you write with; I am in the air you breathe; and I am in diseases. My essence touches everything on the planet. Know in your heart, my dear, that these words are true." I then asked, "Why do I not feel overwhelming feelings when I communicate with Archangels, Moses, Jesus or Mary etc.?" He then told me that my emotions need to be on an even keel in order to work with them.

Next, I had a vision of a woman who is the mother of my childhood friends. This woman passed away to spirit this very morning. She smiled at me very peacefully and said, "Hello Orange Juice Head" (it was what she always called me as a child). I said, "Hello Arlene" and then she left. I knew that she has crossed over and I could feel she was at peace.

December 3rd 2016: St. Therese stepped forward today and she told me that consequence for bold actions against other souls would be dealt with on a karmic level. "The reason that we ask for kindness and empathy towards each other is so souls don't go towards the darkness. The fidelity of mankind as a whole brings disgrace to the union of marriage. The rough patches in our lives can be smoothed out by a steady flow of faith. If the world leaders were omnipresent, the world would run with a flow of energy that was smooth as silk. The leaders are too self-involved to actually put the energy out that the world deserves. The incumbency of most men in business-like positions tear a hole in the universe because their intentions are not of the highest standards, or for the good of all involved. Medication can also stop the flow of one's energy, which in turn, causes turmoil physically, mentally, spiritually, and emotionally."

December 4th 2016: One of my guides, named Samantha from the angelic realm stepped forth to tell me that there is a celebration of joy in the hearts of the angels for my commitment as a light worker. I heard "Job well done, Helene" and then St. Therese stepped forward again today. She said that our parents and I are proud of the work that you are doing on the earth realm. We give you courage, strength and support from the essence of our light. Therese then said, "My Sister," as she bent over and held my hands; she told me that she has put healing qualities in me. She then said, "We love you dearly and look forward to watching you blossom in the work you will do in the future."

Samantha then said that the communication between realms and the angels is more open than anyone realizes. She said it is as simple as speaking words or a thought that brings them joy. "There is no shortage of angels or the help we can give to every soul upon earth. We stand beside you, turn to us and tell us what you need and we will help in ways that you would of never thought of. Don't ever be afraid to ask for help even from earth angels, you should only be afraid of not asking. We are all here from every single realm to help one another and our main purpose is for the welfare of all souls. We are all connected in our life forces for we are all of the creator's children. Make each day count so you may strengthen your soul for your life's purpose."

December 5th 2016: My guide Agnes came forth today and told me that there is a message of hope in the air. "It rings in the bells and flows through our consciousness like a whisper of light. The holiday season brings much joy and happiness to some while others sit in grief and pain. The distinctions between the two are what lead us to growth on our path or the direction of our journey. Each soul must carry their own load in order to release this burden from their soul. Once the soul is cleansed and free of burdens, then it is filled with white light to start anew. Each person must go through the doors of our heavenly father asking for help in self-forgiveness. Our heavenly father always grants everyone grace so that your soul will project into the world with kindness and love. The protectors of our universe are called "Light Warriors" who stop at nothing to keep our universe safe. An eye for an eye or a tooth for a tooth is true statements for a Light Warrior. They stop the darkness from seeping into our energy fields. Glory be to God."

December 6th 2016: An angel in a white robe trimmed in gold came forth in my connection today. I asked him his name and he gave me the name of Jonathan. He told me that the trial and tribulations of mankind are often due to their own doings and mistakes. "The freewill of mankind is a freedom but yet it is a burden to many souls. Some souls need others to control their actions and behaviors because they are not able to choose the right path with their own freewill. The choice must be made by the soul itself in order for the soul to grow. Some souls grow incredibly quick while others take numerous lifetimes and lessons just to take a step forth. In actuality freewill can hinder or help you, and the choice is up to each and every soul. Progress made along the routes of your life can also be determined by the priorities you possess within you. By asking the angels for help on a daily basis your growth can be accelerated. The angels' intentions are to help you get over hurdles and through rocky paths to a place of peace, love and kindness. We, the angels, ask that the people of the world call upon us for the slightest intervention. We love you and we are here to help."

December 7th 2016: My guide Joseph stepped forth today and he told me that the angelic realm and the spirit realm are both on different wavelengths. "The accessibility between the two is higher frequency and pure intentions. Doves bring messages of love, light and hope upon their wings as they fly through the realms. Think of your guardian angels as the three musketeers gallantly protecting your honor.

There will be a false prophet who steps forth like a hero, but in your heart of hearts, you will know the truth. Every step you take is a step closer to the magnificent rewards you will reap. Go forth, my child, your path couldn't be any smoother. The artistry of your life has just begun."

December 8th 2016: As I was saying my prayers today and praying for different celebrities that have passed, specifically I was praying for the older group of people who has passed like Lucille Ball and Desi Arnaz when suddenly Imogene Coca stepped forth with a huge smile on her face and said to me, "Hey what about me?" I was slightly surprised by this but amused and since that day I have added Imogene in my daily prayers. Those from the spirit realm will never cease to amaze me.

Mary Magdalene stepped forth in today's connection and she said that the Holy Land of the Apostles is built with the blood, sweat, and tears of Jesus. "Without pain and sacrifice the future wouldn't hold the promise of tomorrow. Each nugget of gold in the treasure box of life is based upon the love and purity that seeps from our souls. Each turn that is taken in the direction of our Lord brings you closer to the ultimate treasure, which is a healed soul, full of white light and love. There is no other prize or final destination greater than that. When they say, "The meek will inherit the earth; "it is due to their kindness and empathy for others."

December 9th 2016: Mother Mary stepped forth today and told me that the angels give love, light and messages that are carried on the wings of butterflies. "They bring hope to a new day in to the hearts of the suffering souls. A new day is dawning next spring as the world has a chance to start anew. Light filled souls will travel to the earth encompassed in nothing more than the shell of a human. They will be placed strategically throughout the world and they will bring new hope in the future. They are courageous souls, for their missions will be tireless and self-sacrificing. Their main purpose is to awaken and enlighten as many souls as possible. Each white light filled soul has been hand picked by the Creator in an attempt to draw out the darkness that is embedded throughout the world. Some dark souls must perish in order for the light to seep in. It is a battle that those in the light will win because in the end good will triumph over all. We ask that you openly and graciously accept all light workers with love and kindness as they do for you. Go in peace children."

December 10th 2016: Jesus came forth today in my connection and said that the consequences paid during difficult times in your life are due to your own infractions upon your soul. "Each soul must progress in the universe or the energy flow would be at a standstill. The next step forth for anyone in the universe is to be grateful and you will naturally progress. The progression of ten million souls at once increases the energy flow tri-fold and the outcome would be magnificent.

 Many millionaires have no self-worth in their souls and the lesson that they learn is harder than those with meager means. Money might rule the world in the minds of mankind but love is the ultimate ruler. Those who feel sadness because they have no materialistic gifts for Christmas must remember that you have the gifts of love and kindness from the Creator within you, and that is a gift above all gifts. Materialistic things on the earth are worthless to our soul and its purpose. What we need to survive are food, water, shelter, love, empathy and kindness. Anything other than that is useless to your body and soul. Don't take for granted the extravagance of all that you have. Be grateful and much will follow; this is the word of the Lord."

December 11th 2016: Today a man in a green robe stepped in and he somehow seemed familiar to me. I asked him his name and he replied, "I am Jude apostle of Jesus." At this time I innately recognized him as Jude and not Judas Iscariot whom betrayed Jesus. These are the words that he spoke: "the free flow of thoughts in the universe brings about ideas that encourage many actions of faith. Hopelessness in the world is brought on by a loss of faith. Each soul must come to grips with their inner turmoil. This turmoil can either rip you apart or bring you to your knees to succumb to your faith knowing that the Lord is your salvation and the center of all that is good. The Creator our Father will not let us suffer needlessly. Each situation and every action will bring us to where we need to be on our paths, to learn the lessons we have agreed upon for our soul to grow until we go home again. That warm, comfortable loving feeling you have felt in your lives at times is not even one tenth of what you feel when you are home in the presence of God your loving Father. To have those feelings upon earth would be too overwhelming for the human experience and would also not be self-serving to our soul's lesson and growth. Keep on diligently striving to be a better soul till it is your turn to climb the stairway to heaven."

December 12th 2016: My guide Joseph stepped forth in today's connection and said that the worst situations in life can be quickly turned around with faith, belief and devotion to a better way of life. "The stigma of those who are encapsulated under the rules of the government shall take the reigns to bring truth and light shining upon the dark souls of the government. A new day is dawning for the presidential election. Hillary Clinton will triumph in her life over the negativity and bad intentions of those involved. Shared communities shall try and help change the minds of electoral voters, for many of them are afraid of the outcome of Trump for president. Eventually a new light will be shed upon Russia and how deep Trump is intertwined with them and his business dealings. There will be uproar of Trump supporters who believe this to be false but in the end, the country will have suffered. Many different events will take place from now to the end of his time in office. Do your best to stay upbeat for positive results. Citywide, statewide and nationwide--all will be revealed eventually. Have faith and go forth, for the angels stand by the side of those who will triumph."

December 13th 2016: Archangel Haniel came forth today and said that a conversation between an angel and a human is as simple as an everyday task and there is no need for an out of body experiences or tests of faith. "All you have to do is believe and be quiet within yourself to communicate between realms. Each and every soul has the ability to communicate and a little belief will go a long way. Angelic tarot cards are another way of communicating with those in the angelic realm. Believe in yourself and your intentions and the messages that you receive will be for your highest good. Be more open, honest, and kind on a daily basis and let the angels enter your thoughts, hearts and minds. Working with the angels is as easy as asking for their help. Angels are all around and are interwoven into your daily lives. You never know when it will be an angel you encounter who was sent to earth for a variety of reasons. Be good to each other; trust each other with kindness, respect and love because one day it just might be an angel that crosses your path."

December 14th 2016: As I was saying my prayers today, once again as I was praying for certain celebrities, Anna Nicole Smith stepped forth. She had shown herself to me as beautiful as I had remembered her. She told me that she came forth to thank me for my daily prayers for her and her son. She then proceeded to tell me how proud she was of her beautiful daughter and how grateful she was to her daughter's father for raising her. She gave me an incredible feeling of peace and love. I went on with my prayers as she lingered for a short time.

Mother Mary came forth in today's connection and told me that I try to be a bright light to the souls who have darkness in their lives. She went on to say these things about my work and myself: "You pull souls out of the darkness and into the light as a service to your brothers and sisters. As a well-meaning soul, others have misunderstood your purpose on this earth. It is your soul that is free and filled with white light while their souls are weighted down by earthly worries. You truly understand your existence on the earth and that is worth more than any pot of gold. As you go through your life tell your brothers and sisters of all the good that is within them and the power that they possess to do good on earth. Courage and strength will help them to go forth in their everyday lives as they seek the truth of their everyday existence. Light candles for the souls who seek to find the truth. The abstract truth of our own inner guidance will be revealed at the time of their awakening. Each soul must go forth on a daily basis spreading love and kindness in order to find enlightenment and awaken their true soul's purpose on earth."

December 15th 2016: Today I did a reading for someone that was the most confusing disappointing reading I had ever done. The spirit that this woman wanted to step forth, did not step forth. Most of the spirits that did step forth she said she did not know them. This has never happened to me before and I was questioning my abilities as a medium. I was very upset so I contacted Gail Moffat about it. I explained to Gail everything that had happened during the reading. As I was telling her about it her guides told her that this reading was a learning lesson for me. The spirit that this woman wanted to step forth was not ready to speak to her. He had to work through some issues that happened between them when he was on earth. It was set up so that he was not allowed to come through. During the reading I told the woman I feel as if your grandmother is stopping him from stepping forth. She told me that there is no reason for her grandmother to do that. I let this woman know that I would try to give her another reading in a couple of months. After I spoke to Gail I felt better about my abilities as a medium. I was nervous to go forward in doing readings but I have had no problems since.

In my connection today Archangel Gabriel told me that the imagination of the human mind is so powerful that it can overtake the existence of reality. "Many people upon the earth have thought that they have imagined an angel when in truth we were really there. It is easier for some to believe that their imagination is working overtime. The help that we the angels give to the people of the world is so subtle as to not interfere with anyone's freewill. We will step forth with much power when we are called upon. We work side-by-side with the souls who ask for our help. As we are messengers of God, we bring messages to and from all the realms. As made in our Creator's eyes we represent light and love and are here to serve all who ask. The light at the end of the tunnel is filled with the presence of many angels and we offer assistance to all souls regardless of realms. We offer you the safety of a best friend, the love of a parent, and the peace within you."

December 16th 2016: St. Therese stepped forth today in my connection and said that the progression of one's soul is clearly based upon their own free will. "Each mistake should be a learning experience, and the fact that your soul will grow from it. Some souls never learn from their mistakes and their soul's growth is halted to a standstill, which sends out negative energy waves into the universe. The period of reproduction for a human being is meant to be a portal so that souls may enter the world. It was made to be a pleasurable experience and not looked at like a chore so souls would be more willing to accept the responsibility of other souls upon their entrance into the world. The souls that are born to parents are chosen long before the parent enters the earth realm. More than likely each soul born into your family is part of your soul's family, and you are together to learn a life lesson or to work on some unfinished business from another lifetime together. Sometimes the souls aren't of your soul family and the reason you are together is on a much deeper level. The variables of all this might not make sense to you while you are on the earth realm but in the spirit realm everything and every reason is seen so clearly. If you have ever wondered why you feel such a strong bond with one family member over another, more than likely that person was in another life with you, and you carry that bond into this lifetime. If this person was your child in this life quite possibly this person could have been your parent in your last life. There is a reason for everything you go through in life whether good or bad, they are for the purpose of you and your loved one's soul's growth."

December 18th 2016: My guide Joseph stepped forth today and he said that the revolution of the world depends upon the opening of the hearts and minds of the world leaders. "Each step they take forward is a step towards peace. Due to egos and stubbornness many world leaders put the energy of the world at a standstill or in a backward motion. The negative effect it can have on the world can hinder the progression of many souls and their purpose. The angels try to cut through the negativity of some, but free will stops much of the help the angels are able to give. A soul's continued energy field could be filled with love, hatred or anger depending on the soul and their intentions on earth. The disposition of an angry soul will send out negative waves, which in turn can bring down the energy of another soul. The ripple effect works in many ways in the world. Those who accept God's white light must throw out all the love and light within them so it will flow through the universe, uplifting others. It will always be a fight between positive and negative but at the end of it all, love and kindness is what will rule the universe."

December 19th 2016: My guide Samantha came forth today and told me that the infinite intelligence on earth is nothing more than a flower, or a child that weeps for its mother. "The connection between realms is so simple if you believe, and have the faith within you. The outer limits of each realm are beyond human experience. Patience is huge when it comes to the connection between realms. Each day is a new chance to connect to those in spirit, or any being in God's white light such as an angel. The opportunity to connect has always been there for anyone willing to take that leap of faith. After all we are all connected on a soul level, it is a false feeling of disconnection for some on the earth realm. The strongest trees have grown from the smallest seedlings with faith and trust within you. Make the most out of each day in this life, for each day is the beginning of another step towards your soul's purpose."

December 20th 2016: John the Apostle stepped forth in today's connection and said that the souls who rest upon the holy land are souls that have been forgiven from deep within from the core of their being. "The plot that lies in the deep thick air of humanity is so clouded with intense judgment, that no one can see clearly in front of their face. The hope and dignity for the Republican Party is to bring a united front to those who stand strong in wealth. The plan to stomp on those in poverty is an evil gesture on their part. The Bipartisan people of America are no longer allowed to think for themselves. Each minute they spend in the darkness has a backward effect on the energy of the world as a tear trickles down the cheek of Jesus. Free will choices can literally tear the world to pieces by those who have bad intentions. You must all rise up as a nation against poverty, homelessness and all that comes with it. The power is in each and every one of you to reverse the effects of all that has gone wrong. Peace towards each other will bring warmth to your heart and uplift you in ways that you can't imagine for the longevity of your soul."

December 21st 2016: Archangel Michael came forth with an incredible strong presence today and said that the souls of turmoil in this world wreak havoc in the lives of many. "They project their anger, hate and prejudice out in to the world in very destructive ways. The angels of peace have spread white light around trying to salvage what is left behind of all the destruction. The major targets that they chose are those of the innocent and the weak as to assure their success. A much-needed wrath placed upon these souls of turmoil cannot come soon enough. Every soul has a direction and a consciousness and when the two move in the same direction, nothing can stop them unless a Divine Intervention stops it. Each soul must pay a price, whether good or bad for the choices they have made on earth. Death of a body does not excuse anyone; on the contrary it brings you much closer to examine your true self and the changes to be made. No one is ever free from his or her mistakes and they will follow you from life to life, unless you are willing to forgive yourself and others and to improve your soul by going on a higher learning journey."

December 22nd 2016: Moses stepped forth in my connection today and said that the weight of the world lies on the shoulders of the less fortunate souls. "The fortunate ones don't feel the struggle to survive on a daily basis. Each soul brought forth through propaganda is less fortunate than all. Their suffering is deep within and can only be alleviated by true enlightenment. The deeper the wounds the more salt should be poured upon them so they can feel the sting of the thorns of Jesus Christ. There is a lesson of empathy that must be learned in order to fully accept the challenges put before you. The harsh truth of learning a lesson can be pain and suffering, but the end result will bring you where you need to be in order to fulfill your soul's purpose. Each mountain climbed will bring great joy to your very being. The love within each of us is the most powerful tool imaginable."

December 23rd 2016: Archangel Gabriel stepped forth in my connection today and said that the miracles of Christmas have begun, and the righteous will prevail over the lost dark souls. "The angelic realm is singing praises of joy and love throughout the nation to send out peace and love to the souls of the world. The magnificence and beauty that we behold as Jesus Christ, King of the Jews, is a worthy Soul like no other. Those who protest in the streets that He is not real are the ones who sit in darkness within their souls. They are to be pitied for the sadness that dwells within them for they cannot feel the light of the Lord. Each moment that they are silent to the word of God is a moment not truly worthy of existence. There are some who can be pulled out of the dark and others cannot, for they will choose to sit in their pain and misery forever. Freewill plays a part in every aspect of every realm. Each turn taken should be a turn for the better, not for the worse. Every day should be lived to the fullest for every moment counts in this human experience. Do not judge others while the shoe is on the other foot for you all have been there in some way, one time or another. Love is the key and forgiveness is instrumental for peace on earth."

December 24th 2016: Before I started today's connection I heard someone say, "You don't have to work tonight." I was filled with an incredible feeling of déjà vu. I knew someone in spirit had already told me this in a conversation that they had with me in my dreams.

Mother Mary stepped forth in my connection and she said to surrender my will to God and let the emotional upheaval of myself be aware of the truth inside of me. "Be one with God in order to fulfill the prophecy of your legacy. Give of yourself spiritually and we will come anoint you with the wisdom and the knowledge to awaken and enlighten the souls of the world. Free yourself of earthly possessions and be grateful to just be alive on earth. The next step will take you higher than you ever imagined. In your dream state we will sprinkle the necessary information for the uprising of your journey. Preparations are being made for your arrival to the next level. Don't be afraid, my child, for we will sustain you every step of the way. Your hopes, fears and dreams will all come to light as we open the door to our heavenly graces. Hallelujah and welcome, each day will begin anew and each step will bring you closer on your journey. The light will shine upon you in your finest hour."

December 25th 2016: Mother Mary has stepped forth again in today's connection and she said that the bright brilliant light that shines on the mountain top known as the moon holds powers of healing for the entire universe. "There is so much more kindness in the universe than mankind has experienced, it is like a tropical forest full of light, love and gentleness. The more we reveal through words, the closer you are to being one with the universe. Each follicle of hair on your head is a symbol of the cellular dimensions in a human body, which is way more complex than the construction of one's soul. Each flight pattern that a soul seeks is unique and accustomed to your soul's growth pattern. The patterns align with each other so each soul will benefit accordingly. Each generation on earth learns a little more than the next until one day when the ultimate goal of peace has been reached."

December 26th 2016: Jesus stepped forth in today's connection and said that the resilience of one's soul is so strong and courageous that it is the only thing that will truly withstand time. "Preparation of one's soul for the purpose of time is a unique experience for each soul. The continuity between time and space in each realm flows effortlessly like a butterfly through a meadow of sunflowers and daisies. There is no procrastination in the spirit realm for healing or going forth on a learning journey. Each soul determines the amount of time needed and the pace that they will go forth with. Souls will work on improving themselves on many levels to achieve the peace within. We are able to time travel on a soul level in other realms. Mankind will never experience time travel on earth as they view it. Time was not meant to go backwards for there would be no progression of one's soul. Changing an outcome in the past would lead to a trickling of many other unpleasant events, which were not meant to be. The only words that should be said after a statement of "If I could go back and change that" should be, "I would be kinder and more loving," otherwise it has no meaning to your purpose on earth. Strive for the day you will have no regrets because you were kind and loving to all your brothers and sisters without prejudice."

December 27th 2016: Mary Magdalene came forth today and said that the gifts of hope and freedom are what many people seek. "The righteous shall remain in thunderous glory. The meek shall take a step forth to give glory to God. Each and every moment wasted in negativity holds us back from our true purpose on earth. Those who waste this time will suffer in the long run due to the lack of their soul's growth. The precious moments that we have with our brothers and sisters are far beyond the measure of love. The predominant offender of their moral compass weighs heavily upon Jesus." (I was then shown a vision of Jesus carrying the cross and I had a knowing of the cross representing our sins.) Each soul must take the burden off of Jesus and take responsibility for their actions and live their lives with the highest moral values as I have." As I was writing this last sentence of the message a beautiful orb of white light floated directly over my paper.

December 28th 2016: My guide Agnes came forward today and said to me: you give of yourself without expecting anything in return. "You, my child, are the flower that has blossomed perfectly in divine timing. Each soul that you encounter with your work will benefit greatly in many different ways. Thank you for your devotion. Though we tell you all of this, we know that you understand that you are just like all the souls on earth. You are no better and no worse, that is why you were chosen. Each step forward for a suffering soul can be long and tedious, though their steps forth are great strides for all of mankind with helping themselves brings strength and courage to those around them. The most powerful messages in this world will come from great suffering. Pontius Pilate showed how he was weak in character and mind and how Jesus suffered because of it. The suffering of our brothers and sisters is not something we should ignore. We must support and stand up for those who are of weak character and minds. We were put on the earth to help each other in times of trouble and need. Stand by your sisters and brothers, as you would want them to stand by you."

December 29th 2016: Jesus stepped forth in my connection today and he said that the tragedies of the world are based on the atoms that split upon interference of the molecules in a molecular structure such as the earth off of its axis. "The homecoming of the souls who passed away in 2016 was gifts that were returned on a timed basis. Contracts were broken, and souls were impaired because of it. The highest and best good for the souls of the world were looked at as a whole. The program of our souls can be altered in a flash by a single thought from our Creator. The dialect that goes on between souls in the spirit realm is so subtle and gentle, and is meant only for peace. Those souls who were collected have brought their highest value to earth and had met their soul's purpose. It was a gift and an honor for them to return home once again. The gift of happiness lies within each of us and it is up to each soul whether you choose one path or the other. Don't wallow in self-pity for it serves no purpose for your soul."(He is speaking of all souls as well as the many well-known souls that returned home in 2016).

December 30th 2016: An absolutely beautiful angel came forth today. Rays of light surrounded this angel. I asked the angel for a name and I heard "Hope is what you can call me." This angel then said that the equality that each soul projects into the universe brings great hope for the future of the world. "The minute details of each projection are based upon the purity of each soul. The most horrendous days that have come forth are from the souls that float in the darkness. Each day that dawns is a new chance for each soul for a fresh start. Everyday is a gift to start over and many souls are blind to this fact. It is an incredible gift from God to have these chances to start over instead of being stuck in mistakes and bad decisions. Our hopes from the angelic realm are that each soul opens themselves to let the sunshine in and be aware of this precious gift of a new day everyday. The transformation of a soul can be so subtle yet worth every step forward. Stand up and do what's right for yourselves and each other to make this world a better place."

December 31st 2016: Archangel Michael stepped forth today and he said that the trials and tribulations of mankind have gone on for centuries due to a lack of courage and strength against the dark forces. "You must all be willing to forgive yourselves and others as the first step toward redemption. The projection of one's freewill into the universe can harm the outer crust of each cycle that the earth revolves around. If the magnificence and beauty of our inner souls were brought to the surface, then peace on earth would exist. Souls choose to keep the beauty hidden as a way to control their freewill. To those in the spiritual realm it is viewed as a fight against the tides. The angels can only uplift the souls of the world so much, for it is up to each soul to complete their work on this journey. We can uplift you but if you don't stand, then our work goes unnoticed. Each pied piper that plays a tune has a mission that is certainly worth dancing to."

January 1st 2017: I have been feeling very lonely and blue, and in my communication today my guide Agnes said I was to seize life and the moments that come with it. "Don't sit in self-pity, for it does not serve your purpose on earth. Go forth with a gusto and do your highest and best good to uphold the laws of the universe, and the path that you took to better the planet for yourselves and your brothers and sisters. The highest value placed upon you is your own self worth. Your devotion to yourself is just as important as your devotion to God. Everything will change this year and you will reap the benefits of your work. Do your highest and best good each day and it will all follow you. You are the product of our Savior's work and His devotion to His children. Everyday that you spend uplifting another soul is a day that is filled with white light and devotion to our Lord. You are blessed and you will be honored for all that you have done."

January 2nd 2017: Archangel Uriel came forth today in my connection and said that the rising of the sun on a new day and the beginning of a new life correlate on a universal level. Souls are flown in on the wings of angels to begin their human experience on earth. The angelic realm works very closely with the earth realm in a very gentle, loving capacity. Each chord or note written musically brings great joy to all of the realms. The celebration of joy and music bring us to a new understanding of the purity of our souls and all that it contains. Each sweet, gentle action that is performed on earth rises up the levels of energy throughout all the realms. No matter how big or small, every act of kindness counts as a token of humanity on earth. On the other hand, acts of deceitfulness and darkness send out negative energy so it is a constant fight of white light against darkness. The more souls that are awakened and enlightened make a better chance for peace on earth.

Behold the new born King, for He is the center of all that is good, and the choice is yours."

January 3rd 2017: Three very playful angels came in and were flying around me in a circle today. They told me to use 'The Saints & Angels Oracle Cards' by Doreen Virtue this week for the daily readings that I give to my Internet followers. As I read one of the cards that were chosen for today, I realized why they wanted me to use these cards. This particular card was titled "Activist," with a picture of St. Mother Teresa on it. I found information in the guidebook for these cards that I never knew before and it made a connection for me. She was born Agnes Gonxha Bojaxhiu but out of respect for St. Therese of Lisieux she took the name of Teresa. This was a major epiphany for me since St. Therese is my sister and I have been told by several mediums and my guides that I will be carrying on the work of St. Mother Teresa. This new information made me understand the connection among the three of us and I'm very excited to go forward with this work as God sees fit.

Mother Mary stepped forth today and she said to let the outer circle of those who cross your path help bring you to your destiny. "A new circle of friends like myself in white light will cross your path in this winter solstice. They will help bring you to a new level of understanding on your journey. Unconventional methods will be used as a way to reach this enlightenment more efficiently and proactively. Tell the world what it meant for you to be enlightened by these souls." As you read on, I have been enlightened in the winter solstice by such incredible souls of white light. Connecting to these pure souls from other realms is the most magnificent experience I could have ever thought possible. It is the most unimaginable warmest, purist feeling of love, light and trust. It is an experience that I wish every soul on earth could experience for themselves. I am honored to connect and communicate with these incredible holy beings of pure love and light. She went on to say that the closer you feel to God, the more love will seep from your soul. "Spread the word of God throughout your day so others can choose their paths. Every soul that becomes enlightened is priceless. The mission of the army of light workers is so vital to the essence of all that is God, and all that he has created. Keeping your hearts open is a big step in keeping the universal flow of energy moving forward. Choose everything that is good and just for today nothing negative can stop you from living your soul's purpose."

January 4th 2017: As I was saying my prayers today, my son Matthew's friend, a young man named Derek came to me in spirit. He had passed away two days prior. He stepped forth and showed himself clearly to me. He even showed me where he used to live because he was desperately trying to let me know who he was. He was in a state of chaos and I could feel so much regret and sadness from him for his passing. I told him to calm down and let the angels help him. I then asked the angels and Archangels to please help him to get where he is supposed to be and settle him in. In an instant he was gone, and I knew he received the help he needed though I was left feeling upset from the sadness and regret I felt from him. I do believe he tried to come to me the day prior because I could feel someone who was sad but he wasn't able to clearly make himself known.

January 5th 2017: My guide Agnes came forth today and said that the progression of one's soul in this world starts with a smile or a loving touch of warmth from another. "The simplest acts of kindness can move your soul along on the path of its growth towards your future purpose. Life on earth was meant to be simple, but mankind has added many complications along the way. These complications cause needless stress and unhappiness. The souls that become enlightened to a better way of living can clearly see their way around these complications so they stay on a smoother path. A soul comes to earth pure and free of any disillusionment until the standards of mankind are set upon them. Freewill is a gift from God that unfortunately can cause a human to destroy themselves and others if the wrong choices are made. The choices made upon earth must be looked at closely, and to show kindness to others so you may live more closely to God's will and to be the soul you were created to be."

January 7th 2017: A man wearing a robe from the biblical days stepped forth. He seemed to be middle aged and had lost some hair on top of his head. I asked him who he was and he responded, "I am James the greater." At first I didn't realize it but later I realized he is James, the Apostle of Jesus. James began by telling me that the uplifting of souls on this earth is a job that requires courage and strength. "Each soul must be connected through linear space and time in order for the soul to be uplifted. Plagiarisms of such connections can be found throughout the world. The time and space continuum is real and necessary, and takes place on the equator of the earth. Listen carefully to our words, for the light that falls upon the hearts of many will turn to darkness if the equator slips between the sun and the moon's brow. Watch carefully for the reversal of effects that the world has on each other, for these are telltale signs of the world coming to an end. The reversal of these effects is legitimate and can be stopped by a single tear from our Lord Jesus Christ. Faith and belief in humanity encompassed with kindness and love is all that is asked by our Heavenly Father. Trust your instincts and do what is best for everyone in order for the world to survive. Take heed my brothers and sisters."

January 8th 2017: The day that Debbie Reynolds passed away, I asked my guides and angels if they could please let me know at some point if Carrie Fisher and Debbie Reynolds had crossed over and were doing okay. Today, to my surprise my guides set up a visit from Carrie and her mother. As I was starting my daily communication, I saw Carrie and her mother sitting on a grey stone bench. Sunshine and beautiful clouds surrounded them. Carrie stood up and walked over to me and the following communication pursued. Carrie: "Take your time to help the troubled souls for they are your ticket to heaven." Me: "I am my ticket to heaven." Carrie: "You will see what I mean. It's a vast world of responsibility but you seem to have the bulls by the horn." Me: "When I go to heaven, will I meet you?" Carrie: "We have already met my dear. May the force be with you." Me: "I am not a Star Wars fan; I am a Carrie Fisher fan." Carrie: "I knew that I liked you." I thanked her and then told her I was sorry for the suffering she endured on the earth. Our communication finished with Carrie telling me that our visit felt just like doing one more interview. She blew me a kiss and walked away. Debbie Reynolds sat on the bench the whole time and smiled at me sweetly. I could sense that she was very weak and tired and that she needed healing. I called up my friend Heather and told her about the visit I just had. Our friend Tim then beeped in on her end and she told him about the communication that I had with Carrie. Tim's response was "Wow, I can't believe that." Heather then said what part can't you believe and Tim said the part that Dawn has never seen Star Wars. Amusing that Tim had no trouble believing any part of my encounter with Carrie or Debbie, but was flabbergasted that I had never seen Star Wars.

Archangel Gabriel came forth today and he said that the lunar eclipse of the sun can be more powerful than moon beams, which can cause it to be frightening due to it's power. "The overbearing beam from the moon can cause chaos in the universe with its empathetic power. Each step closer to learning the power of the moon is a step forward for mankind. Each soul deserves kindness and love throughout each day in order to reach the height of their progression. A backward flip in time would not change any souls' auras or the outcome of a soul's progression. A timekeeper of sorts is an important figure when it comes to the length of a soul's time on earth. Unfortunately, those souls whose time has been cut short due to mankind must learn their lessons in other ways. There is a spiritual university where souls go to learn about themselves, their mistakes, and how to correct the negative within them. A higher learning journey is an honor, and must be embarked on with the best of intentions. Each journey completed is like a bright shining light that emits incredible joy, love and kindness into the universe. No matter which realm you are in, whether spirit or the earth realm, you will somehow always be working on your soul and its purpose towards peace throughout all eternity."

January 9th 2017: John the Baptist came forth today. He said that there are many treacherous points of entry into the world for souls, because mankind cannot overcome their many addictions, or cannot break the chain of abuse that they were born into. "Part of each soul's purpose is to overcome these struggles and make life for the next generation easier, and more loving. Some have fought and won, but many have failed, which brings their karmic energy into a swirling vortex of nowhere. The promise of a new day was given to all, and those who do not grab it will not reap the benefits of it. Each day, each dawn, you may start anew, to bring your life, your soul, and its purpose to the place it is suppose to be, and that you deserve. Fear and self-pity hold many souls back from moving forward and seeing the true light within them and others. Make the most out of each situation, each moment and each day and you will see and feel the difference to a new way of living and just being."

January 10th 2017: Archangel Haniel stepped forth today. She said that the tormented souls on earth and their burdens could be lessened by their willingness to believe in God and all that he has created. "A mutual respect for each other on earth is like a hidden treasure. Gifted souls can only give so much without their energy being drained by those who act as leaches. Pick yourself up and go forth with your daily routine. Every soul that you help, every step that you take helps you to climb higher in the majestic mountain. Through the hills of this mountain there will be magic, and miraculous events that unfold, that will be revealed within everyone that passes along that path. The proper required ID for those that pass are good intentions, and a bright light that burns within them. The souls of agony will be helped by the souls that burn bright. Each accomplishment along any soul's path makes life on earth worthwhile. If you could forecast your sins, then you could control the amount of damage that would be done. Make the most of each day for they will be gone before you know it."

January 11th 2017: Today as I was starting my connection to the other realm, St. Catherine stepped forth. She said, "I am here to ease your loneliness and help release the anger and frustration within you." (She bent down and was dipping a cloth in a bowl of water and wiped my forehead with it). She said, "Please allow me to wash away the pain and suffering in you. You, my child, should feel free of any earth-bound responsibilities to carry on with the work of God, and the path that is yours. We in the heavens are at your side in the blink of an eye. In order for you to carry on with the work of Mother Teresa, you must be humbler and less caring about earthly possessions. We don't want suffering for you and we will sustain you every step of the way. You have a team of angels and saints who will never let you fall. Your life's work will be magnificent, so go forth in the knowledge and wisdom that we can feel your soul and all that goes on within you. Clouds rose to meet the sun the day that grace was poured upon you. Don't let your neighbors suffering go unnoticed, extend your hand, and offer the kindness that you would hope someone would offer to you."

January 12th 2017: Mother Mary came forth today and she said that beauty is all around if you open your eyes to the hidden treasures right in front of you. "Magnificence seeps out of the pores of every being; it is only at certain times that these beauties are seen. The most common error that humankind makes is treating another soul like they don't matter. When a soul (particularly a child) is abused, it is felt with complete sadness throughout all the heavens. This is an action that is not looked upon lightly, and it serves no purpose for one soul to hurt another. Love is the key to all that is good. Part of this love includes empathy and kindness for others as well as yourself. These are the basic human qualities that every human is born with. Part of the human experience is to learn and grow from the hurt and pain that is endured in this lifetime, and to overcome it and make it better for the new incoming souls. The souls (especially the children), who choose to come home early because their time on earth was too much to bear due to the actions of others, sadden us. Accept each other for who they are, for each soul on earth deserves the love and kindness just like the next one. Make peace within yourselves so you are able to extend a hand to someone in need."

January 13th 2017: A man stepped forth wearing clothing that looked like he was from royalty in another era. The clothing looked satiny and velvet. He had a beard and moustache and seemed rather short. I asked him who he was and he replied, "I am King James." James told me that the coronation of Queen Elizabeth was an epic event in the history of England. "In the eyes of the people, Kings John, Henry and Charles were not fit to sit on the throne. The multitudes of facets that go on in the workings of Buckingham Palace are so intricate and interwoven into their daily lives. The Queen's guards never stand at ease due to terrorist threats against the Palace. Their momentum is reached by their daily practices of stability within their unit. Behind each closed door is a different secret that keeps them united. The heavenly force that has been felt in the palace has been crushed many times over and over again, though they stand tall and pure in their own right with the help of the archangels. Never again will a woman sit on the throne in England. Each cord that is cut will represent a male in power. Hail the Queen for when her time comes her people will revere her as a great warrior in heaven. Follow your heart in the direction of the light and the goodness that you seek will fall at your feet."

January 14th 2017: Archangel Raphael came forth today and said that the courage and strength within each person determines how far the progression of one's soul will go. "Sometimes a blind leap of faith is the best faith possible depending on the state that your soul is in. When you come to a junction on your path in which a decision must be made whether to go left or right, your soul must be open and willing to let the light in, in order for you to choose the right direction. The common denominator for those who choose the wrong path and ingest substances is that it blocks your energy. The white winged dove can bring healing and light to those who need it upon request. A conversation with a soul in the angelic realm is as easy as having a thought or speaking one word. We in the angelic realm are willing, open and ready to communicate with the souls who ask with the best of intentions. Children of God, you are not alone for we stand at your side with love and grace."

January 15th 2017: My guide Joseph came forth and said that the viewpoint that America has of Donald Trump has been embedded in each mind. These viewpoints can't and won't be changed but for the good of America you must all uphold the standard that each soul is worthy, until proven otherwise. Sooner or later you will feel like you live in an asylum in the greatest country on earth, due to all the chaos. Uplift your soul, and the souls of your brothers and sisters to overcome all the confusion. Choose your battles wisely for many will fight to no avail. Make the most out of each day as you all go forward in your daily lives. You must view the world with the eyes of a child and focus on everything like it is new."

January 16th 2017: My guide Margaret stepped forth today and she said that hope and courage fill the hearts of those who stand strong in their convictions. "The illusions that many cannot overcome have to do with the rulers of the world. The land of the Holy in which souls are free is the best possible existence. In this land there in no turmoil due to other's decisions. Every soul offers love and kindness to another in order for peace to exist and a free will choice of one on earth can destroy many lives. World leaders must learn to coexist and with the best intentions for their people in order to strive for peace on earth. The angelic realm works with world leaders, though the leader must willingly and openly, without reservation accept this help for the good of their nation. Each seed that is planted in the soil with love helps bring souls closer to the roots of mother earth and all her divine healing properties."

As I continued on in my communication, Mother Teresa stepped forth. She told me that the sadness of the world falls upon my shoulders. She continued on, saying, "I am honored for you to carry on with my work. You will be loved by the world though it is hard, lonely work. Each soul that you touch is a miracle of light and love. Go forth with peace in your heart and soul for that is the only way you will make it through all the desperation, suffering and sadness you will encounter. Take these lives and make a difference; for your presence alone will uplift souls to continue on in life. You will be able to handle the face of adversity more easily than I, due to the adversity you have already faced. You will be the keeper of the gate for the suffering souls to emerge to a new beginning. Peace is with you my child." (She then stepped closer to me and blessed my forehead).

After my connection to spirit today I video chatted with Gail Moffat. I told her I had been thinking that in order for us to help Lizzie Borden clear her name we should wait till we are more recognized in the world. Suddenly Gail said Lizzie had just stepped forth quickly. Lizzie apologized for stepping forth so quickly but she saw an opportunity to step in while we were speaking of her. Lizzie went on to say many things starting with she was very grateful to us for listening to her. She went on to say that we couldn't understand the awful, lonely life that she led after the murders. The pain and suffering she endured was almost like a leper. She thanked us for having some understanding of what she went through. She said in the spirit realm she still suffers because all the negative thoughts and words that people have about her on the earth plane go directly to her in the spirit realm. She then said it was her uncle who killed her father and stepmother. He was angry at the way Lizzie was being treated by her father, and her stepmother allowing the abuse. She also said that her father raped her, and this enraged her uncle and other family members. Gail said that her uncle and her sister were now standing at Lizzie's side. Her father and stepmother were also in the room but they stood across the room separate from Lizzie. Gail said this symbolizes that Lizzie has not reconciled with them in the spirit realm. Lizzie then went on to say that the entire family knew that her uncle was the one who killed her parents. It was kept a secret because the family knew Lizzie would be acquitted due to her innocence. Lizzie kept quiet out of loyalty to her uncle. She carried this burden due to her love and loyalty for him. Immediately after we hung up, I could feel Lizzie and her family with me. Lizzie clearly and loudly whispered in my ear that John is the name of the uncle that murdered her parents. It felt as if she was standing by my side in the flesh, as I swear I felt her breath as she spoke. I then saw him standing there with her and he told me it is now okay to tell the world that he was the "one." John has already paid his penance for his actions in the spirit realm and now things must be set right on earth. After my communication with them ended, I did research to see if Lizzie's biological mother Sarah Anthony Morse Borden had any siblings. She had several siblings and one of them was a brother named John Vinnicum Morse. This is the Uncle John who Lizzie said that murdered her parents. Nothing is ever a coincidence and I truly believe that the spirit realm had set up the entire communication between Gail and myself with Lizzie and her Uncle.

January 17th 2017: Agnes said today that spirituality is a gift from the heavens that resides in each of us. "Whether you choose to let the spirituality in or let the spiritualty out, is up to each soul depending how you view it. The magnificence of the world surrounds us at all times just like spirituality does. It doesn't come when it feels like it; it is always there for the taking on a daily basis. Much anger in this world could be stopped with an ounce of spirituality. People look at it as a religion when in truth it is a way of living, a way of being and existing. Take the hands of your brothers and sisters and show them the path of this incredible fulfilling journey called spirituality. The more spiritual you are, the brighter your life will become. Trivial things will no longer bother you, and you will see the importance of your time on earth and the soul you are to become. Peace on earth and good will towards all is the goal in the process of everyone's awakening."

January 18th 2017: John the Apostle stepped forth today and he said that memories created on earth are everlasting in the spirit realm. "Each soul that steps forth in the spirit realm to connect to those on earth is forbidden to reveal the secrets of their realm. Every soul must learn these secrets in divine order and timing. To learn of these realms ahead of time would disconnect souls from there paths and in turn would cause harm and chaos throughout the universe. Too much information would be a big problem for mankind. As a soul progresses, the learning progresses and everything eventually falls into place. Every little piece of information that is received from the other realms is important and is given in a timely manner. The existence of all that is good from our Creator has been carried on by strong courageous souls that have come before you. Open your hearts, souls and minds to the words in this book for the truth is in them. Let us come together as one under the reign of our Heavenly Father."

January 19th 2017: Mary Magdalene stepped forth today and she said that one of the most precious gifts that we shall ever receive is the gift of knowing and understanding our true selves. "As souls fight against the darkness, their inner light and beauty emerges to overcome this darkness. The most prevalent amenity in our souls is kindness and empathy for others. Heed the Lord's words that these amenities can bring peace on earth to all. Take the time to show love and caring to one soul a day and your purpose would be served. Extend a kind hand to another on their rocky path and in return, your path will be made smoother. Perform acts of kindness for others without expecting anything in return, and your light will shine brightly to illuminate others on their path. Your guides stand by your side waiting to be of assistance so they may help you, and you may help others. Karmic balance is a 360-degree revolution and there is no escaping the results of your actions, good or bad."

January 20th 2017: My guide Joseph stepped forth and said that the blessed are the ones who light the way for others. "The souls who choose to sit in darkness will never take one step forth on their path. As a soul goes through life there are many layers that must be peeled back to reveal your true selves like a butterfly from a cocoon. There is beauty in each soul and it is up to each soul to work towards finding it. Some souls just shine brightly naturally because that is their soul's purpose on earth. In a human body, souls get angry at their lives and existence, when in actuality each soul has chosen their lesson to learn, and their path to take before they came to earth. For your soul to evolve and learn lessons, you must overcome the hardships and mountains that are put in front of you. Fear causes people to suffer needlessly, but if you could feel the true essence of your soul, then you would understand that there is nothing to fear. The angels, your guides and all those in the other realms will help and protect you if you ask with faith and good intentions."

January 22nd 2017: Today Mother Theresa stepped forth again. As I viewed her from across the room, I said, "Mother Theresa is that really you?" She then sat beside me and said, "My essence is with you my child." She then proceeded to tell me this message: "the beauty and magnificence of the world will be toppled over by the anger within each other. Mankind will destroy the hospitality of souls from other realms. Each level a soul has accomplished will be meaningless during the chaos of all that is to come. Keep each other safe by repeating these words, "Hail Mary the Queen of the throne, and all of her accomplishments throughout all eternity, help bring peace to the earth, settle the souls and quiet the minds of those who have gone astray during this war amongst each other." Make it known to the world that the accomplishments of each individual soul in this journey to bring peace will not go unnoticed. The rewards you seek will help you go forth on your mission. Take heed to these words my friends, for your souls are at stake. She then said I was a good soul and left.

January 23rd 2017: In my connection today I saw what looked like an army of angels banding together. This is the message that I then received; the souls who have been tortured would take vengeance on those who caused the torture. "A new day will rise from this vengeance. A brighter future for the world is coming through pain and suffering. Change is inevitable for the world's anger and despair is upon us. Hope will come in the form of many adversities and open many minds to a new way of thinking. War will be obsolete after the new day rises. Monuments will be erected in honor of the fallen heroes. Peace will no longer be a pipe dream but a reality. Hardships will be looked at as symbols of gratitude to our creator. Monarchies will exist in order for peace to be established. Life will become pure and simple, as it was in the beginning. Newness will coarse through your veins as you continue to spread peace and love throughout the land. Have hope for the future for it can only enlighten your soul, and your purpose to better this planet for all."

January 24th 2017: Once again in my connection I saw a group of angels. I felt such seriousness from them while they were in my presence. I was then told that hollow ground is sacred ground and it will be disturbed. Hope for the future will be renewed once the light workers step in place and make their presence known. Each soul on earth will help commence building in one way or another. Know that the true essence of heaven is in your heart making sure that the plans on earth go forth as needed. It is a new day, a new dawn and freewill will be adjusted accordingly to the soul in order for darkness to not seep back in. Empathy should be used in your daily communication with your brothers and sisters with no judgment, for it would hurt others and yourself."

January 25th 2017: Archangel Gabriel said today that the challenges we face on a daily basis have rewards that come in unexpected ways. "The fight or flight mode comes in to effect when we are faced with challenges that include disaster. The final outcome to many disasters is negative but the hope of the new world rising begins with each soul opening themselves to the light and releasing any darkness within to God and the angels. Your world will face many difficult challenges but in the end it will be worth every drop of blood, sweat and tears that seeped out of your bodies. Eventually, no soul will ever suffer again the way that many are suffering on earth now. The unifying of souls will bring your world to a new way of living and being. Each day a soul is born, they bring with them the hope of a new world."

January 26th 2017: My guide Joseph stepped forth today and said that magnificent mountains with hills upon hills would be covered with majestic love from the heavens. "Each soul that steps on these hills will bring forth to the world love, kindness and empathy. Each breath that is taken in the existence of these hills is far more compelling towards peace on earth. Each neighbor that you help clothe, feed or comfort brings great joy to the universe and to the connection of your Creator. The last thing that is wanted for any soul is suffering. Follow your heart and help those in need regardless of race, orientation or creed. There is a fiber that connects each soul to the next and it cannot be broken. The world must stand as one so each soul gets the love and kindness that they deserve. Many souls have tried for peace on earth and have failed because in a sense, the world as we know it must end in order to start anew. Self-love is the only key to open the door of true happiness."

January 27th 2017: My guide Joseph stepped forth and said that the revolution of the world is upon us. "The dire need for some in leadership to step down would be a step in the right direction. Muslims will be overcome by grief and hatred due to the negativity being thrown out in to the world. The rising of each nation is very important to the new world. "Thy Kingdom come, Thy will be done" is true of what is to come on earth, all brought on by mankind. The true essence of each soul will be shown during the chaos that is already taking place. Freedom rings for all those who are willing to stand strong with love, kindness and empathy for each other without judgment."

January 28th 2017: The army of angels came forth again today and said that the most inconceivable way that some souls will deal with the chaos and catastrophes to come would be through suicide. "The fear of the future on earth will cause great harm to many souls. The souls that have faith, belief and trust will find the courage within them to go on and help make this world a better place for all." (These lyrics started playing in my head: "Let there be peace on earth and let it begin with me." I then heard someone say that this should be the motto of each soul on earth). "The tyrants will be forced to vacate their positions of leadership. As these tyrants step down, light will begin to seep in and bring hope for a new day. We, the angels, ask that souls upon the earth remain as calm as possible for this will benefit you in many ways. Army's of angels and light workers will walk the earth helping, comforting and doing all that is asked of them from our heavenly father. Miracles upon miracles will be witnessed and life on earth will be better than ever before."

January 29th 2017: As I was sitting on my couch today, Mother Mary and Mother Theresa both came forth. Mother Mary was there for the support of the message to me because lately, I have been feeling very sad, lonely, and angry. The message was a combination between the both of them and it started with, "My dear child, progression will come through your daily life, don't despair for life is one step at a time. Your monthly expenses are sustained and the guidance we give you is for your highest and best good. The friendships that you seek are yet to be. Hope for the future is all around you and the progression of one's soul comes in time. The outcome of a life that has been lived fully brings so much more to the earth than just living in self-pity and anger. Each message that you have received from other realms is a notch on the totem pole. It is a puzzle that is being put together in slow motion. When the last piece has been put in this puzzle of your journey, you will return home once again. Take notice to the everyday goings on in the world. There is much more for you to accomplish in the time you have left on earth. Let go of material items, unburden and unshackle yourself for your only prized possessions are your children. Go with peace and love in your heart knowing that we stand beside you."

As I was doing some dishes in the afternoon, still feeling very sad, I started crying talking to my mother out loud, and telling her how much I missed her, and how hard life is without her. Within a half hour after this happened, I received a phone call from my sister Gail to tell me that as she was washing dishes a woman loudly called her name twice. Gail lives alone so she knew nobody was actually there. She asked me if I knew who had called out her name. I told her to give me a minute to try and find out and instantly my mother came to tell me it was she. I then told Gail it was my mother who called her name and Gail said I knew that it was her voice but I didn't want to say it. My mother came forth to Gail because she knew Gail would call me about it. She knew how down I was feeling and she wanted me to know she was around me. This visit from my mother brought me right out of my sadness and I felt a calmness and peace within me. I am only human like everyone else and there are some days that are tougher than others, and I need that reassurance that my loved ones are by my side.

January 30th 2017: As I started today's connection Mary Tyler Moore stepped forth. She presented herself young and she was wearing a brownish suede Native American outfit. I thought to myself it looks like she is going to do a skit. I said to her, "Mary, are you okay?" She replied, "I am fabulous!" She went on to give me this message; "I left the earth with a sadness for the people of the world. Native Americans are the only true settlers of America. No one should hold prejudice or anger against another for the fate of the world relies on it. I beg the people of America to come together before it is too late. Nations will fall upon each other and sacrifices will be made. Many will hang their heads in shame at the outcome of Donald Trump as president. I can see everything very clearly from this side. Please put this message in your book and get this out to the world. You are the spokeswoman for many souls in all of the realms. This was in your contract that you signed before coming to earth. There will be visits from many other souls."

January 31st 2017: St. Therese came forth today and said that miraculous events have unfolded throughout my life and whether I was younger or older, these gifts were meant to be. "Each sunrise is a step closer on the path to your journey, so take the hand of those who have come before you and follow their lead. Each soul will offer you something different toward your eminent success. Reach out to the celebrities who step forth from the spirit realm because they step forth for a reason. You will be dubbed, "The Star Whisperer" receiving messages from the grave. Open your heart to all who comes your way. This type of platform is needed in order for you to accomplish your soul's purpose on earth. The Native American people accept you as one of their ancestors and thank you for your prayers. Chief Riding Red Bull has blessed you on your journey. The wall of finance will fall down for you eventually and a flood of abundance will start pouring in. The block has been broken and you are open to receive all." (I was then shown a wall made of stone that had a hole in it with light shining through it). "A request has been made on your behalf."

As soon as they told me that a request has been made, I knew immediately that it was Rosie Cepero who had made this request. Rosie and I spoke earlier in the day. She did a blessing and said a prayer for me because of my financial struggles.

February 1st 2017: Mother Mary stepped forth today and gave me this message: "The light of the world falls upon the shoulders of many. Don't be alarmed at the outcome of hate and prejudice. The suffering souls upon the earth will be freed in the wake of many disasters. Every action will have a reaction and this will bring many to the destinations that they belong. The rapid river that flows with the time of our world will be interrupted by the earth's constant flow of negativity. Each soul on earth is responsible for what they put out in to the world. Every shred of negativity can be counteracted with an act, or even just a thought of kindness. The inherent ability that each soul has to survive is the base of everyone's courage and strength. In hard times, you must dig deep for this courage and strength, for my son did not send anyone into the world without it. Those who are more vulnerable are protected in many different ways. The abuse of souls on earth sends waves of sadness throughout the other realms and a change is needed to raise earth to the moral standards that was meant for it from the beginning.

February 2nd 2017: St. Therese stepped forth in today's connection and said that the road to freedom for many has a path that is stacked with obstacles. "In order to remove these obstacles, you must have belief and faith not only in God, but also in yourself. Everyone has a pattern that is sort of sewn into your soul, which allows each soul to be unique and also to be identified correctly for his or her soul's purpose. When someone attempts to change the pattern of his or her soul, which is when chaos ensues. Going against the grain of what you were meant for will only bring distress and unhappiness to you. We ask that you go forth each day as you wake up to a new sunrise to stay open in all ways. Ask God and the angels to help you accept each day and all that was meant to be in that day with love, kindness and empathy for yourself and each other. The "Proof is in the pudding" is a perfect statement of your daily life. The effort that you put in to your daily life will determine your success or failure for that day."

February 3rd 2017: Archangel Raphael came forth and said that many of the inventions from mankind have made life easier but they cannot relieve one's soul of the turmoil that's within. "Modern medicine can only go so far for it is the soul's job to begin the actual healing of one's self. Everyone has the ability within them to cure any ailments that arise; but many souls don't believe in themselves or the abilities given to them by the Creator. Our own souls can inherently relieve ourselves of anything if we just allow it to. Faith and belief are much more powerful than many even considered. God just doesn't allow all this suffering on earth, mankind has brought some of the suffering and some of it was chosen as life lessons. Everyone is given the ability to heal within but it is useless without the belief in yourself. Take the words from these messages and tuck them into your heart and soul for use in the future. May every soul who sets their eyes upon these words know and feel how much they are loved from the angels."

February 4th 2017: Before you read this next entry in my communication journal of the other realms, I must say that I have no physical proof of any abuse to anyone I only know of what spirit has told me. As I started my connection today, I had seen Rue McClanahan standing there in a sparkly bright blue pantsuit. I said, "Rue is that really you?" and she came closer to me so I could see her face more clearly. This is the message that I received from Rue: "There is much suffering in the world and each step that is taken to alleviate the suffering will allow more light to seep in from other realms. I have had my fair share of suffering on the earth. Now I am an advocate for suffering souls. Peace in one's heart cannot exist unless kindness has been offered. The challenges that many face on a daily basis are heart wrenching. As part of your journey you are asked to share these words in the hope that others will open their hearts, souls and eyes so the suffering doesn't go unnoticed. I myself was a victim of elder abuse; it can happen to anyone." (I then said to her I don't know if I can put this in my book and Rue replied with: "Tight lips sink ships").

I asked her if she had anything else to say; she smiled at me with sparkly eyes and said to me: "Spread my words and you will be surprised."

February 5th 2017: Joseph stepped forth today and said that the challenges that some souls deal with on a daily basis prove to be overwhelming. "These daunting responsibilities can overtake one's purpose on earth. Many of these responsibilities are unnecessary, and are factors in hindering many souls on their paths and the purpose that they came to earth for. At the end of many lives these souls returned home without having fulfilled their purpose. Lessons that were not learned while on earth will have to be learned in other ways. If everyone lived each day in the present with love, empathy and kindness for each other, the future would automatically take care of itself. In turn, each soul would be nurtured independently and they would rise to new heights in every way possible. The kindness and love that you seek for yourself is the same kindness and love you should be extending to others unconditionally."

February 6th 2017: My guide Margaret said today that the process of elimination of things gone wrong are a biased opinion by those in the Government. The American flag and constitution represents freedom for all, but as we look on from the heavens the basic human rights are not being upheld and will play a part in the downfall of the nation. Those in power are misguided in their thoughts and beliefs while egos play a big part in the downfall of mankind. Each decision that is made with the intention of holding back others throws out negative karmic vibes to those involved. If you cannot extend a hand to your brother or sister, then the least you can do is to not take negative action against them with the intentions of holding them down. The innocence of the young brings so much love and light in to the world. As adults you must break free of all that has hindered your souls so that you can feel the love and light that the world so needs once again."

February 7th 2017: Archangel Michael has come forth today to say: "The terminally ill can sense the souls of those who have crossed over before them, for it is a thin veil between worlds at this point. If you reach your arms out before you then you will be touching our world. This is something that the human mind cannot digest which makes humans unaware of how close the other realms really are to each other. On earth humans substitute many things in place of grief and pain. If everyone would just go through these emotions and feelings purely, then getting to the other side of it would be so much quicker, and your journey much easier. Regardless of how anyone numbs his or her emotions and pain, it won't go away until it is dealt with. Humans tend to prolong their own suffering, but to feel these emotions, whether pleasant or not, are part of the human experience and the soul's journey."

February 8th 2017: Mother Mary stepped forth today and said that the plight of mankind is an ongoing battle. "No matter how many steps forth are taken, there will always be someone there to push you back. Human's egos are such a hindrance to the soul's progression. The main target in everyone's life should be love, not materialistic items. There are wealthy people in the world that would give up everything to have unconditional love in their life, for their loneliness overtakes anything that money can buy. So many souls neglect themselves and what is truly important, for love, kindness and empathy is the base of our souls and all that our Creator stands for. Break through the chains that bind you by stepping forth without judgment for all of God's children. By not offering a helping hand or allowing your brothers and sisters entrance to a free land, then you are not doing your soul or the soul of others any justice. Helping those who are less fortunate in any way should be priority. May you always remember the golden rule: Do unto your brothers, as you would have them do unto you."

February 9th 2017: As I started my connection today, St. Jude stepped forth and told me the helpless, hopeless children in the world that cry in pain due to hunger, abuse, neglect and poverty shall be the souls that raise this world out of the darkness and in to the light. "The empathy these souls will possess due to their own suffering will instill the courage and strength within them for what is needed. It is said that when a soul feels hopeless, they pray to me, so I ask that souls pray to me before they feel hopeless. I can uplift souls before the hopelessness and darkness sets in. I clearly see how souls give up so easily when many times help is just around the corner. Everyone possesses the strength within them to carry the weight of the world on their shoulders. It is the loss of belief within yourselves that bring you down into darkness. So, as I am called upon in their time of need, I will continue to help the hopeless. But as I convey these words to you, I want the people of earth to know that I am here for much more than they ask of me. Bless you, my child, and peace be with you."

February 10th 2017: John the Apostle came forth today and said to live life to the fullest, regardless of what others say or think of you. "This is your life, and your mission, as you bring the highest value and importance to it. The nay sayers of the world are the ones who hold themselves back from the amazing feats they could accomplish. Don't hesitate to be one with the earth, for the root of your being is directly connected to the center of it. The illumination of souls on earth brings such brilliance, joy and positivity to the entire universe. Each accomplishment on earth is felt throughout the entire universe, and vice versa. The thread that connects each being to another is the most incredible work of our Creator. Life on earth could be so much better if humans would be humbler and let go of their egos. Freewill and egos are two wonderful gifts from our Heavenly Father, though humans have chosen to take these gifts and turn them into mountains they are unable to climb."

February 11th 2017: My guide Margaret came forth and said that the fight for the future of America will be an ongoing battle, no matter who is president. "Chaos will ensue over policies, wars will continue and the wreckage of planes is coming. Hope and trust must be instilled in the souls of the world so that they will be open to receive all that is to come. Visions will be given to the light workers to bring forth the new existence of mankind. Peace and joy will fill the hearts and souls of everyone. It will feel like it is a dream or a story out of a book, and people's monologues will no longer carry negative tones. Souls will return to earth that were chosen to better the planet and to also bring peace and harmony with them. There will no longer be madness upon the earth. Listen to those who speak from the light and you will not go wrong on your path. Remember, each day is a chance to start anew."

February 12th 2017: Archangel Gabriel has come forth today and said that man has compromised the revelations from the book of Jesus. "The revelations are true within their own rights without the added twists that were put upon them. The gospel of our Lord is one of true pure faith and while it has been tainted through the years it still holds the energy of His true essence and existence. Mankind bends every aspect of the world to fit their own needs without respect to the nature for which it was created. Improvements in the world are well noted though mankind always goes a step beyond and intrudes on the ideas of the Creator. Monuments have been erected to honor our Heavenly Father and others, but many times words do not match these actions. As angels roam the world in search of light workers, they come across souls who sit in darkness. These souls need to be uplifted, which makes the angels search that much more important to help save the suffering souls. As you go through your day and show kindness to another, then you have done the work of the Lord and you would have carried on His gospel in its truest form."

February 13th 2017: I gave a reading today to the woman I previously gave a reading to on December 15th 2016 in which I wrote about because it was a very disappointing reading. The reading was disappointing because the person who she wanted to connect to never stepped forward. Since I gave her the last reading, the spirit realm has worked with her loved one on some of the things that needed to be healed and dealt with before he stepped forward to communicate. He came forth today very clearly and loudly. He told me he committed suicide, and wasn't ready to communicate with his sister at the time of the first reading. It was a wonderful reading, full of healing and love for both the spirit realm and the earth realm. He stepped forth at the time that was meant to be, and it was wonderful. I learn as I go along to never doubt the spirit realm, or whatever happens in a reading.

St. Therese stepped forth today and gave me this message. "The most unique way to help others is by self-sacrificing. These unselfish acts of kindness help your soul to rise to a new level of awareness. Healing begins from the center of your soul and your self worth will help speed up or slow down the process of healing, depending how you view yourself. You must go on a healing path to help the souls who need to forgive themselves and I will help you every step of the way. Our family is honored that you have chosen this path in life. Your soul will always remind you who you truly are and your self-worth. You have taken big strides on your path though there is much more work to be done. The Blessed Mother has watched over you your entire lifetime as you went through the dark times and struggles to become the soul that was needed for the rest of your journey. We all thank you for your devotion to our Heavenly Father and your soul's purpose. You will see much pain and destruction on your path, but know that you are there to help make it better for all. I leave you with blessings and love, my sister."

February 14th 2017: Archangel Haniel stepped forth today and she said that faith and hope are brought in these messages to the people of the world. "Each significant event that occurs in someone's life is a reminder of the reason they are on earth. Sometimes a reminder comes in the form of a loss, and other times it is something that is uplifting, either way, these reminders are important to the direction of our paths. An overdeveloped sense of progression on our journey can prove to be fatal to our main purpose on earth. The hovering of one's soul between realms is caused by a lack of self-faith on the final journey before you return home. While on earth if you live your life to its truest form, then no number of obstacles will hold you back from accomplishing your soul's purpose in its entirety. The angelic realm is set up to help any soul who sincerely asks for help. The mission of any angel is to guide, protect, love and offer assistance to the souls who need it. We, the angels, are always here for every soul, we never go far away and if you could bring your faith and trust to the next level then you could feel and hear us. Each word that is spoken out of love and belief will bring you closer to any angelic being. Souls who are childlike and playful from any realm are considered to be in their purest form. Muslim people are good people and will rise above the hatred and prejudice."

February 15th 2017: The last few days I have had conflicting feelings and confusion about what the next step I should be taking in my mediumship and spirituality. Today, as I started connecting to the other realm, Mother Mary stepped forth and said to me: "Free yourself from the guidelines of the spiritual community. You must act freely from your heart and soul. Step forth with confidence in your decisions, and do not let others' opinions embark upon your true calling. Allow your guides to guide you towards your true purpose on earth of helping the souls of the world. You, my child, are special in your own right and will be looked upon with grace as you continue to step forth into the light. Your life will interweave with others but, your path is your own. You were chosen for a specific mission on earth, and to stay on this journey you must trust your inner guidance. Know that you have made a difference in the lives you have already touched. I have been with you since the day that you entered the earth, and I will continue to be with you till the day you return home once again. I know that you can feel my love as I bestow grace upon you."

February 16th 2017: I did a reading yesterday and it was the best reading I have ever done for anyone; and I was very proud of myself for improving. Today as I connected to the spirit realm my guide Joseph stepped forth. Today Joseph reminded me of Professor Dumbledore from Harry Potter except he is very regal looking in his long sort of king-like robe. He told me to trust my inner guidance to take me to the next level of my mediumship. He went on to say that yesterday's reading was a small glance into the development of my mediumship that is coming my way. "Take heed in these words and know I will guide you through incredible journeys on your path. We ask that you do your highest and best good on a daily basis as part of your life's journey. Big changes and rewards are coming soon for you. You have earned them by your constant devotion to the spiritual and earth realms. Feel the inner peace within you and take life one day at a time so you're not overwhelmed. I have been assigned to you to help you accomplish great feats through your life. I am the head of the angelic team that will help raise your soul to everlasting glory. We are one; we are together, and know that we will never leave your side. Glory be to God and hosanna in the highest."

February 17th 2017: I see, feel, and hear many spiritual beings very closely around me today. I can see them as sparkles of brilliant light. So, today's communication made a lot of sense to me. Jesus came forth and said that the most prominent souls in the spiritual realms have stepped forth to assist me in my upcoming endeavors. "The tides are rolling in to help your final journey on this level. Each step forth will open a door to another chapter on your journey. Don't be alarmed at the loss of people around you for this personal space is needed to complete the next step. You have been shown that big changes are coming and you have verbally confirmed that you are ready for them. Immerse yourself in the body of our presence, and we will fill you up with what is needed to continue your work. Take our hands and we will lead you to a higher purpose. The world will see the radiance of light that will emit from you and you will be honored as you carry on the work of our Heavenly Father. Each day's struggles and accomplishments have brought you to the place you are today." Mother Mary then showed herself to me and said, "You have done well, my child, and now is the time. She then bent down and kissed my head and said, open yourself up and accept all that we have to offer."

February 18th 2017: My guide Samantha from the angelic realm came forth today and said to take the time to smell the flowers and not to rush through each day as if it is a chore. "Beauty is all around you, and you must learn to live in the moment in order to fulfill the next portion of your journey. Feel the love of the angels as they surround you. Don't hesitate to belong to any group on earth and look beyond what the average person sees to find something spiritual in all that comes your way. When opportunity comes knocking, answer the door with a positive attitude and a smile. Make the most out of situations that put rocks in your path. The door to the angelic realm is right in front of you, all you have to do is turn the knob." (I was then shown a vision of a door opening up and I stepped inside. Beautiful flowers were everywhere, and birds were flying around. Red hearts floated through the air. The grass was very green, and there were waterfalls of bright sparkling white light. Animals were walking around and angels were going about their daily business. There were trees that had colorful flowers all through them, and the sky a brilliant blue. I felt serenity and peace and I have never seen anything so beautiful in my life. I looked across a lake of white sparkling lights and saw my orange tabby cat, Max, who passed away in 2012 sitting there. I wanted to go to him but I didn't know how to get over the lake. I then noticed a wooden arched bridge to cross to the other side. I ran towards the bridge and when I got half way over an angel appeared in front of me and put his hand up to stop me. He said to me; it is not time yet. Then everything disappeared and the vision was gone).

As I told my vision to a friend, she assumed it was about me dying. I did not get any feeling like that from this vision. If you remember earlier in the book how I stated that Max would be returned to me sometime in this lifetime. I feel this vision was about Max returning to me but it is not time yet. I have this sense of him returning to me towards the end of my life. I believe he will be my spiritual animal guide in the last years of my life before we both return home again.

February 19th 2017: My guide Margaret came forth and said that vulnerable souls are treated with disrespect so you must be cautious as how to approach these souls because of their dignity. "The truly selfish souls will always show their true colors, but stay on the path of enlightenment and forgiveness towards them. Do your highest and best good to honor yourself and don't let the actions of others affect your self worth. As souls go through life, they feel a merry-go-round of emotions that can spin them out of control. It is during these times when faith should remain strong so your self worth goes undamaged. Extend your hand to raise another up and in turn this will raise you up even further. Loved ones can hurt us without ever realizing the pain they have caused, but forgive them and go forth for they are only human. Life lessons can be extremely difficult but ultimately, your soul will reap the benefits from them. No soul is perfect, but to love without judgment is as close as you would get to it. Kindness, empathy, and love are the formula at the base of all God's creations."

February 20th 2017: Archangel Michael came forth today and said that the untold stories of the angelic realm would be told in bits and pieces as I go through my journey. "The secrets that lie within your mind in a mountain of knowledge will slowly be retrieved as needed. Your connection to the angelic realm is much closer than you realize for you have worked in many lifetimes with the angels and your quest each time is admirable. In every lifetime you always start as a broken soul who is lifted up by your own intervention, which brings you to the point of the spirituality that you need in order to help others. You have learned many life lessons and your soul is ready to embark upon a higher level of learning so that your soul can acquire the knowledge and wisdom that you thirst for. Go forth each day and don't worry about minute details, and the next chapter in your life will be revealed to you. The people you have encountered on this journey have served as stepping-stones along the way. Some of these souls will play a role equal to yours for the remainder of this lifetime. Go forth, my child, with no trepidation for the future. We have your back, as you have always been loyal."

February 21st 2017: As I connected today, I could not see anyone but I felt many beings of light around and I heard someone say, "At the tender age of 6 you were told to follow your heart and soul by Margaret. I was then told there is a magical door you can enter at anytime that you wish. Just close your eyes and connect to the other side. On each visit you will be taken on a magical journey to help you better understand the goings-on of heaven. You possess a dynamic mix of energy that allows you this passage. As you begin on this journey, do not focus on earth but on us."

As I kept on connecting, I saw myself walking in a forest with very tall trees on both sides of me. Suddenly I was above the forest and there was a white door with a few steps leading to it. I went in the door and there was nothing but white inside and I tried looking around, but still, all I could see was white. Suddenly, to my right I saw an old wooden chair so I sat in it. I sat there for a minute until I saw another door to my right again, so I got up and opened it. I had seen beautiful colors of grass, trees and flowers. Looking around, I realized I was still in the same room, and I was looking at a painting on the wall. I then pulled the painting forward to reveal a golden hidden wall safe and then I was told the numbers 12-24-36. I opened the safe with those numbers and inside was a beautiful sparkling silver skeleton key. As I turned around, I saw a large beautiful gate surrounded in clouds. I used the key to open the gate and walked inside. All I could see were clouds everywhere. Suddenly, I felt a presence and I instantly knew her name was Margaret. I then realized that my guide Margaret has been with me since birth. She took my hand and I saw myself as a young child, but then my age kept changing through the years to the age I am now. I asked her where are we going, Margaret? Then everything disappeared, and I was told that today's journey was "to show you what's what, who's who, and how to get where you're going."

February 22nd 2017: Archangel Raphael came forth in my connection today, he was immersed in a glowing beautiful green color and said to me, "Thank you for spreading healing with your messages of love to the world. Sunshine is a form of emotional healing; when the sun is bright, the soul also shines. The animals of this world need tender loving care and in return they bring healing to the souls of the world. The negativity of one's soul can bring sickness to the body. Gratefulness and appreciation of life on earth is far and in between. Tell the suffering souls of earth to pray to me for healing and I will immerse upon them my emerald green source of energy. Not all humans can be healed for I cannot interfere with a soul's contract; but I can bring comfort to those in need. Each life lesson must be learned in order for the soul's progression. Each day that a soul sits in darkness will cause damage to their overall well-being. Put your troubles on the back burner, get on your knees and ask for help from the heavens. No one can go through this life alone, for teamwork is God's work. Let the healing begin."

I then closed my eyes to see if I was going to be taken on a journey. I suddenly saw vibrant purple, and then felt severe pain in my left breast. I automatically knew I was receiving a healing from Raphael and other healing angels. The pain lasted 3 to 4 minutes and I sat there and just felt the pain because I knew it was for my own welfare. This was the same type of pain I felt when I was standing in front of the St. Therese statue at St. Anne's Shrine when I was receiving a healing from St. Therese. When the pain subsided, the colors changed from purple to pink and yellow. I always see purple when healing angels are around and it is such a spiritual empowerment color, which signifies becoming one with spirit. Pink represents unconditional love, while yellow is happiness, creativity and spiritual development.

For the past 5 days I have not had any readings to do which is unusual since I started doing readings. I was feeling kind of down wondering what this meant. I have been asking the angels and my guides to show me what is going on with my journey. Five minutes after I received this healing, I was contacted to do 2 readings. I must learn to never question my journey and to have faith in my guides and the angels.

February 23rd 2017: As I connected today, I was shown tulips and a white bunny. My guide Margaret then stepped forth and said that Easter is going to be a time of rebirth. "Your soul has evolved in many ways through each lifetime. Congratulations; a celebration of sorts is coming your way. Each milestone is an equator to your entire well-being. The turntable of time is on your side for you have made great strides on your personal journey. Life is going to be filled with craziness and excitement for you in the upcoming years. A brainstorm of ideas will come your way and these ideas will be shown to the world in the hopes of helping mankind. You will be shown the downtrodden lives of many souls and this is your chance to uplift them through your spiritual being. At times crowds of people who will be touched by your spirituality will surround you. Your book is a testament to the people who have endured much suffering, but can't see what is right in front of them. You are a plain Jane and an ordinary soul who has blossomed into so much more. The people of the world should see this and realize that this greatness is in each and every soul."

February 24th 2017: Today an angel wearing all white with wavy blonde hair who was named Christopher stepped forth. I felt a very different and special presence from him like he was up in the hierarchy of angels, though he is not an archangel. He told me that the tunnel of light that is seen at the end of a soul's journey on earth coagulates the soul from one dimension to the other upon entrance and exit. "The dimensions have many levels and upon entrance into each level, the soul must be adjusted accordingly. These dimensions are filled with many angelic beings that guide the souls to where they belong. The weaker souls need more help in adjusting while the stronger souls are more independent and evolve more quickly to where they need to be. This is all part of the cosmic consciousness of a soul. There is a never-ending cycling of souls into and out of the world. The soul who chooses to enter the world must be fully prepared in order to fulfill their purpose on their journey. The soul who is ready to exit has hopefully done their best and highest good on their journey. If their purpose has not been met, then there will be meetings with ascended masters and a resolution will be found. Each resolution is different for every soul and the resolution will be to better that soul and it will always be done with love and kindness."

February 25th 2017: Archangel Gabriel stepped forth today and he said that people must come to resolutions in their lives for the sake of their own salvation. "Each soul must step forth and conquer the demons within in order to fulfill their soul's main purpose. It is like a jungle of turmoil that must be cut through to clear the way and to go forward freely on your path. Once you stand on the other side of this emotional turmoil, everything including yourself will feel lighter and brighter. The motions that some souls go through in a day can set them at a standstill, with no growth spiritually, mentally, emotionally or physically. As the saying goes "Damned if you do and damned if you don't" is not true because "If you do" regardless of how you view the outcome there is always some progression no matter how small. The world is full of angelic beings ready to assist anyone who is open and willing to ask for assistance. It might not be in the form that you imagined but it is always done with your best interest in mind. Our Heavenly Father spreads His love continuously for all of His children so go forth knowing that you are never alone in this world. Everyone has an angelic being by his or her side everyday, so feel the magical touch of the angels for they can help make your life easier, all you have to do is ask."

February 26th 2017: As I started my connection today, I was taken on a journey and the first thing I was shown was a trail that I was walking on. Both sides of this trail had beautiful trees with low hanging branches that had colorful flowers on them. As I got to the end of the trail there was a lake. I stood at the lake for a minute before an angel appeared with a gondola-type boat and then the angel helped me to step inside. The angel then floated to the front of the boat where he started effortlessly pushing the boat. We went down a couple of small waterfalls until we reached a piece of land that had many rocks in the water. I stepped out on to the land and at first I thought that I had seen Jesus, but it was a man who had a long gray hair and a beard. He was wearing a black suit and a black hat and his attire reminded me of that of a Jewish gentleman. I asked him who he was and he answered, "I am Abraham." There was a narrow stream with narrow paths on both sides of it. I walked in front of Abraham down the path and not a word was spoken between us. We reached a cliff and below the cliff I could see a forest as if it was in another world and Abraham was no longer with me. I became a little frightened because of the height of the cliff. Suddenly a rope bridge appeared in front of me but because of my fear of heights I was apprehensive of crossing the bridge. I mustered the courage because I wanted to know where the bridge leads. I was half way across it when it curled up in a circle like a roller coaster but I kept trying to walk. Next thing I know I was sitting on the grass and the bridge was gone. I then saw an old-fashioned baby buggy that a wealthy person would have owned but I couldn't see the baby. I realized I was in a park and then I saw my mother and father from this lifetime. They were young and dressed very well as they were standing at the baby buggy. I could feel their happiness and love for each other. I went over to look inside to see the baby and it was a newborn girl. I was then told; "This is a life you could have lived but instead you chose the other in order to help the souls of the world. Your pain and suffering are not for nothing for the story of your life will awaken and enlighten many souls. You are a strong courageous soul who through your devotion will have made an immense difference in the lives of those who suffer. Each time that you have struggled it brought you closer to God and to the spiritual being that you set out to be. We surround you with our love, guidance and protection."

February 27th 2017: John the Apostle stepped forth today and said that the wonders of the world start with a rainbow for it is the simplest wonder. "The energy of incarnated souls flow through rainbows to bring color to the world. The deception that comes out of the mouths of mankind as they speak of their faith in Jesus does not match their intentions or actions. The alignment of faith, intentions and actions are important to the essence of each individual soul for it is not Jesus who gets fooled, it is you. In order to completely step out of the dark and into the light, you must be willing to forgive others and yourself; this will completely free you of your burdens upon earth. One of the biggest challenges that can be faced is being true to yourself for that is where it all begins. Accept the differences in each soul as they are released into the earth, for it is not just male and female, it is anyway that God chooses for His children. In many ways this is a test of acceptance for mankind."

February 28th 2017: My guide Joseph came forth today and said that the promise of being true to yourself is a promise worth keeping. "The longer a soul stays in solitude, the harder it is to become free of judgment from within. Every soul has an obligation to find the love within and spread this love into the world. Love triggers a domino effect and everyone reaps the benefits. Acts of kindness are looked upon as great feats of unselfishness in heaven and will benefit the soul who takes on these acts of kindness. Rare and unforeseen circumstances can cause great harm to unsuspecting souls who have done no wrong. The karmic balance will even out these doings out eventually whether it be for the positive or negative according to a soul's actions. Take the time to enjoy each day and rest assured that all your needs are being met by heaven."

As I was saying the rosary today, I glanced out my kitchen window and saw a female cardinal sitting on a tree branch. A visit from a cardinal is said to be a visit from a loved one in heaven. This cardinal kept looking in the window at me and she stayed on that branch over half an hour. I was very curious as to the reason for the visit from this bird. I connected to spirit and asked my guide Margaret what the reason was for this visit. She said that this cardinal is a representation from heaven to show they are supporting you as big changes are coming up on your journey. "It is a collective of souls who will guide you through this time in your life. There are many changes coming, and know that you are not alone."

March 1st 2017: An angel with brown hair and wearing a blue dress named Elizabeth stepped forth today and told me that a deeper meaning of one's life can be ascertained through the significance of the cross. "Each time a soul makes the sign of the cross it opens up a tunnel of positive energy in to the other realms. This energy is then stored for future use in that soul's life, for what you put in to the universe you get back. Every soul deserves love and kindness, though karma will always be balanced. A step in to the angelic realm would reveal much more than is needed to know upon the earth. Trickles of information are passed forth so souls may see the magnificence of our Heavenly Father. Teardrops of white light are sprinkled out onto the earth as needed. There is a reason for everything and all will be revealed upon your journey home."

March 2nd 2017: As I connected to the spirit realm today, I was shown a vision of a man blowing some sort of dust from his hand into the face of a woman. The woman had half of a veil on her face and they both reminded me of genies. I could also sense the presence of someone from the angelic realm. I then heard someone say, "This is magic dust to give her the sight of the dead." I looked around and everyone looked like skeletons. I was then told there could be darkness in the work of the dead and to be careful for what you wish for. Not every soul has good intentions upon entering other realms. You must face your fears and be strong against these so-called monsters that will try to bring you down. The upward motion of your soul is like a ladder for the darker souls to climb so you must protect yourself in light and love. Watch out for light workers who are jealous of your impending success. Not all souls realize that there is enough for everyone, and that the world is plentiful. This is why you have been handed the earth angel Heather who assists you in many ways. (They are speaking of my California friend Heather who bought me the television after the fire). Heather and I speak almost daily, and she uplifts me spiritually with tremendous emotional support. Her belief and confidence in me is overwhelming, and greatly appreciated. She has helped me with ideas for my book and she listens to my daily communications as I read them to her. She is also helping me pick my book apart and edit it for grammar. In many ways Heather is my rock and I can't thank the heavens enough for her). Then this angelic being said to me that the love of this friendship is tremendous and it will be carried into the spiritual realm.

March 3rd 2017: As I connected to spirit today my guide Agnes told to go play the daily lottery numbers to win the money to pay for Matthew's probation. I have been praying for a long time asking to please help us find a way to get the money to release him from probation. I had seen the numbers 1 and 4. I thought I saw 1144 so I decided to go play that number without questioning anything because that is where I always go wrong, over thinking, and questioning too much. I then asked, am I supposed to play it for the afternoon or evening, and I heard, "go play now," which would be for the afternoon draw. As I continued in my connection, I saw the numbers 3 and 7 so I said come on now, this is getting too confusing, and I'm going to stick to the numbers I originally saw, so I don't mess this up. I then looked down at my journal and seen I wrote the numbers 3-3-17 for today's date and I decided I must have seen those numbers on the paper and that is how they got in my head. I went to the store and played 1144, pretty confident in my decision because this time I didn't overthink anything. The winning numbers that afternoon were 1374. Sometimes I don't have complete faith and confidence in myself. I should of just paid attention to everything that they showed me and I would have had almost enough money to pay off of Matthew's probation. My guides and angels won't give up on me; they will find another way to help us because I never doubt that they are by my side. I sometimes doubt myself because after all, I am only human.

As I went on in my connection Agnes said that there is an abundance of souls whose fate lies in the hands of the government. "The government's opposition waits patiently to gloat about the failures though this serves no purpose to the uprising of America. Instead of spewing out negativity, an offering of a hand would help for a more positive outcome for the people. Each nation has their own demons to fight and usually these demons are from within their own nations. As angels walk amongst humans, they can see the destruction of them. Praise the Lord on a daily basis and ask for forgiveness, if not for yourself, then for your brothers and sisters. Each time that a hand is offered, take it, and each time a soul is in need, find a way to extend your hand. Simple acts of kindness will help any soul reach their goal of fulfilling their soul's purpose. For the souls who go above and beyond, it fills the realms with joy and gratitude for their devotion."

March 4th 2017: Yesterday I asked my guide Joseph if he could please come into my dream and give me a message. Last night in my dream I was with a man that I couldn't see and he threw some trash on the ground and he also threw Max, my dead orange tabby, on the ground next to it. I wasn't upset because I knew that Max was dead and I thought to myself I have to pick that trash up and then Max and put him in a plastic bag. I was picking up the trash first and when I was almost done I heard someone take a huge deep breath so I turned around quickly and it was Max who took the deep breath, then opened his eyes. He looked right into my eyes and got up and started walking around. I was yelling he is alive and I was trying to find the man I was with but I couldn't see him and then woke up.

As I connected to the spirit today, I felt a little fear and I was told by a being of white light that I had connected to a higher level today. I then let go of my fear because I wanted to be connected to that higher level. I was then told that Max is sleeping in wait to be returned to the earth realm to be your guide once again. His spirit has never left your side. It is with gratitude and love that he will be returned to you upon request from God the Father. Your souls are woven together throughout eternity because you have chosen this. You have a tight knit soul family, and you know who they are for you can feel them by your side.

This being of white light also said that a blanket of love has been provided for those in need. "The angels will go throughout the earth to spread these blankets on the suffering grieving souls. Grief on the earth is overwhelming and is felt tremendously in all the other realms. There are needless departures of souls from earth being brought on daily by mankind. In turn this puts the cosmic consciousness out of balance and it forces other souls to go astray and fall off of their paths. Souls have lost faith in themselves and the power of God. You must all come together as a spiritual community to uplift the souls of the world. Beware, for the many faces of evil presents themselves in the most cunning ways. If you stay open, pure and honest then no harm shall come to you."

March 5th 2017: As I connected today, I could see the color pink, then Archangel Haniel stepped forth. She told me that my spiritual development of intuition has climbed to a new level. "Don't worry about your abilities as a medium you must focus on becoming a humanitarian. Your path has been set in stone and we are opening up the gates of wisdom and knowledge for you." (As she told me about the gate, she also showed me a beautiful golden gate opening surrounded by clouds and I received the most loving warm feeling imaginable). "Your link to the spiritual community is deep, though you need to take a step inside. Some will challenge the reason you step through but don't fret for we will guide you along. Human egos will try to bring you down but stand firm. If you have peace in your heart and treat others with love, then no one shall knock you down. The taking down of the Berlin Wall is a good example of human strength, courage, character and unification. Be true to yourself and everything will follow in the order it is suppose to."

March 6th 2017: Archangel Gabriel came forth today and said that on your journey you will meet souls who uplift you and souls who will try to discourage you. "Open the door with the key that we gave you and your heart will stay pure, true to yourself and your mission. The light that dwells within each of us is God's true essence and the embers can be relit at any time on a soul's journey. Speak; feel and see the truth on a daily basis and you will welcome success. Each tear that is shed due to the pain and hurt of mankind causes a backwards ripple effect in the universe. This effect puts a strain on all of those who feel it and it stops the progression of peace. The angels feel the vulnerability of those who are left behind from human tragedies though these suffering souls don't go unnoticed. The suffering of some of the souls was not the intended purpose, but the doing of mankind themselves. We in the angelic realm extend our love and offer comfort and help to those in need though it is unfortunate that some souls are not open to our offerings."

March 7th 2017: As I connected today my guide Joseph stepped forth and told me that the recognition of my soul's growth has been rewarded. "The level to which your conscious consciousness exists is of pure white light. You have made steady progress throughout your journey and the enfoldment of your life's purpose is about to be revealed. You will take a turn as if in a rotary and this road will take you on your heart's desire where your success will be personal, spiritual, financial and, above all, filled with love. You will meet his holiness (I feel he was referring to the Pope) for the purpose of continuing on your journey. Each step solidifies a solution to the problems of hunger, homelessness, sickness and so on. The progression of your soul is outstanding and a celebration is being planned in heaven as we speak. The west coast will offer you much more than you can imagine."

EIGHTEEN

Mythical and Angelic Beings

March 8th 2017: In my connection today, St. Therese stepped forward and told me to go forth and tell the souls of the world to know your inner truths for they will awaken your spiritual path and calm the demons within. "The Holy Ghost feast is a day of recognizing souls who have opened themselves to Jesus Christ, and God the Father. God is an all-powerful energy and he instills that energy into each soul as they enter the earth. Unfortunately, souls do not have the belief or faith in themselves or the power of God to feel this energy and use it wisely upon earth. I knew of this energy within myself and though I did well upon my journey, there was so much more that I could have accomplished, for I let the human ego control my actions and me. The soul that can illuminate their faith and belief with disregard to the human ego will have achieved holiness upon earth. You must overcome your fear of self worth and belief to become the best humanitarian possible. (Mother Theresa then stepped forth). She said, "My child, I am waiting for your work to begin. In the future you will be shown a path of devastation for the poor, hungry and suffering souls. You must take a step forth to help these souls as I guide you on your journey." (I then said I love having my two Theresa's here). As I said that, we held hands and I was told that the three of us are connected as one. We have great faith in you and we love you." Mother Theresa then told me to break bread in the name of the most holy.

Today I went on a shamanic journey of inner discovery through meditation. As I started out on the journey I was walking in a desert, then realized I wasn't alone. There was man with me who was dressed as a pirate. This man had brown hair, brown eyes and yellow teeth. He had a scruffy beard and was dirty looking. I couldn't understand why he was with me on my journey. As I kept walking, I realized that my hands were tied behind my back. The pirate was holding a sword and I was his prisoner. We continued walking until the sky ripped open like a piece of paper and I fell on to the ground and suddenly I was in the yard I grew up in on Buffinton St. I looked around the yard and saw a small tent that we had as children and I knew that my brother David was inside of it. Suddenly, I was walking on a different path and the pirate was gone. There was a circle of rocks in which I stepped inside to rest. There was an Adirondack chair that I sat in. As I sat down a tiger came and sat to my right and I knew instantly he was there as my protector. I lit a fire for us to stay warm. As I watched the fire and all its colors, the smoke from it formed into a Native American man and a buffalo. I knew they were there for me as my spirit guides. I got up and continued on the path with the tiger by my side and the man and buffalo was in front of us leading the way. We continued walking until we came to stairs that were made out of clouds. We all climbed these stairs with me being the last one. When I reached the top, I could not see anything but the color purple. I didn't feel any fear then suddenly everything became bright like sunlight and I was back home on earth again.

March 9th 2017: As I connected today, I saw two men. Both men had long white hair; long robes, and they were wearing crowns. The younger of the men sat in a chair to my right and the older man sat in a chair facing me. I asked them who they were and I was told they were Poseidon and his son Triton. I was very taken back by who they said they were. As far as I know Poseidon and Triton is Sea Greek gods who are spirits of the sea in Greek mythology. I asked them what the message was that they came to give me. I was then told, "Where the sea meets the land is considered a conjugal relationship toward each other. The healing properties of the sea go far beyond any healing properties on land. With the combination of the two, miraculous cures are to be found. Sea creatures have venom within them that can cure many diseases. We are the gatekeepers for these creatures and we ask for respect of the sea and all within it. Getting help from the sea is as easy as asking for it. These creatures can be brought upon the shore with a flick of our wrist. We work in conjunction with the God of the universe. Miracles and cures are readily available to mankind if you would open your minds, hearts and souls to the wonders of the world. The source and energy of the sea is derived from those who protect and guard it and they are never ending cycles of energy."

March 10th 2017: Today as I connected to the other realm a woman with long blonde hair appeared. She was wearing a long red robe that was trimmed with white fur with black spots. Underneath the robe she was wearing a light blue dress. I couldn't see her face clearly but as I was trying to get a look at it her face changed into a wolf's face and then back to a woman's face again. I asked her who she was and she spelled the name E-t-h-e-r-e-a-l. Honestly, I never heard that word before and did not know it's meaning. I found that to be an odd name and so I looked it up on the Internet and found the meaning of it, which is extremely delicate and light in a way that seems too perfect for this world. She told me she is a messenger of hope and justice for all. She said she had come forth to instill peace in the hearts of lost, lonely souls. She went on to say that the magic is in the words of the messages that are spread throughout the world. "Throughout all of eternity souls have brought doom upon themselves. I am the gatekeeper of hope for these souls. As innocent souls are trampled upon, I seek justice for them. I am only able to come forth to those souls who have a pure open heart and the highest intentions towards others. Each step that you take forth on earth towards helping mankind helps me in my mission. A simple solution for mankind would be to let go of any fear and doubt and this would allow hope and peace to flow throughout the universe. The universal symbol of peace is a handshake, which sends out positive energy into the other dimensions. As other dimensions step forth, the earth is always slightly behind in all that goes on. Celebrate yourselves and each other daily for that is the best way to honor the Creator."

March 11th 2017: In my connection today, an angelic looking woman with long blonde hair stepped forth. She was wearing a long pink gown, a crown on her head, and a wand in her right hand. I asked her, "Who are you?" and she answered, "I am the Queen of the crystal-healing palace." I then asked her what her name was and she said, "I have no name, I am only love." I thought to myself she looks like Glenda the Good Witch from the Wizard of Oz. She then said to me "I do like that name Glenda; you may refer to me as Glenda. She then went on to say, "I have stepped forth to welcome you to a new level of healing. This is the emotional healing of yourself and in return you will project this healing on to the souls who cross your path. The empathy that is in you can become overwhelming in many ways. I have been asked to guide you on this path as it unfolds on your journey for I am a teacher of sorts. Any aggression within you is being transmitted into healthy outlets on your path. I have been watching you since your first visit to the crystal-healing palace and I am amazed at the purity of your soul. You, my dear, are on your way to being angelic. You have proven yourself in many lifetimes in which you have gone have through all the tragedies that have come your way, and you have emerged on the other side with love and empathy for others. You're a seed that was planted by the Creator and you have blossomed beautifully."

March 12ᵗʰ 2017: My guide Joseph stepped forth today and told me that the messages I receive are to be shared with the world. Some of them are secrets from the vaults of heaven. He said, "Hopefully as these messages are revealed in your book, souls will be open to receive them in a positive manner. With the harvest of the full moon tonight, abundance is yours. You reap what you sow in each lifetime and the rewards are limitless. The conjuring of energy between worlds relies upon a much-needed solution to the revolution of the world. Inform the souls of the world just how much energy is needed to connect to the other realms." (All the energy you need to connect is within each and every one of us. The first thing someone should do to connect is to sit in the quiet within yourself and listen to your breathing. Ask your angels to help you increase your spiritual energy to a higher vibration. While in a state of meditation, picture raising your energy, which in essence is white light, and letting it hover above your head for a while. This is called "sitting in the power," and when you do this you must have the best of intentions, with an open heart and soul, and a willingness to help the souls of the world. With practice everyday you will find it easier to raise your energy. Just listen to what comes to your thoughts and don't doubt any messages that come to you for the angels and our guides love to connect to us.) Joseph continued on telling me that the vaults he has spoke of contain secrets to the various plights of mankind. "Upon request and with permission from the Creator these secrets can be revealed upon entrance in to the spirit realm or to settle debts brought on by mankind. Either way there will always be an unknown origin to them, and will be used as needed. It is almost like an eight ball in the pocket for some souls."

March 13ᵗʰ 2017: My guide Joseph came forth and said that the intellectual souls of the world can feel a force that pulls them to their original identity but can be blinded to the reason they have begun this journey. "The music of a harp is felt at the center of the soul and it was originally played by angelic beings. It is a gift from the angelic realm and is not played or listened to nearly enough on earth. Mankind seems to let the true importance of their soul's journey fall at the wayside."

March 14ᵗʰ 2017: A tall being of light with shoulder length hair and a long white robe stepped forth today. He had the presence of a king and when I asked him his name he answered, "I am Archangel Raguel." Raguel began his message by saying that the propaganda of the world had been bestowed upon us by the greatest lawmaker of all time through Moses and the Ten Commandments. "The lawsuits in your world are frivolous and frowned upon by the heavens. The laws that you must abide by are those that protect humanity and all that it encompasses. The legal system is for justice for all, though many times we witness the failures of it. Innocent souls suffer needlessly, while the guilty are free. The karmic balance of these acts of injustice will be set straight in the spiritual realms. There is no escaping the injustices that are done to others. We see all, we hear all, and we know all; that is why we ask you all to treat each other with kindness, empathy and love. In the end it will only be yourself that suffers. We can't stress enough to do unto others as you would have them do unto you."

March 15th 2017: As I connected today, I kept seeing the Blessed Mother everywhere; it looked almost like a movie in slow motion. Mary Magdalene stepped forth and told me that there are traces of the Blessed Mother everywhere on earth. "Her energy and her essence were purposely left behind so that all those who are open to connect to her may feel her loving warmth, and are able to connect upon request. The love between mother and child are important for the nurturing of one's soul. Mother Mary's love is abundant and is spread throughout the world. Jesus would not have become the soul that He became without the undying love of the Blessed Mother. If every nation under God were to pay homage to the Blessed Mother unconditionally, then peace on earth would exist in its purest form. How much love can one person give is not a question that should be asked, but it should be felt with the soul, openly, and honestly. Praise God, praise Jesus but don't forget about the Blessed Mother. She is a staple in the time that Jesus spent upon earth. She is just as important to the survival of the world as any heavenly being. We watch as Mother Mary has been forgotten by many souls, which saddens those in other realms. Love is more powerful in each of us than any hatred brought on by mankind."

March 16th 2017: My guide Joseph came forth and said that heaven isn't all fun and play. "There is a lot of hard work that is done in order to heal souls and correct situations where souls have gone astray on their paths. Souls need to learn and train in order to fulfill a future life to the highest of their ability. Angels are sent in armies to try and stop decisions that can bring on a war. The freewill of mankind, combined with anger and egos, is a tough war to fight in itself. The deviance of the souls in government can bring this nation to its knees. The light of the truth shall be brought forth and it will be up to the republic to have the courage to take the necessary actions needed to save this country from destruction. An update on foreign policy is needed in order to appeal to other countries. As of now the United States looks selfish and arrogant to other countries and if this continues the damage will be irreparable."

March 17th 2017: Archangel Gabriel said today that there would be a turning of the tides in the United States. The welfare of many people is at risk and the population of the homeless will increase over time. It will be like a revolution and an awakening of souls who were previously blinded to their distain over another. Governmental funding will decrease, causing many states to suffer. The angels are spreading their wings over America for protection and to project love and light to those in need.

March 19th 2017: As I connected to the other realm today St. Therese stepped forth, then Mother Theresa. They both motioned the three of us in a circle letting me know that we are connected. St. Therese said the wisdom of your soul comes from within. The purity of this wisdom attests to the soul that you are. Our bond can never be broken because we are sisters of the earth. Our Lord is interweaving our human experiences as one unit. This is being done in order for you to perform at the highest level available to you on earth. We guide you day and night, in your dreams and while wake. We are preparing you for your future endeavors and all that comes with it." Mother Theresa then said, "you are in the process of an emotional healing, which will be for your benefit in the future. Continue your daily guidance to those who need it. The offerings of your time to others have been beneficial in many ways.

March 20th 2017: My guide Joseph came forth and said that challenges in the world would make for a difficult week. "Tune out the negative around you and try to focus on the positive. The policies trying to be enforced are gutless and will cause damage to the heart of the country Souls will wander aimlessly until anger brings it all to a head. The destruction of lives is at stake and the innocent will pay the biggest price. Hope, love and kindness for others will help to prevail during the most difficult times. Hunger and homelessness will be at an all time high. In today's age these atrocities should be a thing of the past though with dark souls sitting at the throne you will only get negative results. The combination of two dark souls conspiring can bring many nations to their knees. Everyone needs to elevate his or her thoughts and prayers to a highly positive and energetic level. If souls would ask for the angels to intervene, we will help upon request. The most joyous times in life are those times that are shared with those you love. You are blessed by the memories that are left behind."

March 21st 2017: Mother Mary came forth today and said that protection and guidance is important in my line of work. She then told me to say this protection prayer on a daily basis. "May the four elements of the world surround me and protect me from negative energy. May the forces of nature be my friend and promote calming and healing within me." She continued by saying that by surrounding yourself in positive energy, the negative energy won't be able to break through. "Hope, faith and love are the three signs that can be collectively associated with the signs of the cross. The cross has a deeper meaning than mankind is aware of. The meaning is so pure it can only be felt and understood by a heavenly presence. As a soul enters earth they have agreed to let go of their heavenly knowledge on many levels. Though the higher self of every soul retains all the knowledge that the heavens offer. There is no justification for the wrong doings on earth because every soul knows what is right and wrong."

March 23rd 2017: Today a beautiful angelic being stepped forth. I asked her what her name was and she told me it was Crystalline. I later looked up her name and the meaning of it, which is having the structure and form of a crystal. She told me, "I am from the crystal-healing palace and I am inviting you to join us in a healing of the world. In your dream state your soul will enter the crystal-healing palace. We are calling upon certain light workers to help with their pure healing energy. The Creator has chosen you for your loyalty and devotion on a daily basis. The decision to call upon you has been based upon the healing you have given to others, and the humanitarian level to which you will reach. Tonight as you rest, open your heart, mind and soul so that we may retrieve you. Do not fear for you will be safer than anyone on earth. Tomorrow you will feel the effects; rest for a 24-hour period and all will be well. In your work you truly convey the meaning of heaven on earth. Each step that you chose to take is bringing you closer to a bright future. Like the stars and sun that shine bright in the sky, an act of kindness towards another will make your soul shine even brighter."

March 24th 2017: Last night a man awakened me by speaking in my ear. He actually scared me because his voice was so loud and clear. He said to me, "In this form I don't trust you." The rest of the night I had interrupted sleep and dreams. I contacted Gail Moffat today to tell her of my experience because she herself has a deep connection to her guides and the other realms. Her guide Arthur said they didn't mean to frighten me. They were just experimenting with helping me to develop my clairaudience, which is hearing the spirit realm. He said that they apologized and said that they will go about it in a different way as to not frighten me again. He also told Gail they are trying to help me develop my mediumship to the next level with clearer clairvoyance "seeing" and clairaudience "hearing" of the other realms. He said they have been working with me since infancy and I agreed to all of this before I entered the earth realm. They also thanked me for my prayers that I not only send out to the earth and spirit realm but to the angelic realm also. They appreciate it because the angelic realm (like everyone else) also needs the prayers and love sent out to them. Lastly, he said they are preparing me because in the next five years there will be tragedies and disasters in the world and I will be needed to help the suffering souls.

March 25th 2017: When I woke up today, I had been given a knowing during the night that the voice that spoke to me the other night was someone I knew from the angelic realm. I know that I have visited the angelic realm and worked with them in many lifetimes. It was an exciting and confusing revelation. All in all, it helped me understand the personnel connection I felt to that voice. Also, I feel like the angelic realm had worked with me during the night to improve my mediumship and today I am exhausted and nauseous.

A beautiful angelic being shining brilliant light came forth today and told me that the end of an era is done. The demolition of human emotion is put to the test in which willpower verses freewill. The sacred souls upon earth will step forth when they are needed in their mission. Angelic beings are in place to be called upon for upcoming disasters in the world. The negativity that is spewed out into the world also has an impact on the other realms. We do not impose upon mankind's freewill so we ask that mankind does not impose their negativity towards us. The angelic realm offers love, kindness and help freely to the earth realm. We ask that mankind send positive thoughts and love to the angelic realm. The bravest of souls is a soul that is willing to take a stand for their brothers or sisters.

March 26th 2017: Once again I woke today knowing that the spirit world worked with me during the night and I once again felt exhausted and nauseous. During my communication Mother Mary stepped forth and told me that the pay equality of women on earth does not measure up to that of man. "Some of the thoughts and actions of mankind are like those of the Stone Age. Though some of the damage is irreversible, it can be repaired with loving thoughts, kindness and acts of redemption. The prejudice on earth seems to be never ending in one way or another. If it is not race, then it is gender, or religion and so on. "Take heed my children for God has created everyone equal. The damnation of another will be dealt with in the next realm. There is no escaping the misfortunes that a soul has caused their brother or sister. No soul can escape karmic balance. "Do unto others as you would have them do unto you' is a far truer statement and has a much deeper meaning than any of you realize. The heavens are pleased by the kindness that souls show to each other, though we are not pleased with the intentions that some in leadership want to impose. They have the mindset of the Romans where the rulers are wealthy and the people are poor in order to gain complete control over them. I will bestow grace upon any soul who calls upon me 'The Blessed

Mother' in the name of my son Jesus. I ask you all to be strong and wise and do not let your egos control your freewill. May your day sparkle with the light that shines down from heaven upon your soul and may you share this gift of light with another."

March 27th 2017: My guide Joseph stepped forth today. He said to me, "I will continue to guide you on the path of enlightenment towards a more humanitarian lifestyle. Each corner that is turned will be filled with glorious feelings of joy and hope. The next step you are to embark upon is a step higher on the next level. The light of heaven is shining upon you so you may light the way for others. Be bold in your decisions and know that we are behind you one hundred percent. Choose your friends carefully, for envy is terrible and can cause harm to your mission. Prayer can alleviate the feelings of angst in your world. The angels have formed a circle of love and protection around the world in order to try and control the negativity. Not only are they protecting the world but they are also protecting the universe from the world. Go forth and be strong on your journey for there will be hills and valleys along the way. Each time that you dip, we will lift you up. Again, we thank you for your support and devotion. Every soul must attend to their own needs before tending to others; otherwise the foundation of the bridge will fall. Keep your eyes wide open and keep your eye on the prize, which is the salvation of souls."

March 28th 2017: Archangel Haniel came forth today and said that the tantalizing tidbits of information passed on from the angelic realm are meant to help souls progress on their journey. "Each and every sentence given might not be a revelation, but know that they come from the purest of love and intentions. Sometimes we feel as though our hard work goes unnoticed on earth. Though our love and help is never ending, mankind's appreciation would increase the angelic vibration to higher energy levels. We are grateful to the light workers who spread their knowledge of our realm. We can work very closely with those who openly accept us into their hearts and souls. The world needs our help and love, but we cannot interfere unless asked. The final outcome of a situation can depend upon the faith and belief in the angels and other angelic beings. We ask that you take one step forth a day by throwing out positive energy in one form or another into the world. The chain reaction from this energy will be tremendous."

March 29th 2017: My guide Margaret stepped forth and said that there is a swirling turmoil in the heads of those who make decisions in the government. Fear, disappointment and embarrassment are playing a huge role in this turmoil. Pray and send positive energy so that these officials gather the strength and courage to make the right decisions. The magnificence and beauty of this world is that no matter what happens to anyone, you all have the ability to rise again. The harvest of the next new moon will bring subtle changes to the earth that will help improve the lives of many (the next new moon will be on April 11th 2017).

The last couple of weeks I keep seeing the numbers 9494. Seeing repeating numbers mean the angels are trying to give you a message. Those particular numbers mean to let go of a situation that has run its course. The angels are reminding you as one door closes, another one opens and they want you to look ahead, not behind. The angels are also helping to open these doors and heal pain or sorrow that you might go through in your next transition. Today I have been speaking to my guides and angels about feeling, but not really knowing what is ahead for me. I can feel the difference in the energy around me. No one has contacted me for a reading and suddenly less people have been choosing my daily tarot cards online. As I am typing this in to my book I put on my Pandora music and the first song that played was "Lady" by Stevie Nicks. I always receive this song when I am unsure of what lies next for me. The lyrics are, "And the time keeps going on by, and I wonder what is to become of me, and I'm unsure I can't see my way, And he says, Lady you don't need to see." When it comes to the part of "Lady you don't need to see" I get a knowing that these words are specifically for me from my guides and the angels. I am very spiritual, but I am also only human, and, like anyone else, I need to be reminded of my path and the reason I am here on earth. This song brings me much comfort when I hear it because I now connect it to the angelic realm.

March 30th 2017: Archangel Michael came forth and said that the idle tuning of my soul has begun. "You are being prepared to walk amongst the evil doings of man. Your spiritual senses will not be like any other, and this must be done in order for your physical, mental and emotional survival. The long road that has led you to this path has finally opened. Relax and enjoy your quiet time for that will be changing in the future. You will drink from the Holy Grail upon your entrance into heaven. This Grail has been shared by many of your predecessors. We of the angelic realm welcome you as you step into our graces."

Mother Teresa then stepped forth and touched me on my nose. She then said to me, "Now you see my child, go and spread love throughout the world. You will do this by healings, kindness, empathy and purity to those in need. Bless you child." At that moment I could feel someone touching my nose but it was an actual physical feeling that I never felt from any realm before, except for earth.

April 1st 2017: St. Therese stepped forth today and said that those who practice certain levels of cosmic consciousness could experience mediumship. "The connection to spirit can be considered omnipresent in the cosmos. A spiritual being would be none other than your brother or sister for we are all created equal. The advancement of some souls over others depends upon the awakening of their soul. The freewill and egos of mankind are of great assistance to some and a hindrance to others. The most likely candidates to improve their future are the souls who have struggled. The effervescent glowing light that illuminates our souls can never be put out. We must trudge forward on our journeys even if it is a half a step at a time otherwise you will not be honoring the Creator and all that He has given to us. Make the most out of each day whether it is gray or sunny, and remember we in this world are always by your side loving you unconditionally."

April 2nd 2017: John the Apostle came forth today and told me that patience is a virtue for the financial flow of prosperity is coming. "Seize the day and feel the energy all around you. The angels are walking upon earth in abundance to help bring peace to the hearts of those who suffer. In this Holy month of the resurrection of your brother Jesus Christ, we ask that an act of kindness be done in his honor. One act of kindness from each soul upon earth would send out an incredible amount of positive energy, which in turn would increase the peace and happiness worldwide. These positive effects would then trickle out into the universe impacting all the realms; every being would benefit in one way or another. Don't ever underestimate what you as one human being can do to make a difference in your lifetime on earth. In one form or another there are armies of angels who march upon earth to protect and spread their love. If you have had the feeling you have crossed paths with an angel, don't ever doubt it, for the intuition of each soul is one gift from the Creator while the interaction with angels is another. All of God's children and creations are of equal importance regardless of your earthly stature.

April 3rd 2017: John the Baptist stepped forth today and said that the purity of one's soul is directly connected to self-sacrificing. "The enlightenment of one's soul is connected to trials and tribulations encountered upon their journey. There is a correlation between each and everything that is encountered on earth and the purpose of our soul's journey. Each soul must find the courage and strength within themselves to step forth for no other soul can do it for you. Other souls may lift you up in times of need but in the end every soul is responsible for their own actions and destiny. To be freed from the imprisonment of earthly emotions is a miracle in itself. Just allowing yourself the ability to accept all that goes on in your life and the lives of others can do this. Do not hold on to anger, resentment, hurt or pain for it is only you who suffer while those who caused this turmoil walk freely in their paths. The outcome of your own lives could be truly magnificent if you just "Let Go and Let God." It truly saddens the Creator to see those imprisoned by their own soul."

April 4th 2017: Archangel Gabriel came forth today and said that we the angels welcome your presence in the angelic realm as you learn better ways to awaken the souls of the world. We will work hand in hand with you to offer you the guidance of your life's purpose. More will be revealed to you as you progress on your journey. You must be at an even keel in order to be of assistance to anyone. Since we have worked with you in many lifetimes, we understand every dimension of your soul. This lifetime was difficult for you in many ways so we applaud you for being able to become the soul that was needed for this mission. Part of your journey is to uplift others, which we see you do on a daily basis. You have always felt our presence and we thank you for not casting us aside with anger due to events that have occurred in your life. We are pleased with your work; just go forth one step at a time."

April 7th 2017: Archangel Michael came forth and said that the ultimate goal for every living creature is peace on earth. "The souls that have passed in vain due to the efforts of mankind in Syria are being retrieved to heaven. The man behind the chemical warfare is a man who sits in power as he peers out from behind a safety shield proving the coward that he is. The angels have put a shield around the children who have been affected from these heinous acts so they may not feel anymore suffering. The Syrian war will trudge on with more activity from other countries. There is and will continue to be a tremendous loss of lives from this war and the after effects. We, the angels, want the people of the world to know that we have heard your prayer. We are putting shields of protection around those who ask for it but unfortunately the freewill of the dark souls involved somewhat interfere with our protection. We ask that you have faith, hope, and most importantly, pray for the safety of all and ultimately for peace on earth. This is a special blessing for all those who lay their eyes upon these words: "Angels of Mercy, we ask for your divine intervention in any war or destruction upon earth. Please protect my family, myself and all my brothers and sisters."

April 8th 2017: Joseph came forth and said that the good fortune of others can't be looked upon with envy and that you should have gratitude for even the simplest things in life. "A rag to richest story is in reach of every soul on earth. It is how you go about manifesting your dreams and goals as to what you would like to enter your life. A block of energy can be brought on by sadness and you must do your part in asking the angels to lift you out of the dark and into the light. There are many lessons to learn in being humble, as this quality will connect you on your path of humanitarianism. We watch as you sit in sadness and still help others. Your time has arrived and you must be willing to accept it for what it is. If you never put expectations on people, then you will not get disappointed and this mindset will continue to help you on your journey. You must go forth on a daily basis until you reach the altar in which you will kneel to meet your Heavenly Father. There is a reason for your poverty, and it will be revealed in the future. Keep the faith and trust in us."

April 9th 2017: Mother Mary stepped forth and said to me, "I walk in a garden of tulips as a celebration for my son Jesus who ascended from earth. The time that is spent in prayer upon my Son's ascension brings powerful energy and light to the heavens, which are then transmitted into the universe. Children are taught about fairy tales of the celebration of my Son's ascension. Do not worry of damaging the children's souls for there are much worse things that can happen to them than these tales. The propaganda of lies that are hidden in the truth of the everyday on goings on earth is more damaging than not. Mankind needs to learn to step up and accept responsibility for their mistakes so they can be corrected. The correction of mistakes will make life easier for the next generation. The brighter your soul shines the brighter your future will be. A little belief in yourself will take you farther than you could imagine."

April 10th 2017: As I connected to the other realm today, a man stepped forward. He seemed very familiar to me. He had long gray hair, a beard and was dressed in a long garment like the men would have worn in biblical days. He said, "I am Joseph, husband of Mary and your guide that has been stripped down to my truest form. I knew that he looked familiar but I'm used to Joseph showing himself to me in a long king-like robe. He went on to say, "You must trust in the guidance I give you to follow. To be a humanitarian is a different path than most. You will be stripped down to your truest form as I am. Don't doubt what is in front of you on your path. In the upcoming months I shall work very closely with you. Trust and believe in the words that you hear. Your momentum is picking up with your connection to the other realms. We are pleased with your gratitude and devotion. A healing has been placed upon your daughter. Everything will fall off at the wayside for your son eventually. Your family has been blessed and will be settled so you may go about your business on your journey. It was time I introduced myself properly and I am pleased to make your acquaintance.

April 11th 2017: As I connected to the angelic realm today, Archangel Haniel stepped forth and she said to me, "The full moon tonight will bring many spiritual awakenings to those on earth. The power of this moon is supreme compared to the power of the harvest moon. For the souls who open themselves to this power there will be many spiritual rewards on a personal level. Spread the truth about the power of this moon to those who will listen. Each step forth for a soul to be spiritually awakened is a step towards peace on earth for all. I ask you to carry the torch of love and light to your brothers and sisters. I also ask you to carry the light within you to every soul you encounter that needs your assistance and I will work with you and in you to help these souls. As you step forth on your journey all you have to do is think of me and I will be there. You may also call upon me for spiritual protection in your time of need. Spread our words with peace and love in your heart."

April 12th 2017: Archangel Raphael came forth today and said that the acoustics of one's mind is so pure, yet it gets filled with negativity against one's self. "The physical body is the temple that holds our souls in place upon earth and many mistreat these temples. The quality of one's life upon earth depends upon the quality and standard that you hold yourself to. The rubble of the ancient ruins can be compared as to what many do to their own souls. Souls are pure love and light made from the essence of God our Father. There is no reason a soul should turn dark, because the light is always available to all. The higher the value you place upon yourself, the higher level you will reach on your journey to fulfill your souls purpose, and in doing so you honor the Creator and all that He stands for. The rejuvenation of one's soul is possible by surrendering yourself to our Heavenly Father and trusting in His love for you. Belief, hope, faith, kindness, trust and love are all the ingredients for a happy fulfilled soul. This is all possible if you would just open up and ask for help. We, the angels, are not preaching but we are spreading the truth so that all souls have a chance at a better life. We love you all and only want the best for you."

April 13th 2017: As I connected to the other realm today, I saw a couple of men. One I recognized as John The Baptist, and the other man was a monk. The monk told me he is Arthur and that he is Gail Moffat's guide. Arthur then said, "We guides are interchangeable between Gail and yourself as you work together. He went on to say the positive outcome of your work with Gail and us will help both of your nations as a whole. It has been decided that we will band together, united for a stronger presence in the world and a brighter outcome. Tell Gail she will receive a surprise visit from your guide Joseph for we are all connected in order for the highest and best good for all. Your guide Margaret will also pay a visit to Gail. Make her aware and pay close attention to what is said for these will be important words for your journeys. Then John the Baptiste said to me, "I have come in good faith to honor the words of the Lord. I join you on your journey to help guide you both on your paths in ways the others cannot. I am considered a friend in the hearts of many. Take my hand and open your hearts as I fill it with positive energy and acceptance of others. I will work with the both of you on your tolerance of others so no soul shall be able to instill their negative emotions toward you. Praise the Lord Jesus Christ my brother, my friend."

April 14th 2017: Archangel Haniel came forth today and said that common sense in a spiritual form is something that everyone innately has within his or her soul. "Awakening this common spiritual sense would bring depth and so much greatness to one's life. Awakening souls is a matter of importance, for each soul needs to learn a better way of living. The earth itself is in danger along with humanity for destruction is inevitable if souls don't start taking responsibility for themselves and their actions. The light workers must help others to see what is right in front of them. It is going to get worse before it gets better but by not giving up on yourself and others will enable you to reach the other side of it. The light of heaven will shine like a beacon of hope through the souls who spread the word of the Lord on earth. The souls who open themselves up and trust in the Lord and his followers to a new way of living and being will have the light of heaven shine upon them also. Belief, hope, faith and trust will take you farther than you can imagine."

April 15th 2017: John the Apostle came forth today and said that the irony that goes on in the world with the bombs and the missiles being thrown around from mankind like they are God in the taking of lives upon earth. "Mankind oversteps their power in the world on a daily basis as far as determining the outcome of another's life. These bad decisions cause a negative ripple effect in to the universe and also in the karmic balance of their own lives. Nothing good comes from hurting another. The destruction brought on by the wars between mankind is doing way more harm than anyone is able to see at this point. Everyone will suffer in one way or another and it will affect everyone upon earth. It lies in the power of mankind to stop the fighting and destruction by overcoming their egos and anger. Kind words and good intentions are a good first step. The world leaders are not looking at the bigger picture and they are being selfish in their actions. Those who order mass murders will be dealt with in the other realm for there is no escaping karmic balance."

April 17th 2017: As I connected today, I was shown a vision of a beaming light in the form of a crucifix. I then saw three beautiful angels all in white who were holding hands in a circle. I heard these words; "We have set forth on a journey of instilling peace and harmony in the lives of the grieving souls. We ask that you follow our lead as we bring these souls to your doorstep. Working hand in hand with us is an agreement that you are fulfilling very nicely. Protect yourself from the dark souls and you will be able to tell the difference between them. The training of your soul had begun before you entered the earth realm. It was a deep emotional training that brought you much suffering so that you could completely open yourself up to those who need you. There will be a welcoming of sorts into the next phase of your journey. The current phase is coming to a completion and you will become busy with much activity soon. We ask that you accept the new ideas and people into your life, as this will start you on the path of a humanitarian. The lessons you have learned in each phase of your journey will be for the good of all mankind. Hope, faith and dignity are prized possessions that are deep in your soul and will be very useful in your work. The light from the angelic realm will always shine upon you, my dear. Do not ever doubt our loyalty to you, for your soul shines brightly as you will continue to have our support."

April 18th 2017: Mother Mary came forth today and said that the fortitude of man that relies upon war, as an answer to the problems in the world is by far the biggest mistake made. "It is the exact opposite of what God intended for mankind. War has been going on for eternity and it is time for a change. This change is needed in order to fulfill the prophecy of peace on earth. The change starts with each and every soul on earth no matter what the contribution is. Take a seedling of kindness, plant it, and watch the miracles that will unfold before your eyes. The souls of the world are too materialistic in their needs and wants. Going back to basics and simplicity does a soul good. That is why some souls are stripped of their materialistic life. Items and luxury will not help a soul to grow; depending on the soul, it can actually stop their growth. You must be able to find the peace and happiness within yourself to be able to offer assistance to your brothers and sisters to the best of your ability. Do not let others' words or actions tear you down in anyway for you should all know your soul's worth. We are all made from the essence of God; therefore, we have God within us and are all extremely worthy like anyone else is. Shine your heart brightly for the world to see and you will be amazed at the positive response you will receive. Spread Love and it will be returned to you."

April 19th 2017: As I connected to the other realm today, I saw Mother Mary, then Mother Teresa, and lastly St. Therese appeared. As a collective they told me that we are bonding together as they circled around me with protection and blessings that will be needed in the upcoming months. They went on to say that we will be your support as you stumble backwards and we will not let you hit the ground. "We also welcome you in to our close-knit unit of divine interventions for the good of all. There will be many purposes that your journey serves and know that on your journey, we will always be close to you and you will never be alone. There are souls who will wreak havoc in your life but you will never falter. An example of your not faltering would be what happened today." (They are referring to my financial difficulties and me joining the National Debt program. One of the creditors has threatened to sue me and today it was all resolved without a lawsuit).

I then asked, "What is my job going to entail on my journey?" Mother Mary said I would be teaching souls about the angels and the different realms and spheres. "You will open the hearts and souls of the ones who have lost their way and instill the faith and trust of the Lord into many others. We will work through you to enlighten and awaken numerous people. You will feed the hungry and help the poor and destitute. You will comfort grieving souls through your gift of mediumship. You will touch many lives and make a difference in the world. My child, just go through your journey one day at a time in order for you to do your highest good for your brothers and sisters."

April 20th 2017: Mother Teresa stepped forth today and said that the fundamental writing of theories and experiments on a scientific level will not increase the chances of a better way of life. "A better way of life comes from within the soul. To be true to your own self is a fact in which everyone should live by. Science and mankind can make life better in some ways but it cannot feed the soul. The importance of the self care of one's soul is extremely important for everyone's survival in the upcoming future of the world. Nourish your soul and you will have the ability to survive in the hardest of times. While it is of a human nature to miss another's presence upon earth, in all reality it is wasted time and energy. If you are not spiritually awakened in the human form you are blinded to the reality of a soul's crossing over. It is a cause for celebration in the spiritual realm as a soul returns home again. Most souls do not come to the realization of the wasted time and energy of constant grieving until they themselves have crossed over. Grieving is part of the human experience but nothing in excess is good for anyone. Emotional pain and suffering cause more damage than any physical pain. Treat your soul with tender loving care for it is the center of who you are and you are worth it."

April 21st 2017: My guide Joseph stepped forth and said that the purity of the universal energy is so simple but yet so powerful. "When the laws of the universe are tampered with it knocks the flow of all types of abundances out of whack. There is a hovering of lower energies that try to take advantage when the universe is most vulnerable due to the tampering of it. As a soul upon earth, your responsibility is to take care of whatever is set in front of you, whether it is yourself, others, mother nature etc. The tampering and destruction done by mankind acts like a domino effect into the universe and it also affects other realms. We ask if you could please show an act of kindness each day and you will eventually feel the peace within your soul. Kindness is beneficial to everyone in every realm. The actions and reactions that you carry out upon earth will follow you in to the spiritual realm. The harboring of negative feelings will only erode your soul. Smiling at someone is a simple way to start cleansing your soul. It is easier to live in the light than it is to live in the dark.

NINETEEN

Mother Therese's 12 Days of Messages

April 22nd 2017: As I connected to the other realm today, I could see Mother Mary but I could also see another woman who was similar to Mary in her clothing and looks. This woman kept making me feel the love of a sister towards Mary. I asked her who she was and she replied I am Elizabeth. I asked her if she was Mary's sister but she did not answer me she just kept giving the feeling of the love of a sister. She then gave me this message: "The most Holy Mother who reigns in heaven and is blessed among woman instills her essence and energy in the core of the souls who take on the responsibility of caring for there loved ones. Her love and caring is at the foundation of family values. There is much to be grateful for that is received from the Blessed Mother and she is not honored nearly enough. The love that carries from one generation to the next stems from the core values that the Blessed Mother has shown to her Son, Jesus. The center of any family or relationship is love. Without love then nothing in life will fall into place or make sense, and can make your journey feel useless. I ask that you open your hearts to the Blessed Mother and allow her love to fill your soul and make you feel as safe as a mother should."

I was intrigued as to who Elizabeth was since she gave me the strong feeling of sisterly love for Mary. I researched to find out if Mary had any siblings and I found that she has a sister named Mary of Islam. So I researched Elizabeth from the biblical days and here is what I found. Elizabeth was the wife of a priest named Zechariah and she is also the cousin of Mary. Elizabeth and Zechariah are called "righteous and blameless" people who walked in all the commandments of the Lord (Luke 1:6). Elizabeth was unable to have children. (Luke 1:7). When Zechariah was in the temple offering incense to the Lord, the Angel Gabriel appeared to him, saying that he and Elizabeth would soon be parents and they were to name the baby John. This baby would grow up to be "great before the Lord" and bring joy and gladness to them, as well as to many other people (Luke 1:14-15). Zechariah was doubtful because of his wife's age and the fact that he was old himself (Luke 1:18), so Gabriel--the same angel who later appeared to Mary--told Zechariah that he would be unable to speak until the prophecy was fulfilled in the birth of John (Luke 1:19-20,26-27). Elizabeth, when finding herself pregnant, kept herself in seclusion for five months. She said, "The Lord has done this for me...in these days he has shown his favor and taken away my disgrace among the people" (Luke 1:25). Six months after Elizabeth conceived, Mary also became pregnant and she went to visit Elizabeth, because the angel Gabriel had told her of Elizabeth's pregnancy (Luke 1:36-37). It was a sign of God's love and care that he placed these women in the same family, which gave them mutual comfort and encouragement. Especially for Mary, the experience of being pregnant outside of wedlock must have been frightening. But God provided Elizabeth as a comforting presence--a trusted and known relation and older woman who was going through a similarly miraculous event (Luke 1:38-45). As soon as Mary arrived at Elizabeth's home and Elizabeth heard Mary's greeting, "the baby leaped in her womb, and Elizabeth was filled with the Holy Spirit. In a loud voice she exclaimed: "Blessed are you among women, and blessed is the child you will bear! But why am I so favored, that the mother of my Lord should come to me? As soon as the sound of your greeting reached my ears, the baby in my womb leaped for joy. Blessed is she who has believed that the Lord would fulfill his promises to her!"(Luke 1:41-45). The Holy Spirit told Elizabeth of Mary's condition even before Mary could say a word.

Eight days after Elizabeth's child was born, several neighbors and relatives were there for the circumcision ceremony. It was during this time that children were officially given their names, and Elizabeth declared her baby's name to be John--Zechariah was still unable to speak. The neighbors questioned Elizabeth about the name; none of her relatives had ever been called John--certainly they should name him Zechariah. But Zechariah procured a tablet and wrote on it the name John. In this he showed his faith in the angel's prophecy, and, with that, Zechariah was able to speak again (Luke 1:57-64). Elizabeth's son grew up to be John the Baptist, who ministered "before the Lord, in the spirit and power of Elijah" (Luke 1:17) and was the prophet who prepared the way of the Lord, fulfilling Malachi's prophecy (Luke 1:76.)"

April 23rd 2017: St. Therese stepped forward today and said that the lack of tolerance that humans have for each other is atrocious. "Empathy is so far and in between that it causes many souls to feel lonely and forgotten. Pontius Pilate had empathy for Jesus but he lacked the courage needed to do what was right, causing great harm to Jesus and others. Empathy and courage go hand in hand so that it may enable you to help the souls of the world in the capacity that was meant for you. Each suffering soul can be helped with the empathy, courage, love and kindness that you possess. The path that you seek has been cleared for you, my dear. Incredible changes are starting all around you. You will become a more evolved soul upon the conclusion of your upcoming trip. (I am going to California for six months to be with my daughter). During this time do not let the bond between Gail and yourself be broken for we have worked too hard to bring you both together. One hand washes the other and in the future you will both desperately need each other's help for the salvation of many souls. We trust in you both. Open your mind and heart to the plight of another and it will fulfill a space in your soul that you didn't know existed."

April 24th 2017: My guide Margaret came forth today and said that there will be many times where I feel like the weight of the world is upon my shoulders. "As you tap into your inner self and strength, you will know that you are not alone as we will all be right by your side. You will learn to find self-peace in the darkest of situations as you walk through some of the destruction that will befall the earth. Teams of light workers are being assembled as we communicate today. Each team of light workers is being assigned a team of protection angels for their mission. You may call upon Archangel Michael at any time you feel you need him, and he will rush to your aid as the warrior he is. We have seen that you have learned to separate sympathy from empathy and this will serve you well on your path." (I was then told how I learned to separate sympathy from empathy because lately I have had many people come around me that in another time in my life I would have taken in or helped. These people would have just caused chaos in my life and taken advantage of me. My standing strong and knowing whom I should help and who I should let go is a freeing feeling). Margaret then told me that California is going to be a turning point in my life; that my life will never be the same. She also said to release any negative emotions that I have towards anyone so that I may be neutral in my work for the souls that need me.

April 25th 2017: As I connected to the other realm today Jesus appeared to me. He was crouched down petting a lamb and he smiled warmly at me. The first thing He said to me was that He loved me. He went on to say, "I thank you for your pure true soul that has been stripped of all the riches that the world has to offer. The riches of your heart are overwhelming when compared to that of the average soul. The offerings of yourself and your soul to your brothers and sisters are commendable. In a sense you will walk in My footsteps as you teach the world of the angels and all those who exist in the other realms and spheres. Do not be afraid as you walk through the dark times that are to come on earth, as I will carry you, my child. As you have asked, your children and family will be safe as you walk on the earth to fulfill your mission. Walk in confidence of their safety and trust yourself. There will be a pivotal point in your career as a communicator to the spiritual realm this week whereas there will be no doubt as to your connection to the other realms."   After my visit from Jesus I was filled with joy and confidence.

April 26th 2017: As I connected to the other realm today, I received a message from a combination of Mother Teresa, Mother Mary and St. Theresa. I was told if you have negative thoughts about yourself it throws your entire balance off. "You must rise out of fear to go forth on your path. You are able to accomplish great feats if you believe in yourself. Though God's work is teamwork you do not need another soul to raise you up because your gift is amazing by itself. Many will come and go through your life and each of them will have served a purpose. You are like a butterfly that is evolving on a level of pure consciousness. Miraculous events will unfold before your eyes on this journey. John The Baptist will work through you as you preach to the people of the world. You will be filled with The Holy Spirit so that you may accomplish all that was meant for you. There will be those who doubt you as was done to Jesus, but stay strong in your faith and all will be revealed in divine timing. You are able to accomplish all that you open your mind to for we all work with you and through you. There is no escaping from one's self, and the sooner that a soul deals with their issues, the happier they will be."

April 27th 2017: Today as I connected to the other realm Mother Theresa, Mother Mary and St. Therese came forth and once again gave me a message as a collective. I was told that the time has come to work on a deeper level with me. They went on to say that the makeup of your energy would shift to a higher level. "There will be an advancement of your gift including your mediumship. In the hours that you rest your body, your soul will be transported to "Heaven" to make the necessary adjustments. You are now ready for a new course of action. As you have put your complete faith in us you have accepted the life of being sustained by us in heaven. Your earthly responsibilities will melt off one by one as you prepare for your journey. Whether you realize it or not you have already taught Gail some empathy. You are a conduit for spirit to those in all the realms. You have been chosen to do this due to your loyalty, faith and complete belief of all that is put in front of you.   From this day forth you will experience something new even if it is of the smallest caliber. Drop away any fear for we have your back. As you rise each day, set the intentions in your mind, heart and soul of spreading love and kindness to another and this will increase the positive energy in your soul."

April 28th 2017: Once again as I connected to the other realm Mother Theresa, Mother Mary and St. Therese stepped forward and gave me a message as a collective. They said there would be a total of 12 messages in 12 days from them as a collective and that this is the 3rd message. I was told to be aware of less fortunate souls that cross my path. "Some are being sent to you for the help that you can offer, while others you may refer to someone else for help. The beginning of your humanitarian work has begun. Help the suffering souls that we put in front of you and eventually your work will be on a world level. This is a freedom of choice for you and last night this decision was discussed in detail. During the following nights your physical energy will be drained noticeably while your soul is being worked with." (The last couple of days I kept dragging my feet and tripping myself up because I didn't have the energy to pick my feet up enough and now I understand why. It is because of them working with me while I sleep and my body is tired). "You always knew this day would come as we prepare you for the battle of the world. Take care of your physical being as you go through this process. Make the others aware of these changes and do not fear for there is a seal of protection around all of you."

April 29th 2017: Today I received day 4's messages from Mother Theresa, Mother Mary and St. Therese. I was told that miracles come in the form that is best for the recipient. "Heaven holds many secrets and we can only divulge a limited amount of information, otherwise the world would be in chaos for the human mind would over think, over plan and not focus upon their earthly responsibilities. In reaction to all that would happen, the order of everything in the universe would be thrown off balance. The universal laws are in place for many needed reasons and we have the highest hopes of mankind abiding by them. As we have trickled information out little by little, it is just enough to give earthly souls a peek into our world so they may have some sort of understanding of our purpose in their lives. The most precious and heavenly gift we are able to give is the gift of love for it is the center of all that exist in our realms. We would like the people of the world to know that we offer love and support to anyone that ask. A mention of us in your daily prayers will strengthen the bond between us. We carry the torch of love for you all just like an earthly mother should, but in a heavenly way with no strings attached. As you communicate with us, we will fill you with love and in return we ask that you spread the love among each other."

April 30th 2017: Today is day 5 of my messages from Mother Theresa, St. Therese and Mother Mary. I was told be generous of yourself to those that you meet on your journey even if it is sometimes hard to do. "Giving of yourself freely is a dominant factor for a humanitarian. Your soul has been prepped for this work and as we work with you to bring your soul to full fruition; we ask that you trust us in all that you will encounter. Popular opinions in the heavens is that you are a bright shining star; we have watched as you have been knocked down many times but you always get up and continue to do the work you were meant to do. It has taken many lifetimes for you to get to this point and to fully understand the importance of your work for the battle that is to come on earth. We have never underestimated you and we ask that you never underestimate us. We are here for all of you my children, may you feel our loving presence."

May 1st 2017: Today is the 6th day of connecting to Mother Teresa, St. Therese and Mother Mary. The first thing that I heard was "We are here, my child." Then I heard, "The progression of your soul is growing quite rapidly. You are beginning to hear other people's thoughts without even realizing it. Your attunement to the souls of the world and everything in it has increased ten-fold. We know that you felt it last night (I attended the service at The First Spiritualist Church in Onset last night). As I was sitting there to listening to the music prelude, I kept thinking of Mickey Mouse. I turned to my friend Heidi and said I am waiting for Mickey Mouse to walk out. When the speaker for the night spoke, one of the first things she mentioned was Mickey Mouse. Heidi and I looked at each other in amazement since I had just mentioned Mickey. Then I suddenly thought to myself, I wonder if Larry was sitting behind me. I turned around and Larry was sitting there. He said to me, did you hear my thoughts because I was just thinking; is that Dawn in front of me? After receiving my message today from the other realm, I now fully understand the "coincidences" of last night. They went on to say, "We want to make you fully aware of this powerful gift that you possess. This gift will be useful to you as you climb through the rubble that is going to embark upon earth. Make the most out of the days that lie before you. We weep for the suffering children. Thank you for giving hope in many different ways to the grieving souls that you have encountered along your journey. We commend you for never giving up hope and your resilience and fighting to stay on your destined path of a humanitarian. We send our love out to the world in the hopes of a brighter future. Many souls will come and go in your life but the ones who stand strong and do not leave your side amongst the chaos are the ones worth living for."

May 2nd 2017: Today as I connected to the other realm, I saw a circle of angels flying over my head and they were each holding small banners. I was then shown a picture of two angels and it had words on it. This picture was familiar to me because I downloaded it on to my phone about a year earlier. I was then told to go and read the words because it was a message from the angelic realm. The words on this picture are, "We love you and are always with you." These angels then told me that prolonging the suffering of another is a cruel act. It takes more energy to perform such an act then it does to love. The defenseless souls that are abused upon earth sadden us. Those who carry out this abuse will pay a price with their karmic balance. We can never stress enough to do unto others, as you would have them do unto you. Your soul will only be truly free if you live your life with kindness, empathy and love for yourself and others.

Mother Theresa, St. Therese and Mother Mary then stepped forth for day 7's message. They said there is a trilogy of horrors coming to earth filled with devastation and loss. The impact of these tragedies depends on the willingness of help that souls will offer to each other. We will watch over you as you make your way through the rubble to help your brothers and sisters. Hope will come in many forms; it can be as simple as a glass of water or a slice of bread. The survival rate of any tragedy can be high if souls choose to band together.

May 3rd 2017: Mother Theresa, St. Therese and Mother Mary stepped forth to give me day 8's message. I was told, "The minute details of your journey are being worked upon as the day draws closer to your ultimate mission. Make the most out of your daily routine on earth. There has been an arrangement made between the angelic realm and the earth realm in which you agreed to. Have faith in the upcoming lessons that are coming your way. Health issues will be repaired and all will be well. Trust in the divine appointment of the souls that are headed your way. There has been some confusion as to assignments but now the path is clear. Every step forward for you is a step closer to being on a humanitarian level. Proudly shine your light for the world to see. Dot your I's and cross your T's as you move forward with your book. Your book will be a source of hope to those who have lost faith. I was then told "Peter 3:12" so I looked it up in the bible and here is what it says. 'For the eyes of the Lord are on the righteous and his ears are attentive to their prayer but the face of the Lord is against those who do evil'."

May 4th 2017: Today is the 9th day of messages from Mother Theresa, St. Teresa and Mother Mary. I couldn't get a clear vision of them or their energy today as a collective as I had in the previous messages. During the message I realized it was St. Therese who was speaking to me because she called me Helene. The message started out with me being told that the 9th day is a day of sunshine and free will. It is a birthday celebration (I was then shown a beautiful baby girl who was celebrating her 1st birthday). I was told that, "This baby girl represents the light of the world that is upon us. She will be more powerful than Queen Elizabeth and a warrior like Joan of Arc but on many continents. She will live her life with gusto and a sort of innocence. This child will cross your path, Helene, and you will instantly know that she is the one. You will give her guidance as your paths cross. Your interactions will be meaningful and purposeful to the outcome of her journey. This, my sister, is a huge part of your mission on earth. She is a heavenly soul in a human body so that she may accomplish what needs to be done for the good of the world. We trust in you as you prepare to go forth on your journey. Let us worry about the placement of souls who need to be in your life at the right moment with divine timing. Tell the souls of the world that each smile they fake will eventually bring them to a more genuine feeling of peace for others."

May 5th 2017: On the 10th day of messages I have received from Mother Theresa, St. Therese and Mother Mary I was told to take the time to cleanse your soul of negative energy each day. "The negative energy of others can seep into your soul slowly through the air and could be undetectable until you feel the chaos within you. Daily prayers are a way of cleansing your soul. You must also stay connected to us in the other realms on a daily basis in order to reach your full potential. The help that you give to others is admirable. We are closing a chapter of your life and opening a door to eminent success. We have graced favors upon you for this book to bring you to the forefront of the spiritual community so that you may be known and to spread our words among your brothers and sisters. Technical difficulties will occur but don't let them discourage you for you have the grace of God on your side. We speak to you as a collective, for the unity of three is very powerful. You will need our assistance many times along your journey and we offer it freely. The purity of our love will carry you far and have no fear for you are always safe. Keep fighting the good fight; you can win any personal war with love and good intentions.

May 6th 2017: Day 11's message from Mother Theresa, St. Therese and Mother Mary is that many souls would suffer due to health care decisions but many will fight against this storm. There are many darker souls in the position of authority who have no concern for the welfare of the people. Pray, trust and have faith and know that these darker souls will pay the debt of their actions through karmic balance. As they sit in their towers, they do not realize that their negative actions against mankind will be dealt with accordingly for there is no escaping from themselves. Light workers have been strategically placed in the health field in one way or another so that they may help the souls who will need it. The wrath of mankind upon themselves is destroying the world in so many ways. Look around at your neighbors, family and friends and you will see the truth as to what is upon all of mankind.

May 7th 2017: Today is day 12 and the final day of messages from Mother

Theresa, St. Therese and Mother Mary as a collective. I was told that the completion of one's life upon the end of their journey should not be about the success of finances or items that they have acquired. "It should be about the service that they offered to the world and their unselfishness, for it is detrimental to the well being of the soul. The fulfillment that is felt within when you have freely offered your services to another is the main purpose of everyone's existence. It doesn't matter what you think you have done wrong in your life for when you reach the place of empathy and kindness for others then you are doing God's work. If you give of yourself without worrying about your own needs, be confident that you also will always be taken care of. Have faith and trust in the Creator for no one is put on this earth without a plan, or without being sustained by the heavens. It is when the human ego and freewill kick in that your life goes awry. You can veer off the plan of God and cause yourself suffering. The biggest test of faith in life is to let God take care of everything. You and God are one so if you don't love yourself than how can you love God? This can bring on physical challenges in the human body. A monarch butterfly is a symbol of the challenges that go on within a soul in the human body." (What I personally know of Monarch butterflies is that they face many hurdles in their fight for survival. They are threatened by global warming and they are offered protection in sanctuaries in the United States. Though delicate, their wings have a strong framework).

May 8th 2017: My guide Joseph came forth and said to take time out of each day to help a grieving soul, that this would be good practice for my upcoming work. "The manipulation of your soul as you sleep has been quite a task due to the fear within. Your next project will be related to the healing of your aura. You have come to a stand still in part of your development as we have worked on the other part of your soul. It will all melt together as you meet souls on the other coast. You are on a sort of vacation now as we prepare you for your upcoming trip and the work it will entail. We are all pleased with the unselfish help you have given to your brothers and sisters. Your two feet are planted firmly on the path of a humanitarian. Tell the people of the world that they are able to change the future by waking up each day doing the right thing for themselves and each other, for everyone has the power within them. By believing in yourself you believe in God, and with God everything is possible."

May 9th 2017: As I was going though my Facebook today a video came up on my feed. It was a four-minute video with John Lennon speaking about peace and the government. As I watched it he said: "Keep fighting the good fight" which I thought was quite a coincidence because four days earlier in my connection to the angelic realm I was also told "Keep fighting the good fight." I actually put the entire statement I was given out on social media yesterday which was "Keep fighting the good fight, you can win any personal war with love and good intentions." As I connected to the other realm today, I kept seeing a vision of John Lennon and I was told there is no such thing as a coincidence. I questioned myself and thought this must be in my mind because of the coincidence earlier. I asked my guide Joseph to help clear my mind so that they could enter my thoughts and I could hear clearly. I again heard: "How many times have we told you there is no such thing as a coincidence?" And the vision of John Lennon was still there. I then knew for sure it was not my own thoughts so I then said, "Could you please give me the message?" An angel came forth but he would not give me a name. He said, "I am the Angel of Peace" then he told me that John Lennon was a messenger of peace on earth. His time on earth was cut short due to the ignorance of mankind. He continues his work from the spiritual realm. His job is to instill peace in the hearts of those who need it, and to teach light workers the truth about how to walk on a more peaceful path. Though his work might go unnoticed on the earth realm, we are highly conscious of it in the other realms. He has made great strides for the future of mankind. He is an honorary member of the angelic realm for his pure heart and soul. The angel then said that John would like to extend love and peace by the bushels to the people of the world. He was committed to this purpose before he came to earth, while he was on earth, and after he left earth. As John steps forward he is letting the world know of his role in the spiritual realm and he is hoping to convince the people of the world to stay true to his words of "Let there be peace." John then said to me, "If you truly believe in your own hopes and dreams then the world would be a better place for all. I apologize for the mishaps I had upon the earth with anyone for my human form was not perfect." (As he said this to me, he showed me Yoko One and his band mates from "The Beatles"). Lastly, he said to me, "Thank you for spreading this message with no fear of those who will tear you down. Namaste--which he pronounced as Nam-as-kar. Peace to you my friend." Then he was gone.

May 10th 2017: As I connected to the other realm today, I was shown a vision of St. Therese and other nuns wearing old fashioned habits standing in front of a red brick building near a beautiful garden. St. Therese then said to me that she was showing me a sacred part of her life. She said this is where she did her learning and she also walked in this garden. She told me that the place she lived in on earth and the place that I live in on earth are of equal value, which serves the same purpose for the both of us. She told me that my apartment is my convent. "You see, my child, it doesn't matter where you are, for if you have faith and desire within, then your soul can grow and miracles can happen anywhere. As I watch all that you do, I beam with pride and my heart feels full. There are many souls that I help though I will never leave your side, my sister. The violence in the world makes me overwhelmingly sad and sometimes I project my sadness onto you and for that I am sorry. As your son walks in empathy, he will be of great assistance to you. This was all agreed upon before you both came to earth. You have both chosen paths with difficult lessons on many levels. You are each other's saving grace for you carry each other when it is needed. Tell Matthew there is plentiful abundance coming both your ways and you have each worked hard for it, keep going forward." She then gave me a knowing that she knows Matthew from another lifetime and that the three of us have been together before. I did some research online and found pictures and videos of the Carmelite Monastery in Lisieux, Normandy where St. Therese lived and worked. I was pleasantly surprised to find that it was a beautiful red brick building with a beautiful garden. I should never doubt any message or vision I receive from spirit.

May 11th 2017: As I connected today, a beautiful angel with long honey colored hair, in all white, with white wings appeared. I am beginning to feel a much more personal connection to those I have been connecting with lately. This angel began by telling me that they don't actually have wings. He said this is the way they appear because this is the way they are depicted and you don't need wings for your soul to fly. He showed himself to me as a man, then as a woman, and said to me, "I am androgynous" and he called himself Nathaniel. He then said to me the word "Azera." I never heard this word before so being curious to it's meaning I looked it up. In the urban dictionary the meaning is: Beautiful, powerful, magical woman. Wise one. An enigma to most. Faithful, and full of love. People person, but can be reclusive at times. Understands "Oneness." Because he is androgynous, I can only assume he was speaking of himself with the word Azera. Nathaniel went on to tell me that the prophet Isaiah spoke of the coming of the Lord. The truest words in his testament are of how evil can spread rapidly. Make no mistake for in the eyes of the Lord evil is the wrath that human kind has put upon themselves. There is no correlation of the New Testament verses the Old Testament for you cannot change the words of the Lord. Seek evil and you will find it, seek good and you will find that. The people of the world must be aware that they truly rule their own destiny. What you put into your life you get out of it. Each soul must secure their own life and the future of the world. Nathaniel then told me he is an angel of the prophet Isaiah and he has come to correct some of the wrongs in the New

Testament. You can call upon me anytime there are words that seem untrue to you. In your world I am a sort of librarian and truthsayer. I speak the truth and I know all the information from each realm.

May 12th 2017: In my connection today, I felt an overwhelming presence but I couldn't see anyone. I asked, "Who is there?" and I heard, "I am the Son of God, do not have self doubt for I stand by your side. The portrayal of me on earth is the form in which the people have chosen to see me. I was a mere mortal five feet tall with short brown hair and luminous green eyes. I walked the earth like every other man as I carried on with the work of our Heavenly Father. It is with great distress that I step forth to bring the news of eminent world disasters. There also are false prophets to come. Souls run amuck on earth and do not listen to their instincts. I must warn you all to get in touch with your true inner guidance or you will follow the false prophet. Take the time each day to search for your inner guidance in preparation for the upcoming disasters. Do not hesitate to protect your family and friends because in the end you will be saving yourself. As I sit beside you, I open my Sacred Heart to you for your devotion through many lifetimes." (I then felt a breeze and heard "But for the grace of God"). Though I have received other messages from Jesus before this one, he had only appeared to me looking like the man in the statues I had seen my entire life. He will appear to me from now on as the form he was on earth.

May 13th 2017: As I connected to the other realm today, I heard "You have the magical touch of angels on your side." I then saw something I have never seen before-little fairies flying around flowers. I can't accurately describe what I saw because though I knew they were fairies, they didn't look like the ones we think of on earth. The best description may be that they were all the color of a bright green blade of grass. They moved around quickly and busily through the air, and I wasn't shown any real detail of them. I was then told that nature is God's way of spreading beauty throughout the earth. These little creatures are considered angels for nature. They are protectors that bring love and light to wherever they go. They are preparing for the future of the world, protecting what will be needed in the aftermath. These protectors welcome each visitor that has come to earth. Any myths of them would be in the way they are seen, not how they actually are. They are a gift from the Creator and have been in existence since day one. I then asked if they are called "Fairies" and the answer given to me was they are "Soldiers of the Soil." Their most important job is for the protection of nature. They send love and light and nurture nature on a daily basis. They sometimes feel distraught over the devastation that has been brought on by mankind to their centuries of work. They ask for love and kindness for all that stands sacred to them.

May 14th 2017: I was feeling a little down today because it is Mother's Day and I miss my mother. As I connected to the other realm I heard, open your heart to the suffering of others and do not sit in self-pity for it serves your journey no purpose. Mother Mary then stepped forth and said we want you to know and understand that mankind cannot hinder you on your journey. "Your soul is fueled with the energy to carry on with your purpose so don't let human emotions stand in the way. Those who are in the greatest need will knock at your door and we ask that you let them in for comfort and support. You will become a world traveler in the hopes of bringing peace to others. You will accomplish great feats in your travels and beyond. This is a great day of celebration on earth so be grateful that you don't sit in grief and loneliness at this time in your life like so many others are. There will be a reconciliation of souls in the spirit realm honoring this day of celebration. Take the time each day to feel your angels around you. This will make them happy and in turn bring you joy."

May 15th 2017: Mother Mary came forth and said that the New Testament will be brought to light of the untruths within it. "Each paragraph that was changed was custom fit by mankind. There are unholy truths in the New Testament of the violence and torture that was put upon mankind. These suffering souls still struggle to heal on a certain level in the spiritual realm. The audacity of mankind to change the words of the Lord is beyond disrespectful and dishonest. The Lord loves all of his children no matter the race, gender or sexual orientation. Each step that mankind makes towards accepting each other for their true selves will only bring you closer to God. There is no wrong or right in male or female genders and the diversity of this is God's way of asking everyone to accept each other as they are."

Then my guide Joseph stepped forth and said, "I am here though I know that you haven't felt me. I am waiting to step forth at a certain time on your path when I will be needed. You are making great strides in your soul's development and I am proud of you. Do not feel guilty on your lazy days for you deserve breaks. You may call upon me at any time and I will be of assistance to you for I am here to support and guide you. Grab the future by the horns for your destiny waits with all the abundance that the universe has to offer."

May 17th 2017: As I connected to the other realm today, Mother Theresa stepped forth and said to me, "As I guide you to your destiny of helping others, may you see just how fortunate you are in life. Spread the fortune that befalls you by feeding the hungry, clothing the poor, and donating to the sick. Always go one step further on your mission than necessary as to not leave out any stragglers.

Those who are in the greatest need and who are the poorest will always be more grateful than the rest. It will be up to you to make sure the funds get distributed evenly. Be gentle and kind to the souls that you meet on this journey for they will feel my presence and know that you are the one with whom they shall work. Follow the path as we guide you and success will be yours and in turn success will be for all. I am always near you, my child, and you may call upon me anytime that you need me. Take a leap of faith one step at a time and it will eventually lead you to somewhere that you never could have imagined."

Today I passed by the property that Lizzie Borden owned and lived in after the murders till the day she passed. I only viewed the property from the outside but it is a huge old gorgeous house that seemed very inviting to me. As I walked home, I started speaking to Lizzie and told her that I hoped to be able to enter that house one day to get a better energy of her. The house is called "Maplecroft" and is located on French St. in Fall River, Ma. After my communication with Mother Theresa, I heard someone say, "A soul-to-soul connection can be made by anyone at anytime with good intentions and some effort. Lizzie then stepped forward and told me that "Maplecroft" is a place of dynamic energy and she would love for me to do a soul-to-soul connection there. "The energy runs high there and I would disclose many details to you. It would be a start as to getting the public's attention to my plight of innocence. Go forth in the direction that you are set on and you are to wait for further instructions. This will be the beginning to opening the doors to my innocence. Remember there are no coincidences and you were drawn to view that house for a reason."

May 18th 2017: My guide Agnes came forth today and said that the deeper your faith and trust is in us, the deeper connection you will have with us. "Your yearning for a bright future has not gone unnoticed but everything has to happen in divine timing. The disappointment of not winning the Powerball has put your soul in a negative space when we have not forgotten you my dear." (I felt drawn to play the Powerball and I thought maybe there was a chance I was going to win some money to help me, but I was wrong. Sometimes I have no patience waiting for divine timing). "There is a divine plan and you will be taken care of every step of the way. There are many steps yet to be taken for future events to unfold. Be kind, patient, and generous to those you meet along the way in preparation for your ultimate sacrifice. The magnitude of your soul's connection to God depends on the magnitude of your faith in Him."

May 19th 2017: Archangel Michael came forth and said that sometimes the main concern for the leaders in government is the struggle for power. This can be a prime example of ego overtaking mankind. The road to peace is not paved with bombs. It is paved with kindness, gratitude, fortitude and the willingness to extend a hand in times of need. Each life that is lost in this struggle of power is needless. The tragedies and sufferings that come out of all this nonsense should be the top priority in the world. It is like a mystical illusion for some people and it doesn't even faze them. We are truly saddened as we watch this chaos from the other realms. A change in the world is needed; but unfortunately to get to a place of peace, much chaos and tragedies will have to ensue first. We, the angels, ask the souls of earth to please take your place in this world by offering love, kindness and a helping hand to your brothers and sisters. And we ask that you do this without judgment. The more souls that project love and light, the better and the easier it will be."

May 20th 2017: As I connected today, Mother Mary stepped forth and told me I was receiving a healing and a cleansing. She said my soul was crying out to be nurtured by nature. I was then shown myself helping the poorest of the poor with Mother Theresa by my side. I was covered in dirt as I was kneeling down with some people. Mother Mary went on to say that I would be taken to the same area where Jesus died on the cross as part of my work, without even realizing it until I arrive. "Your work will bring you far and wide as you cross country into country supporting, comforting and guiding the souls of the world. Jesus works in you and through you and he has taught you well. Remember to remind souls that the doorway to reformation is never closed. Accept each soul as they come forth looking for forgiveness. It is only in their darkest hour upon earth that many souls want to connect to God, when all along the connection should have been strong. Remind them that God has never broken His connection with them for it is they who have not had enough faith to feel Him in their souls. The lives of many will be changed by tragedy and they will rebuild from humble beginnings and learn it is time to live with peace on earth. We are proud of you to keep going forth my child."

May 21st 2017: I went on a walk today and an enormous pure black butterfly flew in front of my face. This is the first time in my life I had seen a pure black butterfly. I felt it was a sign of something so I looked up on google what a pure black butterfly means. It said it is a source of strength and through the darkness you are reborn.

As I connected to the other realm today my guide Margaret stepped forth and said to me the signs have been all around you. "Your gratitude has been well noticed and the advancement of your career is forthcoming. We eagerly wait to assist you with your upcoming project. Each door that is opened will have a spiritually based gift behind it. The longitude of your self-esteem now matches the magnitude of your dreams. There will be a tri-fold of spiritual presence that helps you to unlock these doors. There will be a moment of realization that you have arrived at the place you need to be. Always take the high road, for the low road will only bring you to a roadblock that will negatively affect every aspect of your life."

May 22nd 2017: As I was saying my prayers today and once again as I was praying for celebrities that have passed, a man came forth and asked me to add him to my daily prayers. His face was familiar to me and I knew that he overdosed from heroin but I couldn't remember his name. I looked him up online and found that his name was Phillip Seymour Hoffman and I have now added him to my prayers.

Archangel Haniel came forth and said that the force of nature and the natural surroundings of one's soul in a human body could be devoured by another, which can contribute to the downfall of a human being. These downfalls can cause great chaos in their lives and in the flow of the universe. There are many afflictions that are put upon humans that are willfully caused by another soul. If a soul has enough belief in themselves and God the Father, then they can rise above anything. A soul can temporarily be out of commission but never permanently, for a soul can never die. We want everyone to realize that no one soul has control over another for each soul in the universe controls his or her own destiny. The future of the world depends upon the strength and courage of the souls as time goes forth. Each decision should be based upon love in order to bring the world to a level of peace. The progression of one's soul should outweigh the progression of war and all that it entails. Make the most out of each day and cherish each moment, for it can slip from your fingertips in a split second. Financial abundance may help your life to be easier, but it cannot replace love in any form. The angels and archangels have descended upon earth to help the suffering souls." (I wondered why I was told that the angels have descended upon earth today. Sometime after I received this message today, I heard about the terrorist attack in Manchester, England, then it all made sense).

May 23rd 2017: As I connected to the other realm today my guides Joseph and Margaret both stepped forth to give me this message: "The Queen of England is disheartened by the terrorist attacks. These attacks have caused an uprising and a revolution in the hearts of many. There will be more tragedy and loss in the future for England. They are seen as a wide-open target in the eyes of the terrorists and war is eminent. As the scepter is passed from Queen to King there will be bolder choices made in order to protect the country. The angelic realm has collected all the souls who have passed from this tragedy. Those who are injured are receiving healing as you write this. Unfortunately, there is much more disaster that will happen in many countries-all due to the ignorance of mankind. The terrorists do not care or think about the consequences of their actions. There will be years of poverty, destitution, and suffering for those who have not experienced this before. Each day as you walk through the rubble of people's lives, know that there is a light at the end of the path. Souls must choose a better way of living and a better way of being so that eventually there will be peace on earth. Always keep your eye on the prize, which is the welfare of your brothers and sisters. Be humble my child."

May 24th 2017: As I started today's communication Mother Mary stepped forth to give me this message: "The human error of mankind lies in their hearts. The chaos that they feel within them is like being trapped in a jungle of emotion and feelings with no way out. The terrorists have their wires crossed in the human body and they do not think or see clearly. They follow the false prophets of the world and in turn cause tremendous damage to the innocent. Each individual soul should take charge of there own welfare and of those that they are responsible for. Do not live in fear for this only feeds the terrorist and their actions. Band together and unite for this will be stronger than anything a terrorist can bring forth. Help, hope and charity are three words that are prime examples of extending a hand to another in their time of need. These three actions will help bring you to the other side of the chaos and destruction. The souls who have passed in the Manchester attacks are being healed in the angelic realm. These souls have been chosen to go on higher learning journeys as part of their mission so that they may work with the souls who will cross from the devastation of the world. Tell their families their passing was not in vain. I am personally sending love and light to the families of these souls. It won't always be easy but we ask for faith and trust from all. Joy constitutes being true to yourself and to the ones who matter the most."

May 25th 2017: As I connected to the other realm today St. Therese stepped forth and said to me, "Hello my sister, welcome to the world of hierarchy in which you will be placed on a ladder according to your mission and all it entails to benefit the world. The upheaval of souls in the United Kingdom has brought much distress to the kingdom of God our Father. So as the saying goes, 'If you have lemons make lemonade' and that is what we have done with the souls who have passed from that tragedy. The work that they will do is the highest way we know how to honor them for this injustice. As I stand in a garden of roses, I am projecting healing light out to those in Manchester and also to the souls who have asked for my intercession. Karmic balance waits in the wings for those souls who have caused sufferings to others." I then told St. Therese, "I am very happy that you have stepped forth today and I now feel a sisterly bond with you." She then replied to me that the level on which we connect is a bond like no other, and it is eternal. "Do not fear the future, my sister, for there is much joy and happiness to come. I have connected to your earthly mother "Alice" who is of great importance to you." She then showed me my mother sitting in a chair with St. Therese standing by her side. I could feel complete joy beaming from my mother as she was in the presence of St. Therese and her pride of me for the work I am doing. This vision made me feel very peaceful and thankful to St. Therese. Lastly St. Therese told me that she would send me a rose filled with love.

May 26th 2017: Today an angel named Christopher stepped forth. He came forth to me one other time on February 24th 2016. At that time, and even now, I felt something special about this angel. I asked him, "What kind of angel are you?" and he told me that he is the brother of the Archangels. That was all he told me about himself, so I can only assume it is not meant for me to know at this time. Christopher told me that the triangulation of the people on earth within their communication with each other creates problems of distance between souls. "The people of the world have gotten so comfortable with their interactions in electronics that many have forgotten how it feels to interact with another human being. This has caused people, and especially the future generation to be less empathetic towards others. The more distance that everyone on earth puts between each other will make it harder when the time comes to lift each other up. Everyone must put down the electronics and have a face-to-face conversation with their brother or sister. We also ask that you all keep your eyes wide open on a daily basis with the intentions of helping another. This all is for the preparation of the future and also for your soul's growth. Every act of kindness, love or good intention will never go unnoticed and it will help to fulfill your life's purpose in some way."

May 27th 2017: As I connected to the angelic realm today, I was shown a vision of a group of angels wearing all white. Suddenly all these angels started to change in to what looked like ornaments. Next, I was shown a Christmas tree that I was kneeling in front of when I was a child in our living room while my father was sitting on the couch looking very angry. An angel came forth and told me he is Nathaniel one of my guardian angels. He told me that he has been with me since birth and he has always protected me from the physical harm from my father. He told me that he would continue to be with me till I transition home again. He said, "I will always protect you from physical harm." Then Nathaniel showed me myself when I was pregnant and I fell in the road in which I broke both my ankles. He showed me that he gave me a push on my back so that I would fall. Nathaniel went on to say that this was asked of him from our Heavenly Father in order to change the path that I was on with my alcoholism. He said it had to be done to secure the future of my unborn son and myself. He said, "You had gone too far off of the path and you needed to be brought back in. Otherwise, the dynamics of your life's purpose would have changed and you would never be at the place you are in your mission today. Your life's purpose is too important to just let you go askew. Contracts were signed and promises were made that we had to uphold you to. You were right in your intuition when you had said that God had a hand in it, though you didn't realize the importance of it all. The physical suffering that was brought upon you in turn had healed you in other ways. We did not over step our boundaries by stepping in, for this intercession was agreed to ahead of time. We are all proud of the leaps and bounds that you have taken in this lifetime. We wanted to offer an explanation to you at this point in your life, for your book and work would help change the lives of many upon the earth. Bless you child, go forth in peace."

May 29th 2017: As I connected to the other realm today, I saw an older man with a long white beard. He had no hair on top of his head but hair on the sides of it and he was wearing a long white tunic. I asked him, "Who are you?" He replied, "I am what you would call a wizard on earth, but in my realm, I am a magical mentor of sorts. I teach and guide beings of white light. These beings start out as my apprentices until they grow and form into what is referred to as pixie dust angels. The so-called pixie dust is actually healing white light that they spread in the universe to the souls who are in need of assistance. We from the other realms are stepping forth one-by-one to introduce ourselves to help you understand just how many different beings are in our realms. All these beings are for the purpose of doing good for others." I then asked him, "What is your name?" and he replied, "You may call me 'Merlin' if that makes it easier for you." I told him "I would rather know your real name." He told me his name is Saguaris. He then said there are millions of these white light beings in the universe and they are limitless. "You may call upon us anytime you need us child; all you have to do is ask. I am a sort of father figure to them."

May 30th 2017: Archangel Haniel came forth today and said that I will be brought on a higher level of learning and worshipping, so that I may teach others. She said this higher level would allow me the opportunity to express my beliefs more openly and freely. She went on to say that my teachings would bring me to the Buddhist temples along my path. "The cylinders of your soul hold information from other lifetimes. As these cylinders are accessed from your higher self they will appear in the form of intuition. This information will be valuable to you on your journey. The highest form of spiritual education comes from your own soul. If everyone's information from his or her souls came together it would complete the puzzle of the universe in its entirety. This makes every single soul just as important as the next one. We ask that you do your best to complete your piece of the puzzle. Rewards are headed your way from the riches this world has to offer."(I have a feeling and knowing that these rewards that are headed my way are not materialistic but spiritually based). "If your heart has jumped for joy at the sight of another then your heart has been blessed."

May 31st 2017: As I connected to the other realm today, I saw a Franciscan Monk who kept showing me how he protects children. I asked his name and he said to me that his name wasn't important. He proceeded to give me this message: "In this era of televised events around the world you would assume that there isn't much that is hidden. But on the contrary the most important news that must be brought to the people is hidden in the corners of the world in a circle of dark souls. White light must be shed upon this information. News outlets have been spreading false information that has caused harm to their reputations. When the time is right for this information to be brought to the surface it will be doubted due to their previous actions. False imprisonment of the innocent will arise from the chaos. Follow the hearts of those in the light and seek the truth for there will be many winding roads at your feet. These revelations are all part of your upcoming journey to help those in need."

TWENTY

Some Message Are a Double Edged Sword

June 1st 2017: As I connected to the other realm today, I could see the color pink and I felt a sense of peace. I asked if this was Archangel Haniel and I was told this is Uriel. She said to me, "As you walk on the earth spreading your love and light, the purpose of your soul's journey to enlighten others becomes that much more important. As you descend forward on your journey to California, many changes will be taking place on both coasts. These changes are needed in order for your mission to come to fruition. We have watched you closely in your everyday life to make sure you are on the right path. There have been many interventions in your life to keep you on your path, for the road forth is too important to waiver from. You have been blessed and will be surrounded by many spiritual beings and souls. As you take a step forward one day at a time you are taking a step higher toward your heavenly father. You have our support from all of the realms and we appreciate your gratitude. I am offering peace in your heart as you embark on a new journey in this life. May every soul feel the peace and love that the angels offer as they go forth in their daily lives."

June 3rd 2017: As I connected today, I saw the colors blue and purple. I wasn't sure who was connecting to me but I was thinking it was Archangel Michael because those are the colors I usually see when he connects to me. When I asked who it was, I heard Jophiel. I have heard of Archangel Jophiel before but I do not know anything about her. I later found out that people usually see the colors orange and yellow with Jophiel. I had seen the blue and purple because I was told that Archangel Michael was the one who had brought her forth. She told me that the healing properties of the world come from within each of us. A talisman for this healing can come from the sun, the sea or the richest of the earth. Each soul has the power to manifest their own positive outcome in life. As you take a step backwards in negativity, I am always there to push you forward with positive affirmations and brilliant sparks of creative ideas. My team of angels and I have guided you through every step of this book. I thought it appropriate to step forth at this time as the book is coming to a close. I will continue to help you in your future endeavors for there is much more to come. It was a pleasure to work with someone so willingly devoted to helping others upon earth. Your work will not go unnoticed in any realm. Have faith and leave the details of what is to come next to us.

June 4th 2017: Today as Archangel Michael came forth, I could feel his great strength and power. He said, "There is a concern of future terrorist acts in England for they are seen as a target of vulnerability. The Parliament's structure possibly holds a weakness into which the terrorist activity could seep in. As a protector I have deferred a few threats of terrorism but they are insistent of instilling terror in the hearts of the people. Some of these dark acts will plague the world until there is no choice but to rebuild. His holiness "The Pope" will spread blessings throughout the world to help build a new day. Angels will roam the earth to comfort and love the souls of the world. Each time that a community is rebuilt, a door will open that will bring a new beginning. Stand strong against these terrorists and do not let them overtake your world. Call upon me in your time of need and I will fight against the darkness for you. The angelic realm is willing to instill peace in the hearts of those who ask. Go forward and do your highest and best good in your daily lives."

June 5th 2017: Today is my first day in San Diego staying with my daughter while her husband is away on deployment. In today's connection Archangel Gabriel stepped forward and said to me, "I bring you a message of joy and hope. Hang in there, child, for the rewards will be limitless and we will help you to rise up in your emotions. Due to your lack of rest your emotions are running high. You feel as though you have given up on life in the hopes of advancing your career. Know that you have also been placed with your daughter at this time to heal her in her current and future emotional upheaval. The struggle within you is real and you should no longer settle for anything less than love. As you transition from one coast to the next your spiritual view will broaden. As you go forward on your path, we will nudge you in order for you to meet the souls who we have all agreed that you will work with. The pied piper will be playing a tune and you must follow the music. You will see the picture a little brighter as you catch up on rest. We welcome you into the next step of your spiritual advancement."

June 6th 2017: As I connected today, I didn't see anyone step forward but I could feel a male presence and I heard, "This is the prophet Isaiah." He told me, "The role of a good leader is to be honest and true in integrity and have the welfare of the people at the center of their intentions as to bring peace and light in the path that they walk. Many leaders in the world do not possess these qualities and therefore are not productive in taking any steps forward for peace on earth. The nature of their business is usually self-serving. Eventually a new day will be dawning and everything that the world knows as the government will cease to exist. All matters will be handled on a more spiritual basis and this path will lead to a better way of living and being. The final product of this outcome will be peace on earth. Have faith as the world goes through tragedies for there will be a rainbow at the end of it all. Be good to each other for there is always time for redemption. Take heed in these words, my friends, for this is the word of the Lord."

June 7th 2017: Archangel Gabriel came forth again today and said, "The foundation of life is based on our spiritual truth. Each failure and mistake help bring us closer to seeing what lies beneath the surface so that the truth may be revealed. Many souls on earth go round and round in circles when actually what they seek is right in front of them. They are too interwoven in their own egos to be fully aware or even understand that the process of a spiritual awakening is as simple as pulling the reigns back on your life and surrendering to all that is good. With continued faith in God there is no doubt a soul will become enlightened to their purpose on earth. There will be souls who lose their faith with the upcoming tragedies but that is when your faith should be it's strongest. There is no need to worry about the end of earth for it will be only the end of earth, as you know it. The so-called apocalypse is the destruction brought on by mankind. Fear not what is to come but fear the here and now and the underlying root of it all. Take my hand and I shall lead you to the Promised Land."

June 8th 2017: As I was saying my prayers today my brother David's wife Cindy, who passed away many years ago, appeared. She said to me "Make sure you see my daughter Melanie" so I replied, "Yes of course I will see Melanie." Melanie is David and Cindy's child from their marriage while David lived in California. Her grandparents raised Melanie in California after Cindy passed away. That same day I sent Melanie a message and told her I was in San Diego for a long stay and that I would like her to meet up with my daughter Sarah and myself. Melanie replied that same day saying she would love to come to San Diego and to finally meet my daughter Sarah. Melanie has lived in the Los Angeles area her whole life but had never been to San Diego before so she was excited to come visit. We both said we would be in touch to make specific plans. I was waiting to tell Melanie in person how her mother came to me and asked me to see her because I knew the happiness this would bring to her. I figured we had plenty of time to make plans because I was in San Diego for seven months.

On October 2nd 2017: Mother Mary has come forth for the last three days to tell me there would be a tragedy in my family. I completely ignored theses messages out of fear. I told her I can't go through another tragedy and I denied the message. I could feel that this tragedy was someone young and I feared it was one of my children so I shut myself off from it. I was wrong in doing so because they were only trying to prepare me for what was to come.

Matthew came down to San Diego to visit Sarah and myself the week of October 8th. Sarah, Matthew and myself were sitting in Sarah's car in a mall parking lot on October 14th when I was looking on Facebook. I started seeing a lot of pictures of Melanie from different people saying things like, "I can't believe this happened." At first I didn't know what was going on and I started to panic and as I read on I saw things like, "Rest in peace Melanie." I immediately started crying and shaking as I was trying to tell my kids that Melanie had passed away. Melanie was a piece of my brother David and I couldn't help but feel the loss of David once again. She was driving back from one of her friend's houses on her way to visit another friend who lived in her own neighborhood. A 23-year-old man was driving drunk and racing his car. He lost control and crossed over to the opposite side of the road were Melanie was driving and struck her. He hit her at 105 miles per hour, which instantly crushed her body. She passed to spirit that day on October 13th 2017 at the age of 25 years old. I never had the chance to get together with her before she passed. I now understand why Cindy came to me and asked me to make sure that I saw her daughter. I had the spirit realm warning me of a tragedy, but out of fear I didn't pay attention to their messages. The spirit realm was trying to give me the opportunity to say goodbye to her. Even as a medium and with the communication that I received, I didn't take that opportunity and now I will be forever regretful.

October 15th 2017: Mother Mary and Jesus, who was holding the Sacred Heart stepped forth today. Mother Mary did the talking and she said told me that my sorrow is felt in their world due to Melanie's passing. She went on to say to remember the turmoil you are feeling in your soul for a life gone too soon from the earth. "This feeling will help you on your journey as you go forth helping souls in grief. There are many lessons to be learned though unfortunately these lessons can be difficult. We come to you today with the love of sacred heart upon us. Each generation will suffer their own misfortunes. This is what makes those on earth stronger and able to conquer their demons. The reuniting of souls in heaven is felt with the same amount of joy that those on earth feel grief. The homecoming of your niece was quite beautiful. Her family in the spirit world has embraced her with complete joy and love. Rest assured that her soul is being taken care of."

June 9th 2017: Archangel Michael came forth and said that in future events; disappointments will come in many forms. "Terrorist's attacks will be done randomly, making no sense at all to their targets as if they are trying to start a world war. Many terrorists are planted in cells since infancy and are raised and taught the destruction of others. It is not who you let in your country, but it is who is already in your country that is alarming. The best protection against these dark souls is using your intuition. Many people don't take the time to listen to their inner guidance. A daily routine of meditation and connecting to yourself and your guides will immensely increase your awareness to what and who are around you. These steps will not stop the terrorist actions but it is a step in the right direction to keep you safe. Do not go forth in fear, go forth in dignity knowing that you choose what's right in life, for there is no promise of tomorrow."

June 10th 2017: As I connected to the other realm today my guides Joseph and Margaret stepped forth along with Mother Theresa. Mother Theresa did the speaking and she said: "The road to redemption for many is a road worth traveling. The highest point of a mountaintop is where peace and the true essence of God exist. Each member of society must take on all that the world has to offer. As you spring forward in March and fall back in September, so does the progression of your soul. Each negative connotation in the world has negative consequences. That is why we should speak only from a place of love and if you cannot find that place, then that is when silence is golden. The rules of life are simple, 'Treat and love others as you would want them to treat and love you.' With this simple rule you will not go wrong in how you live your life. Push ahead in your daily life for the good of all."

June 11th 2017: Archangel Gabriel came forth today and said: "The consequences of one's actions doesn't lie in the soul who is the innocent victim, but in the soul of the one who purposely caused harm to another whether it be physical, verbal or spiritual. The consequences of the perpetrator are embedded into their soul and will be dealt with at a later time. There are many suffering souls upon this earth whose needs are neglected by those around them. Do not feel threatened by the words of another but feel empowered by your strength to carry on as the pure soul that you are. The days shall blend together as the future gets closer to your true purpose on earth. Rise above the pettiness of others as you reach your goal of helping your brothers and sisters. Trudge through this portion of your journey even though you can't see what lies ahead for hope comes in many forms. Each day that you awake, another step has been taken to the unraveling of the mystery of your complete self."

June 12th 2017: In today's connection St. Catherine of Augustine stepped forward to give me the following message, and as I was writing the first sentence down a huge orb of white light hovered over the words. "I have seen the damage that financial wealth can bring upon a person. I have stepped forth today to warn you to not let wealth overtake your life. You must live a simple life in order to be true to yourself and your purpose upon earth. Feed the hungry and reach out to the destitute that have no other means to survive except for someone like you who God has entrusted this work to. Live a modest life but with meager means and do not let those around you influence your thoughts and decisions. This is your journey and you will be in control of the financial flow to help others. This is where the lesson you have learned of empathy and sympathy will come in to play. Tell your son to hang in there and know that patience is a virtue. We sustain the both of you and do not go above your means. These lessons are interwoven into your lives to help you upon your future journey."

In the communications that I receive I get many messages from those who worked with the poor and destitute because of my purpose on earth. Blessed Catherine of St. Augustine was an Augustinian Hospitaller sister of "The Mary of Jesus" who ministered to the poor and sick in Quebec. It makes sense to me that these souls would step forth to give me messages and help guide my work.

June 13th 2017: At my daughter's house I have started doing some of my connections up in her spare room in which she has a picture of Jesus hanging. This picture is from the painting that Akiane Kramarik painted from the vision that she was shown as a child. As I connected today, Jesus came forth and he stood to the left of the painting and he looked exactly like the painting. He said these words to me: "You are ready my child for you have reached a new level of awareness. In this awareness you know that one's soul has the ability to heal oneself. I have taught you many lessons through the steps of your life. Sometimes you have fallen but each time you have gotten back up to carry on in this world. Your generous spirit towards others has caused you a mishmash of events throughout your life. Some have seen you for the soul that you are while others have tried to darken your good intentions. Those are the ones who I have helped fall off at the wayside of your life. Do not ever question why someone is taken out of your life because it will always be for your highest good. Many souls are set in place to bring you to the place you need to be on your journey. It is time to go forward rather quickly. Don't be alarmed for we are all at your side for I will never leave you alone. The rewards owed to you are limitless for your devotion to all of us in all the realms. You have been blessed with children who have gifts that will be revealed to you in the future.

June 14th 2017: Today Jesus stepped forth once again but this time he looked different. He looked like the statues I have seen of him and he said to me, "I am the Sacred Heart of Jesus." This is the message that he gave to me: "The reverence of mankind on earth is no longer a plausible factor in the uprising of the world. Each time that a soul comes forth in the light they should be revered as warriors in the fight against darkness. Each moment in time will be revealed as an experience in the space-time continuum. Light workers need to prepare themselves for the next chapter in this world. Memories of days past will serve as a negotiator for future events. These memories will also be used as a way to mentally and emotionally torture souls. We are asking all light workers to step forth and open themselves up to the commitment of helping their brothers and sisters due to the upcoming events in the world. Many souls will be able to testify through a message they have received through God's light workers. When the hard times come upon you that is when the faith of our Creator must withstand all of time. We will keep you safe in your travels as you help the souls of the world. Peace be with you all.

June 15th 2017: As I connected today, I saw a group of angels and I heard, "We are your support team of angels." They said: "The messages that we convey to you on a daily basis come from a place of pure love. These messages aren't meant to cause harm to anyone or hinder their life. They are information to give the souls of the world a glimpse into our world and to also help you prepare for future events. There will be souls who cast their negativity upon you, but remember that it is their negativity, not yours. We ask that you as a light worker go forth in your mission and do not let them cause you distress. Their unpleasant words will not only dishonor you but also God the Father and all those in the other realms who have stepped forth with good intentions. Take all that you have been taught with you on this journey that lies ahead and remember that peace is the ultimate goal. This is the word of the Lord."

June 17th 2017: In today's connection my guide Joseph came forth and said: "Hope and faith are embedded in those whose human bodies were separated from their souls due to tragedy or the violence of another. The next chapter for these souls is to become whole again on earth so they may help those who are in similar situations. There is a certain amount of time that must pass for these souls to be renewed. There are lessons to be learned and contracts to be signed before the process can begin again. As days pass upon earth, souls in our realm make leaps and bounds in their progression forward. Time has no meaning to us for the essence of our souls is what is most important. We ask the people of earth to start taking better care of their souls and in return your souls will take better care of your bodies. The prohibition in the late 1920's was a time of deception and also the conception of mankind and the harm that it caused to a human body. Please heed the words in this message for it is for the benefit of all."

June 19th 2017: My guide Agnes came forth and said these words: "The light of the world will shine upon the souls who have committed themselves to serving others. England will continue to have terrorist acts brought upon them by mentally ill souls and actual terrorists. These acts will be random and spread out across the country. Queen Elizabeth will hold her position with prominence until there is a need for her to step down in one way or another. Prince Charles will become King Charles and he will run the country in a bit more of a modern manner. The purpose of this information is to be enlightened to the bad times that England will suffer and the support they will need from their allies. One hand washes the other for in the future the shoe will be on the other foot and you will always get back what you give out. Every soul should shine their light bright to work towards peace on earth.

June 21st 2017: In today's communication my guide Joseph stepped forward and said: "Communication goes both ways between the worlds. As long as there is a communicator and a receiver, the information can rapidly flow through. Each turn of events that happen on earth can cause a ripple effect in the communication causing a static electric effect. When the time comes of peace on earth then everyone will be able to step into each other's worlds more easily. With the acceptance of other realms there will be so much more that can be done for the universe. Take the hand of the nearest Christian who offers you help so that you may see the world and the different aspects you will be exposed to more clearly."

June 22nd 2017: In today's communication to the spirit realm a combination of women stepped forward. These women were Mother Mary, Mother Theresa, Mary Magdalene and St. Therese and this is what was said to me: "A future event will lead you on a path of humanitarian work. You will have the support from each of us during this difficult transition. You will be guided each step forward that you take as we whisper words of encouragement to you. You truly are our sister of the cloth as you come from the same print as us. Healing has begun for you and your daughter and a friendship will eventually grow. The diversity of your soul's pattern and growth has exceeded our expectations. Your devotion and willingness towards your purpose brings us great pride and joy. You will see a difference in your financial abundance and this growth will accumulate over time." (I then asked them, "What do you see for my book because I can't see anything before me?") The answer they gave me was: "There is a plan my child. There is no need to worry for you cannot put the carriage before the horse. Have faith and believe that we know what we are doing. We understand about earthly frustrations and worries. We have your back, your front, and your side...and they laughed. We love you dear one, and we would never let you fall by the way side."

June 23rd 2017: In today's communication an angel stepped forth and said, "I am the one you call Glenda." This is the message she gave me: "The answers that you seek on the west coast are embedded in the minds of the people you shall meet. As a form of abuse the forefront of humanity is dangled in front of the people in North Korea and these people must be freed from their evil dictator. They must not flee their country but they must be willing to fight for their freedom. These people have been abused for so long that it is a daily acceptance in their lives. They don't understand that there are many people against this dictator who would be willing to overthrow him. They need the support of another nation who looks at them as pure souls of light that want to emerge from the darkness. The United States should do all it can in supporting those people. There will be shields of protection around those who set out to help the people of North Korea with good intentions. Each standardized rule that is broken in that country causes great suffering to those people. We are making a plea for earth angels in any form to step forth and help these souls. It can be as simple as a prayer or an act of kindness that will reach them. We ask that you do your highest and best good to help these suffering souls and this will also bring to light many souls' purposes on earth.

June 24th 2017: In today's communication Blessed Catherine of St. Augustine stepped forth. She showed me a vision of a young girl with a blue cloth on her head and told me this is Bernadette from Lourdes. Catherine then gave me this message: "She was a child of God with light as her protector. Though she was blessed with the presence of Mother Mary, her life would not be easy. She is an example of devotion to God on earth. Her family benefited from the difficult times in her life and she had chosen this in her contract to help others through her own strife. The innocence of the little girl that Mary appeared to was an innocence that she carried with her for the remainder of her lifetime on earth. Each soul has their own glory, their own suffering and their own journey. There is no soul that is better than another for in our purpose, we are all of equal importance to God. Those children who Mary appeared to are revered as blessed when in truth each soul on earth are just as blessed as them. Bernadette led a good life regardless of her strife because she chose to and her faith never wavered. Regardless of your circumstances in life everyone chooses to live with or without God. The choices that a soul makes directly affect the life that they live. Blessings to all upon earth."

June 25th 2017: As I connected to the other realm today a man step forward with long white hair. I asked him his name and he told me it was Melchizedek, whom is an ascended master. This is the message that he gave to me: "The teachings of our soul can help us to divide good and evil. The emotional and physical part of our human bodies interacts with our soul, helping us to differentiate things about others. We all have internal signals warning us of others or bad situations. Though many ignore this warning and go forth with putting themselves in harms way. While a soul is in a human body some will try to push down the truth of their souls. If they were to accept the truth of the pure souls that they are then their life and their purpose would go much more smoothly. Many do not trust themselves and in turn they do not trust God but God is truly in each and every being in the universe that He has created. I myself have been a teacher in many lifetimes and I come forth today to share these words so that I may show even just one soul how magnificent and powerful they really are. Spread these words so you may become one with the road less traveled. Thank you for all that you do."

June 26th 2017: In my communication today John the Baptist stepped forth and gave me this message: "I have come forth as an extension of your true self and your inner guidance that has brought you to the place you are now. It is time to show the world your true colors as you rise up on the shoulders of another. In this life you and Gail Moffat will continue to help each other take a step up like a ladder until you both reach the top. You both understand the meaning of prosperity for all. This is a chance to prove yourself that you are worthy of all that the world offers. As you grasp your portion of the rope you will be connected to all light workers in the universe so that they may help you when the time is right. This is another level and another part of your life that was meant to be for a long time. No matter how long it took you to get here, the timing is perfect for the part that you will play in the world. There will be difficulties but do not be discouraged for the outcome will be magnificent. Success is on the horizon and each day does matter. This is the word of the Lord."

June 27th 2017: Today in my communication my guide Joseph stepped forth and gave me this message: "Alchemy is the desired outcome for your soul. Steps will be taken to preserve your heritage of heaven on earth though your soul will be free to roam the universe doing good for others. The next steps on your path will be crucial to the support and help you will receive in the future. Be tender and kind in your decisions as to not hurt others. The alchemy of your soul has begun and this is a process that will take place for the rest of this lifetime. You will innately know future events so trust yourself and believe in the power that your soul has to offer this world. In your human form you have been given many glimpses into other realms and you have received messages from those that you already know. This should be more of a natural process for you as time goes on for you have reached the level of awareness that was forthcoming. Your mother, brother and father are stepping forth to say how proud they are of you. This is a day of celebration in heaven without you even realizing that you are at a place of grace within yourself. We don't promise everything to be easy we only promise that you will succeed as we are by your side. Hope, faith and belief are the three main factors that have brought you to this place of grace."

June 29th 2017: Today Mother Mary stepped forth in my communication and she gave me this message: "Your connection to my son Jesus is remarkable for you understand the essence of His existence and the nature of His teachings. Your daily gratitude towards His kindness and peaceful soul are to be commended. You will continue on with my Son's teachings to bring awareness to the souls on earth of all the different realms and those that exist in them. Your soul is pure with the willingness to help with good intentions on fulfilling your soul's purpose. That is why you are a trusted soul in each lifetime for you always fulfill your purpose and complete your journey as expected. We are sorry for the heartbreaks and tragedies that you had to encounter in this lifetime but they were in your contract and deemed necessary in order for you to carry out your mission. The object of your affection in your true home is waiting with patience and virtue upon your return. Each step that you take on earth is a step closer to all that is good. Seize opportunities that you know in your heart will open the right doors for you."

June 30th 2017: As I connected to the other realm today, I heard someone say, "Dawn it is me, this is Peter from the house fire. I have come forth with gratitude to thank you for helping me to cross over. I am now safe, protected and happy. I was not able to step forth sooner due to the penance that I had to pay and as I have worked on myself, I have become enlightened. I am a changed soul and it started with your help. Never stop doing what you do because you make a difference in the lives of those on earth and those in the other realms. Your work is important to us and I step forth today as the leader in a group of souls who you have changed for the better. You ask for nothing in return and that is what makes your soul shine. We offer you much gratitude, love and blessings from us all."

July 2nd 2017: In today's communication a cherub angel named Harriet stepped forth and this is the message she gave me: "Powerful enemies will try to enforce their religious points of views on the weaker countries. The countries that abide by the universal laws will need assistance to reach their goals. They will receive this assistance from the angelic realm as a reward for abiding by the laws of the universe. Each good deed deserves a reward as proven in the laws of karmic balance. Some souls will dissipate into the universe as though they never existed in order to cleanse the earth of their negative vibes. Every action, tragedy or situation is happening in natural order to get the world ready for what is to come. Blessed be my child."

July 3rd 2017: In my communication to the other realm today King Solomon stepped forth and this is the message I received from him: "In my time on earth I had many treasures but none were more precious than the gift of family. I now clearly see how I didn't cherish my family or anyone else while I was on earth. I have paid my penance for the pain and sufferings that I have caused to others. When it comes to matters of the heart, money is worthless, while trust, love and kindness are worth everything. I come forth today to share with you the wrong doings of my journey on earth and the price that I eventually paid for them. Power can turn the hearts of some for it is a strong courageous soul that stays pure of good intentions while they are in control. The wisest words that I can say to anyone is to stay true to yourself and never forget that you are put on the earth to help, not hurt others. In the long run you will reap what you have sowed. Peace be with you."

July 4th 2017: In today's communication the four ladies stepped forth again, Mother Mary, Mother Theresa, St. Therese and Mary Magdalene. Mother Mary did the speaking. She said: "We, my child, are at your side and do not ever doubt us for it will only weaken our connection to you. For some unknown reasons to you, the physical ailment that you are suffering is helping you spiritually (I am having a difficult time seeing out of my left eye). We had to tone down your vision in the physical world in order for it to open up in the spiritual world. This process had been ongoing for some time but you are coming to the end of it. Big changes in your world are around the corner. We are solidarity of sisters united as a positive force of energy to help bring in a new world to correct the way people are living. Your work on earth is a strong connection that you share with my Son. Bless you, my child, and may the grace of God fall upon your face each morning."

July 6th 2017: My guide Joseph stepped forward and said that every soul has inner turmoil and this turmoil will lead you on one path or another, depending on your soul's purpose and your freewill choices. The amount of souls that do not complete their soul's purpose is astronomical; the reason souls return lifetime after lifetime. Some souls that have fulfilled their purpose choose to come back in another lifetime to help others fulfill their purpose. These are unselfish acts of kindness that one soul will do for another and shows without a shadow of a doubt what type of souls they are. When one soul bludgeons another whether it is physically, emotionally or spiritually, then that soul will have a penance to pay. They will have to go through intense self-learning. They will not be allowed to return to another lifetime until their sins have been stripped away by their own doings. Self-forgiveness is a major issue that many souls have trouble working on. If you can forgive yourself, then you can forgive others and the doorway to reformation will be wide open. It is as simple as if you don't harm yourself or another then your path is clear and limitless."

July 8th 2017: In today's communication with the other realm, Jesus stepped forth and this is the message that I received: "The most ordinary of souls have passed through our realm. When these souls had the best of intentions is when their souls shine bright. No matter who you are, there are no restraints on how your soul can go forward spiritually. You must become aware of those who will try to pull you into the darkness so that they are not alone. As a soul grows stronger you may extend your hand to another who is in the darkness, but you must understand the difference between helping and hindering in its truest form. The outcome of your mission will be beyond anything you could imagine. Do not feel forsaken for we have not left your side my child. We surround you and protect you as always, just have faith on this winding road where you can't see what is before you."

July 9th 2017: Archangel Gabriel came forth and said that the turmoil on one's soul depends upon the actions they have taken in life. The more questions that we answer about the universe the more attuned you will become to our way of being. Your guides will remain at your side till the time of your transition into the spirit realm. Each guide is for a particular purpose. When a guide steps back and you can no longer sense them, it is because their purpose as your guide has been served. Regardless, there is always one or more guides around you and available to help you. There is a reason for every second that you are alive on earth, regardless of how unimportant a day seems to you. The most important lesson that anyone on earth can learn is that love is at the center of all that exists. If you choose not to experience this love, then negativity and sadness will be what you have chosen to be at the center of your existence. Everything on earth is a choice whether some believe that or not, though some choices are very difficult. Souls must go through painful experiences for a number of reasons. On the other side of pain and sorrow is light and love. Many souls do not allow themselves to truly feel the pain by dulling it with whatever way they have chosen and this is why they never get to the light and love on the other side. To fully experience human emotion is to have great strength and courage. We offer our assistance in the angelic realm to those who ask for it."

July 10th 2017: St. Therese stepped forward in today's communication and gave me this message: "It is with great sadness that I step forth to reveal a mystery of the universe. There are 10 steps to heaven and these 10 steps coordinate with the 10 commandments from Moses. As a soul goes through their lives and they falter on the commandments it will make it that much harder to reach the top step. Self-forgiveness and commitment of the soul must be worked on or else a soul will remain stagnant on the stairs, which means your soul will also be stagnant. Your soul is not able to reach other levels unless you are willing to put in the work. Living the right way ensures the progression of your soul on earth and in other realms. Everyone should have a daily conversation with God in order to stay connected to the Divine. I was not perfect by any means but I did devote myself to God and being a good person. Not every soul will have the devotion I did but a daily prayer of devotion will bring you closer to what and who you are in God's white light. I am proud of you, my sister."

July 11th 2017: John the Baptist stepped forth and gave me this message: "I am your friend or as the saying goes, 'A brother from another mother.' Your brother David has taught that saying to me. David and I have connected on a deep level due to the work he does in the angelic realm. As another saying goes 'It's a small world' for you have no idea how every soul is connected to another. I have stepped forth to let you know that your mission is being refurbished. Do not fret for the finer things in life are ahead for you. There will be a bump in the road but this is for your highest good. We will never leave you though this is something that you must learn along the way so that your future work will benefit from it. My sister I no longer have to hide in the shadows for I am free to step forth and communicate with you at any time. I waited with great patience for you to be reunited with me. I know that you feel our bond though you don't quite understand it. By the time you transition here you will be fully awakened and you will be completely aware of all that you truly know. I will accompany you on your trip home for a difficult time is coming. Trust and have faith for if you only knew what I know then you would have no fear." (I feel such closeness to John the Baptist that I cannot explain but now I realize there is some past life connection between us).

July 12th 2017: A beautiful angel wearing white but had golden yellow light dancing around him stepped forth and gave me this message: "Please take advantage of all that the universe throws your way. These unselfish acts from others are helping you to step forward on your journey. Each soul that has assisted you will be rewarded in divine timing. Tim has stepped up to the plate with minimal nudging from the angels. His career will rise ten-fold, as he is part of the equation as a member of the spiritual team. (What this angel is speaking of about Tim and his stepping up to the plate is that he bought an airplane ticket for me to go back and forth from California to Massachusetts so I could go see my eye doctor because I was having trouble with my vision. This was such a generous act of kindness from him and I will always be grateful to him for it). "Heather also continues to offer her assistance as she supports you and shows her gratitude to the angels. She has made great strides in her endeavors in this life in her soul's progression and she has earned a place in our fold. As you relay this message to her this should bring comfort to her. Adoration comes in many forms but the sincerest form of admiration comes from pure love. That is the admiration that we the angels have for all those who are willing to help others and us. Thank you for taking the time to communicate with us daily and receive these messages. May the grace of God fall upon you."

July 13th 2017: Blessed Catherine of St. Augustine came forth today and said to me: "The light that surrounds your heart can be overbearing for you. The sensitivity of your being is easily hurt by other people's words. You have strength and courage in so many ways but not much empathy for yourself. I have come forth to help you with the strength and courage that you will need for the remainder of your journey. I will be the pillar of strength for the times that you cannot stand on your own. It is my honor to work with you for the rest of this lifetime on the earth. I have been chosen for this mission due to the adversities that I have overcome while on earth. I shall guide you down the path of righteousness with a mighty sword to illuminate the way. Though I have stepped forward earlier, it is now time to let you know that we will work side by side as I join others on the team to help you on this journey. Behold Jesus Christ the King and His loving Mother Mary who stand in our presence with love, virtue and kindness."

July 14th 2017: Jesus stepped forth today in my communication and this is the message that I received: "The most remarkable times in life are when people choose to come together. The epiphanies that people have are extraordinary and can be life changing. They do not realize that these epiphanies are coming from the center of their soul and as they are brought to the surface, they can be amazing. I am speaking of this because you, my child, will experience one in the future and this epiphany will make everything much more clearly to you for the remainder of your journey. You will then be able to understand why and how events have happened over the course of many lifetimes. As you trudge on in your daily life the sequence of events that unfold before you are nothing short of a miracle. As you put two and two together you will become more aware of what I speak of. My sister, as you go through earthly worries, we hope you are aware of the magnificence of your soul. Please continue to spread comfort and peace in the hearts of those who suffer."

July 15th 2017: St. Therese stepped forth today in my communication and gave me this message: "The equivalent of one man's sorrow is another man's joy. The combinations of the two are what help to keep your soul sewn to the human body. There are appropriate reactions to the many cycles in life in which your soul resides and they are important key factors in the balance of your soul on earth. The magnificence and beauty that surround everyone on earth should be admired and not looked upon as an everyday normalcy for one day it might not exist. Humankind tend to appreciate others or things only after they are gone. Instead of looking down the path at the future of the world many only look at what is right in front of them for immediate gratification. Patience is a virtue and will only improve the lives of those who attain it."

July 16th 2017: St. Christopher stepped forth today in my communication and said: "The land of the most holy is serene and peaceful with souls who light up the world and these souls are known as peace trackers. They are able to sense the peaceful souls throughout the universe. When they connect to these souls a path will be set in stone to eventually bring them to the holy land. Any negativity that enters this holy land would cause great chaos and destruction. The purpose of these soul's existence and everyone in the universe would suffer in some way from it. Though mankind is unable to view the bigger picture especially when life seems to have no rhyme or reason, there is a place for everyone and every event in the universe. You must have faith in your lives even when things don't make sense for there is always a reason. Mankind tends to not have patience and they force things to happen-the end result is not good. Temporary fixes are a big downfall for humans. If souls upon earth could have patience, trust, and faith in all that is to come, then the seeds that you plant would be very fruitful for the entirety of your lives. Sometimes we sound like a broken record but mankind tends not to listen."

July 17th 2017: In today's communication I saw a man with brown hair. I knew he was from the biblical days and I heard, "I am Jude, brother of James." I then knew he was the apostle Jude. He said: "The completion of one's journey upon earth is a great feat in the eyes of our Creator. The wrong doings that a soul has done to another will vary in the pattern of your soul until these injustices have been cleared and the karmic balance evens out. I myself have had to deal with injustices and karmic balance. There are no secrets from the universe or the Creator, for all is known whether it be good or bad. The turbulence that dwells in some souls is due to past life regrets. The moral of any story should be truth and justice for all. My biggest regret was my lack of courage that strayed me off my path. The door to reformation is never closed to anyone willing to step through it and change for the better. Today I am revered, as a saint of saints when at one time I was diverted from my path, for no soul is perfect. Love, kindness, forgiveness and truth are just a few of the things that a soul should live by on a daily basis. I instill in you courage and strength so that you may go forward to help souls in their time of need."

July 18th 2017: Mother Mary stepped forth in today's communication and said to take the time each day to nourish the spirit within you. "There are consequences for ignoring one's soul. The visions we have shown you or told you would not be possible if you did not care for your soul and let your light shine each day. My child, I appreciate your visits at the shrine and I feel your love and devotion but I also feel the self-doubt you have in yourself. You are very capable of all that we ask of you and more. You were chosen to walk this path so you can show others how to climb out of any turmoil within and rise to the top as a new day is dawning. There is no holding back any soul who wants to change for the better. Take the time to nourish your soul for it is important for yourself and others. You have been blessed with the grace of God so never doubt yourself. Each time you need a lift in spirit think of me and I will help you instantaneously. Remember as much as we chose you, you also chose this path for the good of others. Keep going forward my child; you are almost around the corner."

July 19th 2017: Archangel Ariel came forth today and said that the lesson of the day is virtue. "If you live with virtue in your heart, then there are no limits to what a soul can reach and these moral standards are quite becoming of a light worker. Your destiny, my child, is set in stone and you have no need to fear. As long as you wake up each day and go forth with the purest of intentions then your path will be followed accordingly. Each moment that a soul sheds a tear, has a regret or a doubt, brings sadness to the other realms. The goal of everyone in the entire universe is for each soul to be happy and to experience peace within him or her, for this is the fundamental law of the universe. Without the universal laws in place, no one would be able to exist in peace, love and beauty that is abundant in the world. We watch as many souls on earth experience an emotional and spiritual roller coaster ride throughout their lifetime. There is nothing we, the angels, can do unless we are asked because Freewill takes precedence over all."

July 20th 2017: When I connected today, I was shown a group of people and was told, "We are from your home, the angelic realm" and this is the message that I received: "You have worked with us, in us and through us in every lifetime that you have lived. Your soul's purpose is not only to offer assistance to your brothers and sisters on earth, but also to us in the angelic realm. We don't want you to forget who you are and we certainly don't want you sitting in self-pity, for your emotional state affects all of us. You have a deep connection to us as your friend, John the Baptist, has told you. Around the corner is the goal that you seek for patience has never been your strong point. Every person and place that you need on your journey has been set up and will go off without a hitch. What you ask of us you really are asking of yourself for we are interwoven like a beautiful piece of fabric created by our Father. Do not sell yourself short for once you transition back into our realm you will be kicking yourself for the hesitations and fear you instilled in yourself on your journey. Go forward full steam ahead for that is how you truly wanted to live this lifetime. We got you and will never let you go."

July 21st 2017: As I connected to the other realm today, I was shown St. Therese on my left side, Mother Theresa sitting on the floor behind her with her legs crossed, Mary Magdalene standing to the left of Mother Theresa, while Mother Mary was standing to the right side in front of all of them. Mother Mary did the speaking and this is the message she gave me: "The world as people know it will be coming to an end and changing right before their eyes. Each stone that is cast at another slowly rips apart the bond between humanity. The road less traveled is a course of action that we ask of the people on earth. Each step forward will help the outcome in your world but any step sideways or backwards will only hinder it. It is a time to take action in helping the souls that you see who need it and please do not forsake a suffering soul. You always get back what you put out and if you want help when you are at your lowest, then you must step up to the plate when help is asked of you. Your daily devotion, my child, has brought you to a state of grace and enlightenment that you are not fully aware of yet. We are proud of the work you are doing. We told you that you would be busy but do not feel overwhelmed for we are here for you every step of the way. Bless you, my child." (I have been very busy with giving people readings and putting together events for Gail to work at when she arrives in California).

July 22nd 2017: Joseph my guide stepped forth today in my communication and he gave me this message: "Space and Time are in existence because of the Creator, though there is freewill, He still controls the universe. There is nothing that happens in this space or time that He does not know of. The flawless energy that He possesses is so much greater than any mind could imagine or embark on trying to understand. His greatness is indescribable; you would have to stand in His presence to fully understand. Beauty and purity of the angels is just a minute drop of what truly is the Creator. If mankind understood the true essence of our Creator then fear would not exist. As souls transition to the other side they view their lifetime of earth as a jumble of fear, anger, sorrow and love. In the spirit form they then realize that love was the only way they should have lived their life and the other emotions just hindered their soul's growth and their life experience. We offer these words as a way to understand the experience of life on earth and all that accompanies it."

July 23rd 2017: As I connected today, I felt peace and then I heard, "We are your friends from the angelic realm" and this is the message that I received: "The light that shines from the bearer of the soul who helps protect the angelic realm and all those who work with them are considered honored knights of our realm. The cosmic consciousness of these souls is filled with purity, kindness and loyalty to those in God's white light. Regardless of their time on earth or in another realm, their job and mission is the same as protectors of the light. They serve with no agenda or selfish purposes. We are grateful for these souls and the light workers in your world. A common goal of everyone is to serve the Creator to keep working towards peace on earth. The duality role of some souls can be somewhat overwhelming in human form as we sometimes find in your instance. It is the human emotion that is tied to the human body that will sometimes weigh you down. But all in all, the struggle you fight to enlighten the souls of the world will be won. Keep up the good work, my sister, for it is closer than you think."

July 24th 2017: St. Francis of Assisi stepped forth today and said that the laws of the universe are upheld by a strict moral code. "Each soul that comes in contact with the environment in any world has the responsibility to uphold these laws. Mankind is the worst offender of destroying the environment. These laws are in place for the future of the entire universe. Mankind is selfish in this aspect for they act, as if they are the only ones who exist in the universe. I express these words in frustration and in the hope that mankind will awaken to the wrong doings of not protecting the environment as it should be. I come forward with peace and a gentle heart in asking every soul on earth to do their part and take care of the earth in their daily lives. This request is of great importance for the environment to all who exist. Spread these words, my sister, in the hope of enlightening others in many ways."

July 25th 2017: As I connected to the other realm today, I saw a man step forth and then recognized him as the Ascended Master Melchizedek. He escorted me to a different world and though he brought me to this world I entered it alone. He then told me: "As you enter this world of dreams, we ask that you seek solitude in the corners of your soul on this journey. As you progress into the other realm, we want you to be aware of what is around you." (As I descended higher and higher I had seen people standing on grass that looked like islands with a large tree in the center of the other land. The higher I went it reminded me of Jack and the Beanstalk as I kept seeing vines that extend up and down and seemed never ending. As I reached my destination, which looks like a sort of space age town with everything white and bright, I stepped out of a round clear elevator tube. I felt as if I was in a child's toy town and I could see a man's face watching me. He was peering into the town from the sky as if he was a giant. I was aware of him but I was not afraid of him. I feel he's checking up to make sure everything is going OK. I see tall pointed mountains made out of Crystal and further away there's a huge castle in my view. As we walk on this path everything in town starts changing from white to color. There are beautiful green trees with bright red apples on them, also dogs and cats running around. I also saw large birds flying around that remind me of pterodactyls. There were families going about their daily business. I inherently knew that this world was colorless to others, and you can only see the beauty and color of it if you are in it. This is the way of protecting this world to those who aren't allowed to enter. I am then told that they want to make me aware that there are other worlds and realms that are unknown by mankind and I am welcome back anytime. I would like to visit again but I would need a guide to help me reach this world again. Not in a discriminatory way but I am feeling this place is an exclusive type of place for those who are/been truly devoted to God. I also feel a bit of seriousness here, that there's a lot of work that is done by those who are here. After being shown this place and any impressions they gave me and told me it was like someone suddenly picked up the path I was standing on, and I slid all the way back to the clear elevator tube to return home again.

July 26th 2017: As I connected today my guide Joseph stepped forth and said today's message is from him with the help of my higher self. This is the message that I received: "As energy flows through the universe it disperses itself to areas that are in need of it. There are many types of energy in the universe and each type is used according to the universal laws. The energy supply is unlimited and can be recycled if it comes in contact with negativity. The ultimate goal is for energy to flow freely and without hesitation as an every day occurrence. Human emotions can change energy from good to bad and some souls enter the spiritual world with the same negative energy that they had on earth. These souls can choose to change and learn how to be better souls. Help is always offered and available to any soul in any realm. A soul's free will is not only exercised on the earth realm but also in the spirit realm. Some choices that one makes can linger with them for eternity if they so choose, whether it is good or bad. We ask souls to change your thinking to not just the here and now but for everlasting peace within. Bad decisions can corrupt a soul and follow them for many lifetimes."

July 27th 2017: In my communication today St. Francis of Assisi stepped forth again and this was the message that I received: "Your patronage at the church is appreciated for you emit a good energy as you walk through it. My child we understand your appreciation for the saints and angels but you must focus upon the souls on earth. These souls are your purpose and have faith that we will always be by your side. Your connection to us is strong enough that you needn't doubt our help in anyway. When you need a spiritual lift all you have to do is ask us. Show your brothers and sisters the purity of your soul and teach them all about us in the other realms. Let them know that we also stand by their sides and with faith and belief anything is possible. You have been asking us for help with financial abundance but you must have patience. This abundance will free you from earthly responsibilities that hold you down by worry. You will be free to go forth on your path in helping the souls of the world. Peace be with you on your journey."

July 28th 2017: As I was saying my prayers today Jon Benet Ramsey stepped forth. She was wearing a light pink leotard top with a brighter pink tutu. She smiled at me and told me she was grateful for the prayers I say for her each day. Suddenly she was standing with her mom and they were holding hands. She told me that all has been forgiven and I felt a wonderful feeling of mutual love between them. She then showed me her father living in darkness. She didn't actually say the words that her parents were involved in her death but the feeling she gave me was that her father was the cause of it and her mother was aware of what went on. I told her I would continue to keep her in my daily prayers and to rest in peace. She left me with the feeling that she is happy in the spirit realm and holds no bad feelings towards anyone. As I was writing this down just now a beautiful orb hovered over the words on my paper, which is confirmation for me that Jon Benet is at peace and wanted the communication between us to be written about.

In today's communication with the other realm St. Christopher came forward and gave me this message: "There are many messages that need to be told to the people of the world. These messages come in layers a little at a time for if they came in bulk, they would get lost in translation for too much information at once is overwhelming, and it would not be understood properly. The images that are shown to you are similar to pieces of a movie in your world. The temptation that a soul goes through in a lifetime and how they choose to deal with these temptations determines the character of that soul. After a human vessel has served their purpose there is nothing more beautiful than a soul on their journey home. The soul is greeted with love, kindness and healing upon the entrance until they are whole again. They are looked after by angels and loved ones until the healing is complete. At this point there will be meetings and conversations that take place as to make decisions in the next step in the soul's progression. The soul itself is also involved in the decision-making. There are many possibilities for a soul and freewill always is a factor in every realm. The human mind would not be able to comprehend every step that a soul goes through. The trickles and layers of information that are communicated to mankind are so you may all have a basic understanding of what goes on in the spirit realm. We would also like you to know that every soul is completely protected in our realm."

July 29th 2017: My guide Agnes stepped forth and gave me this message: "Carry the light of the world in your hand as you go on your path so others can see the way. The adoration of Jesus Christ is well received in all the realms. There is a tubular balance that lies between worlds and the structure of the tubular balance is easily accessed through a portal that consist of pure white light. Each cell that passes through this portal is affected in a positive way. The changes that a soul goes through in the spiritual realm are somewhat similar to the changes one goes through in a lifetime on earth. The only difference is a soul in the spirit realm understands that they are completely safe from harm. The balance between worlds will never even out because mankind wraps their souls in fear. Fear tremendously hinders the progression of a soul, and can actually stop a soul from crossing from the earth to the spirit realm and can also cause a margin line error in the crossing. This error can off set the balance between worlds though this is not common and it can take some time to set things back on course. It will cause souls in all the realms to feel off-balance or out of sorts. This information is to help understand a soul in its many forms. If there is a willingness to understand, then there is a willingness to accept and help the souls who struggle in human form."

TWENTY ONE

The Ever Changing Circle of Life

July 30th 2017: I am feeling somewhat homesick in California and I am also feeling stressed about a house party at Heather's house today in which I am giving a large group of people private readings. In today's communication with the other realm Mother Mary stepped forth and gave me this message: "Relax my child, today will be miraculous in more ways than one. As each step is taken there will be some more difficult than others. You will adjust accordingly and eventually realize how could you have ever doubted yourself or us. Your life on earth has been a difficult one and the time you spent renewing your soul is commendable. Each rosary that you pray and each soul that you help brings you closer to the revelation that you seek. In the time we have spent together throughout eternity I have chosen to take you under my wing and I have taught you the evolution of one's soul and the reasons behind it. You have always been a faithful student and child of God and now you are at a crossroads in this lifetime with others who might try to shed doubt upon you and your gifts. But I urge you, my child, to stand strong in your beliefs and for the life you have chosen to live. There is no better cure for the soul than self-salvation for it is pure and comes from within. Those who live outwardly will live sad, shallow lives. Be strong, my dear, I am always a thought away."

The readings that I gave to those at Heather's house today were extraordinary. Though I know I am only the conduit for spirit but I impressed myself, also the people that I gave readings to. I do believe you are only as good as the spirit you are working with, and the spirit realm never lets me down. One of the people that I read for that day was a man named Todd. He asked me to connect to his spiritual father so as I looked for this man to step in, I saw a man with long white hair and a beard. I didn't know who this man was till Todd showed me a picture of him on his phone. It was Merlin the magician. Merlin said that I am to connect with him and ask him for magic and to help find my beloved. He also said I am to connect to the fairies. And then someone named Seraphina came forward and I thought she was an angel at first but soon realized that she was a fairy. I felt a very different energy about her than I do from the Angels. She had a different look on her face and she floated above as if she was sitting with her legs crossed. I could feel her joy and happiness and she came forward to just introduce herself. The interactions in these connections were very different from the ones I was used to. If I didn't see Merlin and Seraphina with my own eyes unfortunately, I would have had doubts. I am truly beginning to understand just how many beings and realm there are in the universe.

July 31st 2017: Mother Teresa stepped forth today and said that those who neglect their souls will suffer consequences in the future. "These consequences will be of a spiritual nature and will affect them in many lifetimes. Many souls ask for forgiveness just before the transition back to the spiritual realm. While forgiveness is always available to any soul, it takes time for a neglected soul to heal and learn from their mistakes. There are a number of souls on earth who walk on the path of God's white light, which brings great joy to the Creator. The Muslim people are people of great faith and should be looked upon as pillars in the religious community. They are being looked upon as a negative community when in reality they are true servants of God and trailblazers in their own right. The damage control it would take to restore their community and image, as it should be would take the help of the world. The treatment, disrespect and bullying of these people make them feel as though their lives are going in slow motion due to their own unhappiness. This is not fair to the Muslims or anyone else who lives this way, which is very disheartening to God the Father as He watches His children abuse each other."

August 1st 2017: Today as I connected, I thought I would give it a try to call upon the fairy realm. Three women appeared before me and they all reminded me of Cinderella's fairy godmother in the Disney cartoon. One of them was wearing pink, the other blue and the other yellow. They said to me, "Welcome to the world of the fairies, we have waited a long time to meet your acquaintance. You have not been aware of our true existence and we are looking forward in getting to know each other. As part of your soul's journey you have been given the gift of nature and a deep connection to mother earth. The pinnacles of your path lie in the soil of earth. As the angels help protect your soul, we help protect the earth. It is the light workers of the world who assist us in the protection of earth and the enlightenment of others. We welcome you and thank you for accepting us into your life."

Then my guide Margaret stepped forth and gave me this message: "I beam with pride at the strides you have made, and the souls you have helped not only on earth but in the spirit realm. I feel as though you are one of the easiest souls that I have guided for once you got started there was no stopping you. The angelic realm would like to congratulate you on your acquaintance of Merlin and the fairies. Your views, hopes and dreams are expanding to each new level that you enter. Expect to have fun with the fairies and feel their joy. Merlin will show you magic that you never thought was possible. It is people like you and Todd who are bringing magic back in to the world to make life better for all."

August 2nd 2017: John The Apostle stepped forth and said that the same codes and laws of the universe are similar to the principles of a presidential election. "The only difference is that in our world these principles are always upheld. There have been so-called spiritual outlaws but they are easily contained and removed where they can't cause any harm or chaos. Mankind allows negative behavior to continually repeat itself unlike those in the other realms. The earth is a realm of continuous learning and evading the truth of one's soul and journey. The confusion that mankind has is that they are the center of all that exists in the universe when this is the farthest from the truth. We expect there to be great strides on earth in the next century; souls being enlightened to their purpose on earth, and the reality of our existence and others. The core of distinguishing souls on earth between us and the other realms is a lack of empathy for those who need it. Working together to lift each other up is the common denominator that we are seeking."

August 3rd 2017: As I connected to the other realm today a group of fairies came forward and said to me: "We were the ones who have peaked your interest in flowers and we would like to commune with you on a more spiritual level. Your connection to mother earth is strong though you have resisted it most of your life. At this time in your life many different things will be opening up to you, as you are now more aware of us. If you connect to us on a regular basis, we can help to fill your life with some of what was missing. The protection of this planet is important for mankind to continue to thrive. It is souls like you who have agreed to assist us in protecting the earth. As time goes on you will become more aware of what we ask of you. It will become an ordinary part of your day as you go forth on your path."

Merlin then stepped forth and gave me this message: "Take a drink from the magic cup each day. Connect to my son Todd regularly for in the future you will both be working together at some point on a humanitarian level. I know you feel the magic because you are very open and accepting."

St. Therese than stepped forward and gave me these words: "I struggled many times in life and had self-doubt so I know how hard it is. I have watched you as you have struggled with doubts but as of now, I see how you have come into your own. You have made great strides in going forth though you were filled with fear. That's because your commitment and devotion to God and your brothers and sisters is greater than your fear. I have stepped forth to push you through the next phase of your journey. You must be open to all that comes your way. Nothing will ever happen the way you planned it or the way you imagine it, but remember we always have your back for your highest and best good. I watch you with amazement as you help souls just for the pleasure of it. I love you dearly, my sister."

August 4th 2017: As I connected to the other realm today, I saw Jesus and heard him say "It is Me, my child" and then He preceded to give me this message: "The journey you are embarking on is one of magnificence that includes many emotions, events, triumphs and tragedies along the way. As your journey unfolds, know that the Sacred Heart of Jesus is with you for I have chosen to embark on this journey with you. Our connection is of great value to me and is a connection that we solidified many years ago. By the end of this lifetime on earth you will become aware of our personal bond. Each stone that becomes unturned on your path will make it all a bit clearer. You are a trusted servant and friend of mine and I am proud of how willing you are to share your existence with those who will doubt you and try their best to discredit you. We share a common thread of being disrespected by those that we try to help. Keep going forth as you are turning the corner and will be brought to new heights on your journey. Bless you, my child."

August 6th 2017: The apostle James the Lesser stepped forward and gave me this message: "The angels have asked me to step forth for I also was a conduit of Jesus Christ after his ascension home. I traveled the earth wearily spreading the message of the Lord. As you travel on your journey feel free to call upon me for there will be days that you feel you cannot go on. The souls of the world can drain your energy and your light, so self-care is of the upmost importance to your well-being. At this point in your journey each door that you step through will be more glorious than the next one. You have been patient and valiant in your efforts to help others and you will be rewarded accordingly as you go on your journey. Even though it is said that slow and steady wins the race there are some days you must go at a faster pace. Bless you and know that we are all here to help."

August 7th 2017: In today's communication my guide Joseph has stepped forth. Joseph has told me today that he is the husband of Mary and this is the message that he gave me: "It is time for the people of the world to be awakened from what is to come. Your book and the words in it must be brought forth to the eyes of the world. Divine timing is everything and a publisher will come your way but do not allow this man to change your story or any of the messages from heaven. Allow him cleanup of any grammatical errors but not the main contents, for this is your story, and your story contains the words of our Lord and Savior. It might come to push or shove but hold strong, for this book is to enlighten those who have lost faith and to awaken them to a new way of living and a better way of being. Be proud for this book encompasses this entire lifetime on earth. You have come through the worst of it, my dear, and it is a pleasure to be your guide, for your devotion is everlasting. Your life has been a broken puzzle as you slowly have fixed each piece carefully. The angels sing your praises in heaven, as we know you can feel the connection you have to us. You're starting to realize the connection is deeper than you could have imagined."

August 8th 2017: In my communication today, Jesus stepped forth and gave me this message: "I have stepped forth as I have listened to your conversation with Gail. It is souls like Gail who you will enlighten along your path. Each soul you enlighten brings a better chance for peace on earth. My sisters and brothers of earth can be quite difficult sometimes due to their freewill. I am a master at my trade and a King in my own right. I am a man above men for this was my chosen journey like anyone else. We are all connected through the essence of God the Father and no soul is better than another. Though some souls choose to go down the wrong path in life, redemption is always available to all. I was the chosen Son of God and I was born pure of heart, soul and mind and I never faltered, as I remained the same always. I have a Sacred Heart like no other and I will help anyone who asks. Teaching has been enjoyable to me throughout all of my existence. Many warriors go into battle with dark hearts and they will continue to lose their battles due to their bad intentions. The ways of the world should be about love, peace and kindness and remember that no soul will ever be alone as long as they have faith."

August 9th 2017: In today's communication St. Christopher stepped forth and gave me this message: "A dowry was placed on your head in another lifetime. In this lifetime you were a great warrior and you were wrongly convicted of a crime punishable by death. Because of this injustice your empathy for others is so deep that it affects your happiness. As you go through your day today, a healing has been placed on you to help you recover from any residual fears or pains from this past lifetime. I have brought this information forth so you make go forward on this journey with a healed soul and a brighter vision."

August 11th 2017: Mother Mary stepped forth today in my communication and gave me this message: "My child I ask that you take a leap of faith in your journey. I will put a soul in front of you who will need your help and I ask that you help him. Everyone on this earth is entitled to help though many have left behind this soul. You will encounter her when the time is right and you are able to assist her in her life. Thank you for being a trusted servant and allowing us to guide you on your path. There is a reason you have always felt close to me and in time it shall be revealed. As you have asked, we will keep those you love safe as you go about your journey. The weight of the world does not lie on your shoulders alone for there are many souls that are helping on the earth. Please be vigilant in your prayers for the world for they are truly needed. May the grace of God be with you child."

August 12th 2017: As I connected to the other realm today, I received a vision. In this vision I was walking on a path with bright green grass and tall flowers on each side. I was very content as I was holding hands with a fairy. As I walked along, I saw Jesus standing to the right of the path watching me. A little further down the path I also saw Mother Mary standing on the right watching me. Mary was the last thing I saw before I went into a dark tunnel. I could see light the size of a pin at the end of it but as I continued on all I saw was darkness. It seemed like I was in this darkness forever and then suddenly I was seeing the color purple. Next, the purple was gone and I was back into the light and I was being shown my book cover. It had a blue background with two hands that were cupped holding a butterfly that was just about to fly away as the hands were coming out of the dark tunnel. The spirit realm never ceases to amaze me with the images and information that I receive from them.

August 17th 2017: Today my mother came forward as I connected to the spirit realm and she gave me this message: "A strained relationship with your daughter was inevitable due to the trauma you have all been through. You are both in the process of healing. Have faith, my girl, for better days are coming. Take the high road and turn your cheek to petty arguments. This is your time, Dawn, and nothing can stop your eminent success. I am proud of you and I love you more than you know."

September 3rd 2017: I found it very strange that this next person came forth to give me a message though she is one of the souls that I pray for daily. As I was given her name I was also given a vision of her, which confirmed to me that it was she. Honestly, I know nothing of this woman, except her name and that she was

341

killed in an automobile accident at a younger age. This woman was Princess Grace of Monaco and this is the message that I received: "The opinions of other souls doesn't matter to the outcome of a situation. The most frequent mistake that is made is when someone changes his or her plans due to another's opinion. Each soul inherently knows their own path and the direction in which they should go but there is too much meddling from others. In turn, this will distract a soul from their path and ultimately their purpose. Every dark road a soul has walked on has light at the end, which confirms that they have found their way. It is an every day event for souls to be lost upon earth and when they find their way, this brings glory to the eyes of the Creator. The indigo children are lost souls on earth for they feel they do not fit in with the souls that surround them and it is a huge accomplishment for them to find their way in the world. The acceptance of each other on earth would stop souls from feeling lost and also help others to fulfill their purpose much more easily, also to learn this early on would benefit everyone in many ways. If I didn't listen to the opinions of others, my journey would not have ended so abruptly as I let others influence my decisions. Though I take responsibility for my decisions it is of the greatest importance not to let others influence them."

September 19th 2017: As I connected to the Spirit Realm today, I sat in Sarah's spare room, which is a room I sometimes use for connecting to spirit. Since I first arrived at her house, I could sense a young man in that room who was a Marine and I could sense that he committed suicide. By opening myself up in that room I allowed this young man to come too close in my personal space. I was feeling panic and despair from him that was so bad I felt as though I wanted to kill myself. I had to tell him to back away from me and I called upon the spirit realm to help me. I was feeling better within 10 minutes though I wasn't feeling back to myself. The next day I felt depression and sadness from his energy and I decided I needed to help this young soul. I connected to the spirit realm and called upon Archangel Michael and other angels. I asked them to put a white light of protection around me before I entered the room to speak to the young man. When I first entered the room, I told him he was allowed to step forth but not to enter my personal space. I asked him his name and he told me it was Jeff. He also told me that he had a bad marriage in which his wife was not faithful. This devastated him and triggered him to take his life in which he hung himself. I told Jeff that the angels and I were there to help him and that I understood how he felt upon earth and how he is still feeling but he deserves to free himself from this torture. Next, I told him to trust me and I promised him that he would be so happy and full of joy if he would surrender himself of these negative emotions and go with those who were there to help him.

I could feel how tired he was of feeling the terrible sadness in him. He didn't put up a fight and he easily went with Archangel Michael. Since he left, I haven't felt him and it feels so much brighter and lighter in that room. I feel this is the soul that Mother Mary was speaking of when she said she was putting a soul in front of me to help. I help souls from Heaven and Earth.

September 30th 2017: Lizzie Borden stepped forward once again as she was listening to a conversation that Gail and I were having about her. She thanked us for our willingness to help her and she said when Gail comes to Massachusetts, she is going to show her around. She is very proud to have our friendship and she can't wait until the both of us are back in Massachusetts together. She says she has waited a long time for this and once people receive the truth. Gail's guide Arthur, who is a monk, stepped in and said that many a tear has been shed in their realm due to the way this young woman was treated. They have waited over a century for this behavior of those who create businesses out of her being guilty to come to an end. This is an important aspect of Gail's and my work. He said we in the spirit realm do not tolerate this manipulation of facts to have monetary gain at the expense of any soul.

June 2019 my friend Gail Moffat visited me from England. As we were doing our daily connections to spirit, Lizzie Borden stepped forward. She asked both of us if we could please visit "The Lizzie Borden House" so we could be given more information and details that we weren't previously told. We agreed, and on June 20th 2019, I finally paid a visit to the house were the murders took place. Lizzie said that there were things I needed to add to my book before it publishes in order for the entire truth to be told.

As I sat in the first room of the house I was immediately flooded with information from Lizzie. When spirit floods me this way it is an all-knowing understanding of what they want to tell me. Lizzie made me aware that though she did not murder her father and stepmother, she was quite aware this entire time that it was her uncle John who had done it. She has conversations with her uncle previous to the murders about the abuse her and her sister Emma endured at the hands of their father. They also spoke of financial matters of how her father was beyond frugal. Lizzie felt humiliated for how poorly he forced them to live even though the family was wealthy. Lizzie and her uncle agreed that he needed to have a conversation with Mr. Borden on Lizzie's behalf. This conversation only caused anger between the two men. In this anger Lizzie's uncle decided the only way he could free his nieces from it all was to do away with Mr. Borden. Her uncle did not really want to take the stepmother's life but he needed to in order to secure the girls fortune, otherwise all the money would have gone to her stepmother. Lizzie was aware of her uncle's intentions and was present in the home when the murders took place.

As she gave me all this information I could feel her embarrassment to speak the entire truth. She let me know that higher evolved souls in the spirit world had worked with her and made her understand that though she didn't commit the actual murders, she needed to speak the truth of her role in them. In doing so she will be able to move forward and heal.

Because of her involvement, the information she gave me previously was true, but it was only half true. Although unhappy with how people viewed her, she has always been afraid to speak the entire truth. She said she is grateful to me for being her voice so the truth of Andrew and Abby Borden's murders can be put to rest. I'm hoping that with the release of this book all the souls involved with that horrendous day can finally find peace.

October 2nd 2017: Everyday, I often pray for souls that I feel need it and that includes Andrew Borden, Lizzie Borden's father. As I connected to that spirit realm today Mr. Borden stepped forward and said these words to me: "I ask you to stay out of my business. If I want to be in the light, then I will go there. You are to leave my name out of your mouth. It's that simple, you leave me alone and I will leave you alone. Good day madam." I sensed that he asked permission to step forth to convey this message to me as I could sense the angels around me and I felt protected. Though it wasn't a threat I felt sternness from him. I no longer pray for his soul as he has requested, for his journey even in the spirit realm is his own decision.

October 9th 2017: John the Baptist stepped forth and gave me these words: Back in my time we worked hard regardless of illness or health. There were no excuses or abstinence from a hard day's work. We needed to work this way in order to survive. Our livelihood was more on a day-to-day basis to feed our families and protect our children. Our lives were very hard but we knew no different, as it was a normal way of living. Sometimes we had to eat what you today consider pets in order to survive each day. Our homes were cold, many times our stomachs were empty and sometimes our hearts were heavy. In your world today many live like kings compared to my day. Though the quality of life has improved through the years we see little gratitude in your world today. Many of the souls on earth cause themselves pain by the choices that they make. This is true that this also went on in my time but has grown in enormous numbers since. It seems the more a soul is granted, the less thankful they are and the more they expect. Self-entitlement seems to run rampant among those in your world. This way of living must be brought to a halt and there must be a cleansing of the earth. This cleansing will bring a new light to the earth so it may start anew.

October 23rd 2017: As I connected today, I was shown a vision of the last supper. Then Jesus crunched down in front of me, and touched my chin with his hand. He then said to me; my dear child, you are the one who asked to continue on with the work you are doing. As the journey gets rocky that is when I will carry you. Each day we will give you the gift of the world feeling anew. I offer my condolences with the loss of Melanie. I know you understand there is a place for everything and everyone in time and her passing was meant to be. She is a child of God as she stands by her mother and father. (I was then shown a vision of Melanie standing between her parents Cindy and David).

The magic that appears in the mountains of California is extremely healing to those who believe in it. Many souls go about their busy lives ignoring these majestic mountains. The magic that they possess can offer peace of mind, heart and body but unfortunately many have on blinders to it. As you reach out to the people of the world take that next step in offering them peace of body, mind and soul.

October 30th 2017: As I connected today, Jesus, Mother Mary, and Joseph all stepped forward. Mother Mary did the speaking and here is what she said; in this world of memories whether they are distant or near, there is no greater moment than the one you are in. Each day that you wish to be gone is a waste of your time on earth. The time that you spend in each day is of value to you and those around you. We have come to the conclusion that you must value each day that is put in front of you before you return home. In every lifetime many lessons must be learned and as your mother Alice once told you, "don't wish your children's lives away." Take the time to enjoy what is going on around you. Allow the healings from the mountains to seep into your soul for this journey has much to do with healing for yourself and others. These words my dear is to help your soul with the next steps you are about to embark upon. Take our hand as we lead you to the next part of your journey. Trust and have faith in yourself and us. We love you."

November 1st 2017: As I connected today, I saw Mother Mary, Mary Magdalene, Mother Theresa, and St. Therese. I then heard, "we are the blessed women of your heart along your journey. "Mother Mary did the talking and this is what she said; "We have stepped forth as a collection of support for you my child. In those times that you feel alone or forgotten, know this is not possible for a piece of my soul exists within you. Each time that you feel a door has closed to you, have faith that I am in the process of creating light filled energies of love for your journey. Have patience my child for we know your wants and needs. They will all be addressed in the time that we consider is best for you. If all was to be handed over at once then you would lose sight of your own goals and your determination of your journey would diminish over time. I'm overjoyed that you have always felt the deep connection that we have. You are at a point where you will be awakened to much more. The next portion of your journey may be difficult but I ask that you lean on me in your times of distress for I would hold you up throughout eternity."

November 30th 2017: Today my niece Melanie stepped forward to give this message to Sarah: "Sarah has freed herself emotionally and she is doing okay. She has grown, and she has learned. The next part of her life was meant to be. I'm by her side and I won't leave her. I'll prove to her what a best friend is and it's going to be okay, just sit back and enjoy the ride."(Before I received this message Melanie visited Sarah in her dream to show her something about her upcoming life and to let her know she would be helping her).

In the time that I spent in California with my daughter I was basically there for moral support during her husband's deployment. But this visit turned out to be a journey of healing for both my daughter and myself. Any one who has children knows the trying experiences of being a parent. I was just not prepared for the unwavering at times and what I considered brutal behavior towards me where I was attacked verbally or just dismissed as though she wished I wasn't there. There were times I was just plain hurt and other times where I just wanted to lash out. This went on for months and became very difficult for me. The times that I did want to lash out I could feel the spirit realm close to me and I actually heard someone say "Hold your tongue and have patience with her;" I felt this was my mother who spoke to me. I couldn't understand the reason for the treatment I was receiving but I knew that the spirit realm was by my side. I always knew that Sarah and I needed healing in our relationship due to all that happened in the past. Also, the spirit realm kept telling me I would help her to heal in this visit even though I wasn't able to understand the entire experience at this point. Towards the last two months of my seven months stay with my daughter, she started revealing to me the troubles that she was going through in her marriage and I revealed to her that I was gay. In which she replied, "Mom I already knew," and she felt good that I finally confided in her. We opened up to each other revealing ourselves, and the secrets that we held so close. That day I fully understood why she was so broken inside as she desperately tried to hide her pain from me all those months. This conversation between us was an extraordinary bonding experience for the both of us. I am so grateful to the spirit realm including my mother for talking me down each time I needed it. If I had lashed out at her it would have mortally wounded her and damaged our relationship even further. They helped me to treat her with kindness, love and patience until she was finally able to express her pain to me. My daughter and myself have received a lot of healing from this experience and we are closer than we have ever been before. I can honestly say that both of my children are my best friends in this lifetime. Unfortunately, my daughter and her husband have gone their separate ways and will be officially divorced by the time this book publishes. I will always carry a special place in my heart for Mike, just like I know both of them in some way will always carry love for one another.

December 1st 2017: As I went on my walk today, I was saying my prayers. Since Charles Manson had just passed away I figured I would add him to my prayers and possibly help his soul. Less than 2 minutes after I prayed for him it felt like someone kicked my ankle out from under me. I sat on a bench for a while because my ankle was really hurting. I said to the spirit realm, I guess you don't want me to go on my walk today. I was instantly shown a vision of Charles Manson in my clairvoyance. After a short while I tried to keep going on my walk but it was still hurting me so I went back to Sarah's house. When I returned, I did my daily connection to the spirit realm, Archangel Michael stepped forward and gave me this message: "I am here to protect you. We have condemned him to the house of the damned. We are grateful for the souls that you try to help you must be careful in your choosing for not every soul is worth redemption. He has hurt you my child and that will not happen again but you must keep this soul out of your thoughts and prayers for he is not yours to save. This is a lesson well learned and you as well must abide by the laws of the universe. You may feel the residual affects of his negative energy as the day goes on and I will remain by your side in case I am needed."

My brother David then stepped forward and said these words to me: "Promise me you will stay away from negative energies. There is no need to worry because he is taken care of. The light of your day will be the child that you save." I innately knew he was speaking of my daughter.

My guide Joseph then stepped forth and gave me this message: "You don't understand the damage that could have been done by allowing this negative energy into your thoughts and prayers. By doing this you have allowed him into your space. Keep this lesson close to your heart for you will need it in the future."

December 3rd 2017: Today would have been my brother David's 56th birthday. As I connected to the spirit real today, Charles Manson stepped forth and said to me, "I apologize for my actions." David then came forward and said that this was his own birthday gift to me. David somehow had arranged for this apology to happen because he was upset over what happened to me. This rings exactly true to David and our relationship as my protector.

December 15th 2017: St. Jude stepped forward today and said that the transcription of the words given to me is given in a form of my understanding. "They are presented to you in that manner so that you may understand the meaning of them. We use the dictionary of your mind so you may decipher these messages. We offer you this explanation because there will be some who doubt the form in which we speak. Stay true to yourself Dawn and do not let the doubters put darkness in you, around you, or on you. The path you have traveled is rough, and the road ahead of you will also be rough. It will be rough in different ways as you fight to enlighten souls throughout the remainder of your life on earth. It is a road less traveled to spread the words of the Lord, but it is also a road that will set many on a path of glory. I was once a follower and now I am a leader of many. My soul is quite content with most of the decisions I have made in each lifetime. As I returned home as Jude, I then no longer had the need to return to the earth plane. My place is with my heavenly father so I may serve him as he sees fit. Mark my words, our brother Jesus was more than just a martyr and a savior for he was the beginning of eternity."

December 26th 2017: As I connected today, I saw a man who was scholarly looking with a long beard, and he was wearing a high hat. I asked him who he was and he replied, "I am Nostradamus." Here is the message that I received from him; "You my dear have been awakened to the truths of spirit and to the purity of one's soul. I will not bear witness to the false prophets or the untruth of our realm in your world. I have tried many times to right these wrongs but I have failed due to the ignorance of mankind. There is no task too small when it comes to speaking about the truths of spirit. Though William Shakespeare created the scenario of Romeo and Juliet, it is their devotion to each other that sparks the foundation of the spirit. There is many times in a souls life that they are filled with great revelations but it is up to these souls to decide whether to share these revelations with others. "Does the horse come before the cart or does the cart come before the horse," is a well-known expression that coincides with God and the Universe. I can tell you that God is the Universe and the Universe is God, and there is no separation of our souls in the Universe. The connection of it all is never ending and yet very concrete but it is also too much for mankind to comprehend the continuation of it all. Dawn, you must continue to seek the knowledge to fully understand your own soul and just how very powerful it is. Continue to seek and we will guide you every step of the way.

January 4th 2018: In my communication to the spirit realm today Lizzie Borden stepped forth again and this is the message that I received: "With the selling of my home "Maplecroft" (which is the house that Lizzie lived in and died after the murder Trial was done) I continue to be amazed at the number of people who are interested in my business and at the negative thoughts and words that are thrown my way. My Uncle John and I will work together as a team to help you uncover the truth so that you may clear my name so my soul can move forward in healing. I have waited so long for someone to assist me in this undertaking. I promise you will be pleased with the outcome. Some will attack you verbally and I'm sorry for their ignorance to my cause. Please don't give up when it gets tough for I am counting on you. I am appealing to your gentle soul and kind heart. Please make the souls on earth aware that my Uncle John Morse is the murderer."

On April 16th 2019, I received this message from Abbey Borden, stepmother of Lizzie Borden as I was finishing up and getting ready to publish my book. I take this message as a plea from the spirit world to release Lizzie Borden from all the negative words and actions on earth that hold her back from being fully healed. Mrs. Borden gave me this message; the man responsible for the death of my husband and myself is John Morse, uncle of Lizzie. I was not very sensitive in my lifetime. I showed no sympathy or empathy to Lizzie or her sister Emma. I closed my eyes to many things that went on in my household. Their life or mine was not very pleasant under the rule of my husband. I must atone for my infractions on earth. This is why I step forth today in saying that Lizzie is innocent of murder. Those on earth must know the truth. In this truth, I ask those who damage her name or the goodness of her character in any way to please stop. I have the hope in my coming forth that Lizzie will be released from the stigma of our deaths. I in no way condone the actions of my husband as he was on earth, or how he is in the world of spirit. I have broken all ties to him as I go forth in healing my own soul to a state of purity. Thank you for listening to my words as I ask you all to please understand the importance of them.

In 2017, during my seven-month stay with Sarah in San Diego, Gail Moffat decided to visit California for a month. Before she came she told me that the spirit world prompted her to enlist my help in setting up mediumship events for her while she's in California. Gail would do mediumship readings with a live audience, in different locations throughout the Los Angeles area.

She promised to compensate me for my help. I was hesitant at first because I had never done anything like this before, but, learning as I go. I steam rolled forward in booking venues for her. Our friend Rafael also helped by doing Gail's website, and setting up Event Brite for ticket sales. As I later learned, the hardest part in all of this was the promotion portion of it. The events weren't as successful as we hoped but regardless of the outcome, we both enjoyed ourselves and learned a lot from the business aspect of it all. But we also learned that it is going to be more difficult than we first realized to open the hearts and minds of some to the world of spirit. No matter how difficult it is going to be we are both willing to go forward in our devotion to the world of spirit to enlighten as many souls as possible. Gail flew back to England the end of November and I stayed in California till January 2018. Gail then asked me if I would like a trip to England as compensation for the work I had done for her. Of course my answer was a resounding yes, since I always wanted to visit the place of my many ancestors.

By the time I arrived back home to Fall River in January, I had only two weeks to prepare for my trip to England. During those two weeks I had the flu, ended up with a respiratory infection, and wasn't even sure I was going to make it to England. Just in the nick of time, I felt well enough to travel. England proved to be everything I imagined and more. Every night Gail and I would sit in her lounge, have a cup of tea, and connect to spirit. It felt like a spirit free-for-all, souls from all walks of life stepping forward.] It filled the parts of our soul that felt empty, and that in itself was exhilarating. Gail's home in England was the first time that I was introduced to trance mediumship. It's when mediums allow spirits to use their mind and body ro communicate, a form of channeling spirit through a medium. Gail started a circle for her trance mediumship in order to develop it. Four other ladies would come to her home every Tuesday evening and sit in front of Gail as she connects to spirit. I joined them on Tuesdays, which was a little frightening, but at the same time exciting, because I really didn't know what to expect. In one of Gail's trance medium connections that we did without the other ladies present on January 17th 2018, Confucius came through Gail to speak. He promised me that as Gail improved in her trance in the future, I would see my mother full on. This would be called physical mediumship in which spirit manipulates energy to materialize spirit bodies. I am very excited at the prospect of seeing my mother full on in spiritual form. In my connection to spirit the next day Confucius came forth and gave me this message; I have promised you a gift from this realm and it shall be. In my time there were great warriors of not only the sword, but of the soul. Your kind words and devotion to spirit have helped to open up a blockage between worlds. In our eyes you are helping to wage this war of Enlightenment between worlds. Not only have you opened other's eyes but also you have helped to heal the grief within them. There is no greater reward on earth than to enlighten others to the purpose of those in our world. It goes without saying the love and devotion that we have for the souls on earth. Without those who choose to carry the torch of light there would be no communication between worlds and this would bring us great sadness. As you continue on your journey we ask that you enlighten as many souls as possible, for we too are helping you from our world.

January 24th 2018, since yesterday I kept getting an overwhelming feeling that Gail and I were going to get in to a car accident. Today, that feeling was even stronger. I did not mention this to Gail because I didn't want to frighten her. Today we spent the day in Rye, a charming village in England. On the drive back home it was dark and raining. I suddenly heard spirit all around me so I closed my eyes to concentrate. Jesus quickly came forth. It felt urgent, even a little jarring. Keeping my eyes shut he started to talk to me about people in my life that Gail and I were speaking of earlier. I listened intently for two minutes, then I felt the car swerve, and I heard Gail gasp. I immediately opened my eyes and saw the headlights of two cars going by us quickly, one car on each side. It all happened so fast but I felt like somehow, the car had been moved. Gail said she couldn't understand how we could fit in between two oncoming cars because there was no room for three cars. We were shocked, shaken, and confused, but of course very grateful. In my connection to spirit later that evening, an angel showed me an image of two angels, one on each side of us at the front of the car. I was then told that they moved the car, and that Jesus came in to distract me from the incident. The following day I received this message in my connection from Jesus (as Mother Mary stood behind him). The light that shines within you has been hidden with fear. Your journey of Enlightenment can only continue to unfold if you release your fears to me. I will handle unnecessarily comes your way. Leave the fate of your journey in my hands. I felt I had to prove to you just how safe you are in your world in order for you to release your needless fears to me. As Mother Mary stands behind me, we profess our love and devotion to you, and those around you. Do not hesitate to call upon me, for the cord between us can never be broken. It is I who comes to your aid in your times of need, for our souls are interwoven.

January 25th 2108: Jesus came forth today with Mother Mary standing behind him. He said the light that shines within you has been hidden with fear. Your journey of enlightenment can only unfold if you release your fears to me. I will handle whatever is unnecessary that comes your way. Leave the fate of your journey in my hands. I felt I had to prove to you just how safe you are in this world, in order for you to release your needless fears to me. As Mother Mary stands behind me, we protest our love and devotion to you and to those around you. Do not hesitate to call upon me for the cord between us can never be broken. It is I who comes to your aid in your time of need for our souls are interwoven. (It was during this time that my daughter Sarah was no longer with her husband, and was going through a very, very, difficult time. As Parents, we all know that if your child suffers, so do you, and you do whatever you can to help them-even if it means sacrificing yourself. This last part of the words Jesus gave me in my connection is referring to this situation.) There is no greater act of love and respect than that of sacrifice for a child. Let your frustration go for all will be well soon. Peace be with you and your children.

August 3rd 2018: Jesus stepped forth as I connected today and he said to me; "May the light of God shine on you in your hour of darkness. There is no need to fear, for I am here. You will go through the five stages of grief but you will be quickly uplifted from our world. When you come to the stage of anger it is then that you will realize the reason for it all. You must fully understand human pain in order to carry on with your purpose on earth. Our world will comfort you as much as possible but your soul will have to overcome the grief itself. Your soul will rise to the next level as you come to the completion of these emotions."(I then started to cry and said to Jesus; "Please don't take either of my children away from me"). At this time Mother Mary stepped in and said; "Child do not fear the worst for your time on earth and your children's have been set in stone. None of you will return home until the agreed time. Your purpose on earth requires your children by your side. They are more important to your journey than any of you realize. We love you and do not want you to suffer anymore than you already have but this upcoming death is necessary for many reasons. Please be assured that your time in California is fruitful."

August 28th 2018: As I connected today, I was pleasantly surprised to see Aretha Franklin stand before me. Here is the message that she gave me: "There is no greater act of kindness in the world than a show of respect for another in accepting them just the way that they are. My time on earth was devoted to God through my music, though I sometimes faltered in my personal life. I am amazed at this communication today and in awe of the connection souls in my world can make with the souls on earth. I was always a believer of the Lord but was a little hazy of the paranormal business that was spoken of. I now clearly see just how wrong I was and I also see that fears were what held me back from the truth of it. My daddy was a good man. He was a man of God though he was no saint. I do not want his name tainted on earth, for negative words and actions affect souls in my world. Though I have not been here long I am a quick learner. My faith in God was strong throughout my life and especially at the time of my transitioning into this world. Thank you for taking the time to listen to my words. I send you love and blessings." She then blew me a kiss before leaving.

35 years ago I met Seeta Narayan through my friend heather Thornton. Though we didn't remain in touch through those years, we have once again reunited through Heather and our love of the spirit world. In July 2016 Heather threw a party in my honor at her home in El Segundo, Ca. She got my favorite food and my favorite cake. Heather asked if I was willing to give a few people mediumship readings while there. Low and behold I never got to enjoy my party because the number of people waiting for a reading was endless. I sat in Heather's bedroom as people filed in one at a time for eight hours. (Heather promises to never throw another party in my honor).

Seeta and her family were flying back from a funeral in Florida that day. They landed at Ontario airport-quite a distance from El Segundo. Seeta wanted she and her sister to get a reading from me. After 7 longs hours of readings, I was secretly hoping they didn't show up. But, as I opened Heather's bedroom door there they were, Seeta and her sister Sandra. It was now dark and everyone else had gone home. I had to give at least one of them a reading since they traveled quite a distance. Seeta without hesitation unselfishly offered her sister the reading. This was the first time that I met Sandra. She was extremely quiet during the reading though she had a lovely energy about her. Afterwards I wasn't sure how Sandra felt about the reading because she was so reserved.

In the fall of 2017 Gail Moffat and myself took a trip to California. Seeta graciously offered for us to stay with us in Ontario. Sometimes, change in any form could be difficult for me. Gail gave me a ride one day to my brother Richard's house in Paramount, CA so that I could attend my niece Melanie's funeral with him and his family. Gail planned to pick me up the following day. However, I received a message from Seeta that her sister Sandra (who worked near my brother's house) would be picking me up instead of Gail. I wasn't happy with the change of plans. I really didn't know Sandra well, and because she was so reserved when I first met her, I wasn't sure how to interact with her. Surprisingly, my ride with Sandra felt comfortable and our conversation was effortless. I somehow felt like I knew her forever.

Afterwards I was very happy that Seeta gave me the opportunity to get acquainted with Sandra for I could feel the beautiful light and energy that emanated from her. A week later Sandra invited Gail and myself to her house for a party for her husband's birthday. We both had a few reservations attending but since I knew what a lovely person Sandra was and also that it meant a lot for us to see her, we decided to go. Sandra expressed to Seeta that she was so glad that she met me and she was so happy that she could talk to me. She made it known that if any of her loved ones were to pass that she would fly to Massachusetts to talk to me so I could contact them. It actually felt really good for her to think so highly of me. I was also pleased that Seeta felt so compelled to push Sandra and myself together for reasons she herself didn't understand.

April 30th, 2018 while in a meeting with her boss Sandra (a manger of medical offices), suddenly couldn't speak. The hospital confirmed a stroke. At this point she was still very much awake and aware of everything. She called her daughter and asked her to bring her some things she figured she would need if she were to be admitted for a few days. Shortly after they administered medication to her, she hemorrhaged, and fell into a coma. Cat scans revealed she was brain dead so 3 days later on May 3rd 2018 her family decided to take her off of life support. Sandra peacefully passed to spirit that day. I was heartbroken for her family especially for her 2 daughters. I was blessed to meet Sandra, but for a brief time I selfishly wished I hadn't because of the sorrow I felt. Spirit works in amazing ways for I believe I was meant to meet Sandra and get the chance to experience her beautiful soul during her brief time on earth. I also got the chance to see the amazing soul she is as she stands in the world of spirit. She has come through to me with great love for her family and amazing messages. I will never forget the first thing that she said to me. It gave me goose bumps because she told Seeta these exact words a few months prior, "I am so happy that I can talk to you". Also in my connections to Sandra she told me that she was grateful to the assistance that I extended to her family. She said that their healing is of the utmost importance to her. She also told me that there were many reasons for us meeting.

On the day that Sandra passed Jesus came forth in my connection and gave me these words. "I expel light into the world and through this light souls can choose to follow me or deny me. There are many things upon Earth that you will not understand until you are home again. Your sister Sandra has been returned home upon the request of our Heavenly Father as her time was well served. Her loss on Earth will affect many as they scramble to make sense out of life. There are lessons to be learned and losses to be felt so everything will eventually fall into Divine order. There will be those who show strength while others seem to wither away. I understand that you prayed for a miracle but we cannot go back on the words of

God. You will eventually help bring some comfort and peace to members of this family, as you are a trusted friend to them. You were put in that position for many reasons because as you know nothing is ever linear. I advise you to take things slowly for this family needs time to adjust. You will do great work for many families."

Sometimes only when looking back at happenings or incidences do we realize the gripping impact people or circumstances can have on us. We go along our lives sometimes feeling put out, or even irritated by people and events, never realizing the countless and eternal impact on your life and others. This happened to me. Well, this happened to all of us. Seeta, myself and somebody that I had never met before July 2016, the beautiful soul called Sandra.

In July of 2018 my sister Gail was diagnosed with Hodgkin's Lymphoma for the 2nd time. The oncologist assured us that she would receive two treatments and then she would be fine. Due to the strong chemotherapy she was unable to receive them in our town. Gail was admitted to Brigham and Women's hospital in Boston on August 13th 2018. This treatment was a 24-hour constant drip in which she had to be in the hospital for a few days to receive it. We texted each other on August 16th and she said she was doing well and only got sick once. She went home a day later. As usual we continued texting back and forth, but on August 22nd she did not respond to me. I also noticed that she hadn't been active on social media. This had me concerned since she goes on Facebook daily leaving me a message that she loves me. When I called her phone, she answered and told me that she was feeling so weak and sick that she wasn't able to answer any text or go on social media. We spoke for a short while and made a deal that as soon as I returned from California the following month that we would go out for a day, because surely by that time she would be stronger. We said we loved each other and hung up. On August 25th I received a call from my nephew Chad who is Gail's grandson informing me that my sister was back in Boston hospital on life support. He said she had pneumonia and the oxygen wasn't getting to her blood. The doctor assured us that this medically induced coma would only be temporary while she was receiving the antibiotics. I checked in with Chad everyday as to Gail's progress but there seemed to be no improvement in her condition. On August 28th (Gail's 68th birthday), I went for a walk in my daughter's neighborhood in San Diego. On my walk I found 13 cents (three pennies and one dime). I associate the number 13 with my mother because she was born on April 13th and she sends me that number as a sign she is near. When I looked at the date on the dime it was 1968. I immediately knew that it was a message from my mother on Gail's 68th birthday letting me know they were by my side during this difficult time. On the walk back as I approached my Sarah's porch there was a huge grasshopper in my path. The spirit world gives me grasshoppers as a sign to go forward regardless of what is going on in my life. When I entered Sarah's apartment I glanced at her patio door and there were two huge yellow butterflies flying right outside her door. My mother also always sends me butterflies as a sign that she is near. Though I felt comforted by these amazing signs from heaven I still couldn't shake how heartsick I was feeling over Gail.

On August 29th I called the hospital myself and spoke to Gail's nurse. She told me that Gail was very ill and she probably wasn't going to survive. I flew home to Massachusetts the very next day. I immediately went to Boston and during my visit the nurse once again told me that Gail was not going to survive. That evening I went over to Chad's house to speak with him about taking her off of life support. Gail had made Chad her health care proxy but he felt even if there was a small chance of survival then he couldn't take her off. As I was driving to his house, I heard Gail say, "Tell Chad to let me go." I told Chad the message that I received but he still wasn't able to let her go. His love for her and his faith in her survival was still strong. On September 1st, Chad's wife Melissa and I were on our way to Boston. On the ride up I suddenly felt a panic attack and within seconds my sister Colleen appeared in my clairvoyant vision. Colleen smiled at me a little slyly and said, "Gail is coming with me today" and I said, "OK." I then said to Colleen please take care of her and Colleen said, "I know, she is MY sister." This interaction did not surprise me at all because this was Colleen's personality. When we arrived at the hospital, we were told that Gail was deteriorating quickly and that her blood pressure was dropping rapidly. We wanted Gail to have her last rites from a catholic priest. Because we had to wait an hour for him to arrive the nurse gave Gail a medicine that brought her blood pressure up temporarily. After the priest arrived and gave Gail her last rites, her body gave out 45 minutes later. Although they had administered the medicine to prolong her life, I felt her spirit standing by my side 45 minutes before her heart took its last beat. I had also seen Colleen, their mother Eva, and Gail's son Dennis standing at the head of her bed waiting to cross her over.

After I returned home that evening, my cats were all excited. They kept trying to climb the walls as they kept looking upward. At first, I thought they were seeing a spirit but when I looked up there was a grasshopper on my ceiling. I instantly knew it was a sign from the spirit world. I know that Gail and all my loved ones in spirit want me to keep going forward even in my grief because it is the best thing for me.

I will now always associate the grasshopper with my sister Gail, and I look forward to her visits from the spirit world. It brings me great comfort that our last words to each other were; "I love you."

For quite some time now I have wanted to try cbd edibles for pain. I heard that a dispensary for recreational marijuana opened up in my town. On February 9th I went to this dispensary to inquire about the edibles. The employee informed me that they didn't have any but he referred me to a smoke shop in my town that carried them. I was very hesitant in going to this shop because I felt they probably didn't carry the highest quality product.

For several months I have been asking those in the spirit world to put someone in my life who can help me to put my book on the Amazon website. I am not very good at anything to do with a computer and I have been feeling very lost in that aspect. On February 12th 2019 Rafael the man whom I met through Gail Moffat who did her website for her events entered my thoughts. The next day I found myself thinking about him again and I wondered if he would help me by building me a website.

When I woke on February 14th 2019 I felt surrounded by spirit and they made me feel as if I was going to receive a gift from them on this Valentine's Day. As the day went on I kept feeling pushed to go to this smoke shop. I was sitting outside of the smoke shop talking to my son on the phone and I said to him "I don't even know why I'm here, I just feel like someone is pushing me to come here". When I went inside I immediately recognized the man behind the counter as Rafael, who had been in my thoughts for a couple of days. I told him that I had been thinking about him and I was wondering if he could do a website for my book. He said he could do the website and he could also put my book on Amazon for me or anything else that I needed help with. This is why I was pushed to go to this store. I asked and I received and this was my gift from the world of spirit on Valentine's Day. When I feel pushed to do something I should never doubt why because the spirit world always has my back. Those who are in spirit will never cease to amaze me at what help they can give to us and how far and wide there reach actually is.

Throughout our lives people enter and leave. During the course of it all we have both wonderful and heartbreaking experiences. These last few years while writing this book I had the honor of living amongst the loveliest family. A family that took me in with no hesitation after my last apartment burnt down. Manny the patriarch of this lovely family is a good man. He is one that would do anything for anyone in need. He took me under his wing from the day that I met him. I went from being homeless and feeling very insecure and lost, to feeling safe and whole once again.

From the time that I moved into that apartment I was told from the world of spirit that Manny, his family and this apartment was put in my life upon the request of God. It was given to me as a scared space in which to write my book.

There was nothing too big or small that this good man wouldn't do for anyone that crossed his path. He would tell me stories of how he drank, and how he found his way out of that darkness. Once again showing me that it doesn't matter where you are in life because you can always find your way to the light.

This past winter of 2018 Manny fell ill with pneumonia. He struggled to recover and though he finally did, you could tell he never again felt 100%. He was up and down all winter and was so looking forward to spring. Regardless of how he felt he kept trudging forward taking care of his grandchildren and everyone else, except himself. He was never properly diagnosed until he became so weak that he was admitted to the hospital. Through a scan they found a tumor in his stomach and something on his liver. After having a biopsy, on Saturday April 20th 2019, the doctors told him he had cancer, and had only two weeks left to live. Five days later (April 25th), as he lay in his hospital bed with his wife by his side, his three sons entered the room. Manny opened his eyes and focused on them. He looked at his sons and said their names one by one. He then closed his eyes and took his last breath, proving once again how a soul can choose the time of their passing. He had waited for his entire family to be by his side before slipping into the next world. This is an example of a man who let go when it was time for him to pass. He had a family that he loved and a family that loved him dearly. His passing was truly heartbreaking but it also represented dignity, while illustrating the connection of purity from this life to the world of spirit. It was as if he knew in the blink of an eye that he would be reunited with those that he loves once again. To those who love him it seems like a tragedy, but to those who wait for him in the world of spirit it is a celebratory homecoming. We all have an everlasting relationship with those in the world of spirit. It is never goodbye; it is I'll see you soon.

I am selfish at the loss of Manny. I feel like every time I am given someone who is like a safety net to me; they are taken away, leaving me feeling insecure and vulnerable. On the other hand, I'm so appreciative for his amazing wife and sons that are still here and treat me with such kindness. They are a living testimony to this incredible soul who was has gone on before them. I am truly grateful for this good man who was put in my life and for all that he has done for me.

I am reminded of a conversation that Manny and I had in Sept 2018, the day that my sister Gail died. He said, "You never know when it is your turn to go, for all we know I could be next". He is a perfect example of how none of us are far from standing in the world of spirit. He is also a perfect example of a life well lived and a life well loved. Choosing to walk in the light is the best decision a soul could make, and Manny made that decision. Thank you God for putting this incredible family in my life. Rest well my friend, till we reunite again.

It touches my heart to think that this book and the messages in it have given those who read it a better understanding and a deeper insight into the other realm. I certainly do not claim to understand each message that I was given, nor the reasons for them, but I have chosen to pass them on without question. They have warned me of the skeptics who will try to ruin the credibility of this book and myself, but I am to remain strong in my faith in spite of all that is to come. I realize that the publishing of these messages will be a difficult journey as I continue to stand strong in the belief of others and myself.

What I hope to accomplish with this book is to enlighten as many souls as possible as I continue to go forward. May every soul on the earth open their hearts to a better way of existing in this world. My brothers Philip and Andrew have done just that as they are both doing better in their lives. They both smoke marijuana for certain issues but they have conquered a lot of demons along the way. I'm very proud of them as they go forward on their journeys. Much love and light to all who read this and to all who need it.

AFTERWORD

It has been my honor to channel the messages that I have received from all of those in the other realms. On a daily basis I will continue on with these communications for they make my soul feel complete. My hope is that some of the words in this book have helped every person who has read it. I was told by the angels to start writing this book so the souls of the world can see the words of spirit and start to have some understanding of them and their world. This is an ongoing relationship and they want us to be aware of the huge part that they play in our lives if we just allow them to. They love us unconditionally and want nothing but the best for each of us. You can call upon them for struggles in your life whether it is big or small. Small enough as looking for a parking spot, by just saying, "Parking angel please help me to find a spot." I also hope that I have shown everyone that it doesn't matter where you start out in life; it only matters where you are going. You will be amazed at how much better your life can be with a little faith and belief, for the ability to change things is within all of us. I have shared with you all my personal journey, and the development of the communications that I had with those in the other realms in the hope that I will help others. This can be a go-to book that you can open up at any time when you are having a personal struggle, with the possibility that it will speak to you and help you. This book is a labor of love not only from myself but also from those in the spirit realm who have entrusted me to relay these messages in the hopes of unifying us all.

ACKNOWLEDGEMENTS

A book is never the effort of just one person. I owe much gratitude to the many people who throughout my life have contributed in one way or another to the person that I have become today. First I would like to thank my amazing supporting and unconditionally loving children Matthew and Sarah. They continue to not judge me for my past or present but help me to look forward to the future. I love you both more that I could ever convey into words. I thank my friend Heather Thornton who I wholeheartedly believe is an earth angel. Your support and belief in me is the greatest gift you could have ever given to me. I can't properly express my gratitude enough and I love you eternally. I would like to thank Gail Moffat for her mentoring, friendship and unconditional support of me. You helped me bring order to the chaos in my mind in my connections to the world of spirit. I thank you for your encouragement and generosity. I can't wait to see were this journey that we are on brings us. I love you my friend. I would also like to thank my many mentors that I have encountered during my development, such as Rosie Cepero, Reverend Kathleen, Ron O' Berry and Tracey Lynn. Thank you all for welcoming me into your circle and into your hearts and helping me to realize I was never alone. I can't forget to thank my childhood friends Frances Dacey and Christine Nardelli for their love and support. Thank you Christine for helping me to choose the title for my book "From Dark To Light". I also thank all my siblings for your love, encouragement and support of me and for not blinking once every time I spoke of spirit. I truly love each and every one of you. A huge Thank You to Seeta Narayan for her dedication to my book and me. The only thing more perfect than your editing is you. We have a bond and a pure friendship that will be everlasting. Thank you to my friend Heidi and her beautiful mother Carole for their constant love and support. I love you both. Thank you to my friend Tim for your support and generosity. I understand why the angels always surround you because you're special. I love you. I could never forget the generous help of Rosemary Carton with the time and work that you put into helping edit my book. Thank you Rosemary for the selfless soul that you are. Much love to you. Many thanks to Rafael A Figueroa for your belief in my book, myself and the world of spirit and also for the hours of your endless incredible work. Thank you to my mother Alice and my brother David for always being there throughout my life regardless of the circumstances. Thank you for still being there and standing by my side so closely as you both stand in the world of spirit. I look forward to the day we reunite. I love you both dearly. To my father, I forgive you and I love you. I thank my sister Gail for her devotion to me. She hung on every word I said when I spoke of the world of spirit with such incredible faith and childlike innocence. Thank you my sister for always being there for me. I miss you everyday and I love will love you forever. Lastly I would like to thank God, Mother Mary, Jesus, my guides and all those that are in spirit that have come forth and have allowed me to communicate their words to the souls of earth. I am honored by the presence of your visits and the ability of this gift.

Resources

Louis Martin and Marie Azelie Guerin on page 134 were sourced from Wikipedia. These are the references they cited:

1. "The first miracle of Louis and Zélie Martin, the Blessed". Sanctuaire d'Alençon Retrieved 4 November 2015.
2. ^ "The second miracle of Louis and Zélie Martin, the Blessed". Sanctuaire d'Alençon. Retrieved 4 November 2015.
3. "Canonization of a model couple". Sanctuaire d'Alençon. Retrieved 4 November 2015.
4. Wooden, Cindy (18 March 2015). "Pope Francis recognizes miracle needed to declare French couple saints". National Catholic Reporter. Retrieved 16 October 2016.
5. ^ Miracle of life in Valencia. YouTube. 25 June 2015. Retrieved 19 December 2015

Elizabeth (biblical figure) on pages 251 &252 were sourced from Wikipedia.

This is the reference they cited:

- Gospel of Luke

Whaley House from page 162 was sourced from: whaleyhouse.org

Made in the USA
Las Vegas, NV
15 June 2021